BRIDGING THE GAP: *College Reading*

Second Edition

BRENDA D. SMITH
Georgia State University

Scott, Foresman and Company

Glenview, Illinois   London, England

An Instructor's Manual is available and may be obtained through a local Scott, Foresman representative or by writing to English Skills Editor, College Division, Scott, Foresman and Company, 1900 East Lake Avenue, Glenview, IL 60025.

Sources for chapter opener art are listed on the page following each piece of art.

ISBN 0-673-18037-9

3 4 5 6 - MVN - 89 88 87 86 85

© Scott, Foresman and Company.

PREFACE

It makes me smile when students tell me they enjoyed using my book. I am thrilled when six months later a former student stops me in the hall to say, "I'm doing great and your reading course really helped. I think everybody ought to take a course like that!" All reading teachers want to hear about such success because we are striving to help students make the transition—bridge the gap—from general reading to the kind of specialized reading required in freshman college courses.

New Features

Helping students succeed in college courses is the goal of both editions of *Bridging the Gap;* the second edition tries to help them even more. Some of the changes are:

1. Eight new reading selections from the fields of science, history, speech, and psychology;
2. More open-ended questions to give students an opportunity to recall previous material covered in the text;
3. An explanation of and exercises on using five thinking strategies to assimilate knowledge while reading;
4. More explanation of and exercises on context clues;
5. A discussion of five methods to organize textbook information for later study;
6. An explanation of and exercises on figurative language;
7. A totally revised chapter on sentence-unraveling and sentence-restatement;
8. Explanations of and exercises on the author's purpose, tone, point of view, and techniques of propaganda;
9. A new chapter on reading flexibility with information on skimming, scanning, and adjusting rate to purpose;
10. An appendix on test-taking strategies.

Content and Organization

The second edition of *Bridging the Gap* continues to deal with difficult college textbook material and is designed for an upper-level course in college reading. Each chapter introduces a new skill, contains short practice exercises to teach the skill, and applies the skill to three longer textbook selections which are arranged according to different levels of readability. A section on vocabulary building is included in each chapter, with words presented in context after each of the longer reading selections.

The presentation of skills in the text moves from the general to the specific. Initial chapters discuss concentration and study strategies, while later chapters teach inference, bias, graphic illustrations, and reading flexibility. Both the reading and study skills in the first portion of the book stress developing the ability to see the main idea of a passage and select significant supporting details. This ability to choose the main idea is then applied to sentences, paragraphs, and longer selections. Appropriate study strategies are suggested for use before reading, while reading, and after reading. Five different methods of organizing textbook information for later study are explained. The vocabulary chapter

© Scott, Foresman and Company.

offers instruction and practice in using context clues and word structure to determine a word's meaning.

Other Features

Some other features of the book are:

1. Actual textbook selections are used for practice exercises;
2. Each chapter contains selections on three different levels of readability for greater individualization;
3. Each selection has both explicit and inferential multiple-choice questions;
4. Each selection has an essay exam question for writing practice;
5. A word count appears at the end of each selection for those who wish to time the selections and calculate the speed of reading;
6. Vocabulary is presented in context, and exercises are included on prefixes, suffixes, and roots;
7. Even though skills build and overlap, each chapter can be taught as a separate unit to fit individual class needs;
8. Pages are perforated so that students can tear out and hand in assignments, especially underlining and outlining exercises;

The Instructor's Manual to accompany this book, available from the publisher, contains the answers to all of the exercises as well as suggestions for additional practice.

Acknowledgments

I would like to express my appreciation to a number of people who helped me put this book together. My initial helpers were my husband and my students. Dick, my husband, read every passage and worked every exercise, a time-consuming task to say the least. My many former students "road tested" my material and gave me suggestions and support.

I am particularly indebted to Patricia Rossi for her insight, persistence, and enthusiasm in putting together this second edition. I appreciate the advice of my colleague, Norman Stahl, who served as a reviewer on the book and gave me many valuable suggestions. I also wish to thank Fred L. Patterson of Mesa Community College, Rudy Gedamke of the City College of New York, and Ruby D. Burleson of Texas Southern University for their insightful reviews.

Others I wish to thank for their valuable suggestions are the members of MADRAC, our local college reading association; Mike Anderson, the editor who initially worked with me on the book; the users of the first edition who answered our questionnaire: Calvin M. Walker, Dalton Junior College; Caldonia D. Davis, Norfolk State University; Janice M. Coffee, Valdosta State College; Margaret A. Hyde, Evergreen Valley College; Lucille Warren-Beck, Sinclair Community College; David A. Hurwitz, Wright State University; Elaine M. Fitzpatrick, Massasoit Community College; Patricia A. McDermott, Northern Essex Community College; Alice V. Robinson, Nassau Community College; Marion G. Duckworth, Valdosta State College; Cindy Hicks, Monterey Peninsula College; Lillian W. Lemke, Kean College of New Jersey; Marianne C. Reynolds, Mercer County Community College; Shelley B. Wepner, William Paterson College; Ruby D. Burleson, Texas Southern University; Rudy Gedamke, the City College of New York; William Walsh, California State University at Northridge; Michael Haynes, Hostos Community College; Fred L. Patterson, Mesa Community College; and Terilyn Turner, Central Piedmont Community College.

Brenda M. Smith

TABLE OF CONTENTS

Chapter 10:   Reading Flexibility   331

Appendix A: Test Taking Strategies   367

Appendix B: Organizational Patterns of Paragraphs

CONCENTRATION

WHAT IS CONCENTRATION?

Answer the following questions honestly:

1. Do you believe the power of concentration is an innate gift that some are born with and others are not?
2. Do you believe that the ability to concentrate is hereditary, like blue eyes or brown hair?
3. If your father's side of the family is fidgety and can't concentrate, does that mean that you will be also?

The answer to all three questions is an obvious *no*. Concentration is a skill that is developed through self-discipline and practice, not a mystical power, a hereditary gift, or a defective gene. It is a *habit* that requires time and effort to develop and careful planning for consistent success.

Concentration is no more than *paying attention*—that is, focusing your full attention on the task at hand. Someone once said that the mark of a genius is the ability to concentrate completely on one thing at a time. This is easy if the task is fun and exciting, but it becomes more difficult when you are required to read something that is new and not very interesting to you. At this point your mind begins to wander, and the words on the page remain just words to pass over rather than becoming meaningful thoughts and ideas.

IMPROVING CONCENTRATION

Analyze the following pop quiz and decide if it has any value for you:

You are completely absorbed and fully engrossed in reading an assignment. Someone calls your name, but you do not hear. The caller proceeds toward you and taps you on the shoulder. You are so deeply involved in your work that you *leap* into the air with a *shout* of surprise.

Pop Quiz Questions:
1. How far into the air do you jump?
2. How loud do you yell?
Score:
The higher you jump and the louder you yell, the higher your concentration score will be.
Evaluation Question:
Is this quiz completely silly or does it ring true?

Sol LeWitt. *Bands of Colour in Four Directions and All Combinations* from the portfolio of sixteen. (1971) Etching, printed in color, 12¾ × 12⁹⁄₁₆″. Collection, The Museum of Modern Art, New York. Gift of the artist. Reprinted courtesy of Parasol Press, Ltd., New York.

If someone gave you this pop quiz, you would find the test to be both silly and true. Think of a time when a similar incident has happened to you. The type of intense concentration that forces us to close the rest of the world out is the state we would all like to achieve each time we sit down with a textbook. Too often the opposite is true.

Students frequently ask, "How can I keep my mind on what I'm doing?" or "I finished the assignment, but I don't know a thing I read." The solution unfortunately is not a simple trick, but rather it involves a series of both short- and long-range plans as well as a genuine desire to learn.

THE CULPRITS: THE CAUSES OF POOR CONCENTRATION

1. External Distractions
   Who was that who just walked by? What is the name of the song playing? What time is it? Why is this room so cold? Where is my chewing gum?
2. Internal Distractions
   Will I ever pass this course? Who is going to the party Saturday night? When is the next car payment? Is my blue shirt clean?
3. Lack of Curiosity
   Who cares about this stuff? Could it be any more boring? How many more pages do I have to go?

THE CURES: PLANNING FOR GOOD CONCENTRATION

External Distractions

External distractions are the temptations of the physical world that divert your attention away from the books. They are the people in the room, the noise in the background—the general where and when that you choose for studying. To control these external distractions, create an environment that says, "Now this is the place and the time for me to get my work done."

Place. Start by establishing your own private study cubicle; it may be in the library, on the dining room table, or in your bedroom. Wherever it may be, choose a straight chair and face the wall. Get rid of gadgets, magazines, and other temptations that trigger the mind to think of *play*. Stay away from the bed because it triggers *sleep*. Spread out your papers, books, and other symbols of studying and create an atmosphere in which the visual stimuli signal *work*.

Time. To be successful, your study hours must be as rigid and fixed in your mind as your class hours. Leave nothing to chance because too often an unplanned activity never gets done. At the beginning of each new term, establish a routine study time for each day of the week and stick scrupulously to your schedule.

Schedule.   On the next page is a weekly activity chart. Analyze your responsibilities and in the squares on the chart write your fixed activities such as class hours, work time, meal time, and bedtime. Next, think about how much time you want to spend studying and how much on recreation and plug those into the chart. For studying, indicate the specific subject involved and the exact place where you will be at a particular time. Make a fresh chart at the beginning of each week since responsibilities and assignments vary with examinations coming one week and term papers another.

Successful people do not let their time slip away; they manage time, rather than letting time manage them. Plan realistically and then follow your schedule.

Ratio.   Even though it is not necessary to write this on the chart, remember that you need short breaks. Few students can study uninterrupted for two hours without becoming fatigued and losing concentration. Try the *50–10 ratio*—study hard for fifty minutes, take a ten-minute break, and then promptly go back to the books for another fifty minutes.

Habit.   Forming study habits is similar to developing the habit of brushing your teeth; the important word is *consistency*. Always study in the same place at the same times and do not tolerate exceptions. After a number of repeated experiences, the places and times should become subconscious psychological signals for concentration.

Internal Distractions

Internal distractions are the concerns that come repeatedly into your mind as you try to keep your attention focused on the assignment. Rather than the noise or the conversation in a room, they are the questions of self-doubt or the nagging responsibilities on your mind that disrupt your work.

Confidence.   Saying "I'll never pass this course" or "I can't get in the mood to study" is a beginning step toward not being successful. Concentration requires self-confidence. If you didn't think you could do it, you would not be in a college class reading this book. Getting a college degree is not a short term goal. Your enrollment indicates that you have made a commitment to a long term goal. Ask yourself the question, "Who do I want to be in five years?" In the space below, describe how you view yourself, both professionally and personally, five years from now.

Five years from now I hope to be _____

_____

Time	Sunday	Monday	Tuesday	Wednesday	Thursday	Friday	Saturday
8:00–9							
9:00–10							
10:00–11							
11:00–12							
12:00–1							
1:00–2							
2:00–3							
3:00–4							
4:00–5							
5:00–6							
6:00–7							
7:00–8							
8:00–9							
9:00–10							
10:00–11							
11:00–12							

Sometimes identifying the traits you admire in others can give you further insight into your own values and desires. Think about the traits you respect in others and your own definition of success. Answer the two questions that follow and consider how your responses mirror your own aspirations and goals.

Who is the person that you admire the most? _____

Why do you admire this person? _____

_____

_____

_____

Self-Concept.   Have faith in yourself and in your ability to be what you want to be. How many people do you know who have passed the particular course that is worrying you? Are they smarter than you? Probably not. Can you do as well as they did? Turn your negative feeling into a positive attitude. What are some of your positive traits? Are you a hard worker, an honest person, a loyal friend? Take a few minutes to pat yourself on the back. Think about your good points and, in the following spaces, list five positive traits that you believe you possess.

Positive Traits

1. _____

2. _____

3. _____

4. _____

5. _____

What have you already accomplished? Did you participate in athletics in high school, win any contests, or master any difficult skills? Recall your previous achievements, and in the following spaces, list three accomplishments that you view with pride.

Accomplishments

1. _____

2. _____

3. _____

Responsibilities.   Unfortunately, students, just like everyone else, have to run errands, pick up laundry, make telephone calls, and pay bills. The world does not stop just because George has to read four chapters for a test in

"Western Civ." by Wednesday. Consequently, when George sits down to read, he worries about getting an inspection sticker for his car or about picking up tickets for Saturday's ball game rather than concentrating completely on the assignment.

Make a List. For the most part, the interferences that pop into the mind and break reading concentration are minor concerns rather than major problems. To gain control over these mental disruptions, make a list of what is bothering you. What is on your mind that is keeping you from concentrating on your studies? Jot down on a piece of paper each mental distraction and then analyze each to determine if immediate action is possible. If so, get up and take action. Make that phone call, write that letter, or finish that chore. Maybe it will take a few minutes or maybe half an hour, but the investment will have been worthwhile if the quality of your study time—your concentration power—has increased. Taking action is the first step in getting something off your mind.

For the big problems about which you can do nothing immediately, ask yourself, "Is it worth the amount of brain time I'm dedicating to it?" Take a few minutes to think and make notes on possible solutions. Jotting down necessary future action and forming a plan of attack will help relieve the worry and clear the mind for studying.

Right now, list five things that are on your mind that you need to remember to do. Alan Lakein, a specialist in time management calls this a "To-Do List." In his book, *How to Get Control of Your Time and Your Life* (New York: Signct, 1974), Lakein says that his research studies show that successful business executives start each day with such a list. Rank the activities on your list in order of priority and then do the most important things first.

<table>
<tr><td>**To-Do List**</td><td>**Sample**</td></tr>
<tr><td>1. _____</td><td>1. Get hair cut</td></tr>
<tr><td>2. _____</td><td>2. Book report due</td></tr>
<tr><td>3. _____</td><td>3. Buy stamps</td></tr>
<tr><td>4. _____</td><td>4. Call power co.</td></tr>
<tr><td>5. _____</td><td>5. Pay phone bill</td></tr>
</table>

At the end of the day all the tasks may not be completed, but the leftovers can be transferred to tomorrow's list. Keep your "To-Do Lists" in a tiny booklet, rather than on different scraps of paper, so that you can refer back to a previous day's activity as well as make notes for several days ahead. If you can't think of five things you need to do, you are not being serious; you will never make it through college with such an unrealistic view of your time and your responsibilities. In fact, most students will probably have more than five "To-Do's."

Anxiety. Have you ever heard people say, "I work better under pressure"? This statement contains a degree of truth. A small amount of tension can help you to force yourself to direct full attention to an immediate task. For example, concentrated study for an exam is usually more intense two nights before, rather than two weeks before, the test.

On the other hand, too much anxiety can cause nervous tension and discomfort which interfere with the ability to concentrate. Students operating under too much tension sometimes mentally "freeze up" and physically experience nervous reactions. The causes can range from fear of failure to lack of organization and preparation; the problem is not easily solved.

Anxiety is a behavior that is learned in response to situations that engender feelings of inadequacy. Since it is a learned behavior, it can also be unlearned. As an immediate, short term response to tension, try muscle relaxation and visualization. For example, if you are reading a particularly difficult section in a chemistry book and becoming frustrated to the point that you can no longer concentrate, stop your reading and take several deep breaths. Use your imagination to visualize a peaceful setting in which you are calm and relaxed. Imagine yourself rocking back and forth in a hammock or lying on a beach listening to the surf. Use the image you created and the deep breathing to help relax your muscles and regain control. Take several deep breaths and force your body to release the tension so that you can resume reading and concentrate on your work.

As a long term solution, nothing works better than success. In the same way that failure fuels tension, success tends to weaken it. Each successful experience helps to desensitize feelings of inadequacy. Early success in a course can make a big psychological difference between final success and failure. Starting off with a passing grade on the first examination means that for the rest of the course the student is working at maintaining a passing grade rather than fighting to overcome a failure. Maintaining a good grade creates far less tension and pressure than trying to overcome a bad one. The counseling center of most colleges offers special help for stress management and test anxiety.

Lack of Curiosity

Lack of curiosity means starting the assignment with no desire to learn and no interest in the subject; it means "putting in time" and "covering the pages." The mindset predicts failure because motivation is dead, progress is sluggish, and the mind is prone to wander to more exciting circumstances. The student feels like a prisoner of the assigned pages and the reading itself seems endless.

Spark an Interest.   Have you ever wondered why it is that the same student who barely plods through Book A can pick up Book B, a text of equal difficulty, and become completely engrossed in the subject matter, read for hours, and later remember most of what was read? This phenomenon has probably happened to you. How can the success of Book B be applied to Book A? The student obviously finds Book B very interesting and therefore enjoyable and easy to read. How then can you generate an interest in material that has not previously seemed exciting?

Potentially dull material, like seemingly dull people, needs some background work. Ask some questions, get some ideas, and do some thinking before starting to read. If the material was assigned, it must have merit and finding it will make your job easier. Make a conscious effort to stimulate your curiosity before reading, even if in a contrived manner. Make yourself want to learn something. First look over the assigned reading for words or phrases that attract your attention, glance at the pictures, check the number of pages, and then ask yourself the following question: What do *I* want to learn about this?

With practice, this method of thinking before reading can create a spark of enthusiasm that will make the actual reading more purposeful and make concentration more direct and intense.

Time Goal.   An additional trick to spark your interest is to set a time goal. Study time is not infinite and short-term goals create a self-imposed pressure to pay attention, speed up, and get the job done. After looking over the material, project the amount of time you will need to finish it. Estimate a reasonable completion time and then push yourself to meet the goal.

The following pages contain some exercises for practicing concentration techniques. The skill-development questions are designed to help you learn to apply the techniques discussed in this chapter.

Selection **1**

PSYCHOLOGY

Konrad Lorenz and goslings
imprinting on him.

Thomas McAvoy, *Life* Magazine © 1955 Time, Inc.

Skill Development: Concentration

Directions: Before reading the first selection, take a few moments to analyze your potential for concentration, preview the selection, and answer the following questions.

1. *Look at your physical environment. Where are you and what time is it?*

   _____

   Is this your usual study time and place or are you deviating today for some special reason?

   _____

   What, if any, are your external distractions?

   _____

   _____

   _____

   _____

2. *Is anything popping into your mind that you need to remember to do? Do you feel confident that you understand the assignment and can do well? What, if any, are your internal distractions?*

   _____

   _____

   _____

   _____

3. *Now the big question is "Do you have any interest in what you are about to read?" The title of the selection is "Imprinting," and it is taken from a psychology book on human behavior. Do you know what "imprinting" means? Glance over the selection and see what words attract your attention. You may notice words and phrases like* critical-period hypothesis, Lorenz, goslings, baby chicks, the maternal instinct in rats, overcoming the critical period, baby geese, *and others. What do you think you would like to know about the topic? What about it is of interest to you?*

   _____

   _____

   _____

4. *Set approximate time goals for yourself. How long do you think it will take you*

© Scott, Foresman and Company.

to read this selection?_____ minutes. Look at the comprehension and vocabulary questions that follow the selection. How long do you think it will take you to answer the questions?_____ minutes.

IMPRINTING*

James V. McConnell, from *Understanding Human Behavior*

There is some evidence that the best time for a child to learn a given skill is at the time the child's body is just mature enough to allow mastery of the behavior in question. This belief is often called the *critical-period hypothesis*—that is, the belief that an organism must have certain experiences at a *particular time* in its developmental sequence if it is
5   to reach its mature state.

There are many studies from animal literature supporting the critical-period hypothesis. For instance, German scientist Konrad Lorenz discovered many years ago that birds, such as ducks and geese, will follow the first moving object they see after they are hatched. Usually the first thing they see is that mother, of course, who has been sitting on the eggs
10   when they are hatched. However, Lorenz showed that if he took goose eggs away from the mother and hatched them in an incubator, the fresh-hatched *goslings* would follow him around instead.

After the goslings had waddled along behind Lorenz for a few hours, they acted as if they thought he was their mother and that they were humans, not geese. When Lorenz
15   returned the goslings to their real mother, they ignored her. Whenever Lorenz appeared, however, they became very excited and flocked to him for protection and affection. It was as if the visual image of the first object they saw moving had become so strongly *imprinted* on their consciousness that, forever after, that object was "mother."

During the past 20 years or so, scientists have spent a great deal of time studying
20   *imprinting* as it now is called. The effect occurs in many but not in all types of birds, and it also seems to occur in mammals such as sheep and seals. Whether it occurs in humans is a matter for debate. Imprinting is very strong in ducks and geese, however, and they have most often been the subjects for study.

The urge to imprint typically reaches its strongest peak 16 to 24 hours after the baby
25   goose is hatched. During this period, the baby bird has an innate tendency to follow anything that moves, and will chase after its mother (if she is around), or a human, a bouncing football or a brightly painted tin can that the experimenter dangles in front of the gosling. The more the baby bird struggles to follow after this moving object, the more strongly the young animal becomes imprinted to the object. Once the goose has been
30   imprinted, this very special form of learning cannot easily be reversed. For example, the geese that first followed Lorenz could not readily be trained to follow their mother instead; indeed, when these geese were grown and sexually mature, they showed no romantic interest in other geese. Instead, they attempted to court and mate with humans.

*LEARNING STRATEGY: Even though most of this excerpt describes animal behavior, the textbook is concerned with human behavior; therefore, be alert to links between the two. Be able to define and give examples of the two major terms in this selection.

From *Understanding Human Behavior* by James V. McConnell, pp. 527–530, 550–556, 562–563. Copyright © 1974 by Holt, Rinehart and Winston, Inc. Reprinted by permission of Holt, Rinehart and Winston, CBS College Publishing.

If a goose is hatched in a dark incubator and is not allowed to see the world until two
or three days later, imprinting often does not occur. At first it was thought that the
"critical period" had passed and hence the bird could never become imprinted to
anything. Now we know differently. The innate urge to follow moving objects does
appear to reach a peak in geese 24 hours after they are hatched, but it does not decline
thereafter. Rather, a second innate urge—that of fearing and avoiding new objects—
begins to develop, and within 48 hours after hatching typically overwhelms the prior
tendency the bird has to follow after anything that moves. To use a human term, the
goose's *attitude* toward strange things is controlled by its genetic blueprint—at first it is
attracted to, then it becomes afraid of, new objects in its environment. As we will see in a
moment, these conflicting "attitudes" may explain much of the data on "critical periods"
in both animals and humans.

(*Question:* How might these two apparently conflicting behavioral tendencies help a baby goose
survive in its usual or natural environment?)

In other experiments, baby chickens have been hatched and raised in the dark for the
first several days of their lives. Chicks have an innate tendency to peck at small objects
soon after they are hatched—an instinctive behavior pattern that helps them get food as
soon as they are born. In the dark, of course, they cannot see grain lying on the ground
and hence do not peck (they must be hand-fed in the dark during this period of time).
Once brought into the light, these chicks do begin to peck, but they do so clumsily and
ineffectively, as if their "critical period" for learning the pecking skill had passed. Birds
such as robins and blue jays learn to fly at about the time their wings are mature enough
to sustain flight (their parents often push them from the nest as a means of encouraging
them to take off on their own). If these young birds are restrained and not allowed to fly
until much later, their flight patterns are often clumsy and they do not naturally gain the
necessary skills to become good fliers.

The "Maternal Instinct" in Rats.   Suppose we take a baby female rat from its mother
at the moment of its birth and raise the rat pup "by bottle" until it is sexually mature.
Since it has never seen other rats during its entire life (its eyes do not open until several
days after birth), any sexual or maternal behavior that it shows will presumably be due to
the natural unfolding of its genetic blueprint—and not due to learning or imitation. Now,
suppose we inseminate this hand-raised female rat artificially—to make certain that she
continues to have no contact with other rats. Will she build a nest for her babies before
they are born, following the usual pattern of female rats, and will she clean and take care
of them during and after the birth itself?

The answer to that question is yes—*if*. If, when the young female rat was growing up,
there were objects such as sticks and sawdust and string and small blocks of wood in her
cage, and which she played with. Then, when inseminated, the pregnant rat will use these
"toys" to build a nest. If the rat grows up in a bare cage, she won't build a nest *even
though we give her the materials to do so once she is impregnated*. If this same rat is forced
to wear a stiff rubber collar around her neck when she is growing up—so that she cannot
clean her sex organs, as rats normally do—she will not usually lick her newborn babies
clean *even though we take off the rubber collar a day or so before she gives birth*. The
genetic blueprint always operates best within a particular environmental setting. If an
organism's early environment is abnormal or particularly unusual, later "innate" behavior
patterns may be disrupted.

Overcoming the "Critical Period."   All of these examples may appear to support the "critical-period" hypothesis—that there is one time in an organism's life when it is best-suited to learn a particular skill. These studies might also seem to violate the general rule that an organism can "catch up" if its development has been delayed. However, the truth is more complicated (as always) than it might seem from the experiments we have *cited* so far.

Baby geese will normally not imprint if we restrict their visual experiences for the first 48 hours of their lives—their fear of strange objects is by then too great. However, if we give the geese tranquilizing drugs to help overcome their fear, they can be imprinted a week or more after hatching. Once imprinting has taken place, it may seem to be irreversible. But we can occasionally get a bird imprinted on a human to accept a goose as its mother, if we coax it enough and give it massive rewards for approaching or following its natural mother. Chicks raised in darkness become clumsy eaters—but what do you think would happen if we gave them special training in how to peck, rather than simply leaving the matter to chance? Birds restrained in the nest too long apparently learn other ways of getting along and soon come to fear heights; what do you think would happen if we gave these birds tranquilizers and rewarded each tiny approximation to flapping their wings properly?

There is not much scientific evidence that human infants have the same types of "critical periods" that birds and rats do. By being born without strong innate behavior patterns (such as imprinting), we seem to be better able to adjust and survive in the wide variety of social environments human babies are born into. Like many other organisms, however, children do appear to have an inborn tendency to imitate the behavior of other organisms around them. A young rat will learn to press a lever in a Skinner box much faster if it is first allowed to watch an adult rat get food by pressing the lever. This learning is even quicker if the adult rat happens to be the young animal's mother.

Different species of birds have characteristic songs or calls. A European thrush, for example, has a song pattern fairly similar to a thrush in the United States, but both sound quite different from blue jays. There are *local dialects* among songbirds, however, and these are learned through imitation. If a baby thrush is isolated from its parents and exposed to blue jay calls when it is very young, the thrush will sound a little like a blue jay but a lot like other thrushes when it grows up. And parrots, of course, pick up very human-sounding speech patterns if they are raised with humans rather than with other parrots.

/1642

Comprehension Questions

After reading the selection, answer the following questions with *a, b, c,* or *d.*

_____   1. The best statement of the main idea of this selection is
   a. studies show that goslings can be imprinted on humans
   b. the first few days of an animal's life are a crucial time for learning or imprinting long-lasting "natural" behavior
   c. imprinting seems to occur in mammals but is very strong in ducks and geese
   d. the "crucial period" of imprinting is important but can be overcome with drugs

2. The critical-period hypothesis is the belief that
   a. there is a "prime time" to experience and learn certain skills
   b. most learning occurs during the first few days of life
   c. fear can inhibit early learning
   d. the "maternal instinct" is not innate but is learned

3. In Lorenz's studies, after imprinting the goslings on himself, the goslings would do all of the following except
   a. follow him around
   b. flock to him for protection
   c. return to their real mother for affection
   d. become excited when Lorenz appeared

4. The author points out that in Lorenz's studies the early imprinting of geese with humans
   a. was easily reversed with training
   b. caused the geese to be poor mothers
   c. produced later sexually abnormal behavior in the geese
   d. made it difficult for the goslings to learn to feed themselves

5. The author suggests that after 24 hours the innate urge to imprint in geese is
   a. decreased significantly
   b. increased
   c. overwhelmed by the avoidance urge
   d. none of the above

6. In its natural environment the purpose of the innate urge to avoid new objects that develops within 48 hours of hatching might be to primarily help a small gosling
   a. learn only the behavior of its species
   b. follow only one mother
   c. escape its genetic blueprint
   d. stay away from predators

7. The author suggests that there is a critical period for all of the following except
   a. eating
   b. pecking
   c. flying
   d. song patterns

8. The studies with rats suggest that nest building and "cleaning behavior" are
   a. totally innate behaviors
   b. totally learned behaviors
   c. a combination of innate and learned behaviors
   d. neither innate nor learned behaviors

9. Abnormal imprinting during the critical period can be overcome by using all of the following except
   a. tranquilizing drugs
   b. natural tendencies

c. special training

d. massive reward

_____ 10. Because humans do not seem to have strong innate behavior patterns, the author feels that humans

 a. are better able to adapt to changing environments

 b. have more difficulty learning early motor skills

 c. find adjustment to change more difficult than animals

 d. need more "mothering" than animals

Answer the following with *T* (true), *F* (false) or *CT* (can't tell).

_____ 11. Because they are easy to train, ducks and geese have been used most often in imprinting studies.

_____ 12. The author implies that a goose can be imprinted on a painted tin can.

_____ 13. In the author's opinion, studies show that organisms can catch up adequately when skill development has been delayed past the "critical period."

_____ 14. If an abandoned bird egg is hatched and raised solely by a human, the author feels that the bird will be abnormal.

_____ 15. The author suggests that the urge to imitate is innate in both humans and animals.

▌▌▌ Vocabulary

According to the way the boldface word was used in the selection, indicate *a, b, c,* or *d* for the word or phrase that gives the best definition.

____ 1. "The critical-period **hypothesis** (03)"

 a. association

 b. theory

 c. law

 d. dilemma

____ 2. "in an **incubator** (11)"

 a. cage

 b. electric enlarger

 c. nest

 d. artificial hatching apparatus

____ 3. "its **genetic** blueprint (42)"

 a. sexual

 b. emotional

 c. hereditary

 d. learned

____ 4. "an **instinctive** behavior pattern (48)"

 a. desirable

 b. natural inclination

 c. early

 d. newly acquired

____ 5. "to **sustain** flight (54)"

 a. support

 b. imitate

 c. begin

 d. imagine

____ 6. "birds are **restrained** (55)"

 a. pressured

 b. pushed

 c. held back

 d. attacked

_____ 7. "suppose we **inseminate** (63)"
   a. imprison
   b. artificially impregnate
   c. injure
   d. frighten

_____ 8. "may be **disrupted** (77)"
   a. thrown into disorder
   b. repeated
   c. lost
   d. destroyed

_____ 9. "seem to be **irreversible** (88)"
   a. temporary
   b. changeable
   c. frequent
   d. permanent

_____ 10. "**coax** it enough (89)"
   a. encourage fondly
   b. punish
   c. feed
   d. drill

▥▤▥ Essay Question

Define the critical-period and give two or three examples, using different animal experiment findings, to support the hypothesis. Use a sheet of notebook paper to record your answer.

▥▤▥ Skill Development: Concentration

When you have finished the assignment evaluate your reading and study time.

How long did it take you to read the selection? _____ minutes

How long did it take to answer the questions? _____ minutes

Did you work steadily or were you interrupted? _____

Did setting a time goal help you keep your mind on your work? _____

If you had been given the concentration pop quiz while reading this selection, would your score have been high _____ , medium _____ , or low _____ ?

SOCIOLOGY

Joseph A. DiChello, Jr.

Skill Development: Concentration

Directions: Before reading the second selection, take a few moments to analyze your potential for concentration, preview the selection, and answer the following questions.

1. Where are you? _____ What time is it? _____

   Is this study time and place written on your weekly time schedule? What, if any, are your external distractions?

   _____

   _____

   _____

   _____

2. Is anything special on your mind at the moment? Are you ready to "attack" the material? What, if any, are your internal distractions?

   _____

   _____

   _____

   _____

3. Do you have any interest in reading the next selection? It is called "The American Man" and comes from a sociology textbook. Do you think the role of the American man is changing? Looking over the pages, you might notice words and phrases like masculine mystique, locker-room culture, costs and benefits of the male role, competitive syndrome, and machismo. Do these phrases give you ideas you may want to explore? What ideas in particular are of interest to you?

   _____

   _____

   _____

   _____

4. Set approximate time goals for yourself.
   How long do you think it will take you to read this selection?

   _____ minutes

   How long do you think it will take you to answer the questions?

   _____ minutes

THE AMERICAN MAN*

Donald Light, Jr. and Suzanne Keller, from *Sociology*

The male role is as deeply tied to the family as the female's, although the connections are not always so obvious. First and foremost a man is expected to be a good provider for his wife and children. Financial independence is a prerequisite for manhood in our society; respect goes to men who are reliable, hardworking, and achieving. Americans do not
5 think it odd for a man to sacrifice leisure, his time at home, even his health to a career. His accomplishments and property are a measure of his worth. Initiative, ambition, and strength are all part of the "masculine mystique." We say a man is mature if he accepts obligations for dependents, takes necessary risks, makes decisions, and provides security and protection for those in his care.

10   It is no wonder, then, that so many American fathers encourage their sons to excel in sports (sometimes ignoring that they are not interested in or built for athletics). Sports are not an end in themselves: very few boys will go on to become professional athletes, and few fathers expect them to. But sports teach a boy to be assertive, aggressive, and competitive—all of which are thought to be essential masculine qualities, as Norman
15 Mailer's description of boxer Muhammad Ali suggests: "Ali had shown what we all had hoped was secretly true. He was a man. He could bear moral and physical torture and he could stand."

Most elementary-school teachers are female and most fathers spend relatively little time at home, so contact with and acceptance by male peers may be especially important to a
20 young boy. To a large degree boys depend on one another for information about the male role. The "locker-room culture" of adults (nights off with the boys, drinking, playing cards, going to a ball game) is reminiscent of youthful team sports. As Joseph Pleck suggests, "It seems hard to get a group of men together for very long without someone suggesting a competitive game." For many American men, realizing that it is too late to
25 become a professional pitcher or linebacker is a sobering reminder that they are growing old.

Sports are one of many object lessons in self-reliance and stoicism. Weakness, doubt, and compromise are signs of failure for men who are raised to conceal or deny such feelings. The taboo on expressing emotions and self-doubt explains the strong silent type
30 in American lore. The 100 percent American he-man is happiest when he is with his buddies or riding the range alone on his horse. Courteous to women, he is also detached and prefers dealing with them on a "man-to-man" basis. (Humphrey Bogart's expression of love to Ingrid Bergman in *Casablanca,* "Here's lookin' at you, kid" would hardly be considered romantic in other countries.) Impervious to pain as well as feelings, he is
35 rugged, resourceful, and enjoys combating overwhelming odds. John Wayne, of course, is the prototype for this "ideal man."

The on-screen John Wayne doesn't feel comfortable around women. He does like them sometimes—God knows he's not *queer.* But at the right time and in the right place—which he chooses. And always his car/horse parked directly outside, in/on which he will ride away to his
40 more important business back in Marlboro country. (Manville, 1969, p. 111)

*LEARNING STRATEGY: Be able to describe the traditional male role and its demands in American society. How and why is that role changing?

From *Sociology* by Donald Light, Jr. and Suzanne Keller, pp. 74–77 and 148–152. Copyright © 1975 by Alfred A. Knopf, Inc. Reprinted by permission of Alfred A. Knopf, Inc.

The ban on male emotions does not extend to sexual matters, however. Heterosexual prowess is essential to American manhood. Men are expected to have nearly unlimited appetites for sexual adventure and to enjoy sex for its own sake (unlike women, who are thought to require at least some romantic feelings). Far more stigma is attached to the effeminate boy than to the masculine girl, who can play the role of tomboy. A woman who displays little interest in heterosexual relationships may be labeled prissy or frigid; a man is assumed to be homosexual. And there is no worse insult to an American man—except perhaps the imputation that someone is "trespassing on" his woman.

Costs and Benefits of the Male Role.   Like the female role, the male role has mixed effects. American men have access to the pinnacles of institutional power; men (white men, that is) not women run the nation's government, churches, corporations, professions, universities, even theaters and art galleries. Men are free to exercise legal and social powers that are denied women and children. With the notable exceptions of the now defunct draft law and alimony statutes, neither law nor custom restricts or discriminates against men solely on the basis of their sex. Men have more opportunities than women to develop their talents and acquire special skills and knowledge to cope with the world. (If a family has only enough income to send one child to college, in all likelihood it will choose their son. Men are overrepresented in all professions.) In general, men earn more than women performing the same work, and are more likely to be promoted to powerful and lucrative executive positions (where they enjoy the ministrations of secretaries, who are nearly always female). The fact that men are encouraged to display initiative and independence from the time they are small must also be counted among the benefits of the male role. Finally, the pervasive myth of male supremacy cannot but buoy the male ego.

It is important to remember, however, that although these potentialities are built into the male role, they are not available to all men. Opportunities for training, economic self-support, and power are clearly more accessible to men at the top of the social pyramid than to those at the bottom. To generalize from the privileged few to the struggling many distorts the actual situation for the vast majority of men, who are not in control of their lives nor anywhere near the seats of economic and political power.

The responsibilities that attach to the male role in America can be a source of great stress and anxiety as well as a source of satisfaction and pride. Being in a position to make decisions is fine if a person knows what he is doing, but it may seem less of a privilege to a man who is uncertain of himself. Complicating this is the fact that men are supposed to maintain the impression of strength and courage at all times. Fear of inadequacy and failure is the dark side of the pressures on men to prove themselves.

Equally costly is the competitive syndrome that asks men to consider all other men as either inferiors or rivals and requires substantial mobilization of psychic aggression. Famed as male solidarity is, male friendships are not necessarily easy relationships.

When stripped of male sex role "props," such as baseball scores, automobiles, and masculine sex boasting and fantasy, many men find great difficulty in relating to other men. A man in a group said, "You know, I have a pretty good idea of what I can get in a relationship with a woman; but I just don't know what I could get from a man. I just don't know." (Pleck, 1972, pp. 8–9)

In very concrete terms, men do not live as long as women and suffer more heart attacks. It is also very revealing that they have more psychosomatic diseases, such as ulcers, spastic colons, asthma, and migraine headaches. The male suicide rate is triple the

© Scott, Foresman and Company.

female rate, and men are fourteen times as likely to become alcoholics. Moreover, men commit 95 percent of all violent crimes and eight times as many murders as women do. Men also have to fight the wars other men make.

90 Finally, as with the female role, a number of conflicts are built into the male role. Men are supposed to be single-minded in the pursuit of success but not neglectful of their families; they should be simultaneously interested and disinterested in women; and they must be strong and self-reliant, yet require the care of a nurturant wife.

As a result, masculinity is in many ways a rather vulnerable and precarious status. The

95 male role is demanding and difficult and the rate of "failure" is high in the best of times. In American society, as in other industrial societies, few men can in fact achieve the wealth, power, and positions of leadership that are held out as ideals for all. *Machismo,* or compulsive masculinity, may be a last resort for men who accept the traditional masculine role but cannot fill it. Machismo has two faces, an overt and a covert one. Overtly it

100 consists of a show of strength and sexual prowess as well as the denigration, exploitation, and often brutalization of women. Covertly, this display masks fears and doubts about self-worth. As an effort to convince other men, women, and above all himself that he is truly all-male, machismo is a front for insecurity, self-doubt, and worldly failure (Aramoni, 1972, pp. 69–72).

105 Serious doubts and anxieties about masculine identity and purpose are bound to occur as many women forego the need for male protection and successfully compete with men in spheres previously considered off-limits to them. For example, 30 percent of male undergraduates in one study experienced some conflict between the desire for female intellectual companionship and the notion that as men, they should be intellectually

110 superior (Komarovsky, 1973).

Some men have begun to see these changes in the female role as a welcome liberation. Is traditional masculinity worth the price? These men seek a new male ideal, less geared toward competition and dominance. Men will be better off, they argue, if they can learn to acknowledge their human vulnerability and limitations and escape the posturing and

115 pretense of the male role. However, others see change as a dethronement from a previously privileged status. The more they feel they have to lose, the more likely men— and women—are to resist change. The days ahead will not be easy for those who are wedded to traditional gender ideals. There is bound to be anger, conflict, misunderstandings—a tug of war as traditional roles change for both men and women.

/1476

▌▊▐ Comprehension Questions

After reading the selection, answer the following questions with *a, b, c,* or *d.*

_____ 1. The best statement of the main idea of this selection is
a. women do not feel the pressure of society's demands as much as men
b. the rewards of the male role far exceed the disadvantages
c. men have been responsible for the changes in sex roles in American society
d. men feel the pressure of living up to an impossible image in American society, but this is changing

_____ 2. In American society, according to the author, the primary male responsibility is to provide
   a. emotional stability
   b. financial security
   c. love and affection
   d. time at home with the family

_____ 3. The author believes that American fathers encourage their sons to do well in athletics because they want them
   a. to become professional athletes
   b. to be assertive, aggressive, and competitive
   c. to build healthy bodies
   d. to be able to enjoy recreational activities

_____ 4. According to the selection, to a large extent, boys learn their male role from
   a. their fathers
   b. their teachers
   c. each other
   d. the movies

_____ 5. The John Wayne stereotype of the "ideal man" is all of the following except
   a. intimately attached to his family
   b. sexually attracted to women
   c. free of emotionalism
   d. confident of his abilities

_____ 6. The author considers all of the following benefits of the male role except
   a. early training to develop initiative and independence
   b. the pressures to achieve success
   c. the ego boost from the illusion of supremacy
   d. the opportunities for professional promotion

_____ 7. This selection suggests that male friendships are difficult relationships because
   a. female relationships interfere
   b. time is limited because of ball games
   c. males are in competition with each to succeed
   d. homosexuality is more prevalent in males

_____ 8. The author suggests that "machismo" is all of the following except
   a. a cover-up for insecurities
   b. a desirable masculine quality
   c. an exploitative attitude toward women
   d. a reaction brought about by failure to achieve success in the ideal male role

_____ 9. The author states that some men believe the changing female role in our society
   a. offers the possibility of greater masculine freedom
   b. insures an increase in the "machismo" attitude
   c. is welcomed by most men and women
   d. threatens the job security of men in our society

10. The author of this selection would probably agree with all of the following except
  a. male roles will become less traditional in the future
  b. women's lib has relieved some of the pressure of the male role
  c. men sacrifice in trying to fulfill the ideal American-man image
  d. men should not express emotions and self doubt

Answer the following with *T* (true), *F* (false), or *CT* (can't tell).

11. The author believes that if only one child in a family can be sent to college, the male child should go.
12. In the author's opinion, the adult male "Friday night poker game" is an example of the "locker room culture."
13. According to the selection, American society condemns the tomboy girl more than the effeminate boy.
14. The author believes that most men are in control of their lives and in powerful positions.
15. The female suicide rate has increased with the increase of women in responsible professional positions.

▌▌▌ Vocabulary

According to the way the boldface word was used in the selection, indicate *a, b, c,* or *d* for the word or phrase that gives the best definition.

1. "a **prerequisite** for manhood (03)"
  a. burden
  b. requirement beforehand
  c. advantage
  d. introduction

2. "of the 'masculine **mystique**' (07)"
  a. human body
  b. puzzling aura
  c. social status
  d. genetic make-up

3. "is **reminiscent** of (22)"
  a. a mockery
  b. in opposite directions
  c. complimentary
  d. suggestive from the past

4. "in American **lore** (30)"
  a. folk history
  b. untruths
  c. imagination
  d. media

5. "**Impervious** to pain (34)"
  a. superior
  b. welcoming
  c. resistant
  d. yielding

6. "Far more **stigma** (44)"
  a. importance
  b. mark of disgrace
  c. power
  d. reward

_____ 7. "**lucrative** executive positions (60)"
a. mobile
b. authoritative
c. profitable
d. successful

_____ 8. "**distorts** the actual situation (69)"
a. explains
b. misrepresents
c. compares
d. simplifies

_____ 9. "**precarious** status (94)"
a. uncertain
b. well deserved
c. unreasonable
d. newly acquired

_____ 10. "**compulsive** masculinity (98)"
a. evil
b. spontaneous
c. destructive
d. compellingly forceful

▐▌▓▐▌ Essay Question

How can the changing female role be seen as a "liberation" of the traditional American man? Describe the traditional male role and its stresses and then give examples of how a stronger female role can relieve some of these pressures for men. Use a sheet of notebook paper to record your answer.

▐▌▓▐▌ Skill Development: Concentration

When you have finished the assignment evaluate your reading and study time.

How long did it take you to read the selection? _____ minutes

How long did it take to answer the questions? _____ minutes

Did you work steadily or were you interrupted? _____

Did setting a time goal help you keep your mind on your work? _____

If you had been given the concentration pop quiz while reading this selection, would your score have been high _____ , medium _____ , or low

_____ ?

© Scott, Foresman and Company.

BIOLOGY

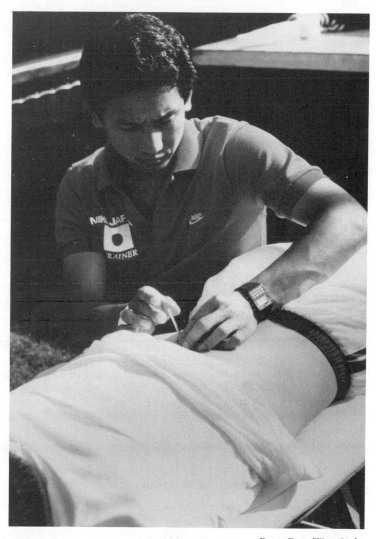

Brent Bear/West Light

Skill Development: Concentration

Directions: The skill questions in this chapter are designed to help you develop the habit of concentration. You are sizing up the situation before getting started and taking steps to increase your chances of success. Our original questions can be condensed and should become an inherent part of your preparation to read any assignment. Answer the following boiled-down version of our original questions before starting on the next selection.

1. Is anything about the present time or place going to disrupt my thinking?

_____

2. Is anything on my mind that will distract me from my studies?

_____

3. What about this article interests me?

_____

4. How long will it take to read?

_____

RELIEF OF PAIN BY ACUPUNCTURE *
Roy Hartenstein, from *Human Anatomy and Physiology*

In recent years, much attention has been focused on acupuncture as a method of relieving pain. This ancient Chinese practice, which dates back to about 3000 B.C., involves the insertion of needles into certain spots on the body. In addition to using needles, acupuncturists may also apply heat and/or pressure to certain sites on the body.

5   Most practitioners of acupuncture, especially Chinese doctors who have not been trained in basic science, use acupuncture not only to relieve pain, but also to treat a variety of diseases, including diabetes, encephalitis, and gout. However, it should be stated that acupuncture theory and practice is based on the principle that basic organic disorders can only be given temporary relief, and that degenerated tissues cannot be

10   treated. Thus, the "cure" of diabetes by acupuncture is possible only if the insulin producing cells of the pancreas have not degenerated and are able to respond to treatment.

    Doctors who have been trained in modern Western medicine are perhaps justifiably skeptical about the curative claims of acupuncture. However, many physicians and

15   scientists believe that it may be of value as a way of relieving pain.

History of Acupuncture

The earliest known document on acupuncture is the "Yellow Emperor's Classic of Internal Medicine," written around 300 B.C. According to legend, acupuncture treatments were established in the course of observing that an injury or the application of pressure

20   to one region of the body would relieve an ongoing pain previously found elsewhere in the body. An injury to the tip of the right index finger, for example, could relieve pain from a toothache; or pressure applied to the crease between an index finger and thumb would provide some relief from a headache. Over a period of many years, numerous observations were made, and maps were made showing points of pain and their

*LEARNING STRATEGY: Use the subtitles in this selection to form questions to answer as you read. The title of the selection will form the overall question to be answered.

From *Human Anatomy and Physiology: Principles and Applications* by Roy Hartenstein. © 1976 by Litton Educational Publishing. Reprinted by permission of Wadsworth Publishing Company.

25 corresponding points of relief. Crude objects, such as pointed sticks and stones, were
used by the earliest acupuncturists to stimulate the sensitive relief points. Later on, with
the development of metals, needles were used instead.

Until about the end of the nineteenth century there was little communication between
Western and Chinese medicine. In 1911 the Chinese Emperor Sonbun, who had received
30 training in Western culture, increased the communication gap by forbidding the practice
of acupuncture. He thus implied that acupuncture was inferior to Western medicine.
Because of the value of acupuncture to the Chinese revolutionaries in 1934–35, however,
Mao TseTung reinstated the practice shortly after he came to power in China in 1949.

Acupuncture was finally introduced into the United States in 1972, when American
35 doctors and journalists visiting China witnessed surgical operations, including chest
surgery and appendectomies, carried out without anesthesia, but under the pain-relieving
effects of acupuncture. By the mid-1970's acupuncture was legalized in more than a
dozen states.

Philosophical Basis for Acupuncture

According to ancient Chinese theory, there are two major forces: yin and yang. These two
40 forces are complete opposites, but nothing is purely either yin or yang. All females, for
example, have some maleness and all males have a certain amount of femaleness.

With regard to health, the Chinese see pain or illness as caused by an excess of either
yin or yang. Acupuncture is aimed at restoring the proper proportions of these vital forces
in the body. Whether Western doctors acknowledge the yin and yang philosophy is
45 unimportant. What is important is that the practice of acupuncture may be more
beneficial to certain individuals than some forms of Western medicine. Acupuncture is
not a form of quackery. Nor is it a form of hypnosis, because it works with infants and
animals.

Practice of Acupuncture

Acupuncture therapy begins with an examination of the patient's ailment. Unlike some of
50 the sophisticated techniques used in Western medicine, however, the diagnostic
techniques are essentially the same from case to case, and no special instruments are
used. Facial expressions and voice qualities are examined, as are the nails, skin, tongue,
breath, and feces. Questions are asked about the location, date, and origin of the illness,
as well as the patient's eating, sleeping, and bowel habits. One of the most important
55 parts of the examination is a simple but subtle procedure in which six different pulse
"readings" are taken from each wrist. You should note that doctors trained in modern
medicine view the pulse-reading information of acupuncturists with deep skepticism.

When the examination is over, a diagnosis is made, and the acupuncturist begins
treatment. Treatment consists of inserting needles into certain select spots on the skin.
60 One or two needles may be used for some illnesses and 30 or more needles for other
ailments. The needles range in thickness from about 0.3 mm to 0.5 mm and are 2 to 10
cm long. Short, thin needles are used for certain regions, such as the face and hands,
while longer, thicker needles are used for the thighs, shoulders, and buttocks. If
treatment is to be effective the needles must "take." That is, the patient must feel a
65 tingling sensation mixed with feelings of numbness or heaviness. The needles are left in
place for 10 to 30 minutes, often with periodic twirling. For certain ailments, only one or
two treatments may be necessary. For other ailments, 20 or 30 treatments are called for.

The effectiveness of acupuncture treatment depends not only on "take" but on the location of the needles. Depending upon the training and point of view of the 70 acupuncturist, one or more of as few as 70 points or as many as 800 points may be selected for the treatment of any kind of pain or disease. These points run along lines that are called *meridians*. Numbering 14 in all, these meridians are believed to carry "vital energy" from one region of the body to another and from one internal organ to another.

There are six pairs of yin meridians, six pairs of yang meridians, a single conception 75 meridian, and a single governor meridian. The yang meridians run along the dorsal surface of the body and head, and along the outer surfaces of the limbs. Three of them carry "vital energy" from the fingertips to the face. The large intestine meridian, for example, begins at the root of the index fingernail and terminates at the side of the nostril. According to basic acupuncture theory, there are 20 points along this meridian. 80 Pressure upon the first point, for example (or the insertion of a needle), may relieve a facial pain.

The other three yang meridians run from the face to the toes. With regard to the yin meridians, three run from the feet to the chest and three run from the chest to the fingertips. The governor and conception meridians run along the back and front 85 meridians of the body, respectively.

Advantages and Disadvantages of Acupuncture

Although modern physicians are generally skeptical about treating diseases with acupuncture, there is a growing acceptance of this practice for the relief of pain and as a substitute for local or general anesthesia. Acupuncture has certain advantages over the use of drugs. Allergic reactions are not provoked, and there are no undesirable side effects, as 90 may occur with drugs. Also, there are no major physiological changes in the body, as in general (inhalation) anesthesia, and the patient is fully conscious during surgery and is sometimes able to assist the surgeon. In addition, the surgeons do not have to wait for the effects of anesthesia to wear off in order to evaluate the consequences of an operation, and no complicated gas-delivering and monitoring devices are needed.

95 Acupuncture also has some disadvantages and complications, however. As a substitute for inhalation anesthesia, it may be only partially effective as a pain remover. Also, there is no muscle relaxation, and this may be troublesome in certain operations. In addition, inflammatory reactions may arise where the needles are inserted, and a nerve may be punctured accidentally. Also, the patient may faint or enter a state of shock.   /1232

© Scott, Foresman and Company.

▌▤▐▐ Comprehension Questions

After reading the selection, answer the following questions with *a, b, c,* or *d.*

_____   1. The best statement of the main idea of this selection is that acupuncture is
    a. a method that originated in China of relieving pain by applying pressure to body points
    b. Chinese cure for pain
    c. the yin and yang forces at work in the body
    d. more valuable than anesthesia in relieving pain

_____ 2. All of the following are used by acupuncturists to affect certain body spots except
    a. needles
    b. heat
    c. tension
    d. pressure

_____ 3. The opinion of the author seems to be that acupuncture
    a. can cure diabetes
    b. probably cannot cure diabetes
    c. can renew degenerated cells
    d. can cure cancer

_____ 4. According to the author, many Western scientists and physicians believe that acupuncture
    a. can cure diabetes, encephalitis, and gout
    b. should replace local anesthesia
    c. is a form of hypnosis
    d. can be helpful in relieving pain

_____ 5. All of the following are true about the history of acupuncture except
    a. it was used as early as 300 B.C.
    b. at one time it was forbidden in China
    c. stones and sticks were used to apply pressure
    d. most Chinese thought Western medicine was superior

_____ 6. Acupuncture has recently become popular in the United States because of
    a. Mao TseTung's leadership
    b. visits to China by doctors and journalists witnessing the technique
    c. Chinese Emperor Sonbun's training in Western culture
    d. legalization in twelve states

_____ 7. In looking at the philosophical basis for acupuncture, Chinese believe yin and yang are
    a. male and female genes
    b. life forces
    c. pressure points in the body
    d. pain and good health in a struggle

_____ 8. In acupuncture treatment, needles or pressure are applied
    a. directly on the area in pain
    b. in a region of the body away from the pain
    c. always on at least one fingertip
    d. in at least 70 points for an average treatment

_____ 9. According to the author all of the following are advantages of acupuncture over anesthesia except
    a. no allergic reactions
    b. the patient is able to assist the surgeon
    c. no muscle relaxation
    d. no physiological change in the body

_____ 10. The best statement of the author's opinion is that acupuncture
   a. should not be used in the West
   b. should be used in cases of allergy
   c. should be considered by Westerners as a pain reliever
   d. should be used in chest surgery and appendectomies

Answer the following with _T_ (true), _F_ (false), _CT_ (can't tell).

_____ 11. In order to be cured by acupuncture, the patient must believe in the philosophy of yin and yang.

_____ 12. The thickness and length of the acupuncture needles depend on the severity of the disease.

_____ 13. In the author's opinion many doctors take a dim view of diagnostic techniques of acupuncture.

_____ 14. If properly inserted, the patient should experience no feeling at all from the acupuncture needles.

_____ 15. The Chinese use acupuncture as a cure for cancer.

▐▬▐ **Vocabulary**

According to the way the boldface word was used in the selection, indicate _a, b, c,_ or _d_ for the word or phrase that gives the best definition.

____ 1. "have not **degenerated** (09)"
   a. bled
   b. divided
   c. deteriorated
   d. renewed

____ 2. "are perhaps **justifiably** skeptical (13)"
   a. with good reason
   b. cautiously
   c. absolutely
   d. undoubtedly

____ 3. "justifiably **skeptical** (14)"
   a. convinced
   b. doubtful
   c. persuaded
   d. knowledgeable

____ 4. "about the **curative** claims (14)"
   a. boastful
   b. assertive
   c. exaggerated
   d. tending to cure disease

____ 5. "a form of **quackery** (47)"
   a. the claims of a faker
   b. ESP
   c. the supernatural
   d. management

____ 6. "of the patient's **ailment** (49)"
   a. body
   b. illness
   c. mind
   d. background

_____ 7. "may be **punctured**
accidentally (99)"
a. pierced
b. divided
c. killed
d. forgotten

_____ 8. "carry '**vital** energy'
(72)"
a. renewed
b. human
c. life-sustaining
d. motor

_____ 9. "a single **governor** meridian
(75)"
a. controller
b. regular
c. necessary
d. vertical

_____ 10. "**terminates** at the side (78)"
a. begins
b. extends
c. continues
d. ends

▦▩▦ Essay Question

Explain how acupuncture can relieve pain. Describe the meridian theory of acupuncture practice, give examples of successful treatment, and point out the advantages of acupuncture. Use a sheet of notebook paper to record your answer.

▦▩▦ Skill Development: Concentration

Did you ask yourself the four boiled down concentration questions before reading "Relief of Pain by Acupuncture?" Did starting with the questions help you focus your reading and remember the important points?

Carlos Cruz-Diez. _Physichromie Number 116._ (1964) Collection Hans Neumann, Caracas.

STUDY STRATEGIES

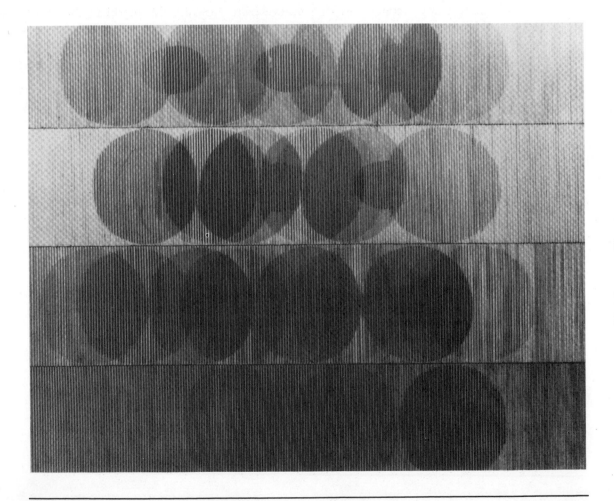

WHY USE A STUDY SYSTEM?

Mindless reading is minus thinking and is a complete waste of time. Calling words is not really reading; reading takes energy. Reading involves anticipation, synthesis, and memory; it is an active rather than a passive process and requires that thinking occur before, during, and after the act.

Because of your purpose, textbook reading demands a more organized approach than recreational reading. Reading a murder mystery might be an escape into intrigue and adventure, whereas, the purpose of textbook reading is to learn and remember a body of information. Each chapter, and even each page of a textbook contains a heavy load for the reader. To be successful, the techniques for reading novels and textbooks must differ.

Psychologists studying learning say that students sometimes "do not know that they don't know." Poor readers pay attention to factual content and tolerate inconsistencies even when the material does not make sense as a whole. Good readers, on the other hand, strive to make their reading relevant and give the material meaning by associating it with past knowledge.

Students need to be aware of the activities involved in the learning process. According to experts on learning theory, students should first analyze the reading task to determine appropriate prereading strategies. As reading progresses, these strategies should be monitored and may need to be altered. To enhance understanding and recall, students should, as they read, engage in predicting, summarizing, self-testing, and establishing relationships to prior knowledge.[1] Obviously, all of these activities involve more than simply opening a book and moving from one word to another.

WHAT IS A STUDY SYSTEM?

In 1946, after years of working with college students at the Ohio State University, Francis P. Robinson developed a textbook-study system called SQ3R. The system was designed to help students efficiently read and learn from textbooks and effectively recall relevant information for subsequent exams. The letters in Robinson's acronym, SQ3R, stands for the following five steps:

1. Survey
2. Question
3. Read
4. Recite
5. Review

Although Robinson's textbook study system remains the most widely recommended, numerous variations have been developed since SQ3R was introduced

[1]Brown, Ann L., Joseph C. Campione, and Jeanne D. Day. "Learning to Learn: On Training Students to Learn from Texts." *Educational Researcher*, vol. 10 (1981), pp. 14–21.

in 1946. One researcher, Norman Stahl, cites at least sixty-five textbook study systems. Most of the variations are modifications of Robinson's SQ3R system. By changing a word, and thus a letter, a new acronym is born. In the *OARWET* system, for example, the initial step is called *overviewing* rather than *surveying*. The second step of OARWET is *ask* rather than Robinson's *question,* the third is *read* which is the same in both systems, and the last are *write, evaluate,* and *test* which are similar in intent to Robinson's *recite* and *review.* In *BFAR* the letters stand for *browse, focus, absorb,* and *reinforce,* and in PQ3R the key words are *preview, question, read, recite,* and *review.* The similarities are obvious, and thus each of the sixty-five textbook study systems is certainly not a totally new way of thinking. Several, however, do vary in purpose and intent. For example, *FAIR* is a study system designed especially for legal texts. The letters in the acronym stand for "What are the *facts, actions, issues,* and *reasons* in a case?" This system, therefore, is appropriate for law students studying court cases. The following list represents a sampling of a few of the variations of SQ3R:

SQRQCQ	PQRST	SOAR	OARWET	PANORAMA
SLOWER	RSVP	OK5R	EARTH	PQ4R
SCORER	SQ4R	C2R	BFAR	PQ6R
SQFR	PARS	REAP	PLORE	PRWR
OR-OR	PQPST	FAIR	PURR	POINT
OR-3	EVOKER	PERU	MURDER	SCORE

In analyzing the sixty-five study systems for his research, Stahl concluded that there are more similarities than differences among the systems. Aside from the XYZ versions of the acronyms, the commonalities in the systems include a previewing stage to ask questions and establish a purpose for reading, a reading stage to answer questions and integrate knowledge, and a final stage of self-testing and ongoing review to improve recall.[2] Strategies used in these stages are depicted in the following chart and are discussed in this chapter.

STAGE 1: PREVIEWING

The Harvard Experiment

In an experiment conducted by Dr. William Perry, Director of the Bureau of Study Counsel at Harvard, 1500 freshmen were instructed to read a thirty page chapter from a history book. The chapter, entitled "The Development of the English State, 1066–1271," was extremely detailed but concluded with a partic-

[2]Stahl, Norman A. *Historical Analysis of Textbook Study-Systems*, Unpublished Doctoral Dissertation, University of Pittsburgh, 1983.

Textbook Study Strategies

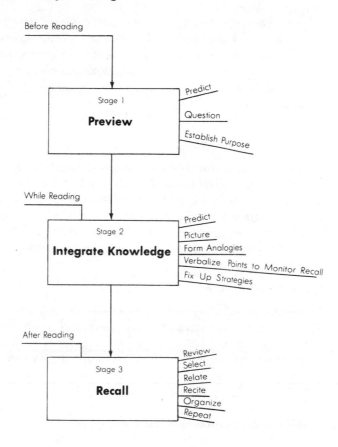

ularly informative summary. The experimenter stated that after "a half minute of study of the last paragraph, the whole development of the chapter would become clear to a reader." Students were told to study the chapter as if they would be taking an hour-examination for which "they would be asked to write a short essay and identify important details." After twenty-two minutes of study time, the students were stopped and asked to describe "what they had been doing." They were given a multiple choice test on the details and all scored extremely high. Perry reported that the ability of the freshmen to recall detail was "remarkable" and "impressive." When asked to write a short statement on what they had read, the freshmen were not quite as impressive. Only 15 of the 1500 freshmen were able to write a brief summary of the chapter. According to their previously written description of their own study strategies, these 15 students were the only ones who had taken the time to preview the chapter and read the summary at the end. The rest, 99 percent, read "from word to word" with an "obedient purposelessness."

Only one percent of the students in this experiment really knew what they had read. They took the time initially to size up the situation rather than start with the first sentence and move to the next and then the next. The 15 students who previewed the material demonstrated superior reading comprehension over the 1,485 who did not; they understood what the assignment was about as opposed to simply recalling details.[3]

What is Previewing?

Previewing is a method of assessing your needs before starting to read by deciding what the material is about, what needs to be done, and how to go about doing it. It is formulating a reading strategy and then reading to meet those goals. Even though it may take a few extra minutes in the beginning, the results are worth the time, as demonstrated by the Harvard study. Previewing is the easy way to approach a text and get involved in your studying.

How to Preview

What to Ask.   To preview, look over the material, think, and ask questions. The process is similar to the concentration technique of sparking an interest before reading, except that in previewing, the questions are more directly related to purpose. The focus is "What do I need to know and how do I go about finding it out?"

More specifically, ask the following questions before beginning to read:

1. *What is* my purpose *for reading?*
   What is the material about? What do I already know about it? What will I need to know when I finish it?

2. *How is the material* organized?
   What is the general outline or framework of the material? Is the author listing reasons, explaining a process, or comparing a trend?

3. *What will be my* plan *of attack?*
   What parts of the textbook seem most important? Do I need to read everything with equal care? Can I skim some parts? Can I skip some sections completely?

What to Read.   A public speaking "rule" says, "Tell them what you are going to tell them, tell them, and then tell them you told them." This same organizational pattern frequently applies to textbook material. An author begins with a

[3]Perry, William G. "Students' Use and Misuse of Reading Skills: A Report to a Faculty." *Harvard Educational Review,* (29) 1959, 193–200.

brief introduction to overview the topic, the ideas are then developed in paragraphs or chapters, and concluding statements at the end summarize the important points the author wants remembered. Although this pattern is not true in every case, it can serve as a guide in determining what to read when previewing textbook material.

Previewing can be a hit or miss activity in that sometimes there is an introductory or concluding statement, and sometimes there is not. Because of differences in writing styles, no one set of rules will work for all material. The following list explains several points that should be considered in previewing.

Title.   Titles are designed to attract attention and reflect the contents of the material. The title of an article, a chapter, or a book is the first and most obvious clue to its content. Think about the title and turn it into a question. If the article is entitled "Imprinting," a major concern in your reading would probably be to find out "What is imprinting?" Use the "Five W Technique" that newspaper stories usually answer in the first paragraph and ask *who, what, when, where,* and *why* of the title.

Introductory Material.   To overview an entire book, refer to the table of contents and preface. Sophisticated students use the table of contents as a study guide, turning the chapter headings into possible exam items. In seeking specific information in parts of books for research, the table of contents can help you quickly locate material relevant to your purpose. For novels, read the book jackets or paperback covers for a preview.

The first paragraphs in textbook chapters and articles frequently introduce the topic to be covered and give the reader a sense of perspective. For both articles and chapters, italicized inserts are sometimes used to overview and highlight the contents.

Subheadings.   Subheadings are titles for small sections within chapters. The subheadings, usually appearing in **boldface print** or *italics*, outline the main points of the author's message and thus give the reader an overview of the organization and the content. Turn these subheadings into questions that need to be answered as you read.

Italics, Boldface Print, and Numbers.   Italics and boldface print are used to highlight words that merit special attention and emphasis. These are usually new words or key words that students should be prepared to define and remember. For example, a discussion of sterilization in a biology text might emphasize the words vasectomy and tubal ligation in italics or boldface print. In another book on the same subject, the two forms of sterilization might be emphasized with enumeration by indicating (1) vasectomy and (2) tubal ligation. Numbers usually signal a list of important details.

Concluding Summary. Many textbooks include summaries at the end of the chapters to highlight the important points within the material. As demonstrated by the Harvard Experiment, the summary can serve, not only as a review to follow reading, but as an introduction for overviewing the chapter.

▪▦▪ Exercise 1: Previewing a Textbook

Respond to the following items by previewing the table of contents of a sociology textbook entitled *Life Designs*. Such previewing can help you get a general idea of the organization and scope of the book, predict possible exam questions, and locate sections that are most important for a particular type of assignment.

1. The book is divided into how many major sections? _____

2. The book follows the individual in society from gender identity in childhood

   to _____

   _____

3. A majority of the chapters in this book focus on what aspect of a person's life

   in society? _____

4. Which seem to be summary chapters? _____

5. What do Chapters 6, 7, and 15 suggest about the authors' approach to the

   subject? _____

6. Suggest an essay exam question for Part 2. (For your classes, you should
   write such questions in the table of contents itself so that the information

   will be there for later study.) _____

   _____

7. Suggest an essay exam question that would cover the information in Parts 3,

   4, and 5. _____

   _____

8. If you were doing a research paper on widows in society, what chapter

   would you read? _____

9. If you were researching how people react in crowds, what chapter would you

   read? _____

10. If you were researching sex before marriage, what chapters would you read?

    _____

Life Designs

J. Gagnon and C. Greenblat

▓▓▓ Exercise 2: Previewing a Textbook Chapter

Respond to the following items by previewing the following chapter from a criminology textbook entitled the "American Police Forces." Since previewing does not necessitate reading the entire chapter, only the introductory paragraphs, the subheadings, and the summary are reprinted for this activity. Allow only five or six minutes for this exercise.

1. This chapter is divided into how many major sections? _____

2. The purpose of this chapter is to describe

   a. _____

   b. _____

   c. _____

   d. _____

3. Chapter 3 of *Criminal Justice in America* is primarily concerned with _____

   _____

   _____

4. How many police activities are categorized under field operations? _____

   _____

5. Suggest an essay exam question concerning the history of the police force.

   _____

   _____

   _____

6. Suggest an essay exam question concerning police activities. _____

   _____

   _____

7. What is the major motivation for entering police work? _____

8. Where is the most money spent in the police force? _____

9. If you were researching police personality structure, what section would you read? _____

10. If you were researching the chain of command in the police department, what section would you read? _____

American Police Forces

As we saw in Chapter 3, the passage of laws is the responsibility of the legislative branches of federal, state, and local governments. When a law has been passed by a legislature, it must then be enforced. In modern societies, enforcing the law is the responsibility of policing agencies.

In this chapter we will briefly discuss the development of police forces and the ways in which American police forces are organized. We will then look at the diverse activities involved in the enforcement of law and end with a consideration of the people who make law enforcement a career.

History of American Police Forces
    European Origins
    The Development of Police Forces in the United States
Structure of American Police Forces
    Types of Policing Agencies
    Types of Department Organization
Police Activities
    Field Operations
        Patrol duties
        Effectiveness of patrol
        Domestic services
        Detective duties
        Special operations
        Juvenile units
        Apprehension of suspects
    Administration
    Technical Services
    Inspectional Services
The Police Personality
    Motivations for Entering Police Work
    Public Image and Private Sentiments

Summary

The origins of the American police system can be traced back to preindustrial England, where policing was a community effort, but the nature of the American experience and the settlement patterns on the North American continent created unique situations that shaped the development of police forces in this country. Most American metropolitan police forces evolved from systems employing a handful of men who were ill-trained and often had questionable credentials to professionalized forces employing hundreds or even thousands of officers who have specialized functions and who use sophisticated technical equipment.

Most law enforcement officers are employed by local police departments. There are also state, federal, and private policing agencies. The most common form of departmental

From *Criminal Justice in America* by Peter C. Kratcoski and Donald B. Walker, pp. 65, 93. Copyright © 1978 by Random House, Inc. Reprinted by permission.

40　organization is the traditional model, characterized by division into four bureaus: field
operations, administrative services, technical services, and inspection. The modified plan,
or team policing, is used in some large departments.

　　Traditionally the most important aspect of field operations, in terms of the resources
allotted it, has been patrol work. The effectiveness of patrol in today's cities has come
45　under serious questioning. Field operations also include domestic services, detective
duties, traffic responsibilities, special operations, juvenile units, and apprehension of
suspects.

　　Activities performed in the administrative services bureau include the formulation of
policy decisions. This bureau is organized in a quasi-military, hierarchical manner
50　characterized by division of labor, unity of command, chain of command, and span of
control.

　　The technical services bureau provides record keeping and analyzing services. It also
takes charge of the lockup or jail and of vehicles and other police equipment.

　　The functions of the inspectional services bureau revolve around inspecting police
55　officers and investigating possible misconduct. Such bureaus also engage in a variety of
intelligence-gathering activities.

　　There are many reasons that individuals give for wanting to become police officers; the
major one seems to be job security. Some police officers may have authoritarian
personality structures, possibly because of the nature of the job. There is hope that better
60　training will help prepare officers for the demands of the job and create more
professional forces.

Peter C. Kratcoski and Donald B. Walker, Criminal Justice in America

STAGE 2:
INTEGRATING KNOWLEDGE WHILE READING

Prior Knowledge

Is it easier to understand a passage if you already know something about the
topic? Read the following paragraphs and decide for yourself.

Passage A

The signal that there will soon be a new member of the earth's most dominant species is
the onset of *labor*, a series of uterine contractions that usually begin at about half-hour
intervals and gradually increase in frequency. Meanwhile, the sphincter muscle around
the cervix dilates, and as the periodic contractions become stronger, the baby's head
pushes through the extended cervical canal to the opening of the vagina. The infant is
finally about to emerge into its new environment, one that, in time, may give it the
chance to propel its own genes into the gene pool of the species.

Robert Wallace, Biology: The World of Life

From *Biology: The World of Life,* 3rd Edition, by Robert A. Wallace. Copyright © 1981 by Scott,
Foresman and Company.

Passage B

Echinoderms have protective skeletal elements embedded in their body walls. They also have an unusual feature called a water vascular system, which is used as a kind of hydraulic pump to extend the soft, pouchlike *tube feet*, with their terminal suckers. They are sluggish creatures with poorly developed nervous systems. However, they are tenacious foragers. Some species feed on shellfish, such as oysters. They wrap around their prey and pull relentlessly until the shells open just a bit. Then they evert their stomachs, squeezing them between the shells, and digest the flesh of the oysters on the spot.

Robert Wallace, *Biology: The World of Life*

Even if you are a biology major, the first passage is probably easier to read than the second. Most people have greater prior knowledge of the human birth process than of echinoderms. This prior knowledge makes reading more interesting, easier to visualize, and therefore easier to understand. By linking the old and the new, there is a structure on which to hang the new ideas.

Before and while reading, good readers ask, "What do I already know about this topic?" and "How does this new information relate to my previous knowledge?" Although textbook topics may at times seem totally unfamiliar, seldom are all of the ideas completely new. Usually there is a link, an old bit of knowledge that you can associate with the new ideas. For example, although you may not be familiar with the echinoderms described in Paragraph B, you probably know what an oyster looks like and can visualize the tenacity needed to open its shell.

Integrating Ideas

Understanding and remembering complex material requires as much thinking as reading. Both consciously and subconsciously, the good reader is predicting, visualizing, and drawing comparisons in order to assimilate new knowledge. The following list, devised by a reading researcher, represents the kind of thinking strategies good readers employ while reading.

1. *Make predictions.* (Develop hypotheses.)
   "From the title, I predict that this section will tell how fishermen used to catch whales."
   "In this next part, I think we'll find out why the men flew into the hurricane."
   "I think this is a description of a computer game."
2. *Describe the picture you're forming in your head from the information.* (Develop images during reading.)
   "I have a picture of this scene in my mind. The car is on a dark, probably narrow, road; there are no other cars around."
3. *Share an analogy.* (Link prior knowledge with new information in text.) We call this the "like-a" step.
   "This is like a time we drove to Boston and had a flat tire. We were worried and we had to walk three miles for help."

© Scott, Foresman and Company.

4. *Verbalize a confusing point.* (Monitor your ongoing comprehension.)
   "This just doesn't make sense."
   "This is different from what I had expected."
5. *Demonstrate fix-up strategies.* (Correct your lagging comprehension.)
   "I'd better reread."
   "Maybe I'll read ahead to see if it gets clearer."
   "I'd better change my picture of the story."
   "This is a new word to me—I'd better check context to figure it out."[4]

The following passage illustrates the use of these thinking strategies with textbook material. The thoughts of the reader are highlighted in parentheses. Keep in mind that each reader reacts differently to material, depending on background and individual differences. This example merely represents one reader's attempt to integrate knowledge.

Example:

With the appearance of tiny pollen (*Flowers have pollen*) that did not require water (*Rain?*) but that could be carried about by drying winds (*Like on deserts?*), the stage was set for the development of another means of pollen transport (*Is this going to say that insects did not always carry pollen?*). As plants were evolving on earth (*Back to the very beginning of time?*), so were other species (*Must mean insects*), and many of them depended on each other in increasingly intricate and complex ways. For example, the insects were broadening into new and unused niches (*Yes, apparently insects did not always eat and transport pollen*), and some of them ultimately began to exploit the food in flowers (*Visualize bees buzzing around flowers on a sunny summer day*). These insects, of course, would have tended to visit one flower after the next, and thus they could have become vehicles for pollen transport (*Was the pollen on their feet?*). Some of those flowers that tended to attract insects, then, would have been better reproducers than their fellows and would have left more offspring (*Reread the last sentence. I wonder what the flowers looked like that were lost*).

Robert Wallace, *Biology: The World of Life*

The example may be confusing to read because many of the thoughts that are highlighted normally occur on the subconscious rather than the conscious level. Stopping to consciously analyze these reactions seems artificial and interrupting. It is important, however, to be aware that you are incorporating these thinking strategies into your reading. The following exercises are designed to make you more aware of this interaction.

From *Biology: The World of Life,* 3rd Edition, by Robert A. Wallace. Copyright © 1981 by Scott, Foresman and Company.

[4] Davey, Beth. "Think Aloud—Modeling the Cognitive Processes of Reading Comprehension." *Journal of Reading,* vol. 27 (October, 1983), pp. 44–47. Reprinted by permission of the author and the International Reading Association.

Exercise 3:
Integrating Knowledge While Reading

For each of the following passages, demonstrate in writing the way you use the five thinking strategies as you read. The passages are double spaced so that you can insert your thoughts and reactions between the lines rather than in parentheses as was demonstrated in the example. Make a special effort to include all of the following strategies as you read:

1. Predict (Develop hypotheses.)
2. Picture (Develop images during reading.)
3. Form analogies (Link prior knowledge with new ideas.)
4. Verbalize points (Monitor your ongoing comprehension.)
5. Fix-up strategies (Correct your lagging comprehension.)

Passage A

The gymnosperms are among the most beautiful and impressive of all plants. After all, the redwoods are gymnosperms. The tallest living thing in the world is a redwood over 100 meters tall that was saved from the lumbering interests. (A taller tree was cut down before the environmentalists could prevent it.) The tree with the greatest bulk is a giant sequoia that reaches 80 meters in height and has a girth of 20 meters at its base. It is about 4,000 years old, but it is a youngster compared to a bristlecone pine almost 5,000 years old in the mountains of eastern Nevada. Other gymnosperms include the hemlocks of Canada, the cypress of the southern swamps, the wiry *ephedra* of the deserts, and the palmlike cycads of the tropics.

Robert Wallace, *Biology: The World of Life*

Did you use all five strategies? Which did you use? _____

Passage B

Bacteria, of course, are extremely small (most are only a few micrometers in length), and they exist in vast numbers on virtually everything on earth. They, or their spores, are found in the upper atmosphere, in hot springs, in the polar ice caps, in raw petroleum, in the deepest reaches of the sea, and in animal guts. Some surfaces, of course are free of the creatures since they tend to dislike acid, high temperatures, and dryness. Nonetheless, they manage to find places to live. It is believed that their mass outweighs that of all plants and animals combined. Obviously, bacteria can't all be bad, and although many, in in fact, do cause a multitude of human diseases and diseases of species humans depend upon, they also act to decompose corpses, releasing their chemical components back into the environment to be used by other living things.

Robert Wallace, *Biology: The World of Life*

Which of the five strategies did you use the most on this passage?

STAGE 3: RECALL

The Classic Spitzer Study

Herbert Spitzer ("Studies in Retention," *Journal of Educational Psychology* 30 [1939]: 641–659) investigated the effects of recall on retention with 3,600 Iowa students. He divided the students into ten groups and gave each group the same article to read. Immediately after reading the article, Groups I and II recalled the important points of what they had read. The other eight groups, however, did not engage in any immediate recall activities.

To measure retention of the articles, tests were given to each group. The time of testing varied; some groups were tested one day after reading the article, some after seven days, and some after 14, 21, 28, and 63 days. Spitzer analyzed the data and found that "more is forgotten on one day without recall than is forgotten in sixty-three days with the aid of recall." In some cases, the recall groups remembered over twice as much as the groups without recall.

The Spitzer study makes a powerful statement about the positive effects of recall on retention, but still students are reluctant to take the time to do it. At the final period of that last sentence, do you stop, breathe a sigh of relief, and say, "Hallelujah, I've finished the assignment!" Do you immediately close the book, never taking the time to mull over what has been read and put it into some type of perspective or order? If you are such a reader, much of what you have learned will be lost because you have given yourself no reminder of what's important, of what you should remember.

What Is Recalling?

Recalling is telling yourself what you have learned, what you wish to remember, and relating it to what you already know. It is taking those few extra minutes to digest what you have read and having a short conversation with yourself or a friend about the new material. Rather than being formal, long, and involved, the recalling process is the natural overviewing step that follows the "Hallelujah Period."

Why Recall?

Engaging in recall immediately after reading forces the reader to (1) select the most important points, (2) relate the supporting information, and (3) repeat what has been learned. These three elements cause the reader to remember better.

1. *Select the most important points.*
   The poor student wants to remember everything—facts have equal importance and thus no priorities are set. In short, no decisions have been made and the student has failed to sift through the reading and pull out the important issues.

2. *Relate the information.*

Facts are difficult to learn in isolation. Memory experts use a technique of linking one item with another and through a series of associations are able to recall an exhaustive amount of seemingly unrelated trivia. To borrow from this technique, students must set up a linking system for each subject-matter area. New facts can then be placed into an overall skeleton of information and be more easily remembered. For example, many students have difficulty with history courses because they have no framework or skeleton into which to fit information. Events are isolated happenings rather than results of previous occurrences or parts of ongoing trends.

3. *Repeat what has been learned.*

How many times did you sing "Twinkle, Twinkle, Little Star" and how well do you know it right now? The rhythm and repetition help you remember the words without much effort. Perhaps this is an exaggerated example of overlearning, yet it represents an important element in memory. That element is repetition. For example, a new word is difficult to incorporate into your vocabulary unless you have the opportunity to use it, see it in print, or hear others use it. The same is true with facts; a review of the information makes it easier to remember. Beyond just pulling the facts into perspective, a review reinforces and cements the ideas in your mind.

How to Recall.

To recall, simply take a few minutes after the "Hallelujah Period" to recap what you have learned. This can be done in your head or it can be done on paper. To visualize the main points graphically, make a recall diagram. On a straight line state briefly the main point of the selection and underneath it, state the significant supporting details. The following is an example of the recall diagram:

What is the material mainly about?

significant supporting examples
(or) significant related facts
(or) significant clarifying phrases

Example

As you probably already know, there are only two basic ways an organism can get its energy, or "food." Plants utilize carbon dioxide, water, and sunlight to make their food. They are called *autotrophs*, meaning "self-feeders." Animals do not normally make their

From *Biology: The World of Life*, 3rd Edition, by Robert A. Wallace. Copyright © 1981 by Scott, Foresman and Company.

own food, but must derive it from other organisms that have made it. They are called *heterotrophs*, meaning "other-feeders."

Robert Wallace, Biology

An organism can get energy in two ways

Autotrophs make their own food (plants)
Heterotrophs feed on other organisms (animals)

▥▤▥ Exercise 4: Recall Diagrams

After reading the following passages, stop and recall what each passage was about. Use the recall diagrams to record the main point and the significant supporting details.

Passage A

Many talented people grew up in families that were headed by talented parents. Johann Sebastian Bach, for instance, did not simply "discover" his musical ability; his father was a court musician and probably taught his son to think in musical terms from an early age. The *situational* factor is thought to be important in developing creativity. Today teachers and parents in western cultures may ask children to "do things their own way" and express themselves as individuals rather than follow the conventional rules. For instance, it has been shown that pupils in "open classrooms" (where they are allowed to choose their own activities and proceed at their own pace) do more productive and original classroom work than pupils who learn on a prearranged or structured schedule (Parnes, 1967). Some freedom to experiment, to develop one's own approach to problems, seems more likely to result in creative and meaningful solutions. If students are always given the answers, they do not need to find answers for themselves.

An important factor in creativity is thought to be *motivation*. To be creative you need an incentive. In experimental situations it has been shown that incentives can come from either some outside reward or from a desire for self-expression and doing something that is personally satisfying.

David Dempsey and Philip Zimbardo, Psychology and You

© Scott, Foresman and Company.

Passage B

A number of factors were responsible for the post-Civil War industrial boom. The United States possessed bountiful raw materials, and the government was willing to turn them over to industry for little or no money. Coupled with the abundance of natural resources was a home market steadily expanding through immigration and a high birth rate. Both capital and labor were plentiful. The increase in trade and manufacturing in the Northeast in the years before the war produced an accumulation of savings, while additional millions of dollars came from European investors. Unbroken waves of European immigration provided American industry with workers as well as with customers. From 1860 to 1900 about 14 million immigrants came to the United States, most of whom settled in cities and became industrial workers.

Carl N. Degler et al., *The Democratic Experience*

Selection **1**

PSYCHOLOGY

Jean-Claude Lejeune

Skill Development

Stage 1: Preview

Before reading the next selection, preview to (1) establish a purpose, (2) size up how the material is organized, and (3) plan an attack. Read any introductory material, the first paragraph, the subheadings, the boldface and italicized print, the first sentence of some paragraphs (if it seems important), and the last paragraph. Think about the selection as a whole and complete the following sentences.

1. *Overlearning seems to mean* _____

_____

_____

2. *After reading this selection, I would like to know* _____

_____

_____

3. *Regarding this topic, I already know* _____

_____

_____

Stage 2: Integrate Knowledge While Reading

Since each reader interacts with material in an individual manner, it would be artificial to require certain thinking strategies to be used in certain places. As you read the following selection, make a note in the margin of at least one instance when you used the following strategies.

1. *Predict*
2. *Picture*
3. *Form analogies*
4. *Verbalize points*
5. *Fix up strategies*

OVERLEARNING*

Jerome Kagan and Ernest Havemann, from *Psychology: An Introduction*

Adults are often surprised by how well they remember something they learned as children but have never practiced in the meantime. A man who has not had a chance to go swimming for years can still swim as well as ever when he gets back in the water. He can get on a bicycle after several decades and still ride away. He can play catch and swing

*LEARNING STRATEGY: Be able to define the terms and to use research findings to support the opinions expressed.

From "Efficiency in Learning" in *Psychology: An Introduction,* 2nd edition by Jerome Kagan and Ernest Havemann. Copyright © 1972 by Harcourt Brace Jovanovich Inc. Reprinted by permission.

5   a baseball bat as well as his son. A mother who has not thought about the words for years can teach her daughter the poem that begins "Twinkle, twinkle, little star" or recite the story of Cinderella or Goldilocks and the three bears.

     One explanation is the *law of overlearning,* which can be stated as follows: Once we have learned something, additional learning trials increase the length of time we will
10   remember it. A laboratory demonstration of this law is shown in the figure.

     In childhood we usually continue to practice such skills as swimming, bicycle riding, and playing baseball long after we have learned them. We continue to listen to and remind ourselves of jingles such as "Twinkle, twinkle, little star" and childhood tales such as Cinderella and Goldilocks. We not only learn but overlearn.

15   Earlier in the chapter, it was mentioned that the multiplication tables are an exception to the general rule that we tend to forget rather quickly the things that we learn in school by rote. An explanation was promised later—and now, of course, you have it, for the multiplication tables are another of the things we overlearn in childhood.

     The law of overlearning explains why cramming for an examination, though it may
20   result in a passing grade, is not a satisfactory way to learn a college course. By cramming, a student may learn the subject well enough to get by on the examination, but he is likely soon to forget almost everything he learned. A little overlearning, on the other hand, is usually a good investment toward the future.

How Overlearning Aids Remembering

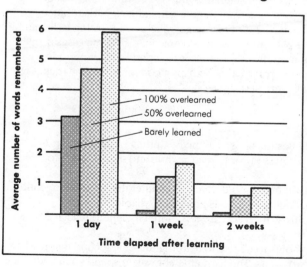

These are the results of an experiment in which subjects learned a list of twelve single-syllable nouns. Sometimes they stopped studying the list as soon as they were able to recall it without error—in the words used in the chart, as soon as they had "barely learned" the words. At other times they were asked to continue studying the list for half again as many trials as bare learning required (50 percent overlearned) or to continue studying for the same number of extra trials as the original learning had required (100 percent overlearned). Whether measured after a day or at later intervals, the subjects who had overlearned by 50 percent remembered considerably more than those who had barely learned, and the subjects who had overlearned by 100 percent remembered most of all. (20)

© Scott, Foresman and Company.

Distribution of Practice

     Another argument against cramming is that it represents an attempt to learn through what
25   is called *massed practice*—that is, a single long learning session. Studies of a wide range of situations involving both human and animal learning have indicated that massed practice is generally less efficient than *distributed practice*—that is, a series of shorter learning periods. The same total amount of time spent in learning is often strikingly more efficient when invested in short, separated periods than all at once.

30   Three possible explanations have been suggested for the superiority of distributed practice:

1. Distributed practice reduces the fatigue that often accompanies massed practice in motor learning and the boredom that often occurs in massed practice in verbal learning.

2. In the intervals between distributed practice sessions the learner may continue to
35 mull over the material he has learned, even without knowing that he is doing so. This process is called *covert rehearsal* and results in what is called *consolidation* of what has been learned.

3. In many kinds of learning it seems likely that we learn not only what we want to learn but a number of useless and irrelevant habits that may actually interfere. A student
40 learning to type, for example, might at the same time learn to grit his teeth, squint, and blink his eyes—habits that do not help his skill but hurt it. During the intervals between distributed practice sessions these extraneous habits may be forgotten more quickly than the basic subject matter of the learning. The process is called *differential forgetting*.

It must be added, however, that distributed practice does not always give such
45 spectacular results. It seems less helpful in learning by logical rule than in learning by rote, possibly because rule learning involves less boredom. In learning situations that require a lot of "cranking up" time—getting out several books and notebooks, finding some reference works on the library shelves, and finding a comfortable and well-lighted place to work—short practice periods may be less efficient than long ones. Moreover,
50 distributed practice does not appear to have much effect if any on how well the learning is remembered; even when it results in substantial savings of the time required for learning, it does not seem to improve retention. But the general idea of distributed practice is a useful tool in the management of learning. Probably all learning tasks can be best accomplished through some pattern of distributed practice—in some cases many
55 short periods separated by long intervals, in some cases fewer and longer periods separated by shorter intervals, and in some cases perhaps a combination. The trick is to find the pattern that best suits the particular situation.

Recitation

We come now to the last of the questions posed at the beginning of the chapter: Is it better just to keep reading when you study or to read a while and then attempt to
60 recite? . . .

Experimenters have found that it makes no difference whether the subjects are children or adults or whether the material being learned is nonsense syllables, spelling, mathematics, or a foreign vocabulary. In every case it is more efficient to read and recite than to read alone.
65 Let us say that you have eight hours to devote to learning this chapter and that reading through the chapter takes you two hours. The least efficient way to spend your study time would be to read through the chapter four times. You would do much better to spend more time in trying to recite what you have learned than in reading—for, . . . devoting as much as 80 percent of study time to recitation may be more efficient by far than mere
70 reading.

Recitation seems to assist learning in a number of ways. It certainly helps make the stimulus more distinctive; it casts a telling searchlight on what you have grasped quickly and what you have not, on what you understand and what you still find obscure. It provides a form of feedback that sharpens your attention. It helps you find meaningful-

© Scott, Foresman and Company.

75 ness and logical principles in the material. Of all study techniques, recitation is the one of
    most clearly proved value.

    Recitation is the heart of a widely recommended study method called the SQ3R system
    (24), which holds that the most efficient way to study a chapter is to approach it through
    five steps:

80 1. *Survey.* That is, study the outline at the beginning of the chapter (if there is one, as
    in this book) and then glance through the chapter to get a general idea of how much
    attention is devoted to each point in the outline and to the subheadings.

    2. *Question.* Look through the chapter again in a more inquisitive fashion, asking
    yourself questions that the headings and subheadings suggest; let the topics you find

85 there whet your curiosity.

    3. *Reading.* Now read the chapter straight through, without taking notes.

    4. *Recitation.* You have made a survey of the chapter, asked some questions about it,
    and read it. Now see how much of the chapter you can recite, either silently to yourself or
    out loud to a cooperative friend.

90 5. *Reviewing.* Go through the chapter again, making another survey of its topics and
    noting how much of it you were able to recite and what points you left out. The
    reviewing process will show you where you must devote further study.   /1328

▌▐▐ Skill Development: Study-Reading

Stage 2:   Review your marginal notes to see if you are using all five thinking
strategies as you read. Which did you use the most?

Stage 3:   Stop and recall what the selection was about. Use the recall diagram
to record from memory the main point and the significant supporting details.

▌▐▐ Comprehension Questions

After reading the selection, answer the following questions with *a, b, c,* or *d.*

SQ3R system from F. P. Robinson, *Effective Study,* Revised Edition, Harper 1961.

_____ 1. The best statement of the main idea of this selection is
   a. recitation explains why cramming for an exam is an ineffectual method of study
   b. overlearning, distributed practice, and recitation improve the efficiency of the learning process
   c. effective learning means remembering the material at least two weeks later
   d. forgetting is caused by a failure to apply the principles of learning in an efficient manner

_____ 2. The author uses all of the following as examples of the success of overlearning except
   a. bicycling
   b. nursery jingles
   c. multiplication tables
   d. examination cramming

_____ 3. The difference between distributed practice and mass practice is
   a. the number of hours spent studying
   b. the complexity of the material studied
   c. the time intervals between study periods
   d. the recitation after study units

_____ 4. The process of covert rehearsal between distributed practice sessions is
   a. a conscious recitation
   b. an unconscious review
   c. an organized consolidation
   d. a selective forgetting

_____ 5. The author implies that the differential forgetting process that occurs between distributed practice sessions would probably be the most important in
   a. learning to play tennis
   b. memorizing a poem
   c. studying for a history examination
   d. learning multiplication tables

_____ 6. Distributed practice sessions have been shown to do all of the following except
   a. cut down on fatigue
   b. improve retention
   c. give an opportunity for covert rehearsal
   d. relieve boredom

_____ 7. The author feels that the most effective method of spending four hours studying a chapter for an exam would be to
   a. read it once and then recite
   b. read it once, recite, and then read it again
   c. read it twice and then recite
   d. read it three times and recite after each reading

_____ 8. The author feels that the key success factor in the SQ3R study method is

a. recitation

b. a combination of distributed practice and recitation

c. the final review that follows the recitation

d. looking over the material and asking questions before beginning the reading

_____ 9. The author feels that the most valuable practice for a college student to use in remembering material is

a. overlearning

b. distribution of practice

c. covert rehearsal

d. recitation

_____ 10. The author would consider an adult's forgetting how to tie a shoe an example of a failure in

a. overlearning

b. distribution of practice

c. recitation

d. SQ3R

Answer the following with *T* (true), *F* (false), or *CT* (can't tell).

_____ 11. The author implies that short distributed practice periods would be the most efficient method for writing a research paper.

_____ 12. The author suggests that recitation is similar to a self-imposed examination.

_____ 13. Remembering the words to a popular hit song usually would combine the laws of overlearning, distributed practice, and recitation.

_____ 14. Recitation lessens fatigue and boredom.

_____ 15. The author considers the initial reading to be the most important key to learning.

▌▌▌ Vocabulary

According to the way the boldface word was used in the selection, indicate *a, b, c,* or *d* for the word or phrase that gives the best definition.

____ 1. "learn in school by **rote** (17)"

a. rules

b. short time sessions

c. logic

d. repetition without meaning

____ 2. "to **mull** over (35)"

a. ponder

b. work

c. progress

d. refine

____ 3. "**covert** rehearsal (36)"

a. planned

b. hidden

c. required

d. repetitious

____ 4. "**consolidation** of what has been learned (36)"

a. unification

b. reorganization

c. magnification

d. repetition

_____ 5. "**Irrelevant** habits (39)"
   a. annoying
   b. conditioned
   c. detrimental
   d. unrelated

_____ 6. "these **extraneous** habits (42)"
   a. extraordinary
   b. nonessential
   c. dangerous
   d. disliked

_____ 7. "still find **obscure** (73)"
   a. unnecessary
   b. ridiculous
   c. vague
   d. uninteresting

_____ 8. "a form of **feedback** (74)"
   a. rekindling
   b. reminding review
   c. instructions
   d. demonstrating

_____ 9. "a more **inquisitive** fashion (83)"
   a. vindictive
   b. intellectual
   c. curious
   d. studious

_____ 10. "**whet** your curiosity (85)"
   a. kill
   b. fancy
   c. find
   d. excite

▪▪▪ Essay Question

Explain why a series of study periods is better than one long cramming session when studying for an exam. In responding, define both methods, point out the advantages of short, separate periods, and use the research findings to corroborate your statements. Use a sheet of notebook paper to record your answer.

Selection **2**

PSYCHOLOGY

Leonard Freed/Magnum

Skill Development

Stage 1: Preview

Before reading the next selection, preview to (1) establish a purpose, (2) size up how the material is organized, and (3) plan an attack. Read any introductory *material, the first paragraph, the subheadings, the boldface and italicized print, the first sentence of some paragraphs, and the last paragraph. Think about the selection as a whole and then complete the following sentences.*

1. Memory retrieval seems to mean _____

_____

_____

2. After reading this selection, I would like to know _____

_____

_____

3. Regarding this topic, I already know _____

_____

Stage 2: Integrate Knowledge While Reading

Since each reader interacts with material in an individual manner, it would be artificial to require certain thinking strategies to be used in certain places. As you read the following selection, make a note in the margin of at least one instance when you used the following strategies.

1. Predict
2. Picture
3. Form analogies
4. Verbalize points
5. Fix up strategies

MEMORY RETRIEVAL*

Bootzin et al., from *Psychology Today*

Retrieval Cues

A **retrieval cue** is a piece of information that helps us to retrieve information from long-term memory. It can be a word, a sight, an odor, a texture that reminds us of the information we are seeking—or that summons unbidden an event from the past. For example, the odor of evergreens may suddenly evoke the memory of Christmases past.

5 Retrieval cues are taken seriously by the legal system and often used in court to remind a witness of some event. In one court decision, the range of possible retrieval cues was described as "the creaking of a hinge, the whistling of a tune, the smell of seaweed, the

*LEARNING STRATEGY: What is known by psychologists about memory and how do memory systems work?

From *Psychology Today: An Introduction*, Fifth Edition by Richard R. Bootzin, et al., pp. 212–220. Copyright © 1975, 1979, 1983 by Random House, Inc. Reprinted by permission of Random House, Inc.

sight of an old photograph, the taste of nutmeg, the touch of a piece of canvas" (*Fanelli* v.
U.S. Gypsum Co., 1944). Many aspects of memory—including recognition and recall, state-
10   dependent memory, and the elusiveness of information that remains stubbornly on the
tip of the tongue—can be understood by applying the concept of retrieval cues.

Recognition and Recall.   Retrieval takes two basic forms: recognition and recall.
Recognition requires us to realize whether something that is before us has been seen or
heard in the past. The process seems to occur automatically and is usually accurate. A
15   familiar act of recognition occurs in answering multiple-choice questions. Three possible
answers are in view; the task is to recognize the correct item. **Recall** requires us to
retrieve specific pieces of information in the information's absence. The process often
demands an active search of long-term memory. To answer the question, "What is your
mother's family name?" the item must be recalled from memory.
20   Recognition is easier than recall because the most effective possible retrieval cue is
present—the original information. There is no need to search long-term memory for it.
Recognition for visual memories is often extraordinarily good. In one experiment (Haber
and Standing, 1969), people looked at 2,560 photographs of various scenes, studying each
for ten seconds. When shown a group of photographs on a subsequent day, the subjects
30   were able to recognize between 85 and 95 percent of the pictures they had seen before.
In contrast, recall is often difficult because retrieval cues may be sparse or absent. The
most common recall failure is the inability to retrieve any information at all, as when
people grope for a word they want or fail to remember a name they thought they knew.
False recall is rare. When it does occur, it can usually be explained in terms of strong
35   familiar associations. For example, most grandchildren are used to having a grandparent
call them by a parent's name.

Relearning.   Sometimes information can be neither recalled nor recognized with
certainty, as when a student seems to have forgotten everything learned in last year's
German class. Yet if that student were to begin studying German again, she would be able
40   to relearn the language in less time than the original learning required. Although the
information is no longer accessible, it apparently leaves a trace in long-term memory that
facilitates new storage and retrieval, when cued by relearning.

State-Dependent Memory.   Many people have experienced an inability to recall on
the following morning events that accompanied heavy drinking the night before. Such
45   losses of memory may be due in part to the absence of retrieval cues, for several
experiments (e.g., Weingartner et al., 1976; Bartlett and Santrock, 1979) have shown that a
person's internal state—whether sober or drunk, happy or sad—can serve as a retrieval
cue. In **state-dependent memory**, information learned while in one physiological state is
difficult to retrieve when a person is in a different state, but when the original condition
50   is restored, the information can again be retrieved.

"Tip-of-the-Tongue" Phenomenon.   Sometimes we produce our own retrieval cues
internally, although they're not always successful, as the **"tip-of-the-tongue"** phenomenon
indicates. When we have a word or a number on the tip of the tongue, we are certain that
we know the word but simply can not pull it out of storage. The condition has been
55   described as "a state of mild torment, something like the brink of a sneeze" and when the

word is finally retrieved, there is a feeling of considerable relief (Brown and McNeill, 1966).

Aiding Retrieval

It is possible for anyone to improve her or his memory. **Mnemonic**, or memory-assisting, systems have been known for thousands of years and were practiced in ancient Greece.
60 Mnemonic systems organize information so that it can be remembered, using imagery, association, and meaning to accomplish their purpose, and they all make use of information already stored in semantic memory. However, the boost to ordinary memory they provide will not take the work out of learning. At first these devices may take more time than traditional rote memorization, but people who learn to use mnemonic systems
65 gain two advantages. First, routine things are memorized more efficiently, freeing their minds for tasks that involve understanding and reason. Second, facts required for tasks involving reasoning and understanding are remembered better (Higbee, 1977).

Method of Loci.   One mnemonic system is called the **method of loci**, and it involves the use of a series of loci, or places, that are firmly implanted in memory. Items to be
70 remembered are placed along a familiar route.

Anyone can use this method. Suppose, for example, that you must learn the names of the presidents of the United States in chronological order. Simply visualize a familiar place—say, the house in which you grew up—and imagine each president in a particular location: George Washington greeting you at the front door, John Adams and Thomas
75 Jefferson talking in the entrance hall, James Madison playing backgammon with John Quincy Adams on the stairway, and so on until you find Ronald Reagan chopping wood in the back yard. Thus, by taking a mental journey through the house along the same route, you will be able to visualize and recall the presidents. The same loci could be used to recall information about each of Shakespeare's plays or the chemical reactions involved
80 in photosynthesis.

Another mnemonic system based on loci is called the peg-word system, which uses twenty simple words as loci. Once memorized, these words act as pegs upon which any arbitrary series of information can be hung. Each of the twenty words stands for one of the numbers from one to twenty. For example:

85 One is a bun.
Two is a shoe.
Three is a tree.
Four is a door.
Five is a hive.
90 Six is sticks.
Seven is heaven.
Eight is a gate.
Nine is a line.
Ten is a hen.

95 Each item to be remembered is visualized as interacting with one of these words. Suppose the memory task involves a shopping list, consisting of tomato soup, potatoes, spaghetti, and pickles. Imagine tomato soup being poured over a large bun, a potato resting in a shoe, strands of spaghetti hanging over a tree limb, and pickles sticking like knives into a door. Once at the market, it's fairly easy to run through the familiar peg
100 words and recall the image that has been hung on each. The list of presidents could

be learned the same way with, for example, George Washington gnawing on a bun, John Adams complaining of a hole in his shoe, and so forth.

Imagery.   The method of loci is based on imagery and uses the principle that it is easier to remember something if the object can be pictured in some way. Imagery is most
110   helpful when the items to be remembered are concrete rather than abstract. For example, compare the word combinations "gorilla-piccolo" and "omniscience-euphony." The first pair of words, both concrete nouns, immediately suggests specific images, but the second pair, both abstract nouns, either suggests no images at all or suggests images that are not uniquely tied to the words to be remembered. Abstract nouns can be remembered
110   through images, but there is always the risk that "choir," chosen as the image for "euphony," will bring "harmony" instead of "euphony" to mind on later recall.

Memory for visual images improves further if the images are woven into some sort of scene. Studies (e.g., Bower, 1973) have shown that when a pair of words, such as "pig-ice," must be remembered, people who imagine the words interacting in some way, such
115   as a pig skating on ice, will remember the words better than someone who creates unconnected images for both words. The images need not be bizarre—ordinary scenes work just as well. But it is helpful to imagine a scene with a strong emotional impact. In one study (Sadalla and Loftness, 1972), people were shown lists of noun pairs and told to form images about the words that would later help them to recall the second noun in the
120   pair when they were given the first. Some of the people were instructed to form neutral images, vivid but without emotional content; others to form positive images, full of pleasant feelings; the rest to form negative images, which were "horrifying" and "uncomfortable to think about." On later memory tests it was clear that associating any strong emotion with an image was more effective than none; both positive and negative
125   images helped people recall missing words far better than did neutral images.

Why imagery is such a powerful tool of memory is not completely understood. It may be because imagery is processed in the nonlinguistic systems of the brain. In this view, words plus images are more likely to be remembered than words alone for the same reason that it is better to have two reminder notes—one at home and one in a pocket—
130   than to have only one. The two kinds of "notes"—verbal and visual—make it twice as likely that the message will be remembered.

Research with people who are totally blind from birth indicates that imagery can be used to improve memory even among those who have never had visual experiences. In one experiment (Jonides, Kahn, and Rozin, 1975), both sighted and congenitally blind
135   adults showed improved memory when they were given word pairs such as "locomotive-dishtowel" and told to imagine a relationship between the words of each pair—for example, the locomotive wrapped in the dishtowel. The fact that imagery instructions improved the memory of blind subjects as well as sighted ones indicates that imagery effects do not rely on vision. The reason for imagery's effectiveness with the blind is
140   unclear; attempts to relate its success to other sensory channels, such as hearing or touch, have been unsuccessful.

The Key Word System.   The key word system has been successfully used to learn foreign languages, and it relies on linking English words (key words) with foreign words that have similar sounds. The imagery used is much like that suggested to the blind. For
145   example, if the word to be learned is *pato* (pronounced "pot-o"), the Spanish word for

© Scott, Foresman and Company.

duck, an effective image is a duck with a *pot* (key word) on its head. To learn the French word for skin, *peau* (pronounced "poe"), imagine Edgar Allan Poe with a beautiful complexion. Students who use this method have learned almost twice as many words in the same study time as students who use rote memorization. In addition, since some key

150 words are better than others, the system works best if an instruction booklet suggests the key word but students create their own images (Bower, 1978).

Rhymes and Acronyms.   Unlike the mnemonic systems we have been discussing, rhymes and acronyms are specific. They can be used only once, so that although they are effective, they require a good deal of effort to create. Most, therefore, are handed down

155 and apply to common information that many people must learn. There are many mnemonic rhymes: "*I* before *E* except after *C*"; "Thirty days hath September, April, June, and November . . ."; and so on. The rhyme system is based on the fact that people have no difficulty remembering the individual items (the letters or the months); the problem is remembering something about them (letter order, number of days). Acronyms are

160 created by taking the first letter of each word in a series that must be remembered and making a word for them. For example, ROY G. BIV represents the order of the colors in the spectrum: red, orange, yellow, green, blue, indigo, violet.

▓▓▓ Skill Development: Study-Reading

Stage 2.   Review your marginal notes to see if you are using all five thinking strategies as you read. Which did you use the most?

Stage 3.   Stop and *recall* what the selection was about. Use the recall diagram to record the main point and the significant supporting details.

© Scott, Foresman and Company.

▦▦▦ Comprehension Questions

After reading the selection, answer the following questions with *a, b, c,* or *d.*

_____ 1. The best statement of the main idea of this selection is
  a. memory is dependent on retrieval clues and can be enhanced by their manipulation
  b. the ability to recall information is more significant than recognition
  c. mnemonic devices can enhance short-term memory
  d. retrieval clues for memory are state-dependent

_____ 2. A retrieval cue can be all of the following except
  a. a bit of information that helps recall thoughts from long-term memory
  b. a word that reminds us of the information we are seeking
  c. an odor or a sight that evokes the past
  d. the word that seems to be on the tip-of-your-tongue but cannot be pulled from storage

_____ 3. Recall is a more difficult memory form than recognition because
  a. the most effective retrieval clue is present
  b. the original information is presented
  c. the retrieval clue must come from the retriever
  d. the information in the long-term memory is sparse

_____ 4. The author attributes the tip-of-the-tongue phenomenon to
  a. state-dependent memory
  b. an inability to produce successful internal retrieval clues
  c. the lack of information in long-term memory
  d. the absence of the information from storage

_____ 5. The author suggests that mnemonic systems
  a. take the work out of learning
  b. use imagery alone
  c. use information already stored in semantic memory
  d. are faster initially than rote memorization

_____ 6. The method of loci is a better memory system than the key word method for learning
  a. foreign languages
  b. items in a series
  c. definitions of vocabulary words
  d. brand names for grocery items

_____ 7. In the peg-word system the learner must first
  a. memorize a peg for each number
  b. make up numbers
  c. visualize the number itself
  d. reverse the order of the images that represent the numbers

_____ 8. The author believes that the types of scenes and images that are most helpful to memory are

a. bizarre
b. neutral
c. strongly emotional
d. positive rather than negative

_____ 9. The initial link or retrieval clue in the key word system of memory is
   a. place
   b. a similar sounding word
   c. numbers in a series
   d. an acronym

_____ 10. According to the author, the disadvantage of rhymes and acronyms as memory systems is
   a. they apply to common information
   b. they have a more generalized use than other systems
   c. they are specific to one bit of information
   d. they apply only to letters rather than concepts

Answer the following questions with *T* (true), *F* (false), or *CT* (can't tell).

_____ 11. According to the author's explanation, answering a multiple choice test would be considered an easier task than answering an essay exam.

_____ 12. Relearning a forgotten foreign language takes less time than the original learning required.

_____ 13. Mnemonic memory systems were first used by scientists in the United States.

_____ 14. Abstract nouns are easier to remember through imagery than concrete nouns.

_____ 15. Blind people are not able to use imagery effectively as a memory system.

▥ ▤ ▥ Vocabulary

According to the way the boldface word was used in the selection, indicate *a, b, c,* or *d* for the word or phrase that gives the best definition.

____ 1. "the **elusiveness** of information (10)"
   a. inaccuracy
   b. hopelessness
   c. frustration
   d. evasiveness

____ 2. "cues may be **sparse** (31)"
   a. few
   b. frequent
   c. forgotten
   d. misleading

____ 3. "people **grope** for a word (33)"
   a. think aloud
   b. search uncertainly
   c. stutter
   d. wish

____ 4. "the **brink** of a sneeze (55)"
   a. end
   b. beginning
   c. verge
   d. threat

_____ 5. "stored in **semantic** memory (62)"
   a. relating to language
   b. relating to nerves
   c. long-term
   d. ordinary

_____ 6. "traditional **rote** memorization (64)"
   a. regular
   b. familiar
   c. reliable
   d. mechanical repetition

_____ 7. "any **arbitrary** series of information (83)"
   a. random
   b. structured
   c. compatible
   d. organized

_____ 8. "Washington **gnawing** on a bun (101)"
   a. agonizing
   b. crying
   c. chewing
   d. banging

_____ 9. "in the **nonlinguistic** systems of the brain (127)"
   a. unmeaningful
   b. without nerves
   c. stationary
   d. not associated with language

_____ 10. "**congenitally** blind adults (134)"
   a. existing from birth
   b. completely
   c. recently
   d. severely

▦▤▥ Essay Question

To associate events in history, certain dates that form crucial reference points must be committed to memory. In United States History, the following dates are reference points. Using imagery and the mnemonic systems discussed in this selection, describe a plan for remembering these dates and events. More than one type of memory system should be used. Use a sheet of notebook paper to record your answer.

1492	Columbus discovers America
1620	_Mayflower_ lands English Pilgrims in Plymouth, Mass.
1775–1783	Revolutionary War
1812–1815	War of 1812
1861–1865	Civil War
1914–1918	World War I
1929	Stock market crash and start of Great Depression
1941–1945	U.S. in World War II

SOCIOLOGY

Ingeborg Lippman/Magnum

Inell Jones

Skill Development

Stage 1: Preview

Before reading the next selection, preview to (1) establish a purpose, (2) size up how the material is organized, and (3) plan an attack. Read any introductory material, the first paragraph, the subheadings, the boldface and italicized print, the first sentence of some paragraphs, and the last paragraph. Think about the selection as a whole and then complete the following sentences.

1. Unity in diversity seems to mean _____

_____

_____

2. After reading this selection, I would like to know _____

_____

_____

3. Regarding this topic, I already know _____

_____

_____

Stage 2: Integrate Knowledge While Reading

Since each reader interacts with material in an individual manner, it would be artificial to require certain thinking strategies to be used in certain places. As you read the following selection, make a note in the margin of at least one instance when you used the following strategies.

1. Predict
2. Picture
3. Form analogies

4. Verbalize points
5. Fix up strategies

UNITY IN DIVERSITY *

Donald Light, Jr. and Suzanne Keller, from *Sociology*

What is more basic, more "natural" than love between a man and woman? Eskimo men offer their wives to guests and friends as a gesture of hospitality; both husband and wife feel extremely offended if the guest declines (Ruesch, 1951, pp. 87–88). The Banaro of New Guinea believe it would be disastrous for a woman to conceive her first child by her husband and not by one of her father's close friends, as is their custom.

5

> The real father is a close friend of the bride's father. . . . Nevertheless the first born child inherits the name and possessions of the husband. An American would deem such a custom immoral, but the Banaro tribesmen would be equally shocked to discover that the first born child of an American couple is the offspring of the husband. (Haring, 1949, p. 33)

10   The Yanomamö of Northern Brazil, whom anthropologist Napoleon A. Chagnon (1968) named "the fierce people," encourage what we would consider extreme disrespect. Small boys are applauded for striking their mothers and fathers in the face. Yanomamö parents would laugh at our efforts to curb aggression in children, much as they laughed at Chagnon's naïveté when he first came to live with them.

15   The variations among cultures are startling, yet all peoples have customs and beliefs about marriage, the bearing and raising of children, sex, and hospitality—to name just a few of the universals anthropologists have discovered in their cross-cultural explorations. But the *details* of cultures do indeed vary: in this country, not so many years ago, when a girl was serious about a boy and he about her, she wore his fraternity pin over her heart;

20   in the Fiji Islands, girls put hibiscus flowers behind their ears when they are in love. The specific gestures are different but the impulse to symbolize feelings, to dress courtship in ceremonies, is the same. How do we explain this unity in diversity?

Cultural Universals

Cultural universals are all of the behavior patterns and institutions that have been found in all known cultures. Anthropologist George Peter Murdock identified over sixty cultural

25   universals, including a system of social status, marriage, body adornments, dancing, myths

·LEARNING STRATEGY: How do the examples explain the different principles and the overall idea of cultural unity?

"Unity in Diversity" from *Sociology*, by Donald Light, Jr. and Suzanne Keller. Copyright © 1975 by Alfred E. Knopf, Inc. Reprinted by permission of Alfred Knopf, Inc.

and legends, cooking, incest taboos, inheritance rules, puberty customs, and religious rituals (Murdock, 1945, p. 124).

The universals of culture may derive from the fact that all societies must perform the same essential functions if they are to survive—including organization, motivation,
30 communication, protection, the socialization of new members, and the replacement of those who die. In meeting these prerequisites for group life, people inevitably design similar—though not identical—patterns for living. As Clyde Kluckhohn wrote, "All cultures constitute somewhat distinct answers to essentially the same questions posed by human biology and by the generalities of the human situation" (1962, p. 317).
35 The way in which a people articulate cultural universals depends in large part on their physical and social environment—that is, on the climate in which they live, the materials they have at hand, and the peoples with whom they establish contact. For example, the wheel has long been considered one of the humankind's greatest inventions, and anthropologists were baffled for a long time by the fact that the great civilizations of
40 South America never discovered it. Then researchers uncovered a number of toys with wheels. Apparently the Aztecs and their neighbors did know about wheels; they simply didn't find them useful in their mountainous environment.

Adaptation, Relativity, and Ethnocentrism

Taken out of context, almost any custom will seem bizarre, perhaps cruel, or just plain ridiculous. To understand why the Yanomamö encourage aggressive behavior in their
45 sons, for example, you have to try to see things through their eyes. The Yanomamö live in a state of chronic warfare; they spend much of their time planning for and defending against raids with neighboring tribes. If Yanomamö parents did *not* encourage aggression in a boy, he would be ill equipped for life in their society. Socializing boys to be aggressive is *adaptive* for the Yanomamö because it enhances their capacity for survival. "In general, culture is . . . adaptive because it often provides people with a means of
50 adjusting to the physiological needs of their own bodies, to their physical-geographical environment and to their social environments as well" (Ember and Ember, 1973, p. 30).

In many tropical societies, there are strong taboos against a mother having sexual intercourse with a man until her child is at least two years old. As a Hausa woman explains,

55 A mother should not go to her husband while she has a child she is sucking . . . if she only sleeps with her husband and does not become pregnant, it will not hurt her child, it will not spoil her milk. But if another child enters in, her milk will make the first one ill. (Smith, in Whiting, 1969, p. 518)

Undoubtedly, people would smirk at a woman who nursed a two-year-old child in our
60 society and abstained from having sex with her husband. Why do Hausa women behave in a way that seems so overprotective and overindulgent to us? In tropical climates protein is scarce. If a mother were to nurse more than one child at a time, or if she were to wean a child before it reached the age of two, the youngster would be prone to *kwashiorkor,* an often fatal disease resulting from protein deficiency. Thus, long
65 postpartum sex taboos are adaptive. In a tropical enviornment a postpartum sex taboo and a long period of breast-feeding solve a serious problem (Whiting, in Goodenough, 1969, pp. 511–24).

No custom is good or bad, right or wrong in itself; each one must be examined in light

© Scott, Foresman and Company

of the culture as a whole and evaluated in terms of how it works in the context of the entire culture. Anthropologists and sociologists call this *cultural relativity*. Although this way of thinking about culture may seem self-evident today, it is a lesson that anthropologists and the missionaries who often preceded them to remote areas learned the hard way, by observing the effects their best intentions had on peoples whose way of life was quite different from their own. In an article on the pitfalls of trying to "uplift" peoples whose ways seem backward and inefficient, Don Adams quotes an old Oriental story:

> Once upon a time there was a great flood, and involved in this flood were two creatures, a monkey and a fish. The monkey, being agile and experienced, was lucky enough to scramble up a tree and escape the raging waters. As he looked down from his safe perch, he saw the poor fish struggling against the swift current. With the very best intentions, he reached down and lifted the fish from the water. The result was inevitable. (1960, p. 22)

Ethnocentrism is the tendency to see one's own way of life, including behaviors, beliefs, values, and norms as the only right way of living. Robin Fox points out that "any human group is ever ready to consign another recognizably different human group to the other side of the boundary. It is not enough to possess culture to be fully human, you have to possess *our* culture" (1970, p. 31).

Values and Norms

The Tangu, who live in a remote part of New Guinea, play a game called *taketak*, which in many ways resembles bowling. The game is played with a top that has been fashioned from a dried fruit and with two groups of coconut stakes that are driven into the ground (more or less like bowling pins). The players divide into two teams. Members of the first team take turns throwing the top into the batch of stakes; every stake the top hits is removed. Then the second team steps to the line and tosses the top into their batch of stakes. The object of the game, surprisingly, is not to knock over as many stakes as possible. Rather, the game continues until both teams have removed the *same* number of stakes. Winning is completely irrelevant (Burridge, 1957, pp. 88–89).

In a sense games are practice for "real life"; they reflect the values of the culture in which they are played. *Values* are the criteria people use in assessing their daily lives, arranging their priorities, measuring their pleasures and pains, choosing between alternative courses of action. The Tangu value equivalence: the idea of one individual or group winning and another losing bothers them, for they believe winning generates ill-will. In fact, when Europeans brought soccer to the Tangu, they altered the rules so that the object of the game was for two teams to score the same number of goals. Sometimes their soccer games went on for days! American games, in contrast, are highly competitive; there are *always* winners and losers. Many rule books include provisions for overtime and "sudden death" to prevent ties, which leave Americans dissatisfied. World Series, Superbowls, championships in basketball and hockey, Olympic Gold Medals are front page news in this country. In the words of the late football coach Vince Lombardi, "Winning isn't everything, it's the only thing."

Norms, the rules that guide behavior in everyday situations, are derived from values, but norms and values can conflict, as we indicated in Chapter 3. You may recall a news item that appeared in American newspapers in December 1972, describing the discovery of survivors of a plane crash 12,000 feet in the Andes. The crash had occurred on October 13; sixteen of the passengers (a rugby team and their supporters) managed to survive for sixty-nine days in near-zero temperatures. The story made headlines because, to stay alive,

© Scott, Foresman and Company.

115 the survivors had eaten parts of their dead companions. Officials, speaking for the group, stressed how valiantly the survivors had tried to save the lives of the injured people and how they had held religious services regularly. The survivors' explanations are quite interesting, for they reveal how important it is to people to justify their actions, to resolve conflicts in norms and values (here, the positive value of survival vs. the taboo against
120 cannibalism). Some of the survivors compared their action to a heart transplant, using parts of a dead person's body to save another person's life. Others equated their act with the sacrament of communion. In the words of one religious survivor, "If we would have died, it would have been suicide, which is condemned by the Roman Catholic faith" (Read, 1974).   /1708

▦▦▦ Skill Development: Study-Reading

Stage 2:   Review your marginal notes to see if you are using all five thinking strategies as you read. Which did you use most?

Stage 3:   Stop and recall what the selection was about. Use the recall diagram to record the main point and the significant supporting details.

▦▦▦ Comprehension Questions

After reading the selection answer the following questions with *a, b, c,* or *d.*

1. The best statement of the main idea of this selection is
   a. the variety of practices and customs in society show few threads of cultural unity
   b. the unusual variations in societies gain acceptability because of the cultural universals in all known societies

    c. a variety of cultural universals provides adaptive choices for specific
      societies

    d. cultural universals are found in all known societies even though the
      details of the cultures may vary widely

_____ 2. The author believes that the primary cultural universal addressed in the
    Eskimo custom of offering wives to guests is

    a. bearing and raising of children

    b. social status

    c. hospitality

    d. incest taboos

_____ 3. The custom of striking practiced by the Yanomamö serves the adaptive
    function of

    a. developing fierce warriors

    b. binding parent and child closer together

    c. developing physical respect for parents

    d. encouraging early independence from parental care

_____ 4. Cultural universals might be defined as

    a. each culture in the universe

    b. similar basic living patterns

    c. the ability for cultures to live together in harmony

    d. the differences among cultures

_____ 5. The author implies that universals of culture exist because of

    a. a social desire to be more alike

    b. the differences in cultural behavior patterns

    c. the competition among societies

    d. the needs of survival in group life

_____ 6. The author suggests that the wheel was not a part of the ancient Aztec
    civilization because the Aztecs

    a. did not need wheels

    b. were not intelligent enough to invent wheels

    c. were baffled by inventions

    d. did not have the materials for development

_____ 7. The underlying reason for the postpartum sexual taboo of the Hausa tribe is

    a. sexual

    b. nutritional

    c. moral

    d. religious

_____ 8. The term cultural relativity explains why a custom can be considered

    a. right or wrong regardless of culture

    b. right or wrong according to the number of people practicing it

    c. right in one culture and wrong in another

    d. wrong if in conflict with cultural universals

_____ 9. The author relates Don Adams' Oriental story to show that missionaries
    working with tribesmen

    a. should be sent back home

b. can do more harm than good

c. purposefully harm tribal culture to seek selfish ends

d. usually do not have a genuine concern for the tribal people

_____ 10. The tendency of ethnocentrism would lead an American to view the Eskimo practice of wife sharing as

a. right

b. wrong

c. right for Eskimos but wrong for Americans

d. a custom about which an outsider should have no opinion

Answer the following questions with *T* (true), *F* (false) or *CT* (can't tell).

_____ 11. An American's acceptance of the Banaro tribal custom of fathering the first born is an example of an understanding by cultural relativity.

_____ 12. The author feels that the need to symbolize feelings in courtship is a cultural universal.

_____ 13. The author feels that culture is not affected by climate.

_____ 14. Among the Harisa, there is a tribal taboo against eating beef.

_____ 15. The Yanomamö are forced to raid neighboring villages because they cannot grow enough food to support their own tribe.

▥ ▤ ▥ Vocabulary

According to the way the boldface word was used in the selection, indicate *a, b, c,* or *d* for the word or phrase that gives the best definition.

____ 1. "efforts to **curb** aggression (13)"

a. stabilize

b. release

c. promote

d. restrain

____ 2. "at Chagnon's **naiveté** (14)"

a. lack of knowledge

b. gentle manner

c. jolly nature

d. clumsiness

____ 3. "body **adornments** (25)"

a. ailments

b. treatments

c. scars

d. decorations

____ 4. "**articulate** cultural universals (35)"

a. remember

b. design

c. express clearly

d. substitute

____ 5. "will seem **bizarre** (43)"

a. phony

b. unjust

c. grotesque

d. unnecessary

____ 6. "**smirk** at a woman (59)"

a. refuse to tolerate

b. smile conceitedly

c. lash out

d. acknowledge approvingly

___ 7. "**abstained** from having sex (60)"
    a. matured
    b. regained
    c. refrained
    d. reluctantly returned

___ 8. "long **postpartum** sex taboos (65)"
    a. after childbirth
    b. awaited
    c. subcultural
    d. complicated

___ 9. "being **agile** and experienced (78)"
    a. eager
    b. nimble
    c. young
    d. knowledgeable

___ 10. "ready to **consign** (84)"
    a. assign
    b. remove
    c. reorganize
    d. overlook

■ ■ ■ Essay Question

Identify elements of unity among diverse cultures of the world by discussing the common needs of group life and illustrating how the cultural concepts listed by the author are found in diverse cultures as well as our own. Use a sheet of notebook paper to record your answer.

VOCABULARY

LOCATING WORD MEANING

While reading, you come across the following words:

stratification   psychopathology   ultracentrifuge

What do they mean?
Should you stop reading immediately, look up each word in the dictionary, and jot down the definitions for future drill? That's ambitious, but unrealistic.

Your purpose for reading is to get information and ideas from the text, not to make word lists. Stopping to look up a particular word in the dictionary may or may not improve your vocabulary, but it definitely interrupts your train of thought and detracts from your comprehension of the material. A good reader can usually employ tools other than the dictionary to get an approximate meaning of a word and still not lose any understanding of the ideas in the passage.

This chapter will explain the use of three such tools: (1) context clues, (2) structural clues, and (3) the glossary. It will also explain how to use the dictionary as more than a word decoder.

CONTEXT CLUES

Context clues are the most frequently used method of unlocking the meaning of unknown words. The context of a word refers to the sentence or paragraph in which the word appears. Readers use several types of context clues. In some cases words are defined directly in the sentences in which they appear, whereas, in other instances, the sentence offers clues or hints which enable the reader to indirectly arrive at the meaning of the word. The following are examples of how each type of clue can be used to figure out word meaning in textbooks.

1. Definition

Complex scientific material has a heavy load of specialized vocabulary. Fortunately, new words are often directly defined as they are introduced in the text. Do you know the meaning of *erythrocytes* and *oxyhemoglobin*? Read the following textbook sentence in which these two words appear and then indicate the correct definition for each word.

When oxygen diffuses into the blood in external respiration, most of it enters the red blood cells, or erythrocytes, and unites with the hemoglobin in these cells, forming a compound called oxyhemoglobin.

Willis H. Johnson, et al., *Essentials of Biology*

From *Alphabets and Images* by Maggie Gordon. © 1977 Charles Scribner's Sons.

erythrocytes means

a. diffused oxygen
b. red blood cells
c. respiration process

oxyhemoglobin means

a. hemoglobin without oxygen
b. dominant oxygen cells
c. combination of oxygen and hemoglobin

The answers are b and c. Notice that the first word is defined as a synonym in an appositive phrase, and the second is defined in the sentence.

2. Elaborating Details

In political science you will come across the term *gerrymander*. Keep reading and see if you can figure out the meaning from the hints in the following sentence.

Since Governor Elbridge Gerry's newly engineered electoral district "had the shape of the salamander," it quickly came to be labeled a "gerrymander," and since its wildly convoluted shape seemed to typify the widespread practice of forming districts with distorted boundaries, the usage of the term spread.

Theodore J. Lowi, *American Government: Incomplete Conquest*

gerrymander means

a. dividing voting districts unevenly to give unfair advantage
b. member of the salamander family
c. voting in a new electoral district

convoluted means

a. twisted
b. inflated
c. reduced

The answers are a. Both of these words can be figured out from details within the sentence.

3. Examples

In psychology you might frequently find a complicated word describing something you have often thought about but had not named. Read the following sentence to find out what *psychokinesis* means.

Another psychic phenomenon is *psychokinesis,* the ability to affect physical events without physical intervention. You can test your powers of psychokinesis by trying to influence the fall of dice from a mechanical shaker. Are you able to have the dice come up a certain number with a greater frequency than would occur by chance?

Douglas W. Matheson, Introductory Psychology: The Modern View

psychokinesis means
a. extrasensory perception
b. an influence on happenings without physical tampering
c. physical intervention affecting physical change

The answer is b. Here the word is first directly defined in a complicated manner and then the definition is clarified by a simple example.

4. Comparison

Economics contains many complex concepts that are difficult to understand. The use of a familiar term in a comparison can help the reader relate to the new idea. Can you explain *monopolistic competition*? The following comparison will help.

Monopolistic competition is similar to monopoly because each individual firm claims to produce a distinctly unique product: the *only* socially accepted toothpaste or haircream, the *only* truly tasteful soft drink, the *only* fully nutritious breakfast cereal. Monopolistic competition is similar to competition because there are many firms in the industry.

Marilu McCarty, Dollars and Sense

monopolistic competition means that industries are competing to sell
a. vastly different products
b. only slightly differentiated products
c. over priced products

The answer is b. In this case, both the comparison and the example aid the reader in understanding the concept.

5. Contrast

Can you explain what transsexuals are and how they differ from homosexuals? The following sentences will give you some clues.

Transsexuals are people (usually males) who feel that they were born into the wrong body. They are not homosexuals in the usual sense. Most homosexuals are satisfied with their anatomy and think of themselves as appropriately male or female; they simply prefer members of their own sex. Transsexuals, in contrast, think of themselves as members of the opposite sex (often from early childhood) and may be so desperately unhappy with

From *Dollars and Sense,* Second Edition, by Marilu Hurt McCarty, Copyright © 1979 by Scott, Foresman and Company.

their physical appearance that they request hormonal and surgical treatment to change their genitals and secondary sex characteristics.

Atkinson et al., Introduction to Psychology

a transsexual is a person who thinks of himself as
a. a homosexual
b. a heterosexual
c. a member of the opposite sex
d. a person without sex drive

The answer is c. By comparing homosexual and transsexual, the reader is better able to understand the latter and distinguish between the two.

Limitations of Context Clues

While the clues in the sentence in which an unknown word appears are certainly helpful in deriving the meaning of a word, these clues will not always give a complete and accurate definition. To totally understand the meaning of a word, it is frequently necessary to take some time after your reading is completed to look the word up in a glossary or a dictionary. Context clues operate just as the name suggests; they are hints, and not necessarily complete definitions.

▎▎▎ Exercise 1: Context Clues

This exercise on the use of context clues is divided into two parts: Part A and Part B.

Part A:

The object of the first part is to see how many words in the following list you can define without the use of context clues. In the twenty spaces below, indicate a, b, c, or d for the definition that best fits each boldface word. When you have finished, check your answers, record the total number correct, and move to Part B.

1. _____   6. _____   11. _____   16. _____

2. _____   7. _____   12. _____   17. _____

3. _____   8. _____   13. _____   18. _____

4. _____   9. _____   14. _____   19. _____

5. _____   10. _____   15. _____   20. _____

Total number correct = _____

Word List

_____ 1. usurped
    a. shortened
    b. acknowledged
    c. aggravated
    d. seized

_____ 2. derived
    a. ridiculed
    b. dismayed
    c. originated
    d. encouraged

_____ 3. adversaries
    a. supporters
    b. soldiers
    c. voters
    d. enemies

_____ 4. assimilationist
    a. one who adopts the habits
       of a larger cultural group
    b. a machinist
    c. typist
    d. one who files
       correspondence

_____ 5. dyad
    a. star
    b. two member group
    c. opposing factor
    d. leader

_____ 6. self-actualization
    a. imitation of self
    b. reality counseling
    c. achievement to fullest
       degree
    d. evaluation of past
       experiences

_____ 7. proximity
    a. substitution
    b. stubbornness
    c. uncertainty
    d. nearness

_____ 8. plausibility
    a. believability
    b. spontaneity
    c. amusement
    d. reversibility

_____ 9. heterogeneous
    a. revolutionary
    b. stagnant
    c. intelligent
    d. dissimilar (different)

_____ 10. gastrovascular
    a. relating to arteries of
       petroleum
    b. explosive
    c. digestive and circulatory in
       nature
    d. cellular interaction

_____ 11. planarians
    a. meteorites
    b. small worms
    c. birds
    d. lizards

_____ 12. anticoagulants
    a. demonstrators
    b. substances against clotting
    c. coal-mining disease agents
    d. germs

_____ 13. ameliorated
    a. improved
    b. finalized
    c. united
    d. exterminated

_____ 14. expropriated
    a. took from its owners
    b. industrialized
    c. approximated
    d. increased in size

_____ 15. **adherents**
   a. children
   b. followers
   c. instigators
   d. detractors

_____ 16. **stimulus**
   a. writing implement
   b. distinguishing mark
   c. something that incites
      action
   d. result

_____ 17. **debilitating**
   a. weakening
   b. reinforcing
   c. exciting
   d. enjoyable

_____ 18. **autocratic**
   a. automatic
   b. democratic
   c. self-starting
   d. dictatorial

_____ 19. **incentive**
   a. debt
   b. sensory agent
   c. encouragement
   d. suggestion

_____ 20. **disseminated**
   a. dissolved
   b. spread
   c. destroyed
   d. originated

Part B:

The purpose of Part B is to demonstrate how context clues assist the reader in clarifying or unlocking the meaning of unknown words. Each of the boldface words on the list appears in a sentence from a college textbook. Using the context clues in the sentences, again indicate a, b, c, or d for the definition that you feel best fits each boldface word. Check your answers, record your total number correct, and compare your scores on Part A and Part B. Did reading the word in context help? Were you uncertain of a word as it appeared on the list, but then able to figure out the meaning after reading it in a sentence?

Words in Context

1. Henry, to the end of his life, thought of himself as a pious and orthodox Catholic who had restored the independent authority of the Church of England _usurped_ centuries before by the Bishop of Rome.

   Shepard B. Clough et al., _A History of the Western World_

2,3. But his own income was _derived_ largely from other sources. He regained much of the royal domain and its revenues that had previously passed out of the crown's hand and added to it by confiscating the estates of his _adversaries_.

   ibid.

4. When members of a minority group wish to give up what is distinctive about them and become just like the majority, they take an _assimilationist_ position. An example is the Urban League.

   Reece McGee et al., _Sociology: An Introduction_

5. Georg Simmel was one of the first sociologists to suggest that the number of members in a group radically transforms its properties. He began with an analysis

of what happens when a dyad, a two member group, becomes a triad, a three member group.

ibid.

6. Rogers believes that everyone has a tendency toward '*self-actualization*,' the realization of one's potentials, and stresses that the human need for acceptance and approval is essential if self-actualization is to occur.

ibid.

7,8,9. However, the United States has lived in rather close *proximity* to its own Constitution and can by virtue of that fact at least claim, with some *plausibility*, that as a country we have managed to maintain conquest over an immensely *heterogeneous* society without falling prey to tyranny.

Theodore J. Lowi, *American Government: Incomplete Conquest*

10. The gut is essentially an elaborate *gastrovascular* cavity.

Willis H. Johnson et al., *Essentials of Biology*

11. Locomotion ranges from the generally nonmotile tapeworms to freely moving flatworms such as *planarians*, that glide on a slime they secrete by ciliary action of their epidermal cells and generalized muscular contractions of the body.

ibid.

12. The body can produce some natural *anticoagulants* such as heparin or dicumarol, which are formed in the liver. Also, some animals that depend on blood for nutrition—such as fleas and leeches—secrete substances to inhibit clotting.

ibid.

13. If France's sharp regional differences in development and prosperity are to be *ameliorated*, the Southeast and the West must be encouraged to grow more rapidly.

Jesse H. Wheeler, Jr., J. Trenton Kostbade and Richard S. Thoman,
Regional Geography of the World

14. Under a decree of September 1952, the government *expropriated* several hundred thousand acres from large landholders and redistributed this land among the peasants.

ibid.

15. One of the fundamental features of Hinduism has been the division of its *adherents* into the most elaborate caste system every known.

ibid.

16. While we are sleeping, for example, we are hardly aware of what is happening around us, but we are aware to some degree. Any loud noise or other abrupt *stimulus* will almost certainly awaken us.

Gardner Lindzey, Calvin Hall and Richard F. Thompson, *Psychology*

17. However, anyone who has passed through several time zones while flying east or west knows how difficult it can be to change from one sleep schedule to another. This "jet lag" can be so *debilitating* that many corporations will not allow their executives to enter negotiations for at least two days after such a trip.

ibid.

18. *Autocratic* leadership can be extremely effective if the people wielding it have enough power to enforce their decisions and if their followers know that they have it. It is especially useful in military situations where speed of decision is critical. Among its disadvantages are the lack of objectivity and the disregard for opinions of subordinates.

David J. Rachman and Michael Mescon, Business Today

19. Many social critics decry profits as an *incentive* but have proposed no practical alternative in a free society. The only other incentive that has worked is the one used most often in communist countries: severe punishment for nonproductive persons.

ibid.

20. Disseminated Magmatic Deposits are the simplest of the magmatic deposits. The valuable mineral is *disseminated* or scattered throughout the igneous body. In the diamond deposits of South Africa, for example, the diamonds are disseminated in unusual rock, somewhat similar to peridotite.

Robert J. Foster, Physical Geology

1. _____   6. _____   11. _____   16. _____

2. _____   7. _____   12. _____   17. _____

3. _____   8. _____   13. _____   18. _____

4. _____   9. _____   14. _____   19. _____

5. _____   10. _____   15. _____   20. _____

Total number correct = _____

▮▤▮ Exercise 2: Context Clues in College Textbooks

The following sentences have teen taken from *Psychology and You* by Dempsey and Zimbardo. The sentences contain the type of context clues that typically appear in textbooks. Using only the context clues, write the meaning for each of the italicized terms.

1. Children grasp the basic, deep structure of language long before they learn all of the adult rules. In fact, when children begin to learn the rules, they overextend them and get into trouble. It is more logical to say foots (for feet) and goed (for went). This tendency is called *overregularization*. Children apply the "normal" rules too strictly and must unlearn them later.

   overregularization: _____

2. Psychologists distinguish between *intrinsic* and extrinsic motives. When you

From *Psychology & You* by David Dempsey and Philip G. Zimbardo. Copyright © 1978 by Scott, Foresman and Company.

do something solely for the fun of doing it, you are said to be intrinsically motivated.

intrinsic: _____

3. An example of a *homeostatic* mechanism is the heating system used in most homes. When the house cools off, the thermostat relays this information to the furnace, which then provides more heat. As the air warms, the thermostat "feeds back" to the furnace a message to shut down. This "steady state" process maintains the house at a comfortable temperature.

homeostatic: _____

4. One hypothesis is that *affiliation* is motivated by a desire to reduce anxiety and fear or, in the everyday phrase, because "misery loves company."

affiliation: _____

5. Unlike the other psychoses, *paranoid* reactions are characterized by one major symptom—persistent delusions, whether they be of grandeur, persecution, reference (chance events are interpreted as being directly aimed at the individual), or all three.

paranoid: _____

6. Freud also believed that creative impulses represent the transfer of psychic energy from meeting basic biological needs into higher and nonsexual channels of behavior. He called this process *sublimation* (meaning, in one sense, to purify).

sublimation: _____

7. *Utilitarianism*, which developed in the 1600s, was a combination of hedonism and rationalism. The seventeenth-century English philosopher Thomas Hobbes maintained that since every person acted in his or her own self-interest, this alone provided "the greatest good for the greatest number." Thus, ethical ideals and social justice came about because they were useful to individuals.

utilitarianism: _____

8. Two widely used *sedatives* are alcohol in its various forms, and the barbiturates, or "sleeping pills." Both are known to depress the central nervous system, but beyond that, their exact biochemical action on the body is unclear.

sedatives: _____

9. Christian mystics aim for oneness with God through prayer and extended periods of contemplation of God. Such approaches require a *renunciation* of physcal pleasures, prolonged disciplining, and an altered lifestyle.

renunciation: _____

© Scott, Foresman and Company.

10. Sometimes we experience stress physically, in the form of physical illness. These *psychosomatic* reactions usually involve the autonomic nervous system, over whose functions we have relatively little conscious control.

psychosomatic: _____

STRUCTURE

What is the longest word in the English language and what does it mean? Maxwell Nurnberg and Morris Rosenblum in *How to Build a Better Vocabulary* (Prentice-Hall, Inc. 1949) say that in 1939 the longest word in Webster's *New International Dictionary* was

pneumonoultramicroscopicsilicovolcanokoniosis

Look at the word again and notice the smaller and more familiar word parts. Do you know enough of the smaller parts to figure out the meaning of the word? Nurnberg and Rosenblum unlock the meaning as follows:

pneumono:	pertaining to the lungs, as in *pneumo*nia
ultra:	beyond, as in *ultra*violet rays
micro:	small, as in *micro*scope
scopic:	from the root of Greek verb *skopein,* to view or look at
silico:	from the element *silicon,* found in quartz, flint, and sand
volcano:	the meaning of this is obvious
koni:	the principal root, from a Greek word for dust
osis:	a suffix indicating illness, as trichin*osis*

Now, putting the parts together again, we deduce that *pneumonoultramicroscopicsilicovolcanokoniosis* is a disease of the lungs caused by extremely small particles of volcanic ash and dust.

This dramatic example demonstrates how an extremely long and technical word can become more manageable by breaking it into smaller parts. The same is true with many of the smaller words that we use everyday. A knowledge of word parts will help you unlock the meaning of literally thousands of words. One vocabulary expert identified a list of thirty prefixes, roots, and suffixes and claims that knowing these thirty word parts will help unlock the meaning to 14,000 words.

Words, like people, have families and, in some cases, an abundance of close relations. Clusters, or what might be called "word families," are comprised of words with the same base or root. For example, *bio* is a root meaning *life*. If you know that *biology* means *the study of life*, it becomes easy to figure out the definition of a word like *biochemistry*.

Prefixes and suffixes are added to root words to change the meaning. A prefix is added to the beginning of a word and a suffix is added to the end. For example, the prefix *il* means *not*. When added to the word *legal*, the resulting word, *illegal*, becomes the opposite of the original. Suffixes can change the meaning or change the way the word can be used in a sentence. The suffix *cide* means to *kill*. When added to *frater* which means *brother*, the resulting word, *fratricide*, means to *kill one's brother*. Adding *ity* or *ize* to *frater* change both the meaning and the way the word can be used grammatically in a sentence.

To demonstrate how prefixes, roots, and suffixes overlap and make families, start with the root *gamy* meaning marriage and ask some questions.

1. What is the state of having only one wife called?
   (*mono* means *one*)
2. What is a man who has two wives called?
   (*bi* means *two* and *ist* means *one who*)
3. What is a man who has many wives called?
   (*poly* means *many*)
4. What is a woman who has many husbands called?
   (*andry* means *man*)
5. What is a hater of marriage called?
   (*miso* means *hater of*)

In several of the *gamy* examples, the letters change slightly to accommodate language sounds. Such variations of a letter or two are typical when working with word parts. Letters are often dropped or added to maintain the rhythm of the language, but the meaning of the word part remains the same regardless of the change in spelling. For example, the prefix *con* means *with* or *together* as in *conduct*. This same prefix is used with variations in many other words:

cooperate   *collection*   *correlate*   *communicate*   *connect*

Thus, *con, co, col, cor,* and *com* are all forms of the prefix that means with or together.

▦ ▦ ▦ Exercise 3: Word Families

Create your own word family from the root word *vert* which means *to turn*. For each of the following definitions, supply a prefix, suffix, or both to make an appropriate word using the root vert.

1. to change one's beliefs: _____vert

2. to go back to old ways again: _____vert

3. a car with a removable top: _____vert_____

4. to change the direction of a stream: _____vert

5. activities intended to undermine or destroy: _____vers_____

6. an outgoing, gregarious person: _____vert

7. a quiet, introspective, shy person: _____vert

8. conditions that are turned against you; misfortune: _____vers_____

9. one who deviates from normal behavior, especially sexual: _____vert

10. the side of a coin bearing the main design: _____verse

Word Part List

The following is a list of prefixes, roots, and suffixes. The list includes some of the most frequently occurring word parts. For example, the list includes the thirty word parts that the vocabulary expert claims will help unlock the meaning to 14,000 words. Study the list and become familiar with the meaning of each word part. For each item on the list, write a definition of the example. In addition, supply a word from your vocabulary that fits the definition following and using each word part.

	PREFIX	MEANING	EXAMPLE	DEFINITION OF EXAMPLE
1.	com, con, co col, cor, syn	with, together	comrade	_____

infectious or catching: _____

| 2. | .ad, ag, as | to, toward | advance | _____ |

one who has a habit for something: _____

| 3. | ab | away from | abstain | _____ |

away from the normal: _____

| 4. | de | down from, | debark | _____ |

to jump from the tracks: _____

| 5. | ex | out of | exodus | _____ |

to breathe out: _____

| 6. | re | back, again | retread | _____ |

to patch up or fix: _____

	PREFIX	MEANING	EXAMPLE	DEFINITION OF EXAMPLE
7.	in, im, en,	into	ingrown	_____
	to blow air into: _____			
8.	in, im, il,	not	incompetent	_____
	ir, a, non			
	not possible: _____			
9.	dis, un	not, opposite of	disinfect	_____
	to get off a horse: _____			
10.	ob, op	against	obliterate	_____
	the reverse of something: _____			
11.	contra, anti	against	contraband	_____
	to speak against another's statement: _____			
12.	uni, mono	one	monogamy	_____
	mythical animal with one horn: _____			
13.	bi, du, di	two	dual	_____
	marriage dissolution: _____			
14.	omni, pan	all	omniscient	_____
	both meat- and plant-eating: _____			
15.	multi, poly	many	multimillionaire	_____
	worship of many gods: _____			
16.	iso, equ	equal	isomagnetic	_____
	equal measure of pressure: _____			
17.	extra, hyper,	above	hyperactive	_____
	senses beyond the normal: _____			
18.	sub, hypo	under	subconscious	_____
	to plunge under water: _____			
19.	ambi, amphi	both	ambivalent	_____
	using both hands equally well: _____			

	PREFIX	MEANING	EXAMPLE	DEFINITION OF EXAMPLE
20.	pre, ante,	before	predict	_____
	room before the main room: _____			
21.	post	after	posthumous	_____
	to delay or set back: _____			
22.	mal, mis	ill, wrong	malady	_____
	discontent, ill-tempered: _____			
23.	bene, eu	well, good	benefactor	_____
	speech praising a dead person: _____			
24.	mega	large	megalomania	_____
	device for amplifying sound: _____			
25.	micro	small	microscope	_____
	a small organism: _____			

	ROOT WORDS	MEANING	EXAMPLE	DEFINITION OF EXAMPLE
1.	port	carry	portable	_____
	to trade or carry goods out of the country: _____			
2.	mit, miss	send	transmit	_____
	a duty one is sent to perform: _____			
3.	duct, duce	lead	conduct	_____
	an artificial channel to carry water: _____			
4.	vers, vert	turn	revert	_____
	usable on both sides: _____			
5.	geo	earth	geodetic	_____
	study of the earth: _____			
6.	spect, spec	to look at	spectacle	_____
	one who looks on, an observer: _____			

	ROOT WORDS	MEANING	EXAMPLE	DEFINITION OF EXAMPLE
7.	cap, cept	take, receive	intercept	_____
	social for receiving guest after a wedding: _____			
8.	fac, fact	make, do	manufacture	_____
	place where products are made: _____			
9.	ven, vent	come	advent	_____
	a meeting for people to come together _____			
10.	fid, fide	faith, trust	confidence	_____
	to trust a friend with a secret: _____			
11.	psych	mind	psychotherapy	_____
	a physician who studies the mind: _____			
12.	morph, soma	body	ectomorphic	_____
	a study of structure of form: _____			
13.	ver, veri	true, genuine	veracity	_____
	opinion of the jury: _____			
14.	pel, puls	drive, push	propel	_____
	to push out of school: _____			
15.	dem, demo	people	demagogue	_____
	government by the people: _____			
16.	idea, ideo	idea	ideology	_____
	visionary or dreamer: _____			
17.	somnus	sleep	somnolent	_____
	person who cannot sleep: _____			
18.	ced, cess, ceed	go, move along	recession	_____
	withdrawal of states from the union: _____			
19.	therma	heat	thermos	_____
	device for regulating furnace heat: _____			

ROOT WORDS	MEANING	EXAMPLE	DEFINITION OF EXAMPLE
20. clud, clus	shut	exclusive	_____
to finish: _____			
21. nil, nul	nothing	nullify	_____
to invalidate a marriage: _____			
22. later	side	equilateral	_____
action that is one-sided: _____			
23. sat, satis	enough	insatiability	_____
thoroughly soak: _____			
24. gest	carry, bear	digestion	_____
clogged and overcrowded: _____			
25. path, pathy	feeling, disease	apathy	_____
physician who studies diseases: _____			

SUFFIX	MEANING	EXAMPLE	DEFINITION OF EXAMPLE
1. er, or, ant,	person who	actor	_____
ist, eer, ee			
one who has a specialty _____			
2. ation, ition	act of	violation	_____
the act of making pure: _____			
3. able, ible	capable of	enjoyable	_____
that which you are able to see: _____			
4. ful	full of	careful	_____
being full of thanks: _____			
5. ology	study of	climatology	_____
study of bacteria: _____			

	SUFFIX	MEANING	EXAMPLE	DEFINITION OF EXAMPLE
6.	al	relating to	natural	_____
	relating to the mouth, spoken: _____			
7.	ify, fy	make, cause to be	exemplify	_____
	to make larger in size: _____			
8.	tude, ance	quality of	solitude	_____
	state of thankfulness: _____			
9.	ism	doctrine	romanticism	_____
	doctrine concerned with common ownership: _____			
10.	age	act of	salvage	_____
	act of storing: _____			
11.	cracy	rule	theocracy	_____
	type of rule by a king or queen: _____			
12.	gon	angle	polygon	_____
	five-sided figure: _____			
13.	log, logue	speak	dialogue	_____
	a soliloquy: _____			
14.	arium, orium	place for	auditorium	_____
	tank for fish: _____			
15.	naut	voyager	astronaut	_____
	voyager in the sea: _____			
16.	oid	in the form of	asteroid	_____
	a newspaper half ordinary size: _____			
17.	meter	measure	thermometer	_____
	instrument to measure pressure: _____			
18.	ics	art, science	mathematics	_____
	study of the action of electrons: _____			
19.	orgy, ary, ery	place for	granary	_____
	cloister for monks: _____			

	SUFFIX	MEANING	EXAMPLE	DEFINITION OF EXAMPLE
20.	chrome	color	heliochrome	_____
	a brand of color film: _____			
21.	archy	rule	monarchy	_____
	state of no rule and disorder: _____			
22.	gamy	marriage	bigamy	_____
	having three or more spouses at a time: _____			
23.	rupt	break, burst	interrupt	_____
	a volcanic explosion: _____			
24.	scope	watch, see	peristyle	_____
	instrument to record earthquakes: _____			
25.	itis	inflammation of	appendicitis	_____
	inflammation of a nerve: _____			

▓▓▓ Exercise 4: Word Parts in College Textbooks

The following sentences have been taken from two different college textbooks: a biology and psychology text. Using your knowledge of word parts and context clues, write the meaning for each of the italicized terms. Refer to the master list of word parts if you need help or want to check your work.

Biology: The World of Life by Robert Wallace

1. It has been found that an animal may not possess all its fixed action patterns when it is very young. Many of these patterns develop as the animal matures, as is the case with *morphological* characteristics.

   morphological: _____

2. For example, an animal may live in a desert habitat, or more specifically, in a briny desert pool. Furthermore, it may live in a certain part of that pool, its *microhabitat.*

   microhabitat: _____

From *Biology: The World of Life*, 3rd Edition, by Robert A. Wallace. Copyright © 1981 by Scott, Foresman and Company.

3. One of the most promising sources of power is *geothermal energy.*

    geothermal energy: _____

4. The hard covering, or *exoskeleton*, of insects is also composed of units of sugar bonded in a way that makes them indigestible.

    exoskeleton: _____

5. Even the most advanced *amphibia*, such as frogs, toads, and salamanders, return to lay eggs in the water, and their early lives are spent there.

    amphibia: _____

6. It has been jokingly said that people who practice the rhythm method of *contraception* are called "parents," although the joke is funnier to some than others.

    contraception: _____

7. On the other hand, it may be difficult to tell a male mouse from a female and the sexes of seagulls are almost identical. Sexual *dimorphism*—or the different appearance of the sexes—varies widely among animals.

    dimorphism: _____

8. In addition, sounds are *transitory*; they don't linger in the environment after they have been emitted.

    transitory: _____

9. The amazing feats accomplished by some practitioners of Yoga are believed to be due to *autonomic* learning.

    autonomic: _____

10. We know that in some species, such as the flatworm, the fate of most cells is never sealed; or how could *regeneration* take place when it is cut in half?

    regeneration: _____

Psychology and You by Dempsey and Zimbardo

1. Certainly, there is no basis for the conjecture that *prenatal* experiences could have such specific effects. Yet what happens in the mother's womb can affect the baby's development in important ways.

    prenatal: _____

2. The *parasympathetic* function (para means "alongside") words in close

From *Psychology & You* by David Dempsey and Philip G. Zimbardo. Copyright © 1978 by Scott, Foresman and Company.

coordination with the sympathetic word of the autonomic system, but plays a more passive role.

parasympathetic: _____

3. Nerves in the *somatic* system do one, and only one, of three things: they receive instructions, give instructions, or pass instructions along to other nerves.

somatic: _____

4. *Interneurons* serve as connectors between sensory and motor nerves, routing nerve impulses toward their destination.

interneurons: _____

5. As you perspire, excrete, and breathe, this *extracellular*, or "outer," fluid becomes depleted.

extracellular: _____

6. Through a process called *transduction*, the receptors translate external energy into a usable form of internal biological energy.

transduction: _____

7. For several minutes, you acted like a *somnambulist*, a person who walks, talks, and performs other actions in a sleeplike trance.

somnambulist: _____

8. From this perspective, the roles that the family members play are crucial *pathogenic* factors.

pathogenic: _____

9. *Heterogeneous* breeding is advantageous for animals, plants, and humans. It generally results in a stronger, more adaptable organism because fewer recessive gene characteristics surface or are passed on, as happens with inbreeding.

heterogeneous: _____

10. Recent claims that *megavitamin* therapy has been used successfully with some schizophrenics suggest that a severe vitamin deficiency accounts for certain aspects of the disorder.

megavitamin: _____

GLOSSARY

The first shock in a new subject area, like sociology or geology, is the vocabulary. Each subject seems to have a language or jargon of its own. Words like *socio-*

cultural, or *socioeconomic* crop up again and again in a sociology text. In truth, these words are somewhat unique to the subject-matter area—they are "made-up words" to describe sociological phenomena. The best explanation of such words and their relation to the subject area can usually be found in the textbook itself rather than in the dictionary. Often, textbooks have definitions inserted in a corner or at the bottom of a page, or more frequently, texts will include a glossary of terms at the end of the book or at the end of a chapter. The glossary defines the words as they are used in the textbook. Examples of two different glossary pages follow, one from a psychology and another from a biology textbook.

▤▤▤ Exercise 5: Using a Psychology Glossary

By referring to the glossary page from *Introductory Psychology*, answer the following with *T* (true) or *F* (false).

_____ 1. A person with neurosis should not be encouraged to hold a full-time job.
_____ 2. An Oedipus complex is associated with a female child.
_____ 3. An obsessive-compulsive neurotic does not have complete control over his own life.
_____ 4. Neurons are an integral part of the nervous system.
_____ 5. "*I* before *e* except after *c*," is an example of a mnemonic device.
_____ 6. Two people who act alike are said to have multiple personalities.
_____ 7. A nonsense syllable is a word whose definition does not fit the meaning of the sentence.
_____ 8. Heroin is considered a narcotic.
_____ 9. Monocular cues are corrective lenses for one eye only.
_____ 10. Negative feedback can reinforce the probability of behavior.

Glossary from Introductory Psychology

mnemonic device   coding technique that facilitates recall, consisting of a system of rules to assist and improve memory.

monocular cues   cues for depth perception involving the use of one eye alone.

moon illusion   fact that the moon looks larger near the horizon than when it is overhead, although it doesn't actually change in size.

moral reasoning   explanation for moral behavior; ideas behind a person's notions of what actions are right and wrong.

morals   learned values or standards by which a person judges his own actions.

From *Introductory Psychology: The Modern View* by Douglas Matheson, Copyright © 1975 by the Dryden Press, a division of Holt, Rinehart and Winston. Reprinted by permission of the author.

motivation   act or process of being activated or directed toward an object or incentive in the environment.

movement   stimulus cue for depth perception.

multiple personality   form of neurotic dissociative reaction in which the person manifests two or more distinct personalities.

narcotic analgesic   pain reliever, such as heroin.

narrative chain   story that ties ideas together in order to facilitate recall of verbal material.

naturalistic observation   method for studying behavior by observing and recording events as they naturally occur in life (subjects' behavior is not manipulated in any way).

negative reinforcers   unpleasant or adverse stimuli that increase the probability of a response if they are terminated or removed following the response.

nervous system   network of neurons that transmit nervous impulses.

neuron   nerve cell, a basic structure in the nervous system.

neurosis   a behavior pattern whose primary characteristic is anxiety or fear, it does not totally impair a person's ability to maintain a job, family, and friends.

neutral stimulus   stimulus that has no meaning to an organism other than generating an orienting reflex.

noncontingent   events that occur randomly, unconnected with any particular stimulus.

nonsense syllables   three-letter nonwords consisting of a consonant, a vowel, and a consonant used in studies of verbal learning and memory.

norms   social rules that guide our behavior.

object permanence   cognition developed during the sensorimotor period that objects do not disappear when we are not doing anything with them or even when they cannot be seen.

obsessions   persistent thoughts that a person may recognize as irrational but still cannot stop thinking.

obsessive-compulsive neurotic   person who has repetitive thoughts or impulses that rule his life.

Oedipus complex   according to Freud, sexual attachment which a boy has to his mother. (A girl's attachment to her father is usually called an Electra complex and doesn't seem to occur as often as the Oedipus complex.)

Douglas W. Matheson,
Introductory Psychology: The Modern View

▦ ▣ ▥ Exercise 6: Using a Biology Glossary

By referring to the glossary page from *Essentials of Biology*, answer the following with *T* (true) or *F* (false).

_____   1. A pollen grain and a pollen tube are the same.

_____   2. Plankton denotes both plant and animal organisms.

_____   3. The placenta is a region for the exchange of nutrients between a mother and an embryo.

_____   4. Photoperiodism includes both a plant and animal response.
_____   5. Chemical waste can be considered pollution.
_____   6. Platelets help stop bleeding.
_____   7. Phototropism is the intensiy of light on a plant.
_____   8. The pistil is not part of the flower.
_____   9. A phylum is organized in a random order.
_____   10. An animal, such as man, with one life form in a life cycle is polymorphic.

Glossary from Essentials of Biology

Phenylketonuria   A metabolic disease characterized by faulty phenylalanine metabolism and mental retardation.

Pheromone   Substances secreted by one individual which elicit a physiological, developmental, or behavioral response from an individual of the same species; an insect sex attractant.

Phloem   A conducting tissue, functioning chiefly in food conduction. Sieve tubes and sieve cells are the important units of conduction.

Phosphoglyceric acid   A three-carbon compound that is the first inter-mediate to appear in photosynthesis; also metabolite in glycolysis.

Photon   A light quantum.

Photoperiodism   Response of plants in growth and development to differing lengths of exposure to light; refers to vegetative organ responses as well as to flowering response; also response of animals to light duration.

Photophosphorylation   ATP production from ADP and P under the direct influence of light.

Photoreactivation   Recovery of microorganisms from ultraviolet damage under the influence of white light.

Photosynthesis   The manufacture of a simple carbohydrate from CO_2 and water in the presence of chlorophyll, with light as a source of energy and with electrons released. Oxygen is generally the electron acceptor.

Phototropism   Movement toward or away from light.

Phylogeny   The evolutionary history of a group of organisms.

Phylum   A taxonomic category; subdivision of a kingdom; a group of next higher rank than a class.

Phytochrome   Pigment that exists in green plants in two forms, one absorbs red light and one far-red light; involved in such processes as flowering, dormancy, leaf formation, and seed germination.

Pinocytosis   The intake of fluid droplets by a cell.

Pistil   The ovule-bearing part of the flower, composed of one to several carpels (megasphorophylls).

Pith   The central area of parenchyma cells in a shoot axis.

Placenta   In plants, a central part of some fruits, such as tomatoes, and to which the seeds are attached. In animals, the combination of

© Scott, Foresman and Company.

From _Essentials of Biology,_ second edition by Willis H. Johnson, Louis E. DeLanney, Thomas A. Cole, and Austin E. Brooks. Copyright © 1969 and 1974 by Holt, Rinehart and Winston, CBS College Publishing. Reprinted by permission of Holt, Rinehart and Winston.

extraembryonic membranes of the embryo and the wall of the uterus of the mother. It is a region for exchanges of nutrients, gases and wastes between the mother and the embryo.

Plankton Free-floating microscopic aquatic organisms, both plant and animal.

Plaque method Determination of the number of bacterial viruses in a sample by counting the clear zones of viral lysis in a layer of bacteria.

Plasma Fluid fraction of blood in which corpuscles are suspended.

Plasmagel The outer region of the endoplasm; stiff and jellylike.

Plasma membrane The very thin membrane that surrounds and differentiates from the cytoplasm of the cell.

Plasmasol The inner part of the endoplasm; fluid in nature.

Plasmodesma Fine thread that leads from the cytoplasm of one plant cell through the wall to the cytoplasm of an adjacent cell.

Plasmolysis Shrinkage of the cytoplasm of a plant cell away from the wall when placed in hypertonic solution due to loss of water.

Platelets Formed elements in the blood that participate in clotting of blood.

Polar body The very small nonfunctioning cells that are produced in the maturation of an egg cell.

Polar nuclei In plants, two nuclei of the endosperm which will triple-fuse with a sperm nucleus.

Pollen grain Young male gametophyte of seed plants.

Pollen sacs Areas in the anthers derived from microsporangia and laden with pollen.

Pollen tube An outgrowth of a germinated pollen grain.

Pollination Mechanical transfer of pollen from where it is formed to where it will germinate.

Pollution Defilement of the environment with solid waste, heat, trash, chemicals, sewage, and so forth.

Polymer A large molecule composed of many similar units; for example, polysaccharides, proteins, and nucleic acids.

Polymorphism The occurrence of more than one body form in the life cycle of an animal.

Polypeptide Many amino acids linked together from amino end to carboxyl end.

Polyploid Containing one or more extra sets of chromosomes.

Polytene The duplication of chromosomes in the absence of cell division. Usually there are many duplications, thereby giving rise to large chromosomes.

Population A group of organisms of the same species that interbreed with one another in a particular geographical area.

Position effect The phenomenon of varying phenotype with the different arrangement of the same number of genes on the chromosomes; for example, bar eye in the fruit fly.

Primary block A metabolic blockage due to a genetically inactivated enzyme.

Primary endosperm nuclei The single triploid nucleus in the ovule of higher plants that is the product of triple fusion.

Willis H. Johnson et al., *Essentials of Biology*

lemon yellow *n* (1807) : a variable color averaging a brilliant greenish yellow

lem·pi·ra \lem-'pir-ə\ *n* [AmerSp, fr. *Lempira,* 16th cent. Indian chief] (ca. 1934) — see MONEY table

le·mur \'lē-mər\ *n* [L *lemures,* pl., ghosts; akin to Gk *lamia* devouring monster] (1795) : any of numerous arboreal chiefly nocturnal mammals that were formerly widespread but are now largely confined to Madagascar, are related to the monkeys but are usu. regarded as constituting a distinct superfamily (Lemuroidea), and usu. have a muzzle like a fox, large eyes, very soft woolly fur, and a long furry tail

le·mu·res \'lem-ə-,rās, 'lem-yə-,rēz\ *n pl* [L] (ca. 1555) : spirits of the unburied dead exorcised from homes in early Roman religious observances

lend \'lend\ *vb* **lent** \'lent\; **lend·ing** [ME *lenen, lenden,* fr. OE *lænan,* fr. *læn* loan — more at LOAN] *vt* (bef. 12c) **1 a** : to give for temporary use on condition that the same or its equivalent be returned **b** : to let out (money) for temporary use on condition of repayment with interest **2 a** : to give the assistance or support of : AFFORD, FURNISH ⟨a dispassionate and scholarly manner which ∼s great force to his criticisms — *Times Lit. Supp.*⟩ **b** : to adapt or apply (oneself) : ACCOMMODATE ⟨a topic that ∼s itself admirably to class discussion⟩ ∼ *vi* : to make a loan — **lend·able** \'len-də-bəl\ *adj* — **lend·er** *n*

lending library *n* (1708) : RENTAL LIBRARY

lend–lease \'len-'dlēs\ *n* [U.S. *Lend-Lease* Act (1941)] (1941) : the transfer of goods and services to an ally to aid in a common cause with payment being made by a return of the original items or their use in the common cause or by a similar transfer of other goods and services — **lend–lease** *vt*

length \'leŋ(k)th, 'len(t)th\ *n, pl* **lengths** \'leŋ(k)ths, 'len(t)ths, 'leŋ(k)s\ [ME *lengthe,* fr. OE *lengthu,* fr. *lang* long] (bef. 12c) **1 a** : the longer or longest dimension of an object **b** : a measured distance or dimension ⟨10-inch ∼⟩ — see METRIC SYSTEM table, WEIGHT table **c** : the quality or state of being long **2 a** : duration or extent in time **b** : relative duration or stress of a sound **3 a** : distance or extent in space **b** : the length of something taken as a unit of measure ⟨his horse led by a ∼⟩ **4** : the degree to which something (as a course of action or a line of thought) is carried — often used in pl. ⟨went to great ∼s to learn the truth⟩ **5 a** : a long expanse or stretch **b** : a piece constituting or usable as part of a whole or of a connected series : SECTION ⟨a ∼ of pipe⟩ **6** : a vertical dimension of an article of clothing — **at length 1** : FULLY, COMPREHENSIVELY **2** : at last : FINALLY

length·en \'leŋ(k)-thən, 'len(t)-\ *vb* **length·ened; length·en·ing** \'leŋ(k)th-(ə-)niŋ, 'len(t)th-\ *vt* (14c) : to make longer ∼ *vi* : to grow longer **syn** see EXTEND — **length·en·er** \'leŋ(k)th-(ə-)nər, 'len(t)th-\ *n*

length·ways \'leŋ(k)th-,wāz, 'len(t)th-\ *adv* (1599) : LENGTHWISE

length·wise \-,wīz\ *adv* (1580) : in the direction of the length : LONGITUDINALLY — **lengthwise** *adj*

lengthy \'leŋ(k)-thē, 'len(t)-\ *adj* **length·i·er; -est** (1689) **1** : protracted excessively : OVERLONG **2** : EXTENDED, LONG — **length·i·ly** \-thə-lē\ *adv* — **length·i·ness** \-thē-nəs\ *n*

le·nience \'lē-nyən(t)s, -nē-ən(t)s\ *n* (1796) : LENIENCY

le·nien·cy \'lē-nē-ən-sē, -nyən-sē\ *n, pl* **-cies** (1780) **1** : the quality or state of being lenient **2** : a lenient disposition or practice

le·nient \'lē-nē-ənt, -nyənt\ *adj* [L *lenient-, leniens,* prp. of *lenire* to soften, soothe, fr. *lenis* soft, mild — more at LET] (1652) **1** : exerting a soothing or easing influence : relieving pain or stress **2** : of mild and tolerant disposition; *esp* : INDULGENT — **le·nient·ly** *adv*

Leni–Le·nape *or* **Len·ni–Le·nape** \,len-ē-lə-'näp-ē, ,len-ē-'len-ə-pē, ,len-ē-lə-'näp\ *n* [Delaware] (1781) : DELAWARE 1

Le·nin·ism \'len-ə-,niz-əm\ *n* (1918) : the political, economic, and social principles and policies advocated by Lenin; *esp* : the theory and practice of communism developed by or associated with Lenin — **Le·nin·ist** \-nəst\ *n or adj* — **Le·nin·ite** \-,nīt\ *n or adj*

le·nis \'lē-nəs, 'lā-\ *adj* [NL, fr. L, mild, smooth] (ca. 1897) : produced with relatively lax articulation and weak expiration ⟨\d\ in *doe* is ∼, \t\ in *toe* is fortis⟩

len·i·tive \'len-ət-iv\ *adj* [ME *lenitif,* fr. MF, fr. ML *lenitivus,* fr. L *lenitus,* pp. of *lenire*] (15c) : alleviating pain or harshness : SOOTHING — **lenitive** *n* — **len·i·tive·ly** *adv*

len·i·ty \'len-ət-ē\ *n* (1548) : the quality or state of being lenient : CLEMENCY **syn** see MERCY

le·no \'lē-(,)nō\ *n* [perh. fr. F *linon* linen fabric, lawn, fr. MF *lin* flax, linen, fr. L *linum* flax] (1821) **1** : an open weave in which pairs of warp yarns cross one another and thereby lock the filling yarn in position **2** : a fabric made with a leno weave

¹lens *also* **lense** \'lenz\ *n* [NL *lent-, lens,* fr. L, lentil; fr. its shape — more at LENTIL] (1693) **1 a** : a piece of transparent material (as glass) that has two opposite regular surfaces either both curved or one curved and the other plane and that is used either singly or combined in an optical instrument for forming an image by focusing rays of light **b** : a combination of two or more simple lenses **2** : a device for directing or

focusing radiation other than light (as sound waves, radio microwaves, or electrons) **3** : something shaped like a double-convex optical lens ⟨∼ of sandstone⟩ **4** : a highly transparent biconvex lens-shaped or nearly spherical body in the eye that focuses light rays (as upon the retina) — see EYE illustration — **lensed** \'lenzd\ *adj* — **lens·less** \'lenz-ləs\ *adj*

²lens *vt* (1942) : to make a motion picture of : FILM

Lent \'lent\ *n* [ME *lente* springtime, Lent, fr. OE *lencten;* akin to OHG *lenzin* spring] (13c) : the 40 weekdays from Ash Wednesday to Easter observed by the Roman Catholic, Eastern, and some Protestant churches as a period of penitence and fasting

len·ta·men·te \,lent-ə-'men-(,)tā\ *adv or adj* [It, fr. *lento* slow] (1724) : LENTO

len·tan·do \len-'tän-(,)dō\ *adv or adj* [It] (ca. 1847) : becoming slower — used as a direction in music

Lent·en \'lent-ⁿn\ *adj* (bef. 12c) : of, relating to, or suitable for Lent; *esp* : MEAGER ⟨∼ fare⟩

len·tic \'lent-ik\ *adj* [L *lentus* sluggish] (ca. 1930) : of, relating to, or living in still waters (as lakes, ponds, or swamps) — compare LOTIC

len·ti·cel \'lent-ə-,sel\ *n* [NL *lenticella,* dim. of L *lent-, lens* lentil] (ca. 1864) : a pore in the stems of woody plants through which gases are exchanged between the atmosphere and the stem tissues

len·tic·u·lar \len-'tik-yə-lər\ *adj* [L *lenticularis* lentil-shaped, fr. *lenticula* lentil] (15c) **1** : having the shape of a double-convex lens **2** : of or relating to a lens **3** : provided with or utilizing lenticules ⟨a ∼ screen⟩

len·tic·u·late \-lət\ *vt* **-lat·ed; -lat·ing** (1925) : to provide with lenticules (as by embossing, molding, or coating) ⟨lenticulated film⟩ — **len·tic·u·la·tion** \-,tik-yə-'lā-shən\ *n*

len·ti·cule \'lent-ə-,kyül\ *n* [L *lenticula*] (1942) **1** : any of the minute lenses on the base side of a film used in stereoscopic or color photography **2** : any of the tiny corrugations or grooves molded or embossed into the surface of a projection screen

len·til \'lent-ᵊl\ *n* [ME, fr. OF *lentille,* fr. L *lenticula,* dim. of *lent-, lens;* akin to Gk *lathyros* vetch] (13c) **1** : a widely cultivated Eurasian annual leguminous plant (*Lens culinaris*) with flattened edible seeds and leafy stalks used as fodder **2** : the seed of the lentil

len·tis·si·mo \len-'tis-ə-,mō\ *adv or adj* [It, superl. of *lento*] (ca. 1903) : in a very slow manner — used as a direction in music

len·to \'len-(,)tō\ *adv or adj* [It, fr. *lento,* adj., slow, fr. L *lentus* pliant, sluggish, slow — more at LITHE] (1724) : in a slow manner — used as a direction in music

Leo \'lē-(,)ō\ *n* [L (gen. *Leonis*), lit., lion — more at LION] **1** : a northern constellation east of Cancer **2 a** : the 5th sign of the zodiac in astrology — see ZODIAC table **b** : one born under this sign — **Le·o·nine** \'lē-ə-,nīn\ *adj*

le·one \lē-'ōn\ *n, pl* **leones** *or* **leone** [*Sierra Leone*] (ca. 1964) — see MONEY table

Le·o·nid \'lē-ə-nəd\ *n, pl* **Leo·nids** *or* **Le·on·i·des** \lē-'än-ə-,dēz\ [L *Leon-, Leo;* fr. their appearing to radiate from a point in Leo] (1876) : one of the shooting stars constituting the meteoric shower that recurs near the 15th of November

le·o·nine \'lē-ə-,nīn\ *adj* [ME, fr. L *leoninus,* fr. *leon-, leo*] (14c) : of, relating to, suggestive of, or resembling a lion

leop·ard \'lep-ərd\ *n* [ME, fr. OF *leupart,* fr. LL *leopardus,* fr. Gk *leopardos,* fr. *leōn* lion + *pardos* leopard] (13c) **1** : a large strong cat (*Felis pardus*) of southern Asia and Africa that is usu. tawny or buff with black spots arranged in broken rings or rosettes — called also *panther* **2** : a heraldic representation of a lion passant guardant — **leop·ard·ess** \-ərd-əs\ *n*

leopard frog *n* (1839) : a common American frog (*Rana pipiens*) that is bright green with large black white-margined blotches on the back; *also* : a similar frog (*R. sphenocephala*) of the southeastern U.S.

le·o·tard \'lē-ə-,tärd\ *n* [Jules *Léotard,* †1870 Fr. aerial gymnast] (1920) : a close-fitting one-piece garment worn by dancers, acrobats, and aerialists; *also* : TIGHTS

Lep·cha \'lep-chə\ *n, pl* **Lepcha** *or* **Lepchas** (1819) **1** : a member of a Mongoloid people of Sikkim, India **2** : the Tibeto-Burman language of the Lepcha people • • •

leopard 1

¹lep·ton \lep-'tän\ *n, pl* **lep·ta** \-'tä\ [NGk, fr. Gk, a small coin, fr. neut. of *leptos* peeled, slender, small, fr. *lepein* to peel — more at LEPER] (ca. 1727) — see *drachma* at MONEY table

²lep·ton \'lep-,tän\ *n* [Gk *leptos* + E ²-*on*] (ca. 1948) : any of a family of particles (as electrons, muons, and neutrinos) that have spin quantum

(right margin, vertical) © Scott, Foresman and Company.

DICTIONARY

Not only does the dictionary contain the definitions of words, but it also provides the following additional information for each word:

Pronunciation. After the boldface main entry, each word is divided into sounds. A key to understanding the sounds usually appears at the bottom of the page.

Spellings. Spellings are given for the plural of the word and for special endings. This is particularly useful in determining whether letters are added or dropped to form the new words.

Origin. For many entries, the foreign word and language from which the word was derived will appear after the pronunciation. For example, L stands for a Latin origin and G for Greek.

Multiple Meanings. A single word can have many shades of meaning or several completely different meanings. Numbers are used to indicate each additional meaning.

Parts of Speech. The part of speech is indicated in an abbreviation for each meaning of a word. A single word, for example, may be a noun with one definition and a verb with another.

Guide Words. The two words at the top of each dictionary page are the first and last entries on the page. They help guide your search for a particular entry by indicating what is covered on that page.

flamingo

By permission. From *Webster's Ninth New Collegiate Dictionary;* © 1984 by Merriam-Webster Inc., publisher of the Merriam-Webster® Dictionaries.

▦▤▥ Exercise 7: Using the Dictionary

Answer the following questions, using page 98 from *Webster's New Collegiate Dictionary*, with *T* (true), *F* (false), and *CT* (can't tell).

_____ 1. *Lent* is eight weekends before Easter.

_____ 2. *Lentils* can be eaten.

_____ 3. The word *leotard* is derived from *leopard*.

_____ 4. A convex *lense* lets in more light than a concave lense.

_____ 5. *Lenient* can be both an adjective and a noun.

_____ 6. The plural of *leone* can be either *leones* or *leone*.

_____ 7. One of the origins of *lemur* is from the Latin word *lemures* meaning ghosts.

_____ 8. The word *lemures* can be correctly pronounced in two different ways.

_____ 9. When the words *lend* and *lease* are used together to mean a transfer of goods, no hyphen is required.

_____ 10. A legitimate word can be formed by adding the suffix *-esque* to the first part of Leonardo da Vinci's name.

MAIN POINT

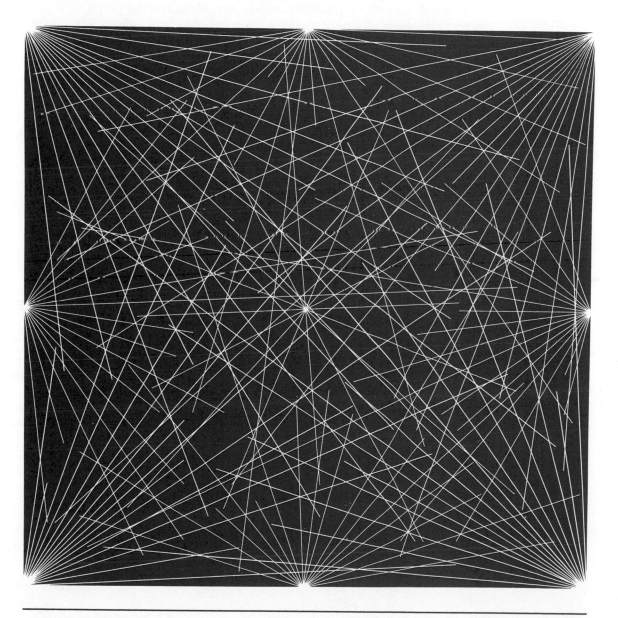

WHAT IS IT ABOUT?

If all reading comprehension skills were reduced to one basic question, that question might possibly be, "What is the main point the author is trying to get across?" In order to answer the question, the reader must first determine the topic being discussed, and then after considering the details, decide what point or statement the author is trying to make about the particular topic. For example, if a friend commented favorably on a recent article, your first question would be "What was it about?" and then you would ask "What was the point?" The first answer is the topic and the second is a statement of the main idea or main point.

TOPIC

The topic of a passage is a word or phrase that labels the subject but does not reveal the specific contents of the passage. The topic is a general, rather than a specific, term and forms an umbrella under which the specific ideas in the passage can be grouped.

Exercise 1: Topics

Each of the following lists contains a general topic as well as four specific ideas related to the topic. Circle the general topic for each list.

1. shirt	2. Psychology	3. democracy	4. Bermuda	5. coffee
pants	Social Sciences	autocracy	Islands	tea
jacket	History	oligarcy	Cuba	caffeine
clothes	Sociology	government	Haiti	cola
sweater	Political	monarchy	Tahiti	chocolate
	Science			

MAIN POINT

The main point of a passage is a statement of what the author says about the topic. Similar to the topic, the main point is general rather than specific and forms a type of summary statement for the specific ideas in the paragraph. Reading specialists use several different terms in referring to the author's main idea. In this book, all of the following terms are synonymous with "main point."

Sol LeWitt. *Lines from Sides, Corners and Center.* (1977) Etching and aquatint, 34¼ × 34⅞". Collection, The Museum of Modern Art, New York. Gift of Mrs. Barbara Pine.

main idea
central focus
gist
controlling idea
central thought

In all cases, the main point of a passage must be stated in a complete sentence. Constructing anything less, such as expanding a phrase or narrowing a subject, remains only a designation of topic. For example, an article on advertising might be quickly narrowed to "New Trends in Advertising," but being more specific by saying, "New Sexual Trends in Advertising" or "Costly New Trends in Advertising" still does not state the author's main point. The point of the passage on new trends in advertising depends on how the passage is developed and thus could be any of a million different ideas. Notice the diversity among the following possibilities:

1. New trends in advertising lack imagination.
2. New trends in advertising capitalize on sex.
3. New trends in advertising abandon sex.
4. New trends in advertising are predicted to cost more money than the old methods.
5. Here is a list of five new trends in advertising.

All of the five statements are about the same general topic, but when stated as a main point, the focus of each differs.

▐▐▐ ▓ ▐▐▐ Exercise 2: Main Point, Topic, or Detail

The following exercise is designed to check your ability to differentiate statements of main point from topics and specific supporting ideas. Beside each of the following, indicate whether the item is a statement of main idea, a topic, or a specific supporting idea. Compare the items within each group and indicate whether each item is a statement of main idea (*MI*), a topic (*T*), or a specific supporting detail (*D*).

Group 1

_____ a. A mother's affection for her small son, for instance, may be very strong; but her respect for her son's judgment may not be.
_____ b. The audience's attitude toward the speaker.
_____ c. The attitude which an audience will have toward you as a speaker will be based in part upon (a) your known reputation and, in part, upon (b) your behavior during the speech.

Ehninger et al., *Principles of Speech Communication*

© Scott, Foresman and Company.

Group 2

_____ a. Convenience goods are those that are convenient for the consumer to purchase.

_____ b. Purchasing convenience goods.

_____ c. People can buy chewing gum in many and diverse outlets, such as grocery stores, service stations, restaurants, drug stores, and through vending machines.

Pickle and Abrahamson, *Introduction to Business*

Group 3

_____ a. Although preschoolers may not have a clear-cut "identity" in the adult sense, each child is certainly aware of being unique, different from other children and with individual qualities shared by no one else.

_____ b. This naiveté is often revealed in children's drawings and paintings.

_____ c. Early individuality in children.

Dempsey and Zimbardo, *Psychology & You, p. 169.*

Group 4

_____ a. Changes in energy throughout the universe.

_____ b. Molecules, physical things, can be rearranged so that they hold more energy.

_____ c. Energy exists in a variety of forms, at different levels, and it ebbs and flows in countless directions throughout the universe.

Robert Wallace, *Biology: The World of Life*

Group 5

_____ a. The type of manufacturing and technology that developed indigenously in Africa is called cottage industry, and as such it was not able to compete with the mass manufacturing and industrialized techniques of the Europeans in the eighteenth and nineteenth centuries.

_____ b. African-produced brass and leather jewelry could not compete with the flood of European glass beads.

_____ c. The ability of African products to compete with European technology.

Wallbank et al., *Civilization Past and Present*

Group 6

_____ a. First, there is a process of gathering information.

_____ b. Regardless of whether group decisions are conservative or bold, they appear to involve common processes.

_____ c. Decision making in groups

Jonathan Turner, *Sociology*

Group 7

_____ a. Problems and expense created by poor morale

_____ b. Poor morale can cause so many undesirable problems that it is easy to see why it is very expensive.

_____ c. For example, some people have such an intense need for authority that, when they become supervisors, they attempt to force an almost master-servant relationship with employees to satisfy their own needs.

Pickle and Abrahamson, _Introduction to Business_

Group 8

_____ a. Self-concept, or the way in which we view ourselves, will influence the manner in which we process information about ourselves.

_____ b. The influence of self-concept on information processing

_____ c. We tend to reject feedback that does not fit our self-concepts.

Derlega and Janda, _Personal Adjustment_

Group 9

_____ a. An attractive appearance creates a "halo effect": this appeal influences all other impressions a person makes on us.

_____ b. Physical attractiveness is another category by which we stereotype people and, unfortunately, we tend to give it disproportionate emphasis as we communicate with them.

_____ c. Stereotyping people according to physical attractiveness

Weaver, _Understanding Interpersonal Communication_

Group 10

_____ a. Along with the confinement of women, the most serious indictment which can be brought against the age was the further growth of the passion for cruelty.

_____ b. When one went down with a disabling wound, it was the privilege of the crowd to decide whether his life should be spared or whether the weapon of his opponent should be plunged into his heart.

_____ c. The growth of cruelty in the Roman Colosseum

Burns et al., _World Civilizations_

STATED AND UNSTATED MAIN IDEAS

Look at the following picture and state the topic of the picture and the main point that the artist is trying to convey.

for the **U.S. ARMY**
ENLIST NOW

World War I Poster, Library of Congress

What is the topic? _____

What is the main point the artist is trying to convey about the topic? _____

_____

The topic is recruitment or joining the military and the main point is that the United States wants you to sign up for service in the military. In this case the main point is stated directly in the slogan that is included with the picture.

Now look at the next picture which does not include a slogan or a directly stated appeal. Again, state the topic of the picture and the main point the artist is trying to get across.

Dorothea Lange for FSA/Library of Congress

What is the topic? _____

What is the main point the artist is trying to convey about the topic?

_____

The topic is poor children and the main point is that the children are living in poverty and need your help.

The main point of the picture is strongly communicated in the faces of the children. Details such as the dirt, their clothes, the background, and their general untidiness support the main idea. Although the point is unstated, why do you think such a picture might make an effective advertisement to appeal for money to help the poor?

Similar to the pictures, the author's main point can be directly stated in the material or it can be unstated. When the main idea is stated in a sentence, the statement is called a topic sentence or thesis statement. Such a general statement is helpful to the reader because it provides an overview of the material. It does not, however, always include the author's opinion of the subject. For that reason, the topic sentence, while helpful in overviewing, may not always form a complete statement of the author's main point.

TOPIC SENTENCES

Topic sentences can be positioned at the beginning, in the middle, or at the end of a paragraph. Parts of them can also be found in the beginning and concluding sentences. The following examples demonstrate the different positions for topic sentences within paragraphs.

1. An introductory statement of the main idea at the beginning of the paragraph

Topic sentence
1. detail
2. detail
3. detail
4. detail

Under hypnosis, people may recall things that they are unable to remember spontaneously. Some police departments employ hypnotists to probe for information that crime victims do not realize they have. In 1976, twenty-six young children were kidnaped from a school bus near Chowchilla, California. The driver of the bus caught a quick glimpse of the license plate of the van in which he and the children were driven away. However, he remembered only the first two digits. Under hypnosis, he recalled the other numbers and the van was traced to its owners.

David Dempsey and Philip Zimbardo, *Psychology and You*

2. A concluding statement of the main idea at the end of the paragraph

1. detail
2. detail
3. detail
4. detail
Topic sentence

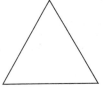

Research is not a once-and-for-all-times job. Even sophisticated companies often waste the value of their research. One of the most common errors is not providing a basis for comparisons. A company may research its market, find a need for a new advertising

From *Psychology & You* by David Dempsey and Philip G. Zimbardo. Copyright © 1978 by Scott, Foresman and Company.

From *Modern Marketing* by Edward J. Fox and Edward W. Wheatley. Copyright © 1978 by Scott, Foresman and Company.

campaign, conduct the campaign, and then neglect to research the results. Another may simply feel the need for a new campaign, conduct it, and research the results. Neither is getting the full benefit of the research. When you fail to research either the results or your position *prior* to the campaign, you cannot know the effects of the campaign. *For good evaluation you must have both before and after data.*

Edward Fox and Edward Wheatley, *Modern Marketing*

3. Beginning with details to arouse interest and then a statement of main idea in the middle of the paragraph

1. detail
2. detail
Topic sentence
3. detail
4. detail

What happens when foreign materials do enter the body by breaking through the skin or epithelial linings of the digestive, circulatory, or respiratory systems and after the clotting process is complete? The next line of defense comes into action. Phagocytic cells (wandering and stationary) may engulf the foreign material and destroy it. But there is another and very complicated aspect of the process. *This is the production of specific antibody molecules. Antibodies may circulate in the blood as mentioned or they may be bound to cells*; less is known about these cell-bound antibodies. Antibodies inactivate or destroy the activity of antigens by combining with them. The reaction is a manifestation of the immune response, and the discipline primarily devoted to its study is immunology. Generally immunity is considered to be peculiar to the vertebrates, but recent evidence suggests that a form of immunity occurs in invertebrate animals also.

Johnson et al., *Essentials of Biology*

4. Both the introductory and concluding sentences state the main idea

Topic sentence
1. detail
2. detail
3. detail
4. detail
Topic sentence

A speech of tribute is designed to create in those who hear it a sense of appreciation for the traits or accomplishments of the person or group to whom tribute is paid. If you cause your audience to realize the essential worth or importance of the person or group, you will have succeeded. But you may go further than this. You may, by honoring a person, arouse deeper devotion to the cause he or she represents. Did this person give distinguished service to community or country? Then strive to enhance the audience's sense of patriotism and service. Was this individual a friend to young people? Then try to arouse the conviction that working to provide opportunities for the young deserves the

From *Principles of Speech Communication,* 9th Brief Edition, by Douglas Ehninger, Bruce E. Gronbeck, and Alan H. Monroe. Copyright © 1984, Scott, Foresman and Company.

audience's support. Create a desire in your listeners to emulate the person or persons honored. *Make them want to develop the same virtues, to demonstrate a like devotion.*

Ehninger et al., Principles of Speech Communication

Unfortunately, readers cannot always rely on a topic statement being provided. For example, fiction writers rarely, if ever, use topic sentences. The following is an example of a paragraph with an unstated topic sentence.

5. Details combine to make a point but the main idea is not directly stated.

1. detail
2. detail
3. detail
4. detail

This creature's career could produce but one result, and it speedily followed. Boy after boy managed to get on the river. The minister's son became an engineer. The doctor's sons became "mud clerks;" the wholesale liquor dealer's son became a bar-keeper on a boat, four sons of the chief merchant, and two sons of the county judge, became pilots. Pilot was the grandest position of all. The pilot, even in those days of trivial wages, had a princely salary—from a hundred and fifty to two hundred and fifty dollars a month, and no board to pay. Two months of his wages would pay a preacher's salary for a year. Now some of us were left disconsolate. We could not get on the river—at least our parents would not let us.

Mark Twain, Life on the Mississippi

Topic Sentence: Young boys in the area have a strong desire to leave home and get a job on the prestigious Mississippi River.

QUESTIONING FOR THE MAIN POINT

In order to determine the main idea of a paragraph, an article, or a book, the reader needs to ask two basic questions. First, the topic should be established by asking, "Who or what is this about?" In responding, the topic should be stated generally, but yet it should be restrictive enough to reflect the details within the material. For example, saying that an article is about politics, state politics, or corruption in state politics might all be correct, but the latter is most descriptive of the actual contents. The second question to ask is "What is the main point the author is trying to convey about the topic?" The statement of the main point should be:

1. A complete sentence
2. General enough to include the specific details
3. Slanted enough to indicate the author's opinion toward the subject

Example:

In the process of getting attention and arousing interest, the salesperson is building up to the sales presentation. In the presentation, the salesperson strives to develop the customer's desire to purchase an item. The salesperson must try to achieve the balance between not pushing too strongly, taking too long to make the sales pitch, and quitting too soon in the sales presentation. The salesperson must be keenly aware of this important problem. Some salespersons are very pushy; some just like to hear themselves talk; and others, by their overbearing nature, lose a sale. By contrast, a salesperson may fail to push the sale and give the appearance of being uninterested. Oftentimes, a demonstration of how a product operates is a useful technique to let the customer handle the goods. Continue to emphasize how the product benefits the customer.

Pickle and Abrahamson, *Introduction to Business*

1. Who or what is this about _____

2. What is the main point the author is trying to convey about the topic? _____

_____

(The passage is about making a sales presentation and the main point is that the salesperson should develop customer desire and achieve a balance between being too pushy and not pushing enough.)

▥▤▥ Exercise 3: Determining Main Point

Read the following passages and use the two question system to determine the author's main point.

A. Crystal balls grow cloudy when it comes to predicting consumer behavior in the market. Who, in the 1960s, could have predicted the success of the CB radio or the disappointing performance of supersonic air travel during the 1970s? Consumers are influenced by such a wide range of circumstances that it is impossible to know for certain what products will sell, what businesses will be profitable, and what training will earn you the highest income.

Marilu Hurt McCarty, *Dollars and Sense*

1. Who or what is this about _____

2. What is the main point the author is trying to convey about the topic? _____

_____

B. The use of cocaine originated with the Indians of the Andes, who chewed the leaves of the coca bush, often as they carried large loads up steep mountain trails. The practice in

From *Dollars and Sense,* Second Edition, by Marilu Hurt McCarty. Copyright © 1979 by Scott, Foresman and Company.
From *Biology: The World of Life,* 3rd Edition, by Robert A. Wallace. Copyright © 1981 by Scott, Foresman and Company.

this country is to pulverize the bitter alkaline extract of the leaves and to sniff the powder. However, this habit causes destruction of the mucous membranes and may even dissolve the partition between the nostrils; a number of celebrated entertainers have ulcerated or even perforated nasal septa from cocaine overuse. Heavy users may inject the cocaine directly into veins.

Robert Wallace, Biology

1. Who or what is this about _____

2. What is the main point the author is trying to convey about the topic? _____

_____

_____

C. The crowded urban centers, particularly in downtown shopping areas, have caused many people to seek out stores that are easily accessible. For example, many customers prefer the convenience of the suburban shopping center with its many stores carrying almost everything a customer needs. Many merchants of downtown stores have joined together to provide free customer parking on lots or have arranged to allow customers to park free on city streets. Some have even built their own parking lots near their stores. With heavy emphasis today on accessibility, a convenient location is an important factor in choosing to shop at a particular store.

Pickle and Abrahamson, Introduction to Business

1. Who or what is this about _____

2. What is the main point the author is trying to convey about the topic? _____

_____

D. If at any one time of my life more than another, I was made to drink the bitterest dregs of slavery, that time was during the first six months of my stay with Mr. Covey. We were worked in all weathers. It was never too hot or too cold; it could never rain, blow, hail, or snow, too hard for us to work in the field. Work, work, work, was scarcely more the order of the day than of the night. The longest days were too short for him, and the shortest nights too long for him. I was somewhat unmanageable when I first went there, but a few months of this discipline tamed me. Mr. Covey succeeded in breaking me. I was broken in body, soul, and spirit. My natural elasticity was crushed, my intellect languished, the disposition to read departed, the cheerful spark that lingered about my eye died; the dark night of slavery closed in upon me; and behold a man transformed into a brute!

Frederick Douglas, Narrative of the Life of Frederick Douglas, an American Slave

1. Who or what is this about _____

2. What is the main point the author is trying to convey about the topic? _____

_____

_____

E. Audiences grasp new facts and ideas more readily when they are able to associate them with what they already know; therefore, in a speech to inform, always try to connect the new with the old. If you are giving instructions or describing a problem, relate your materials to procedures or problems with which your listeners are familiar. A college dean talking to an audience of manufacturers on the problems of higher education presented his ideas under the headings of raw material, casting, machining, polishing, and assembling. He thus "translated" the central ideas into an analogy his audience would understand and appreciate. Indeed, if a speech to inform is to meet the needs and satisfy the curiosities of audiences, *the association of new ideas with familiar ones may well represent the informative speaker's principal intellectual task.*

Ehninger, et al., Principles of Speech Communication

1. Who or what is this about _____

2. What is the main point the author is trying to convey about the topic? _____

_____

F. Delusions and hallucinations may well be the most dramatic of the symptoms of schizophrenia. A **delusion** is a powerful belief in something despite the reality of the situation. It is maintained despite evidence to the contrary. A **hallucination** is a sensory experience that has no basis in reality. A schizophrenic may have the delusion that he is Napoleon or that she is the Virgin Mary. A hallucinating schizophrenic may hear voices that no one else can hear or see a person that no one else can observe. Some patients have reported feeling electrical currents passing through their bodies. Disturbances in speech and thought are also important symptoms. Schizophrenics may use sentences made up of unrelated words (called word salads), or they may come to illogical conclusions. Patients might even claim to be God. The most frequent form of thought disturbance is confusion. Patients seem to know that many of their thoughts are not logical, but they cannot sort them out.

Derlega and Janda, Personal Adjustment

1. Who or what is this about _____

2. What is the main point the author is trying to convey about the topic? _____

_____

DETAILS

Look at the details in the following picture. Determine the topic of the picture, the main point, and then list some of the significant details that support this point.

From *Principles of Speech Communication,* 9th Brief Edition, by Douglas Ehninger, Bruce E. Gronbeck, and Alan Monroe. Copyright © 1984 by Scott, Foresman and Company.
From *Personal Adjustment,* Second Edition, by Valerian J. Derlega and Louis H. Janda. Copyright © 1981 by Scott, Foresman and Company.

L. A. Huffman

What is the topic? _____

What is the point the artist is trying to convey about the topic? _____

What are the significant supporting details? _____

_____

    The topic of the picture is the buffalo slaughter and the main point is that man's slaughter of the buffalo was a cruel waste. The significant supporting details are the dead buffalo, the gun, and the number of buffalo that must have been used for meat as opposed to the unused ones. In this case, the details develop the main idea and make the picture into a strong and moving statement about man's wasteful slaughter of the buffalo.

WHAT DO DETAILS DO?

Details support, develop, and explain a main idea. Specific details can include:

1. Reasons
2. Incidents
3. Facts

4. Examples
5. Steps
6. Definitions

    The task of a reader is, first of all, to organize the details under a main idea, and using that main idea as a focus, sift through the material for the significant supporting details. Textbooks are packed full of details, but fortunately all details are not of equal importance. Ask the following questions to determine which details are significant and which are not:

1. Which details logically develop the main point?
2. Which details help you understand the main point?
3. Which details validate the main point?

Noticing key words can sometimes help the reader distinguish between major and minor details. The following terms are frequently used to signal significance:

Key words for major details:
one, first, another, furthermore, also, finally

Key words for minor details:
for example, to be specific, that is, this means

Exercise 4: Topic, Main Point, and Details

The following passages contain examples of the five different positions of topic sentences within paragraphs. After reading each passage, determine the topic, the author's main point, and the significance of the details.

A. Adolescence is a period in which individuals are expected to express achievement motivation in some concrete fashion. Whether this entails academic success, athletic prowess, or social competence will vary from person to person. The general features of achievement motivation, such as autonomy, planning for the future, mastery of socially relevant skills, a devotion to effort and hard work, ambition, and a desire for upward mobility, all comprise a set of expectations that intrude heavily upon adolescents. Studies have demonstrated that social pressures toward the demonstration of achievement motivation are applied, often abruptly, early in adolescence and increase substantially throughout this period. Aversive behavior, such as the postponement of work activities, tardiness, erratic habits, and other forms of avoidance of responsibility, which would have been condoned in childhood are often severely punished in adolescence. He is expected to be an achiever, and to achieve consistently in many fields.

Burton Wright II, John P. Weiss and Charles M. Unkovic, *Perspective: An Introduction to Sociology*

1. This paragraph is mainly about
    a. the expectation of concrete achievements during adolescence
    b. the variety of avenues open to adolescents for achievement
    c. the aversive behavior caused by achievement pressure
    d. the parental pressure for adolescent achievement
2. What is the main point that the author is trying to convey about this topic?

_____

_____

3. Of the following details, the least significant in support of the main idea of the paragraph is
    a. areas of achievement will vary from person to person
    b. childhood aversive behavior is no longer acceptable

    c. social pressures for achievement increase after early adolescence
    d. academic success is stressed more than social competency
4. Underline the main idea if it is directly stated in the passage.

B. The furor over heart transplants died down as suddenly as it began. Once hailed as a medical triumph, transplants have fallen from grace over a period of a few years because most of the transplanted hearts are quickly rejected by the recipients. The job of actually removing the heart from the donor and suturing it into place was technically feasible from the inception of the idea, but the production of antibodies, which attack foreign cardiac tissue, was never successfully suppressed.

                                        Shelby D. Gerking, *Biological Systems*

_____
1. This paragraph is mainly about
    a. why heart transplants were unsuccessful
    b. how successful heart transplants were
    c. the change in public opinion over heart transplants
    d. the complex nature of heart transplants
2. What is the main point that the author is trying to convey about this topic?

_____

_____

_____
3. Of the following details, the least significant in support of the main idea of the paragraph is
    a. recipients rejected most transplanted hearts
    b. the transplanted heart was a medical triumph
    c. antibodies attack new heart tissue
    d. unsuppressed antibodies cause rejection of a transplant
4. Underline the main idea if it is directly stated in the passage.

C. The water in a breaking wave climbs far up the beach and then, losing its momentum, flows back down the beach under the influence of gravity. In so doing, it passes beneath several subsequent waves, aiding greatly in upsetting them. This seaward-moving current operating beneath the landward-moving waves is called the undertow. When waves are large, the undertow is correspondingly powerful and is able to transport seaward great quantities of material.

                            Henry M. Kendall et al., *Introduction to Geography*

_____
1. This paragraph is mainly about
    a. the influence of gravity
    b. waves
    c. currents in the ocean
    d. undertows
2. What is the main point that the author is trying to convey about this topic?

_____

_____

3. Of the following details, the least significant in support of the main idea is
   a. the undertow passes under waves
   b. if the waves are large, the undertow is therefore powerful
   c. the changes of the tides are governed by the moon
   d. the undertow carries material into sea
4. Underline the main idea if it is directly stated in the passage.

D. In addition to offsetting the tendency to overheat, insensible perspiration may be helpful, insofar as the palms and soles are concerned, for providing friction in order to facilitate the handling of objects and performing of work. The palms and soles do not secrete an oily sebum, as does the skin elsewhere on the body, and in the absence of moisture on their surface, it would be more difficult to get a good grip on certain things. In this connection, the reader may reflect on a baseball batter's habit of spitting on his hands when called to bat.

Roy Hartenstein, *Human Anatomy and Physiology*

1. This paragraph is mainly about
   a. offsetting the tendency to overheat
   b. the benefit of insensible perspiration on palms and soles
   c. the absence of oily sebum in palms and soles
   d. natural creation of friction
2. What is the main point that the author is trying to convey about this topic?

3. Of the following details, the least significant in support of the main idea of the paragraph is
   a. palms and soles do not secrete oily sebum
   b. a baseball batter spits on his hands before batting
   c. palms and soles perspire
   d. insensible perspiration cools the overheated body
4. Underline the main idea if it is directly stated in the passage.

GETTING THE MAIN POINT OF LONGER SELECTIONS

Understanding the main point of longer selections requires a little more thinking than finding the main idea of a single paragraph. Since longer selections such as articles or chapters involve more material, the challenge of tying the ideas together can be confusing and complicated. Each paragraph of a longer selection usually represents a new aspect of a supporting detail. In addition, several major ideas may contribute to developing the overall main point. The reader, therefore, must fit the many pieces together under one central theme.

From *Human Anatomy and Physiology: Principles and Applications* by Roy Hartenstein. © 1976 by Litton Educational Publishing. Reprinted by permission of Wadsworth Publishing Company.

For longer selections, the reader needs to add an extra step between the two questions, "What is the topic?" and "What is the main point the author is trying to convey?" The step involves organizing the material into manageable subunits and then relating those to the whole. Two additional questions to ask are, "Under what subsections can these ideas be grouped?" and "How do these subsections contribute to the whole?"

Use the following suggestions to determine the main point of longer selections. The techniques are similar to those used in previewing and skimming, two skills that also focus on the overall central theme.

1. Think about the significance of the title. What does the title suggest about the topic?
2. Read the first one or two paragraphs for a statement of the topic or thesis. What does the selection seem to be about?
3. Read the subheadings and, if necessary, glance at the first sentences of some of the paragraphs. From these clues what does the article seem to be about?
4. Look for clues that indicate how the material is organized.
   a. Is the purpose to define a term, to prove an opinion, to explain a concept, to describe a situation, or to persuade the reader towards a particular point of view?
   b. Is the material organized into a list of examples, a time order or sequence, a comparison or contrast, or a cause and effect relationship? (Refer to appendix B for examples of these organizational patterns.)
5. As you read, organize the paragraphs into subsections. Give each subsection a title. These become your significant supporting details.
6. Determine how the overall organization and subsections relate to the whole and answer the question, "What is the main point the author is trying to convey in this selection?"

Selection **1**

ANTHROPOLOGY

Fred Bruemmer

Stage 1: Preview

Preview *the selection and complete the following sentence: After reading this selection, I would like to know* _____

_____

_____

Stage 2: Integrate Knowledge While Reading

As you read, use the thinking strategies discussed in Chapter 2:

1. *Predict*
2. *Picture*
3. *Form analogies*
4. *Verbalize points*
5. *Fix up strategies*

THE ESKIMOS*

Conrad Phillip Kottak, from *Anthropology: The Exploration of Human Diversity*

Among foragers, there is nothing that could accurately be called law in the sense of a legal code, including machinery of adjudication and enforcement, that applies to all members of the population. In some foraging societies, there may be a great deal of disorder. The Eskimos can serve as a good example. There are approximately 20,000
5   Eskimos, and the population extends over approximately 6,000 miles in the extreme north, the Arctic region from eastern Siberia to eastern Greenland. The only significant social groups among Eskimos are the nuclear family and the local band. Bands are tied together through personal relationships established by each member individually. Some of the bands have headmen. There are also shamans, diviners, in Eskimo bands. These
10   positions confer little power on those who occupy them.

Why do disputes arise among the Eskimos? Most involve males, and most originate over women. Wife stealing and adultery are common causes for disputes. Although it is acceptable for one man to have intercourse with another man's wife, access is by invitation only. If a man discovers that his wife has been having sexual relations without
15   his sanction, he considers himself wronged, and he is expected to retaliate against the male offender. The manner of retaliation will be examined after discussion of a related reason for disputes—wife stealing.

The Eskimos, you will remember, practice female infanticide. There are several reasons for this. The male's role in Eskimo subsistence activity is primary; people prefer to have
20   sons who can care for them when they become old. Furthermore, men have to travel on land and sea, hunting and fishing in a bitter environment. Their tasks are much more dangerous than those of women. Female infanticide regulates the size of the Eskimo population: since the male role in the division of labor takes more lives, there would be

*LEARNING STRATEGY: Seek to explain how the Eskimo society has adapted and functions in a system that has no set legal code and no machinery for law enforcement.

From *Anthropology: The Exploration of Human Diversity* by Conrad Phillip Kottak, pp. 239, 343–345. Copyright © 1974 by Random House, Inc. Reprinted by permission of Random House, Inc.

an excess of females over males in the adult population if a proportion of female infants
25 were not killed. Even with female infanticide, however, slightly more females survive than
males. This demographic imbalance accommodates polygyny. Some men take two or
three wives. Usually, it is a successful hunter-fisherman who marries plural wives. The
ability to support more than one wife confers a certain amount of prestige. Yet, it also
encourages envy. If it becomes obvious that a man is marrying plural wives merely to
30 increase his status, he is likely to have one of his wives stolen by a rival. This, like
adultery, can lead to conflict.

A wronged man has several alternatives. Community opinion will not let him ignore the
offense; one way of avenging his tarnished honor is to kill the man who has stolen his
wife. However, if he does this, he can be reasonably sure that one of the close kinsmen of
35 the dead man will try to kill him in retaliation. Consider an example. Sam has two wives,
Cynthia and Tricia. Irving, a younger man from another local group, manages to steal
Tricia and take her home. Sam's social status and honor have now been tarnished. He
must avenge himself in some way. One way of doing it is to kill Irving. However, Sam
knows that Irving has a brother, and if he kills Irving, Irving's brother will be bound by
40 kinship to kill Sam. Sam also has a brother who will then be obliged to kill Irving's
brother. One dispute could escalate into several deaths.

Once such a *blood feud* develops, there is no state authority to intervene and stop it.
However, an aggrieved individual always has the alternative of challenging the offending
party to a song contest. This is a means of regaining lost honor. The two parties in the
45 dispute make up insulting songs about one another. The audience listens and judges the
insults. At the end of the song match, one of the two is declared the winner. If the man
whose wife has been stolen wins the song contest, there is no guarantee that his wife will
return to him. The woman appears to have a good bit to say about where she will remain.
Sometimes, she will decide to stay with her abductor.
50 There are several acts of killing which are deemed crimes in the contemporary United
States and in other state-organized societies but which are not considered criminal among
the Eskimos. Individuals who feel that, because of age or infirmity, they are no longer
economically useful may kill themselves or ask others to kill them. An old person or
invalid who wishes to die will ask a close relative, a son perhaps, to end his life. It is
55 necessary to ask a close relative to be sure that the kinsmen of the deceased will not take
revenge on his killer.

Occasionally among the Eskimos we encounter something suggestive of law, the
enforcement of a decision for the public good. An individual who has committed a single
homicide is apt to be attacked and perhaps killed by a close kinsman of his victim.
60 Suppose, however, that before the avenger can kill him, he kills the avenger instead. He
has now committed two murders. The Eskimos fear individuals who murder more than
once. In such cases, there may be a meeting of adult male members of the offender's
local group. It is apparently the headman of the group who initiates this meeting. If there
is unanimous agreement that the individual must die, then one of his close relatives is
65 usually chosen to carry out the execution. Again, this is to avoid the possibility of revenge
by kinsmen. There is some possibility, too, that the headman may do the killing.

To summarize, most disputes which arise among the Eskimos are related to the
disposition of women. Murders must be avenged in some way, often leading to the blood
feud. However, peace may be restored through a song contest. The group may decide to
70 execute a repeated murderer, perceived as a public threat. Disputes also arise if
individuals believe that others are practicing sorcery on them, and Hoebel (1954) reports
that certain individuals have been killed because they are chronic liars.

Perhaps you have noted a major and significant difference between Eskimo conflicts and our own. Theft is not a problem for the Eskimos. Access to resources needed to
75   sustain life is open to everyone. By virtue of his membership in a band, every individual has the right to hunt and fish and to manufacture all the tools he needs for subsistence activities. Individuals may even hunt and fish within the territories of other local groups. Conspicuously absent is the notion of private ownership of strategic resources. To describe the property notions of people who live in nonstratified societies, the
80   anthropologist Elman Service (1966) coined the term *personalty*. Personalty describes items other than strategic resources which are indelibly associated with a specific individual, things like the arrows he makes, the pouch he uses to carry his tobacco, his clothes. Service chose this term to point to the personal relationship between material items and the individual who owns them. So tied to specific individuals in public opinion
85   are personalty items that for another to steal them would be inconceivable. It may be that the grave goods found so often in pre-Neolithic archeological sites represent items of personalty, things which could not be passed on to heirs, so definite and inseparable was their association with the deceased.

Thus, in band-organized society, there is no differential or impeded access to strategic
90   resources; private property is personalty, and if one individual wants something which is owned by another, he simply asks for it and it is given. According to Hoebel, one of the basic postulates of Eskimo life is that "all natural resources are free and common goods." One of the corollaries of this is that "private property is subject to use claims by others than its owners [Hoebel, in Middleton, 1968, p. 96]."   /1312

Stage 3: Recall

Stop *and* recall *what you have read.*
   Review your use of the thinking strategies. Did you use all five?

▌▐▐ Skill Development: Main Point

Directions: Write the answers to the following questions.

1. In the first paragraph what aspect concerning foragers is the author addressing? _____

2. In the second paragraph what point is the author trying to get across about Eskimo disputes? _____

3. In the third paragraph what is the author's point concerning the role of women in Eskimo society? _____

   _____

4. In the fourth paragraph what is the author's main point about the Eskimo method of settling disputes? _____

   _____

5. In the next to the last paragraph what is the author's main point about theft in the Eskimo society? _____

▥▤▥ Comprehension Questions

1. The main point the author is trying to convey in this selection is _____

_____

After reading the selection, answer the following questions with *a, b, d,* or *d.*

_____ 2. According to the article, the Eskimos of the Arctic region from eastern Siberia to eastern Greenland are ruled by
a. the laws of the country in which they reside
b. the headman of the band
c. their desire for passion and revenge
d. a traditional code of justice that is acceptable to the band

_____ 3. Most Eskimo disputes concern sexual relations without the permission of the
a. wife
b. husband
c. father
d. wife stealer

_____ 4. Eskimos practice female infanticide for all of the following reasons except
a. the older people want someone to take care of them
b. the male death rate is higher
c. the male is primarily responsible for family security
d. the successful male wants to have plural wives

_____ 5. The author implies that retaliation for wife stealing is
a. forced by the community
b. more vicious than retaliation for adultery
c. not necessary if the husband is not upset
d. dependent on the wishes of the wife

_____ 6. The purpose and practice of an Eskimo song contest is most similar to the elements of
a. a courtroom trial
b. a minstrel show
c. a carnival
d. an opera

_____ 7. The Eskimos condone killing in all of the following cases except
a. a mother killing a baby girl
b. a son killing an invalid father
c. a murderer killing an avenger
d. a kinsman killing a double murderer

_____ 8. The author suggests that Eskimos do not steal material goods because they
a. have few personal needs

b. lack the concept of private ownership
   c. have little access to manufactured products
   d. have strict laws against it

_____ 9. According to the definition, an item that would be most likely described as *personalty* is a
   a. chair
   b. comb
   c. frying pan
   d. sled dog

_____ 10. The author probably believes the Eskimo practice of revenge by murder is
   a. undesirable because of the many deaths
   b. against the laws of the community
   c. preferable to a song contest
   d. sinful and should be punished

Answer the following with *T* (true), *F* (false), or *CT* (can't tell).

_____ 11. The author suggests that jealousy over prestige often motivates wife stealing.
_____ 12. The winner of the song contest automatically wins the wife.
_____ 13. Without female infanticide, many Eskimos would leave the northern region in search of food.
_____ 14. When requested, the Eskimos kill the old and the sick so they won't be a burden to society.
_____ 15. The author suggests that the Eskimo lifestyle dictates the code by which an Eskimo lives.

▥▤▥ Vocabulary

According to the way the boldface word was used in the selection, indicate *a*, *b*, *c*, or *d* for the word or phrase that gives the best definition.

_____ 1. "machinery of **adjudication** (02)"
   a. court decisions
   b. imprisonment
   c. apprehension
   d. arrest

_____ 2. "some **foraging** societies (03)"
   a. cold weather
   b. foreigners
   c. fighting
   d. searching for food

_____ 3. "without his **sanction** (15)"
   a. attention
   b. approval
   c. noticing
   d. suspicion

_____ 4. "This **demographic** imbalance (26)"
   a. hereditary
   b. democratic rule
   c. scientifically frigid areas
   d. science of vital statistics of populations

_____ 5. "could **escalate** into several deaths (41)"
   a. demand
   b. legislate
   c. expand step by step
   d. eliminate

_____ 6. "are **deemed** crimes (50)"
   a. assigned
   b. disfavored
   c. forgiven
   d. judged

_____ 7. "practicing **sorcery** (71)"
   a. witchcraft
   b. rebellion
   c. bribery
   d. untruths

_____ 8. "**Conspicuously** absent (78)"
   a. frequently
   b. centrally
   c. noticeably
   d. moderately

_____ 9. "are **indelibly** associated with (81)"
   a. narrowly
   b. permanently
   c. marginally
   d. sorrowfully

_____ 10. "**Impeded** access to (89)"
   a. promoted
   b. regretted
   c. obstructed
   d. accelerated

▌▌▌ Essay Question

The Eskimos described in this selection do not live in the United States or Canada; they live in the remote regions of Siberia and Greenland. Analyze how the different parts of the "the code" serve their needs in these remote areas. Use a sheet of notebook paper to record your answer.

Selection **2**

PSYCHOLOGY

Harry F. Harlow, University of Wisconsin Primate Laboratory

Stage 1: Preview

Preview *the selection and complete the following sentence: After reading this selection, I would like to know* _____

_____

_____

Stage 2: Integrate Knowledge While Reading

Use thinking strategies as you read:

1. *Predict*
2. *Picture*
3. *Form analogies*

4. *Verbalize points*
5. *Fix up strategies*

MONKEY LOVE*

James V. McConnell, from *Understanding Human Behavior*

The scientist who has conducted the best long-term laboratory experiments on love is surely Harry Harlow, a psychologist at the University of Wisconsin. Professor Harlow did not set out to study love—it happened by accident. Like many other psychologists, he was at first primarily interested in how organisms learn. Rather than working with rats, Harlow
5 chose to work with monkeys.

Since he needed a place to house and raise the monkeys, he built the *Primate* Laboratory at Wisconsin. Then he began to study the effects of brain lesions on monkey learning. But he soon found that young animals reacted somewhat differently to brain damage than did older monkeys, so he and his wife Margaret devised a breeding program
10 and tried various ways of raising monkeys in the laboratory. They rapidly discovered that monkey infants raised by their mothers often caught diseases from their parents, so the Harlows began taking the infants away from their mothers at birth and tried raising them by hand. The baby monkeys had been given cheesecloth diapers to serve as baby blankets. Almost from the start, it became obvious to the Harlows that their little animals
15 developed such strong attachments to the blankets that, in the Harlows' own terms, it was often hard to tell where the diaper ended and the baby began. Not only this, but if the Harlows removed the "security" blanket in order to clean it, the infant monkey often became greatly disturbed—just as if its own mother had deserted it.

The Surrogate Mother. What the baby monkeys obviously needed was an artificial or
20 *surrogate* mother—something they could cling to as tightly as they typically clung to their own mother's chest. The Harlows sketched out many different designs, but none really appealed to them. Then, in 1957, while enjoying a champagne flight high over the city of

*LEARNING STRATEGY: Be able to explain the needs of the infant monkey and the effect that deprivation of those needs can have on the whole pattern of psychological development. Relate these findings to human behavior.

From *Understanding Human Behavior* by James V. McConnell. Copyright © 1974 by Holt, Rinehart and Winston, CBS College Publishing. Reprinted by permission of Holt, Rinehart and Winston.

Detroit, Harry Harlow glanced out of the airplane window and "saw" an image of an artificial monkey mother. It was a hollow wire cylinder, wrapped with a terry-cloth bath
25 towel, with a silly wooden head at the top. The tiny monkey could cling to this "model mother" as closely as to its real mother's body hair. This surrogate mother could be provided with a functional breast simply by placing a milk bottle so that the nipple stuck through the cloth at an appropriate place on the surrogate's anatomy. The cloth mother could be heated or cooled; it could be rocked mechanically or made to stand still; and,
30 most important, it could be removed at will.

While still sipping his champagne, Harlow mentally outlined much of the research that kept him, his wife, and their associates occupied for many years to come. And without realizing it, Harlow had shifted from studying monkey learning to monkey love.

Infant-Mother Love

The chimpanzee or monkey infant is much more developed at birth than the human
35 infant, and apes develop or mature much faster than we do. Almost from the moment it is born, the monkey infant can move around and hold tightly to its mother. During the first few days of its life the infant will approach and cling to almost any large, warm, and soft object in its environment, particularly if that object also gives it milk. After a week or so, however, the monkey infant begins to avoid newcomers and focuses its attentions on
40 "mother"—real or surrogate.

During the first two weeks of its life warmth is perhaps the most important psychological thing that a monkey mother has to give to its baby. The Harlows discovered this fact by offering infant monkeys a choice of two types of mother-substitutes—one wrapped in terry cloth and one that was made of bare wire. If the two artificial mothers
45 were both the same temperature, the little monkeys always preferred the cloth mother. However, if the wire model was heated, while the cloth model was cool, for the first two weeks after birth the baby primates picked the warm wire mother-substitutes as their favorites. Thereafter they switched and spent most of their time on the more comfortable cloth mother.

50 Why is cloth preferable to bare wire? Something that the Harlows call *contact comfort* seems to be the answer, and a most powerful influence it is. Infant monkeys (and chimps too) spend much of their time rubbing against their mothers' skins, putting themselves in as close contact with the parent as they can. Whenever the young animal is frightened, disturbed, or annoyed, it typically rushes to its mother and rubs itself against her body.
55 Wire doesn't "rub" as well as does soft cloth. Prolonged "contact comfort" with a surrogate cloth mother appears to instill confidence in baby monkeys and is much more rewarding to them than is either warmth or milk. Infant monkeys also prefer a "rocking" surrogate to one that is stationary.

According to the Harlows, the basic quality of an infant's love for its mother is *trust*. If
60 the infant is put into an unfamiliar playroom without its mother, the infant ignores the toys no matter how interesting they might be. It screeches in terror and curls up into a furry little ball. If its cloth mother is now introduced into the playroom, the infant rushes to the surrogate and clings to it for dear life. After a few minutes of contact comfort, it apparently begins to feel more secure. It then climbs down from the mother-substitute
65 and begins tentatively to explore the toys, but often rushes back for a deep embrace as if to reassure itself that its mother is still there and that all is well. Bit by bit its fears of the novel environment are "desensitized" and it spends more and more time playing with the toys and less and less time clinging to its "mother."

Good Mothers and Bad. The Harlows found that, once a baby monkey has come to accept its mother (real or surrogate), the mother can do almost no wrong. In one of their studies, the Harlows tried to create "monster mothers" whose behavior would be so abnormal that the infants would desert the mothers. Their purpose was to determine whether maternal rejection might cause abnormal behavior patterns in the infant monkeys similar to those responses found in human babies whose mothers ignore or punish their children severely. The problem was—how can you get a terry-cloth mother to reject or punish its baby? Their solutions were ingenious—but most of them failed in their main purpose. Four types of "monster mothers" were tried, but none of them was apparently "evil" enough to impart fear or loathing to the infant monkeys. One such "monster" occasionally blasted its babies with compressed air; a second shook so violently that the baby often fell off; a third contained a *catapult* that frequently flung the infant away from it. The most evil-appearing of all had a set of metal spikes buried beneath the terry cloth; from time to time the spikes would poke through the cloth making it impossible for the infant to cling to the surrogate.

The baby monkeys brought up on the "monster mothers" did show a brief period of emotional disturbance when the "wicked" *temperament* of the surrogates first showed up. The infants would cry for a time when displaced from their mothers, but as soon as the surrogates returned to normal, the infant would return to the surrogate and continue clinging, as if all were forgiven. As the Harlows tell the story, the only prolonged distress created by the experiment seemed to be that felt by the experimenters!

There was, however, one type of surrogate that uniformly "turned off" the infant monkeys. S. J. Suomi, working with the Harlows, built a terry-cloth mother with ice water in its veins. Newborn monkeys would attach themselves to this "cold momma" for a brief period of time, but then retreated to a corner of the cage and rejected her forever.

From their many brilliant studies, the Harlows conclude that the love of an infant for its mother is *primarily a response to certain stimuli the mother offers.* Warmth is the most important stimulus for the first two weeks of the monkey's life, then contact comfort becomes *paramount.* Contact comfort is determined by the softness and "rub-ability" of the surface of the mother's body—terry cloth is better than are satin and silk, but all such materials are more effective in creative love and trust than bare metal is. Food and mild "shaking" or "rocking" are important too, but less so than warmth and contact comfort. These needs—and the rather primitive responses the infant makes in order to obtain their satisfaction—are programmed into the monkey's genetic blueprint. The growing infant's requirement for social and intellectual stimulation becomes critical only later in a monkey's life. And yet, as we will see in this (and the next) chapter, if the baby primate is deprived of contact with other young of its own species, its whole pattern of development can be profoundly disturbed.

Mother-Infant Love

The Harlows were eventually able to find ways of getting female isolates pregnant, usually by confining them in a small cage for long periods of time with a patient and highly experienced normal male. At times, however, the Harlows were forced to help matters along by strapping the female to a piece of apparatus. When these isolated females gave birth to their first monkey baby, they turned out to be the "monster mothers" the Harlows had tried to create with mechanical surrogates. Having had no contact with other animals as they grew up, they simply did not know what to do with the furry little strangers that suddenly appeared on the scene. These motherless mothers at

120 first totally ignored their children, although if the infant persisted, the mothers occasionally gave in and provided the baby with some of the contact and comfort it demanded.

Surprisingly enough, once these mothers learned how to handle a baby, they did reasonably well. Then, when they were again impregnated and gave birth to a second
125 infant, they took care of this next baby fairly adequately.

Maternal affection was totally lacking in a few of the motherless monkeys, however. To them the newborn monkey was little more than an object to be abused the way a human child might abuse a doll or a toy train. These motherless mothers stepped on their babies, crushed the infant's face into the floor of the cage, and once or twice chewed off their
130 baby's feet and fingers before they could be stopped. The most terrible mother of all popped her infant's head into her mouth and crunched it like a potato chip.

We tend to think of most mothers—no matter what their species—as having some kind of almost-divine "maternal instinct" that makes them love their children and take care of them no matter what the cost or circumstance. While it is true that most females have
135 built into their genetic blueprint the *tendency* to be interested in (and to care for) their offspring, this inborn tendency is always expressed in a given environment. The "maternal instinct" is strongly influenced by the mother's past experiences. Humans seem to have weaker instincts of all kinds than do other animals—since our behavior patterns are more affected by learning than by our genes, we have greater flexibility in what we do
140 and become. But we pay a sometimes severe price for this freedom from genetic control.

Normal monkey and chimpanzee mothers seldom appear to inflict real physical harm on their children; human mothers and fathers often do. Serapio R. Zalba, writing in a journal called *Trans-action*, estimated in 1971 that in the United States alone, perhaps 250,000 children suffer physical abuse by their parents each year. Of these "battered
145 babies," almost 40,000 may be very badly injured. The number of young boys and girls killed by their parents annually is not known, but Zalba suggests that the figure may run into the thousands. Parents have locked their children in tiny cages, raised them in dark closets, burned them, boiled them, slashed them with knives, shot them, and broken almost every bone in their bodies. How can we reconcile these facts with the much-
150 discussed maternal and paternal "instincts?"

The research by the Harlows on the "motherless mothers" perhaps gives us a clue. Mother monkeys who were themselves socially deprived or isolated when young seemed singularly lacking in affection for their infants. Zalba states that most of the abusive human parents that were studied turned out to have been abused and neglected
155 *themselves* as children. Like the isolated monkeys who seemed unable to control their aggressive impulses when put in contact with normal animals, the abusive parents seem to be greatly deficient in what psychologists call "impulse control" (*see* Chapter 20). Most of these parents also were described as being socially isolated, as having troubles adjusting to marriage, often deeply in debt, and as being unable to build up warm and
160 loving relationships with other people—including their own children. Since they did not learn how to love from their own parents, these mothers and fathers simply did not acquire the social skills necessary for bringing up their own infants in a healthy fashion.

/2207

Stage 3: Recall

Stop *and* recall *what you have read.*
Review your use of the thinking strategies. Did you use all five?

▦▦▦ Skill Development: Main Point

Directions: Write the answers to the following questions.

1. In the first section which includes the first four paragraphs, what is the point the author is trying to convey about Harlow's experiments? _____

   _____

2. In the second section entitled "Infant-Mother Love" what is the point the author is trying to convey about that love? _____

   _____

3. In the beginning of the section entitled "Good Mothers and Bad," what is the point the author is trying to convey about these mothers? _____

   _____

4. In the beginning of the section entitled "Mother-Infant Love," what is the point the author is trying to convey about that love? _____

   _____

5. In the last paragraph, what is the point the author is trying to convey about child abuse? _____

   _____

▦▦▦ Comprehension Questions

After reading the selection, answer the following questions with *a, b, c,* or *d.*

1. The main point the author is trying to get across in this selection is _____

   _____

2. When Harry Harlow originally started his experiments with monkeys, his purpose was to study
   a. love
   b. breeding
   c. learning
   d. disease

3. The reason that the author mentions Harry Harlow's revelations on the airplane is to show
   a. that he had extrasensory perception

    b. that he liked to travel

    c. that he was always thinking of his work

    d. in what an unexpected way brilliant work often starts

_____ 4. In his experiments Harlow used all of the following in designing his surrogate mothers except

    a. a terry-cloth bath towel

    b. real body hair

    c. a rocking movement

    d. temperature controls

_____ 5. Harlow manipulated his experiments to show the early significance of warmth by

    a. heating wire

    b. cooling terry cloth

    c. equalizing temperature

    d. creating "monster mothers"

_____ 6. Harlow feels that for contact comfort the cloth mother was preferable to the wire mother for all of the following reasons except

    a. the cloth mother instilled confidence

    b. the wire mother doesn't "rub" as well

    c. the wire mother was stationary

    d. with the cloth mother, the infant feels a greater sense of security when upset

_____ 7. Harlow's studies show that when abused by its mother, infant monkeys will

    a. leave the mother

    b. seek a new mother

    c. return to the mother

    d. fight with the mother

_____ 8. For an infant to love its mother, Harlow's studies show that in the first two weeks the most important element is

    a. milk

    b. warmth

    c. contact comfort

    d. love expressed by the mother

_____ 9. In Harlow's studies with motherless monkeys he showed that the techniques of mothering are

    a. instinctive

    b. learned

    c. inborn

    d. natural

_____ 10. The Harlows feel that child abuse is caused by all of the following problems except

    a. parents who were abused as children

    b. socially isolated parents

    c. parents who cannot control their impulses

    d. parents who are instinctively evil

Answer the following with *T* (true), *F* (false), or *CT* (can't tell).

_____ 11. The author feels that the studies of love in infant monkeys have a great deal of similarity to love in human children.

_____ 12. The author implies that isolated monkeys have difficulty engaging in normal peer relationships.

_____ 13. When taught how to be good mothers, all of the motherless mothers became fairly good parents.

_____ 14. Zalba's studies confirmed many of the findings of the Harlow studies.

_____ 15. Infant monkeys deprived of warmth become intellectually impaired.

▓▓▓ Vocabulary

According to the way the boldface word was used in the selection, indicate *a, b, c,* or *d* for the word or phrase that gives the best definition.

____ 1. "the **surrogate** mother (19)"
   a. mean
   b. thoughtless
   c. loving
   d. substitute

____ 2. "a **functional** breast (27)"
   a. mechanical
   b. operational
   c. wholesome
   d. imitation

____ 3. "on the surrogate's **anatomy** (28)"
   a. body
   b. head
   c. offspring
   d. personality

____ 4. "begins **tentatively** to explore (65)"
   a. rapidly
   b. hesitantly
   c. aggressively
   d. readily

____ 5. "fears of the **novel** environment (67)"
   a. hostile
   b. literary
   c. dangerous
   d. new

____ 6. "fears . . . are **desensitized** (67)"
   a. made less sensitive
   b. made more sensitive
   c. electrified
   d. communicated

____ 7. "solutions were **ingenious** (76)"
   a. incorrect
   b. noble
   c. clever
   d. honest

____ 8. "**deprived** of contact (110)"
   a. encouraged
   b. denied
   c. assured
   d. ordered into

____ 9. "if the infant **persisted** (120)"
   a. stopped
   b. continued
   c. fought
   d. relaxed

____ 10. "to be greatly **deficient** (157)"
   a. lacking
   b. supplied
   c. overwhelmed
   d. secretive

▞▞▞ Essay Question

Describe infant needs as demonstrated by Harlow's monkeys and use Harlow's study to explain child abuse as a chain reaction. Use a sheet of notebook paper to record your answer.

Selection **3**

HISTORY

Courtesy of the New York Historical Society, New York City

Stage 1: Preview

Preview *the selection and complete the following sentence: After reading this*

selection, I would like to know _____

_____

Stage 2: Integrate Knowledge While Reading

Use thinking strategies as you read:

1. *Predict*
2. *Picture*
3. *Form analogies*

4. *Verbalize points*
5. *Fix up strategies*

WOMEN IN HISTORY*

Leonard Pitt, from *We Americans*

Three Radical Women

Amelia Bloomer (1818–1894) published the first newpaper issue expressly for women. She called it *The Lily*. Her fame, however, rests chiefly in dress reform. For six or eight years she wore an outfit composed of a knee-length skirt over full pants gathered at the ankle, which were soon known everywhere as "bloomers." Wherever she went, this style
5   created great excitement and brought her enormous audiences—including hecklers. She was trying to make the serious point that women's fashions, often designed by men to suit their own tastes, were too restrictive, often to the detriment of the health of those who wore them. Still, some of her contemporaries thought she did the feminist movement as much harm as good.
10   Very few feminists hoped to destroy marriage as such. Most of them had husbands and lived conventional, if hectic, lives. And many of the husbands supported their cause. Yet the feminists did challenge certain marital customs. When Lucy Stone married Henry Blackwell, she insisted on being called "Mrs. Stone," a defiant gesture that brought her a lifetime of ridicule. Both she and her husband signed a marriage contract, vowing "to
15   recognize the wife as an independent, rational being." They agreed to break any law which brought the husband "an injurious and unnatural superiority." But few of the radical feminists indulged in "free love" or joined communal marriage experiments. The movement was intended mainly to help women gain control over their own property and earnings and gain better legal guardianship over their children. Voting also interested
20   them, but women's suffrage did not become a central issue until later in the century.
Many black women were part of the movement, including the legendary Sojourner Truth (1797–1883). Born a slave in New York and forced to marry a man approved by her owner, Sojourner Truth was freed when the state abolished slavery. After participating in religious revivals, she became an active abolitionist and feminist. In 1851 she saved the
25   day at a women's rights convention in Ohio, silencing hecklers and replying to a man who had belittled the weakness of women:

> The man over there says women need to be helped into carriages and lifted over ditches, and to have the best place everywhere. Nobody ever helps me into carriages or over puddles, or gives me the best place—and ain't I a woman? . . . Look at my arm! I have ploughed and planted and
30   gathered into barns, and no man could head me—and ain't I a woman? I could work as much and

*LEARNING STRATEGY: Look at the historical trend toward altering the image of women and note the contributions to this change made by individuals and groups.

Pitt: *We Americans*, Second Edition. Copyright © 1984 Kendall/Hunt Publishing Company. Reprinted with permission.

eat as much as a man—when I could get it—and bear the lash as well! And ain't I a woman? I have borne thirteen children, and seen most of 'em sold into slavery, and when I cried out my mother's grief, none but Jesus heard me—and ain't I a woman?

Changing the Image and the Reality

The accomplishments of a few women who dared pursue professional careers had
35 somewhat altered the image of the submissive and brainless child-woman. Maria Mitchell of Nantucket, whose father was an astronomer, discovered a comet at the age of twenty-eight. She became the first woman professor of astronomy in the U.S. (at Vassar in 1865). Mitchell was also the first woman elected to the American Academy of Arts and Sciences and a founder of the Association for the Advancement of Women. Elizabeth Blackwell
40 applied to twenty-nine medical schools before she was accepted. She attended all classes, even anatomy class, despite the sneers of some male students. As a physician, she went on to make important contributions in sanitation and hygiene.

By about 1860 women had effected notable improvements in their status. Organized feminists had eliminated some of the worst legal disadvantages in fifteen states. The Civil
45 War altered the role—and the image—of women even more drastically than the feminist movement did. As men went off to fight, women flocked into government clerical jobs. And they were accepted in teaching jobs as never before. Tens of thousands of women ran farms and businesses while the men were gone. Anna Howard Shaw, whose mother ran a pioneer farm, recalled:

50 It was an incessant struggle to keep our land, to pay our taxes, and to live. Calico was selling at fifty cents a yard. Coffee was one dollar a pound. There were no men left to grind our corn, to get in our crops, or to care for our livestock; and all around us we saw our struggle reflected in the lives of our neighbors.

55 Women took part in crucial relief efforts. The Sanitary Commission, the Union's volunteer nursing program and a forerunner of the Red Cross, owed much of its success to women. They raised millions of dollars for medicine, bandages, food, hospitals, relief camps, and convalescent homes.

North and South, black and white, many women served as nurses, some as spies and
60 even as soldiers. Dorothea Dix, already famous as a reformer of prisons and insane asylums, became head of the Union army nurse corps. Clara Barton and "Mother" Bickerdyke saved thousands of lives by working close behind the front lines at Antietam, Chancellorsville, and Fredericksburg. Harriet Tubman led a party up the Combahee River to rescue 756 slaves. Late in life she was recognized for her heroic act by being granted a
65 government pension of twenty dollars per month.

Southern white women suffered more from the disruptions of the Civil War than did their northern sisters. The proportion of men who went to war or were killed in battle was greater in the South. This made many women self-sufficient during the war. Still, there was hardly a whisper of feminism in the South.

70 The Civil War also brought women into the political limelight. Anna Dickson sky-rocketed to fame as a Republican speaker, climaxing her career with an address to the House of Representatives on abolition. Stanton and Anthony formed the National Woman's Loyal League to press for a constitutional amendment banning slavery. With Anthony's genius for organization, the League in one year collected 400,000 signatures in
75 favor of the Thirteenth Amendment.

Once abolition was finally assured in 1865, most feminists felt certain that suffrage would follow quickly. They believed that women had earned the vote by their patriotic

wartime efforts. Besides, it appeared certain that black men would soon be allowed to
vote. And once black men had the ballot in hand, how could anyone justify keeping it from
80 white women—or black women? Any feminist who had predicted in 1865 that women
would have to wait another fifty-five years for suffrage would have been called politically
naive.   /1108

Stage 3: Recall

Stop *and* recall *what you have read. Review your use of the thinking strategies.
Did you use all five?*

▮▮▮ Skill Development: Main Point

Directions: Write the answers to the following questions.

1. In the first paragraph what is the author's main point about Amelia Bloomer?

   _____

   _____

2. In the second paragraph what is the author's main point about Lucy Stone?

   _____

   _____

3. In the third paragraph what is the author's main point about Sojourner Truth?

   _____

   _____

4. In the fourth paragraph what is the author's main point about women in
   professional careers? _____

   _____

5. In the last paragraph what is the author's main point about women's
   suffrage? _____

   _____

▮▮▮ Comprehension Questions

1. The main point the author is trying to get across in this selection is _____

   _____

   _____

After reading the selection, answer the following questions with *a, b, c,* or *d.*

_____ 2. In originating "bloomers," Amelia Bloomer's greatest concern was
a. fashion
b. principle
c. expense
d. good taste

_____ 3. The major purpose of Sojourner Truth's quoted speech was to
a. prove that women are stronger than men
b. reprimand men for social courtesy
c. dramatize the strengths of women
d. praise childbearing as a womanly virtue

_____ 4. Lucy Stone's major motive in retaining the name "Mrs. Stone" after marriage was to
a. condone "free love" without marriage
b. de-emphasize the responsibilities of marriage
c. purchase property in her own name
d. be recognized as an independent person equal to her husband

_____ 5. The article states that women worked during the Civil War in all of the following except
a. farms and businesses
b. the military
c. government clerical jobs
d. the Red Cross

_____ 6. The author implies that the eventual assumption of responsible roles by large numbers of women was primarily due to
a. the feminist movement
b. the determination and accomplishments of female professionals
c. a desire to give women a chance
d. economic necessity

_____ 7. The author believes that the Civil War showed southern women to be
a. as capable but less vocal than northern women
b. more capable than their northern sisters
c. capable workers and eager feminists
d. less able to assume responsible roles than northern women

_____ 8. The author's main purpose in mentioning the accomplishments of Maria Mitchell is to point out that
a. she discovered a comet
b. her professional achievements improved the image of women
c. she was the first woman professor of astronomy in the U.S.
d. she was a founder of the Association for the Advancement of Women

9. The article states or implies that all of the following women worked to abolish slavery except
   a. Anna Howard Shaw
   b. Harriet Tubman
   c. Anna Dickson
   d. Stanton and Anthony

10. In the author's opinion, the long wait by women after the Civil War for suffrage
    a. was predictable in 1865
    b. would not have been expected in 1865
    c. was due to the vote of black men
    d. was justified

Answer the following *T* (true), *F* (false), or *CT* (can't tell).

11. Women were granted the right to vote in 1920.
12. Sojourner Truth had been a southern slave.
13. The author implies that feminist leaders were more concerned with their own right to vote than with the abolition of slavery.
14. From the very beginning, the right to vote was the focal point of the woman's movement.
15. Many black slaves were led to freedom along an underground railway by Sojourner Truth.

▌▐▌ Vocabulary

According to the way the boldface word was used in the selection, indicate *a, b, c,* or *d* for the word or phrase that gives the best definition.

___ 1. "were too **restrictive** (07)"
   a. showy
   b. expensive
   c. complicated
   d. confining

___ 2. "to the **detriment** of (07)"
   a. harm
   b. anger
   c. apology
   d. objection

___ 3. "a **defiant** gesture (13)"
   a. unlucky
   b. resistive
   c. admirable
   d. ignorant

___ 4. "**communal** marriage experiments (17)"
   a. permanent
   b. living together in groups
   c. illegal
   d. uncommon

_____ 5. "silencing **hecklers** (25)"
  a. soldiers
  b. rioters
  c. disciples
  d. verbal harassers

_____ 6. "**pursue** professional careers (34)"
  a. strive for
  b. abandon
  c. acknowledge
  d. indicate

_____ 7. "sanitation and **hygiene** (42)"
  a. garbage disposal
  b. biology
  c. health care
  d. mental disorders

_____ 8. "an **incessant** struggle (50)"
  a. earlier
  b. final
  c. novel
  d. unceasing

_____ 9. "**convalescent** homes (58)"
  a. sanitary
  b. government
  c. reclaimed
  d. recuperating

_____ 10. "called politically **naive** (82)"
  a. unsophisticated
  b. well informed
  c. dishonest
  d. unfortunate

▦ ▤ ▥ Essay Question

List five of the women mentioned whose actions represent an altering of accepted ideas and discuss how each changed stereotypical thinking. Use a sheet of notebook paper to record your answer.

Chapter 5

UNRAVELING COMPLEX SENTENCES

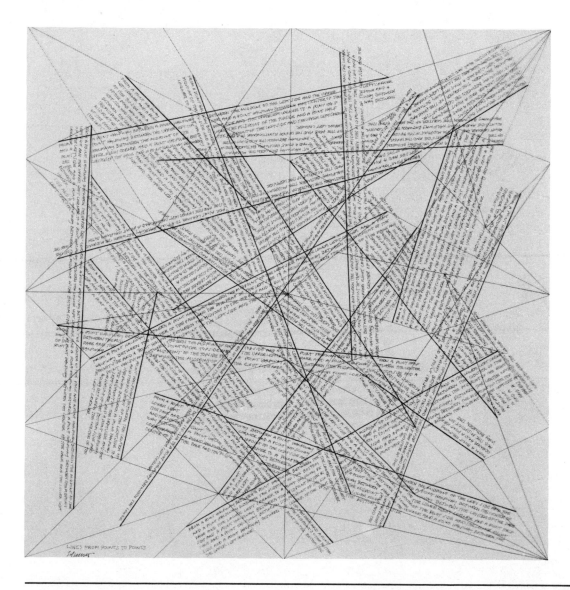

MAIN IDEA FOR SENTENCES

Understanding the sentence is a basic element of reading comprehension. Some sentences are concise and clear, while others are complex and complicated. Similar to finding the main idea in paragraphs, you can find the main idea in sentences by breaking them down into main ideas and significant supporting details. For sentences, the main ideas are called core parts, and the significant details are the essential modifiers. Read the following sentences and determine how they are alike.

I see her.

As the office workers crowd the sidewalks and John and I patiently begin our ten-minute wait at the corner for the last afternoon bus home, I always see her resting on the post-office steps selling bouquets of roses to passersby.

Can you spot the similarity? The first sentence has three words and the second has forty, yet both sentences have the same subject, the same action, and the same receiver of the action. The three-word core, "I see her," forms the heart of both sentences—the other thirty-seven words in the second sentence merely describe the situation more vividly. In restating the sentence, however, some of the essential modifiers would need to be included to effectively communicate the author's meaning. For example, the sentence could be restated as follows:

I always see her selling roses as I wait for the afternoon bus.

Many sentences are simple and easy to understand, but others can present problems that form barriers to reading comprehension. Logic suggests that if you cannot understand the sentences, you cannot hope to understand the paragraphs. Have you ever read a sentence that was so long that you had forgotten how it started by the time you got to the end? Have you ever read a lengthy paragraph that was made up of just one long sentence? Have you ever read a poem in which one sentence meandered through three or four verses? Have you ever read a sentence that was so complicated that you couldn't figure out the meaning?

Surely, the answer to all four questions is "yes." Even for the best readers, some sentences can be monstrosities to unravel. Essential elements lie hidden amid a maze of clauses, phrases, commas, and semicolons. Think of a sentence as having only a few vital parts. Find them, and then relate the remaining words and phrases to those core parts. In other words, find the skeleton of the sentence, and then worry about the "hangers-on."

To unravel the meaning of a sentence, use the following questions to guide your thinking. These are the same questions that you ask to determine the main idea of a paragraph, an article, a chapter, or a book.

Sol LeWitt, *Lines from Points to Points.* (1975) Pen and ink on ink on acetate, 18 × 18″. Private Collection, courtesy New Britain Museum of American Art, New Britain, Connecticut.

1. Who or what is it about?
2. What is the main point the author is trying to convey?
3. Which details validate, develop, or help you understand the main point?

These questions need to be slightly modified when applied to sentences, but the underlying idea remains the same. The following explanation will discuss how to unravel the parts of a sentence.

UNRAVELING THE PARTS OF A SENTENCE

Action and Subject

The first step in determining the core of a sentence is to locate the action word or words. These action words are called verbs and can recount an action like *hit, had slapped,* and *could have driven* or they can be linking verbs that show a state of being like *is, was, seems,* and *could have been.* To locate the verb, ask, "What word or words tell what is happening in the sentence?"

The second step in determining the core is to find the subject of the action. Ask the question, "Who or what is doing the acting?" in order to locate the subject. Apply the two questions to the following sentence to find the verb and then the subject.

Caesar fought the barbarians with all of his forces.
1. What word tells what is happening? *fought*
2. Who is doing the acting? *Caesar*

For an example of a linking verb that shows a state of being, apply the same questions to the following sentence.

Caesar was the leader of the Roman forces.
1. What word tells what is happening? *was*
2. Who is doing the acting? *Caesar*

Notice that inserting a descriptive phrase does not change the core.

Caesar, a man who enjoyed power, was the leader of the Roman forces.
1. What word tells what is happening? *was*
2. Who is doing the acting? *Caesar*

■■■ Exercise 1: Subjects and Verbs

The following sentences are taken from *We Americans*, a history text by Leonard Pitt. For each of the sentences, locate the action word or words (*verb*) and then locate the subject. Put two lines under the action word (s) and one line under the subject.

Example:

Caesar fought hard against the enemy.

1. Tax laws contributed to this rise.
2. In 1873 the evangelist Dwight L. Moody devised the techniques of urban revivals.
3. Charles Darwin's theory of evolution exploded like a time bomb under America's Protestant pulpits.
4. On the other hand church membership was definitely on the increase.
5. A tireless organizer, Tecumseh traveled as far east as New York and south to Florida trying to enlist support for his pan-Indian nation.
6. Lincoln, a former Whig congressman from Illinois, was not the first choice of the GOP party regulars in 1860.
7. In the midst of the Spanish-American War, the Senate reconsidered annexing Hawaii.
8. In April, reluctantly giving in to powerful pressure, President McKinley asked Congress for the power to use armed forces to end the fighting in Cuba and to establish the island's independence.
9. The economic future of ex-slaves remained a key question.
10. To remedy these problems, the art of city planning was revived.

Action, Subject, and Object

In determining the remaining core of a sentence, the third question to ask is "Who or what receives the action?" This receiver of the action is called the direct object, and some sentences contain an object and some do not. In the following example, the first sentence has an object, but the second and third do not.

The Greeks used their knowledge to influence others.

1. What word tells what is happening? used
2. Who is doing the acting? Greeks

3. Who or what receives the action? <u>knowledge</u>

The Greek civilization came to a close.

1. What word tells what is happening? <u>came</u>

2. Who or what is doing the acting? <u>civilization</u>

3. Who or what receives the action? There is no object.

The Greek civilization was an important cultural force.

1. What word tells what is happening? <u>was</u>

2. Who or what is doing the acting? <u>civilization</u>

3. Who or what receives the action? There is no object. *Was* is a linking verb and since *force* renames the subject, it is called a complement.

▦ ▦ ▦ Exercise 2: Subjects, Verbs, and Objects

The following sentences are also from *We Americans* by Leonard Pitt. For each sentence, locate the action word or words, the subject, and then the object. Put two lines under the action word(s), one line under the subject, and a circle around the object.

1. Roosevelt enthusiastically supported the National Reclamation Act of 1902, known also as the Newlands Act.

2. The War of 1812 between Britain and the U.S. had a positive effect on manufacturing.

3. Prized fur-bearing animals suffered wholesale slaughter.

4. To keep beaver and other pelts flowing to Britain instead of France, the English established several trading companies.

5. Sea captains sold the contracts to American employers, who lined up to greet the ships and take away their servants as they came ashore.

6. England enforced its colonial policies through a series of Navigation Acts.

7. In the meantime, France sent adventurers into Canada, through the Great Lakes, and down the Ohio and Mississippi rivers.

8. To encourage females to settle Virginia, the Burgesses granted fifty acres of land to each married woman in the colony.

9. Older infants enjoyed considerable freedom to play and run about.

10. Children learned skills by watching their parents work in the home and around the farm, or by the apprentice system.

Multiple Core Parts

Sentences can contain more than one of either the subject, verb, object, or any combination of the three. In the case of a compound or double sentence, two separate sets of core parts exist. These parts of equal value are connected by words like *and, but, or,* and *nor.* The following sentences are marked to illustrate some of the possible variations.

Multiple Subjects

Republicans and Democrats voted in large numbers.

Multiple Verbs

Farmers returned to the land and planted their crops.

Multiple Objects

The depression hurt the rich and poor.

Multiple Core Sets (Compound Sentence)

The soldiers needed weapons, and the government needed money.

Exercise 3: Compound Sentences

The following sentences, all containing multiple parts, are taken from *We Americans* by Leonard Pitt. For each sentence, locate the action word(s), the subject(s), and the object(s). Put two lines under the action word(s), one line under the subject(s), and circle the object(s).

Example:

The Romans and Greeks worshiped many gods and goddesses.

1. Workers lost their jobs, farmers lost their land, and the middle class lost its savings.

2. Economists and historians are still groping for answers.

3. The rivalries and disagreements initiated by Hamilton's program sharpened in response to the French Revolution.

4. Tutoring in the home was common and remained so in the South.

5. Technology and skilled workers were two major factors that propelled the American economy forward between 1815 and 1860.

6. The Northeast also supplied loans and investments for the other two regions.

7. Each region wanted what another was selling, and leftovers could be sent to Europe.

8. In the large cities notorious slums housed both immigrants and native-born factory workers.

9. Most Americans rejected both the "iron law" and the Socialists.

10. From time to time irate wives, backed by equally irate preachers, tried to close them down, but their efforts rarely had a lasting effect.

Sentence Fragments

Before discussing unequal core parts, it is necessary to recognize the difference between what is and what is not a sentence. A sentence is defined as a group of words that express a complete thought. Sentence fragments or clauses may contain core parts, but they leave questions unanswered and do not express a complete thought. In the following examples, the first is a sentence expressing a complete thought, but the other two are not complete sentences because they do not finish the thought.

Example:

The soldiers were fighting in the snow.
While fighting in the snow.
So that they were fighting in the snow.

▐▌▐ **Exercise 4: Sentence Fragments**

The following sentences and fragments are excerpted from a biology textbook entitled *Biology: The World of Life* by Robert Wallace. Beside each item, write *yes* if it is a complete sentence, and write *no* if it is not a sentence.

_____   1. The molluscs are named for their soft bodies

_____ 2. Although some are encased in hard shells and others have stiff shells inside their bodies

_____ 3. Probably mulluscs have more reason to be afraid of us

_____ 4. For example, the area of elongation may cover several inches

_____ 5. If the terminal bud has been removed

_____ 6. Whereas it's relatively easy to look at a root tip and name the various areas with great authority

_____ 7. The reflex arc is structurally simple

_____ 8. Above the medulla and somewhat further toward the back of the head is the cerebellum

_____ 9. If you should crawl out of your sleeping bag one night and step on a hot coal

_____ 10. While ethologists were seeking to clarify the concept as an explanatory tool

Unequal Core Parts

Some sentences appear at first glance to contain multiple subject-verb sets, but further investigation indicates that the core part sets are not of equal value. In other words, the sentences contain clauses that could not stand by themselves to express a complete thought even though they do have subjects and verbs. In such cases, there is only one subject-verb set that expresses the main thought of the sentence and the other clauses serve as modifiers within the sentence. In the following example, the core parts of the sentence have been marked.

Example:

Although the news came quickly, the senator did not change her vote.

Exercise 5: Unequal Core Parts

The following sentences, each containing unequal core parts, are taken from _Biology: The World of Life_ by Robert Wallace. Disregard the clauses that do not form a complete thought, and mark the core parts of the sentence. Put two lines under the action word, one line under the subject, and circle the object.

1. Nevertheless, several legal appeals have been entered on behalf of men convicted of murder and other violent crimes based on the argument that these men had been "genetically driven" to the crimes.

2. If one looked carefully at the lichen, it was sometimes possible to discern a light-colored moth sitting concealed on the tree.

3. High variation can also be maintained if the environment is "patchy," that is, comprised of markedly different kinds of places.

4. As long as members of different subpopulations continue to interbreed, however, they will tend to dilute each other's adaptations.

5. Interestingly, however, the kind of plant that attracts us may depend on where we were raised.

6. Once conception has taken place, the zygote will continue down through the oviduct to be received by the ready uterus.

7. Since freshwater fish have water to spare, they excrete diluted ammonia directly.

8. In case you are planning to be shipwrecked sometime, you may also be interested in another bit of practical physiology.

9. You would do better eating fish than drinking seawater, of course, since the salt concentration in seawater is about 3.5 percent.

10. As the body's resources of glucose drop below the amount needed to maintain a constant blood level, we have the sensation of hunger and are motivated to go out and find some glucose.

Modifiers

Modifiers describe core parts as well as other words within a sentence. They limit, restrict, or qualify the meaning of the words they modify and answer questions like *when, why, how, how much,* and *how many.* In order to accurately assess the meaning of a sentence, you need to determine which words the modifiers are limiting or describing. The following examples illustrate the variety of ways in which modifiers limit the meaning of other words in the sentence.

The president left office after the announcement.
After the announcement tells when he left.

The river, which had been there for many years, had created a beautiful canyon.
Which had been there for many years describes the river.

Quickly and quietly, the pioneer moved through the woods.
Quickly and quietly describes how he moved.

▮▮▮ Exercise 6: Sentence Parts

The following sentences have been taken from a variety of textbooks. Write in the blanks the answers to the questions about the relationships of the sentence parts.

A. If Homer had tried reading the *Iliad* to the gods on Olympus, they would either have started to fidget and presently asked if he hadn't got something a little lighter, or, taking it as a comic poem, would have roared with laughter or possibly, even, reacting like ourselves to a tear-jerking movie, have poured pleasing tears.

W. H. Auden, *The Dyer's Hand*

1. Who would "have started to fidget"? _____

2. Who "would have roared with laughter"? _____

3. Who would "have poured"? _____

4. "he" takes the place of _____

B. If Sam Fathers had been his mentor and the backyard rabbits and squirrels his kindergarten, then the wilderness the old bear ran was his college and the old male bear itself, so long unwifed and childless as to have become its own ungendered progenitor, was his alma mater.

William Faulkner, "The Bear"

1. What was his alma mater? _____

2. "the old bear ran" modifies _____

3. What was his kindergarten? _____

4. "so long unwifed and childless as to have become its own ungendered progenitor" modifies _____

C. When it occurs to a man that nature does not regard him as important, and that she feels she would not maim the universe by disposing of him, he at first wishes to throw bricks at the temple, and he hates deeply the fact that there are no bricks and no temples.

Stephen Crane, *The Open Boat*

1. Who wishes and hates? _____

2. What does a man want to do that he can't? _____

3. "she" refers to _____

4. How does nature feel about man? _____

D. He lifted his head from his drinking, as cattle do,
And looked at me vaguely, as drinking cattle do,
And flickered his two-forked tongue from his lips, and mused a moment,
And stooped and drank a little more,
Being earth brown, earth golden from the burning
   burning bowels of the earth
On the day of Sicilian July, with Etna smoking.

D. H. Lawrence, from "Snake"

1. Who is the sentence about? _____

2. The subject engages in six different actions. Name them. _____

   _____

3. "Being earth brown" modifies _____

4. When was "Etna smoking"? _____

E. As the depression deepened, as some Americans approached a second winter without employment, as charities and states ran out of funds for relief, as newspapers reported that people were foraging in dumps and garbage heaps, and as malnutrition and exposure came to public attention, Herbert Hoover became the nation's scapegoat.

Henry F. Bedford and Trevor Calbourn, The Americans

1. Who is the sentence about? _____

2. What was Hoover renamed? _____

3. "As the depression deepened" tells which of the following: how? when? where? why? _____

4. "as malnutrition and exposure came to public attention" tells which of the following: how? where? when? why? _____

F. In a sudden and startling break with the worship of Amon, the divine father of the pharaohs of the XVIIIth dynasty, and with all the other gods dear to the tradition of Egyptian polytheism, Akhenaten gave his entire allegiance to a single, all-powerful, and merciful creator, the sun disk or Aten whose rays brought blessings to the earth.

Shepard B. Clough et al., A History of the Western World

1. Who is the sentence about? _____

2. What did Akhenaten do? _____

3. "the divine father of the pharaohs of the XVIIIth dynasty" renames _____

4. "the sun disk or Aten whose rays brought blessings to the earth" renames

_____

G. Under yonder beech-tree single on the green sward,
Couched with her arms behind her golden head,
Knees and tresses folded to slip and ripply idly.
Lies my young love sleeping in the shade.
Had I heart to slide an arm beneath her,
Press her parting lips as her waist I gather slow,
Waking in amazement she could but embrace me
Then would she hold me and never let me go?

George Meredith, "Love in the Valley"

1. Who is the sentence about? _____

2. Where is the girl? _____

3. "Couched with her arms behind her golden head" modifies _____

4. "sleeping in the shade" modifies _____

H. Up to the farmhouse to dinner through the teeming, dusty field, the road under our sneakers was only a two-track road.

E. B. White, from "Once More on the Lake"

1. What is the sentence about? _____

2. "teeming" describes what? _____

3. Where did the road go? _____

4. "under our sneakers" modifies _____

I. Upon my entrance, Usher arose from a sofa on which he had been lying at full length, and greeted me with a vivacious warmth which had much in it, I at first thought, of an overdone cordiality—of the constrained effort of the ennuyé man of the world.

Edgar Allan Poe, The Fall of the House of Usher

1. Who is the sentence about? _____

2. What are the two core actions of the subject? _____

3. "on which he had been lying at full length, and greeted me with a vivacious warmth" modifies _____

4. "which had much in it" modifies _____

J. A wealthy man, addicted to his pleasure and to his profits, finds religion to be a traffic so entangled, and of so many piddling accounts, that of all mysteries he cannot skill to keep a stock going upon that trade. What should he do?

John Milton, Areopagitica

1. Who is the sentence about? _____

2. What is the core action of the subject? _____

3. "addicted to his pleasure and to his profits" modifies _____

4. "to be a traffic so entangled" modifies _____

RESTATING COMPLEX SENTENCES

The ultimate assessment of the understanding of a sentence comes with a restatement of the sentence in your own words. In an appropriate restatement, you present the main idea in the sentence and include the significant supporting details. As mentioned before, you ask the same question that you applied to find the main idea for everything from paragraphs to books. That question is, "What is the point the author is trying to convey about the topic?" As demonstrated by the preceding exercises, this question can be broken down into several smaller steps. Depending on the difficulty of the sentence, the steps may be performed consciously or subconsciously. Use the following questions as preliminary stages in determining the meaning of a sentence and then restate the sentence in a manner that maintains the same meaning as that intended by the author.

1. What word or words tell what is happening in the sentence?
2. Who or what is doing the acting?
3. Who or what receives the action?
4. How do the modifiers change the meaning of the sentence?

The goal to emphasize in restating a sentence is that the restatement must have the *same focus as the original sentence*. In other words, the restatement must express the same main idea. The actual words that are used may or may not be the same as those used by the author, but the meaning must be the same. In the following example, notice that the first sentence restatement expresses the same idea as the original sentence, but the second restatement does not maintain the author's original focus.

Sentence:

Given the massive problems of the poor, the government can no longer accept the responsibility of caring for the needy without the assistance of the private sector.

Correct Restatement:

The government cannot continue to take care of all the poor people without private aid.

Incorrect Restatement:

The government no longer accepts the responsibility for the poor because aid from the private sector has not been forthcoming.

Again, the restatement must express the same focus as the original sentence. Paraphrasing or rearranging the words is not enough to indicate that you have understood the sentence's main point.

▮▮▮ Exercise 7: Restating the Main Idea

The following sentences are taken from a variety of college textbooks. Using your own words, as well as those of the author, restate the main idea of the sentence in a way that maintains the author's original focus.

1. Extended kinship, neighborhoods, and religious organizations are the most salient points of involvement among the poor and those of clear ethnicity.

Jonathan Turner, *Sociology*

_____

_____

_____

2. Science also cannot tell us whether war is good or bad or whether capital punishment or abortion is immoral, since such statements would have to be based on some system of values about what is good or bad.

Robert Wallace, *Biology: The World of Life*

_____

_____

_____

3. For verbal materials, the dominant long-term memory code is neither acoustic nor visual; instead, it seems to be based on the meanings of the items.

Atkinson et al., *Introduction to Psychology*

_____

_____

4. So feeble had the light of learning become by the end of the eighth century that

_____

Charlemagne found it necessary to order the monasteries to revive their schools and resume instruction in the rudiments of "singing, arithmetic, and grammar."

Wallbank et al., Civilization Past and Present

_____

_____

5. Parting is all we know of heaven,
And all we need of hell.

Emily Dickinson

_____

_____

_____

6. The relative levels of athletic activities among boys and girls, and the encouragement of "masculinity" in boys and "femininity" in girls, have greatly accentuated dissimilarities between males and females with respect to size, weight, and strength.

Jonathan Turner, Sociology

_____

_____

_____

7. Beyond the physical world, which is the legitimate realm of science or "pure reason," lies the world of "things-in-themselves," he believed, where science can never penetrate and which is the legitimate realm of faith or "practical reason."

Wallbank et al., Civilization Past and Present

_____

_____

_____

8. If government is to regulate society effectively, it must be able to use its coercive power when people are unwilling to obey its decisions voluntarily.

Mark Amstutz, An Introduction to Political Science

_____

_____

_____

9. In this essay, which appeared in 1798, Malthus pointed out that populations increased in a geometric progression, and if man continued to reproduce at the same rate, he

would inevitably outstrip his food supply and create a teeming world full of misery and vice.

Robert Wallace, Biology: The World of Life

_____

_____

_____

10. That it will never come again
    Is what makes life so sweet.

Emily Dickinson

_____

_____

_____

11. In many cases, we can graph a line by finding its x-intercept and y-intercept; the points (if any) where the line crosses the x-axis and y-axis respectively.

Lial and Miller, Beginning Algebra 3

_____

_____

_____

12. A true son of the Age of Reason, Locke believed that investigation of such basic philosophical questions as the existence of God and the fundamentals of morality would lead men to a state of universal reasonableness and thereby free them from the necessity of relying blindly on authority.

Wallbank et al., Civilization Past and Present

_____

_____

_____

13. Although two eyes help us to perceive depth and distance, we are by no means restricted to binocular effects for depth and distance perception.

Atkinson et al., Introduction to Psychology

_____

_____

_____

_____

14. Abelard's great contribution to medieval thought was freeing logic from barrenness and rerouting it to become again a means to an end rather than an end in itself.

Wallbank et al., *Civilization Past and Present*

_____

_____

_____

15. An aggressive person may have learned that smiling and speaking in low tones reaps him greater rewards, but if his aggression is innate, then we can expect him to be aggressive in small ways, or to direct it into harmless channels, or perhaps to show sporadic outbursts of violence when his guard is down.

Robert Wallace, *Biology: The World of Life*

_____

_____

_____

16. Reactions involving solids usually take place only on the solid's surface and therefore include only a small fraction of the total molecules present in the solid.

Stoker and Slabaugh, *General, Organic, & Biochemistry*

_____

_____

_____

17. This situation may have resulted from the vice-president's having established more rapport with people in other statuses that, on an aggregate level, gives him or her the ability to get things done because more employees are on his or her side.

Jonathan Turner, *Sociology*

_____

_____

_____

18. It has been estimated that as the world's population grows, two people join the ranks of the hungry for each one that will be adequately fed.

Robert Wallace, *Biology: The World of Life*

_____

_____

_____

19. Finally, in the postconventional level, when children have begun to move increasingly away from the family sphere and are interacting with more people with ideas different from their own, their conceptions of good and evil become more complicated.

Jonathan Turner, Sociology

_____

_____

_____

20. From cradle to grave this problem of running order through chaos, direction through space, discipline through freedom, unity through multiplicity, has always been, and must always be, the task of education, as it is the moral of religion, philosophy, science, art, politics, and economy; but a boy's will is his life, and he dies when it is broken, as the colt dies in harness taking a new nature in becoming tame.

Henry Adams, The Education of Henry Adams

_____

_____

_____

Selection 1

BIOLOGY

1. In a classical experiment, Lorenz and Tinbergen showed that the behavior of a greylag goose rolling an egg back to her nest had two components: fixed and orienting. When they removed the egg while she was retrieving it, she continued the chin-tucking movements (the fixed componet) but stopped making the slight side-to-side movements that kept the egg moving in a straight line (the orienting component).

Drawing adapted from "Taxis and Instinkthandlung in der Eirollbewegung der Graugens" by Konrad Lorenz and Niko Tinbergen, _Z. Tierpsychol._ 2: 1–29 (1938).

Stage 1: Preview

Preview *the selection and complete the following sentence: After reading this selection, I would like to know* _____

_____

Use thinking strategies as you read:

1. *Predict*
2. *Picture*
3. *Form analogies*

4. *Verbalize points*
5. *Fix up strategies*

FIXED ACTION PATTERNS AND ORIENTATION *

Robert Wallace, from *Biology: The World of Life*

It has long been known that animals are born with certain behavioral repertoires. The first time a tern chick is given a small fish, it manipulates the fish so that it will be swallowed head first, with the spines safely flattened. Dogs that have spent their entire lives indoors will attempt to bury a bone by making scratching motions on the carpet as if they were
5 moving earth. The same dogs will turn around several times before lying down, although there is no grass to trample nor spiders to chase out. Such patterns, which are innate and characteristic of a given species, are called *fixed action patterns*. When fixed action patterns are coupled with orienting movements, we can speak of an *instinctive pattern*. But this probably isn't too clear just yet.

10   To illustrate the relationship between a fixed action pattern and its orientation, consider the fly-catching movements of a frog. For the fixed action pattern to be effective, the frog must carefully orient itself with respect to the fly's position. The performance of the fixed action pattern, the tongue flick, results in the frog's gaining a fly. It is important to realize, however, that once the fixed action pattern is initiated, it cannot be altered. If
15 the fly should move after the pattern is initiated, the frog misses since the sequence of movements will be completed whether the fly is there or not. When a frog catches a fly, one can easily distinguish the orientation movements from the fixed action pattern.

With other instinctive patterns the orientation may be indistinguishable from the fixed action itself. For example, if a goose sees an egg lying outside her nest, she will roll it
20 back under her chin (Figure 1). She keeps the egg rolling in a straight line by lateral movements of the head. In an interesting experiment, it was found that the fixed and orienting components of the retrieval pattern could be separated. The orienting movements depend on the direction taken by the rolling egg. If the egg is removed during the retrieval the goose will continue to draw her head back (the fixed
25 component)—but in a straight line, without the orienting side-to-side movements. Thus we see that the fixed action pattern, once initiated, is independent of any environmental cue, so that once it starts it continues. The relationship between the fixed action pattern and its orientation component is similar to that between a car's engine and its steering wheel. Once the engine is started, it continues to run, but each change of direction
30 requires a new movement of the steering wheel and thus depends on the specific environmental circumstance.

*LEARNING STRATEGY: Be able to define and explain fixed action patterns and orientation and give examples of each.

From *Biology: The World of Life*, 3rd Edition, by Robert A. Wallace. Copyright © 1981 by Scott, Foresman and Company.

It has been found that an animal may not possess all its fixed action patterns when it is very young. Many of these patterns develop as the animal matures, as is the case with morphological characteristics. For example, wing flapping or other patterns associated with flight normally do not appear until about the time a bird is actually ready to begin flying, although there may be some incipient flapping just prior to this time. Also, the fixed action pattern and its orientation component do not necessarily appear simultaneously in the animal's behavioral repertoire. A baby mouse may scratch vigorously with its leg flailing thin air; later it will come to apply the scratch to the itch.

Now let's consider another drama, one that might put some of this together for us. After daylight a peregrine falcon begins its hunt. At first its behavior is highly variable; it may fly high or low, or bank to the left or the right. It is driven by hunger and would be equally pleased by the sight of a flitting sparrow or a scampering mouse. Suddenly it sees a flock of teal flying below. Its behavior now becomes less random as it swoops toward them in what is the next stage of "teal-hunting behavior." First the random search, and then the swoop.

Almost all falcons perform this dive in just about the same way, although there are some variations. This is a sham pass to scatter the flock, and the falcon is likely to fall through any part of it. The teal, at the sight of the falcon, have closed ranks for mutual protection. (After all, it is hard to pick a single individual out of a tightly packed group. A predator is likely to shift its attention from one individual to another, and in failing to concentrate on a single prey, it may come up empty-handed.) The sham pass works though, and the terrified teal scatter. The falcon immediately beats its way upward, and after picking out an isolated target below, it begins a second dive.

If we were to watch this same falcon perform such a dive on several occasions, we might notice that the procedure is much the same every time. And if we were to watch several different falcons, we might notice that they all perform this action in much the same way. The greatest amount of variation is during the earliest part of such dives, since, at this stage, what the falcon does will be dictated in part by what the teal does. The falcon's options become fewer, and its behavior becomes more and more stereotyped, as it descends. Finally, there is a point at which the falcon's action is no longer variable. It now initiates the last part of the attack, the part that is no longer influenced by anything the teal does. At this instant the falcon's feet are clenched, and it may be traveling at over 150 miles an hour. Unless the teal makes a last split-second change in direction, it will be knocked from the sky, and the falcon's hunt will have been successful.

The falcon's energy will then be spent in following the teal to the ground, where, with rather unvarying and stereotyped movements, it will pluck the teal, tear away its flesh with specific movements of its head, and swallow the meat. The sequence of muscle actions in swallowing is very precise and always the same. The swallowing action itself seems to bring a measure of relief, so that the falcon does not feel like hunting again for a while. Theoretically, it is the desire to perform swallowing movements that brought the falcon out to hunt in the first place. In other words, the falcon was searching for a situation that would enable it to swallow. This probably seems a bit bizarre, but let's go on.

We can derive several points from this example. First, the state of the animal is significant. The falcon had not eaten for a time and was hungry. Hunger thus provided the impetus, or "motivation." In general, if an instinctive action pattern has not been performed for a time, there is an increasing likelihood of its appearance. Second, the earlier stages of this instinctive sequence were highly variable, but the behavior became more and more stereotyped until the final *fixed* action was accomplished. Third, the

85　performance of this final action provided some relief. We have to assume this relief from the fact that once the falcon has performed this final action (swallowing), it does not immediately seek out conditions that will permit it to do so again. You will also note that the fixed action pattern provides the animal with a biologically important element—in this case, food.

Courting behavior in birds is also believed to be instinctive. In one experiment Daniel Lehrman of Rutgers University found that when a male blond ring dove was isolated from females, it soon began to bow and coo to a stuffed model of a female—a model that it had previously ignored. When the model was replaced by a rolled-up cloth, he began to
90　court the cloth; and when this was removed the sex-crazed dove directed his attention to a corner of the cage, where it could at least focus its gaze. It seems that the threshold for release of the behavior pattern became increasingly lower as time went by without the sight of a live female dove. It is almost as though some specific "energy" for performing courting behavior were building up within the male ring dove. As the energy level
95　increased, the *response threshold,* the minimum stimulus necessary to elicit a response, lowered to a point at which almost anything would stimulate the dove.

Invoking a mysterious "energy" seems less necessary to explain the hunting behavior of the falcon, since the reason the falcon hunts seems apparent: it is hungry. But then how do you explain hunting behavior in well-fed animals such as house cats? Perhaps the
100　hunt is an instinctive action pattern in itself, so that its performance provides a measure of relief.　　　　　　　　　　　　　　　　　　　　　　　　　　　　　　/1457

Stage 3: Recall

Stop and recall what you have read. Review your use of the thinking strategies. Did you use all five?

▥ ▨ ▥ Skill Development: Sentence Meaning

Answer the questions about the relationships of the following sentence parts.

1. If the egg is removed during the retrieval the goose will continue to draw her head back (the fixed component)—but in a straight line, without the orienting side-to-side movements.

　1. What "will continue"? _____

　2. "The fixed component" refers to _____

　3. "During the retrieval" modifies _____

　4. "In a straight line" modifies _____

2. The falcon's energy will then be spent in following the teal to the ground, where, with rather unvarying and stereotyped movements, it will pluck the teal, tear away its flesh with specific movements of its head, and swallow the meat.

　1. What "will be spent"? _____

2. "Stereotyped movement" modifies _____

3. "Specific movements of the head" modifies _____

4. "Unvarying" modifes _____

Using your own words, as well as those of the author, restate the main idea of the sentence in a manner that maintains the author's original focus.

3. Thus we see that the fixed action pattern, once initiated, is independent of any environmental cue, so that once it starts it continues.

_____

_____

_____

4. Second, the earlier stages of this instinctive sequence were highly variable, but the behavior became more and more stereotyped until the final *fixed* action was accomplished.

_____

_____

_____

5. We have to assume this relief from the fact that once the falcon has performed this final action (swallowing), it does not immediately seek out conditions that will permit it to do so again.

_____

_____

_____

▥▦▥ Comprehension Questions

1. The main point the author is trying to get across in this selection is_____

_____

_____

After reading the selection, answer the following questions with *a, b, c,* or *d.*

_____ 2. All the following are examples of fixed action patterns except
  a. a dog scratching the carpet to bury a bone
  b. a tern manipulating a fish to swallow it head first

    c. a dog trampling the carpet to chase out spiders

    d. a dog barking to protect a bone

_____ 3. The author implies that fixed action patterns

    a. occur at random without stimulation

    b. are not specific to certain species

    c. are learned rather than instinctive responses

    d. will continue to occur when stimulated even though the need no longer exists

_____ 4. In animals, fixed action patterns are

    a. developed simultaneously with the orientation component

    b. fully developed at birth

    c. developed as the animal gets older

    d. developed after the orientation movement

_____ 5. In hunting the teal, the purpose of the falcon's first dive is to

    a. scatter the prey

    b. isolate a target

    c. practice fixed action patterns

    d. judge the size of the flock

_____ 6. If the teal remained in a tightly packed group during the falcon's hunting dives, the author implies that

    a. the falcon would not be able to kill a teal

    b. the falcon would kill more than one teal

    c. the teals could more easily attack the falcon

    d. the falcon would move to a higher altitude

_____ 7. After killing the teal, the falcon

    a. shares its prey with other family members

    b. immediately eats its prey

    c. hides its prey for a delayed feast

    d. eats only part of its prey and saves the rest for a later time

_____ 8. Once the orientation of the hunting dive and fixed action attack pattern is initiated, the falcon

    a. can vary with the movement of the teal

    b. cannot vary with the movement of the teal

    c. can isolate its target regardless of movement

    d. can vary both the speed and direction of the dive

_____ 9. The minimum stimulus necessary to elicit an instinctive response is called

    a. the orientation movement

    b. the fixed action pattern

    c. the response threshold

    d. the fixed energy

_____ 10. The author concludes that courting behavior is instinctive in ring doves because

    a. the behavior occurs after the removal of the stimulus

    b. the behavior is extinguished after removal of the stimulus

c. the male ring dove has a high energy level

d. sex-crazed doves direct their energy to isolated females

Answer the following questions with *T* (true), *F* (false), or *CT* (can't tell).

_____ 11. In the analogy of the instinctive pattern and the car, the orientation component is compared to the steering wheel.

_____ 12. The falcon can fly at a speed of 150 miles per hour.

_____ 13. The author suggests that the falcon is motivated to hunt by the desire to swallow.

_____ 14. The author implies that falcons usually hunt and kill several times in one day.

_____ 15. Hunger does not provide the motivation for the falcon to hunt.

▉▉▉ Vocabulary

According to the way the boldface word was used in the selection, indicate *a, b, c,* or *d* for the word or phrase that gives the best definition.

_____ 1. "by **lateral** movements of the head (20)"
   a. quick
   b. up and down
   c. rhythmical
   d. side to side

_____ 2. "with **morphological** characteristics (34)"
   a. instinctive
   b. normal
   c. structural
   d. aging

_____ 3. "some **incipient** flapping (36)"
   a. nervous
   b. beginning
   c. unsure
   d. silly

_____ 4. "leg **flailing** thin air (39)"
   a. finding
   b. encountering
   c. thrashing
   d. accepting

_____ 5. "behavior is highly **variable** (41)"
   a. dangerous
   b. exaggerated
   c. noticeable
   d. inconsistent

_____ 6. "a **sham** pass (48)"
   a. fake
   b. evil
   c. shameful
   d. frightening

_____ 7. "swallowing is very **precise** (69)"
   a. strong
   b. aggressive
   c. exact
   d. hungry

_____ 8. "**derive** several points (75)"
   a. agree on
   b. deduce
   c. settle
   d. separate

_____ 9. "provided the **impetus** (77)"
    a. rationale
    b. platform
    c. background
    d. incentive

_____ 10. "to **elicit** a response (95)"
    a. negate
    b. withhold
    c. draw forth
    d. summarize

▮▮▮ Essay Question

Define both fixed action patterns and orientation and give examples of each. Use a sheet of notebook paper to record your answer.

Selection **2**

BIOLOGY

Howard Hall

Stage 1: Preview

Preview the selection and complete the following sentence: After reading this

_selection, I would like to know _____

_____

Use thinking strategies as you read:

1. *Predict*
2. *Picture*
3. *Form analogies*

4. *Verbalize points*
5. *Fix up strategies*

COMMUNICATION BY SOUND*

William T. Keeton, from *Biological Science*

Being vocal animals ourselves, we are very familiar with the use of sound as a medium of communication. No other species has a sound language that even approaches the complexity and refinement of human spoken languages. But many other species can communicate an amazing amount of information via sound, information upon which both
15 the life of the individual and the continued existence of the species may depend.

Sound Communication in Insects.   We have already mentioned two examples of sound communication: Male *Aedes* mosquitoes are attracted by the buzzing sound produced by the female's wings during flight (or by devices such as tuning forks that emit sounds of a similar pitch), and hen chickens respond in a characteristic fashion to the
10 distress calls of their chicks. Let us return to the first of these examples. The head of a male mosquito bears two antennae, each covered with long hairs. When sound waves of certain frequencies strike the antennae, these are caused to vibrate in unison. The vibrations stimulate sensory cells packed tightly into a small segment at the base of each antenna. The male responds to such stimulation by homing in on the source of the
15 sound, thus locating the female and copulating with her. A striking demonstration of the adaptiveness of this communication system is that during the first 24 hours of the adult life of the male, when he is not yet sexually competent, the antennal hairs lie close to the shaft . . . and thus make him nearly deaf. Only after he becomes fully developed sexually do the hairs stand erect . . . , enabling the antennae to receive sound stimuli from the
20 female. Thus the male does not waste energy responding to females before he is sexually competent, but once he becomes competent he has a built-in system for locating a mate without random searching. Furthermore, his built-in receptor system is species-specific; it is stimulated by sounds of the frequency characteristic of females of his own species, not by the frequencies characteristic of other species of mosquitoes. Hence the sound
25 produced by the female's wings functions both as mating call and species recognition signal.
     Many other insects utilize sound in a similar way. For example, male crickets utilize calls produced by rasping together specialized parts of their wings. These calls function in species recognition, in attracting females and stimulating their reproductive behavior, and
30 in warning away other males. So species-specific are the calls of crickets that in several

*LEARNING STRATEGY: From the examples given, be able to explain how and why each uses sound to communicate.

From *Biological Science,* 2nd Edition, by William T. Keeton, pp. 418–422, by permission of W. W. Norton & Company, Inc. Copyright © 1972, 1967 by W. W. Norton & Company, Inc.

© Scott, Foresman and Company.

cases closely related species can best be told apart by human beings on the basis of the calls; the species may be almost indistinguishable on an anatomical basis, but have distinctively different calls.

Sound Communication in Frogs.   The calls of frogs serve functions similar to those
35   of cricket calls, and like these they are very species-specific. The male frogs attract females to their territory by calling. In one experiment, C. M. Bogert of the American Museum of Natural History recorded the call of male toads. He then captured 24 female toads and released them in the dark in the vicinity of a loudspeaker over which he was playing the recorded male call. Thirty minutes later, he turned on the lights and
40   determined the position of each female. Nineteen of the females had moved nearer the loudspeaker, four had moved farther away, and one had escaped. Eighteen of the nineteen females that had moved toward the speaker were physiologically ready to lay eggs; of the four females that moved away from the speaker, three had already laid their eggs and the other was not yet of reproductive age. In a control experiment, Bogert
45   showed that 24 females released in the dark near a silent speaker had scattered randomly in all directions by the time the lights were turned on 30 minutes later. This demonstration that females ready for mating are strongly attracted by the male's vocalizations while other females are not serves to emphasize the effectiveness of a releasing stimulus depends, among other things, on the condition of the recipient of the
50   stimulus; the call of the male frog is an effective releaser for movement by the female toward the male only if the female's reproductive drive is high, largely as a result of a high level of sex hormones.

Bird Songs.   Of all the familiar animal sounds—the buzzing of mosquitoes, the calling of crickets and frogs, the barking, roaring, purring, grunting, etc. of various mammals—perhaps none, with the exception of human speech, has received so much
55   attention as the singing of birds. It has been celebrated in poetry, copied in musical compositions, mimicked by whistlers, adored by lovers, and enthusiastically welcomed by those impatient for spring. The popular "explanation" for bird song is simple: The bird is happy and sings with joy, welcoming the morning and the spring and expressing love for his mate. Probably few other biological phenomena have been so enshrouded in
60   anthropomorphic fancies. But biologists must cast a skeptical eye on such admittedly appealing interpretations. Objective investigation has demonstrated that bird song functions primarily as a species recognition signal, as a display that attracts females to the male and contributes to the synchronization of the reproductive drives (increasing sexual motivation and decreasing attack and escape motivations), and as a display
65   important in defense of territory. In its defensive function, a bird's singing is certainly no indication of "happiness" or "joy"; if such human-oriented concepts could properly be applied to birds, which they cannot, the singing would more accurately be taken as an indication of combativeness.

The role of singing in the establishment and defense of territories is an especially interesting one. A territory may be defined as an area defended by one member of a
70   species against intrusion by other members of the same species (and occasionally against members of other species). A male bird chooses an unoccupied area and begins to sing vigorously within it, thus warning away other males. The boundaries between the territories of two males are regularly patrolled, and the two may sing loudly at each other across the border. Although during early spring there is often much shifting of boundaries
75   as more and more males arrive and begin competing for territories, later in the season the

boundaries usually become fairly well stabilized and each male knows where they are. During the period when the boundaries are being established, it is often the males that can sing loudest and most vigorously that successfully retain large territories or even expand their territories at the expense of other males that sing less loudly and vigorously.

80 **Sound Communication by Whales.** Recent research on whales by Roger Payne of Rockefeller University has revealed that many species sing amazingly elaborate songs. In some cases, a single song may last over half an hour before repetition begins. Because the frequencies of the sounds are ones that can be transmitted over very long distances in water, Payne thinks it is possible that singing whales may be heard by other whales
85 hundreds (or perhaps even thousands) of miles away. The eerie beauty of whale songs, as recorded by Payne, has inspired several new musical compositions in the last few years.
    There is evidence that the small whales called dolphins can produce a great variety of sounds that convey many types of information. One investigator even believes that dolphins have an intelligence approaching that of human beings and that they have a
90 language far more extensive and advanced than that of any other animal except man. Though this is a minority view, there is no denying the desirability of more intensive research on dolphin communication.   /1268

Stage 3: Recall

Stop and recall what you have read. Review your use of the thinking strategies. Did you use all five?

▥ ▤ ▥ Skill Development: Sentence Meaning

Answer the questions about the relationships of the following sentence parts.

1. This demonstration that females ready for mating are strongly attracted by the male's vocalizations while other females are not serves to emphasize the effectiveness of a releasing stimulus depends, among other things, on the condition of the recipient of the stimulus; the call of the male frog is an effective releaser for movement by the female toward the male only if the female's reproductive drive is high, largely as a result of a high level of sex hormones.

    1. What "serves to emphasize the effectiveness"? _____

    2. On what does the "effectiveness of a releasing stimulus" depend? _____

    3. What serves as a releaser of female movement? _____

    4. What makes the female's reproductive drive high? _____

2. In its defensive function, a bird's singing is certainly no indication of "happiness" or "joy"; if such human-oriented concepts could properly be applied to birds, which they cannot, the singing would more accurately be taken as an indication of combativeness.

    1. What does not indicate happiness? _____

2. What indicates combativeness?_____

3. "Which they cannot" describes _____

4. What "could be properly applied"? _____

Using your own words, as well as those of the author, restate the main idea of the sentence in a manner that maintains the author's original focus.

3. Objective investigation has demonstrated that bird song functions primarily as a species recognition signal, as a display that attracts females to the male and contributes to the synchronization of the reproductive drives (increasing sexual motivation and decreasing attack and escape motivations), and as a display important in defense of territory.

_____

_____

_____

4. So species-specific are the calls of crickets that in several cases closely related species can best be told apart by human beings on the basis of the calls; the species may be almost indistinguishable on an anatomical basis, but have distinctively different calls.

_____

_____

_____

5. Probably few other biological phenomena have been so enshrouded in anthropomorphic fancies.

_____

_____

_____

© Scott, Foresman and Company.

▥ ▤ ▥ Comprehension Questions

1. The main point the author is trying to get across in this selection is_____

_____

_____

After reading the selection, answer the following questions with *a, b, c,* or *d.*

_____   2. The female *Aedes* mosquito sexually attracts by
    a. a buzz from its antennae   c. hairs on the wings that stand erect
    b. a device similar to a tuning fork   d. a sound from its wings in flight

_____ 3. In responding to the mating call of the female, the male *Aedes* mosquito experiences all of the following except
a. vibrating antennae
b. stimulation of cells at the base of the antennae
c. a buzzing from his wings
d. erect hairs on the antennae

_____ 4. "Species-specific" behavior refers to a natural attraction for
a. members of related species
b. members of the same limited species group
c. sexually competent mates
d. specific individuals within a species

_____ 5. The main purpose of Bogert's experiment was to show that a female frog will respond to the male mating call only if she is
a. ready to reproduce at that time   c. old enough to reproduce
b. species-specific   d. experienced in reproduction

_____ 6. The primary reason Bogert used the control experiment with the silent speaker was to show that
a. female frogs react to darkness
b. with no sound, thirty minutes is not long enough for a reaction
c. frogs not yet of reproduction age would not respond
d. his first results were not accidental

_____ 7. The author believes that the melodious song of a bird is most likely
a. a welcoming of spring
b. a sign of love
c. an expression of happiness and joy
d. a declaration of ownership

_____ 8. According to the selection, in order to keep competition out of territorial boundaries, a bird must
a. arrive early in the spring
b. sing more forcefully than competing birds
c. engage in physical combat with competing birds
d. attract more female birds than the competition

_____ 9. All of the following are characteristics of the song of the whale except that it
a. is repetitious
b. can be transmitted over long distances
c. can last for over a half an hour
d. has a beauty that has inspired musicians

_____ 10. The author feels that the most complex of all the sound communications mentioned is that of
a. mosquitoes
b. frogs
c. birds
d. whales

Answer the following with *T* (true), *F* (false), or *CT* (can't tell).

_____ 11. The author implies that territorial boundaries are species-specific.

_____ 12. A male *Aedes* mosquito with damaged antennae cannot mate.

_____ 13. The call of the cricket is a vocal sound.

_____ 14. In describing the results of his first experiment, Bogert fails to account for the behavior of one of the frogs.

_____ 15. The author implies that female birds do not establish territorial boundaries.

▮▰▮ Vocabulary

According to the way the boldface word was used in the selection, indicate *a, b, c,* or *d* for the word or phrase that gives the best definition.

____ 1. "not yet sexually **competent** (17)"
- a. older
- b. complete
- c. capable
- d. proven

____ 2. "to vibrate in **unison** (12)"
- a. perfect agreement
- b. opposite directions
- c. total isolation
- d. lower frequencies

____ 3. "insects **utilize** sound (27)"
- a. buzz
- b. ignore
- c. use
- d. sting

____ 4. "in the **vicinity** of (38)"
- a. only in front of
- b. same time period
- c. only to the right of
- d. surrounding region

____ 5. "the **recipient** of the stimulus (49)"
- a. sender
- b. evaluator
- c. receiver
- d. originator

____ 6. "**mimicked** by whistlers (56)"
- a. beloved
- b. imitated
- c. recognized
- d. sought after

____ 7. "few other biological **phenomena** (59)"
- a. mistakes
- b. laws
- c. experiments
- d. extraordinary events

____ 8. "have been so **enshrouded** (59)"
- a. interested
- b. substituted
- c. veiled
- d. unlucky

____ 9. "cast a **skeptical** eye (60)"
- a. approving
- b. doubting
- c. knowledgeable
- d. welcoming

____ 10. "an indication of **combativeness** (68)"
- a. readiness to fight
- b. cooperation
- c. insecurity
- d. anxiety

■■■ Essay Question

Discuss evidence of sound communication in animals. Use a sheet of notebook paper to record your answer.

Selection **3**

HISTORY

The Library of the University of Edinburgh

Stage 1: Preview

Preview the selection and complete the following sentence:

After reading this selection, I would like to know _____

_____

_____

_____

© Scott, Foresman and Company.

Stage 2: Integrate Knowledge While Reading

Use thinking strategies as you read:

1. *Predict*
2. *Picture*
3. *Form analogies*

4. *Verbalize points*
5. *Fix up strategies*

MOHAMMED AND THE RISE OF THE ARAB EMPIRE*

Joseph R. Strayer, et al., from *The Mainstream of Civilization to 1715*

A few years after the death of Justinian in 565, a child was born in Arabia who was to found a religion that spread more rapidly than Christianity and an empire that was larger than that of Rome at the height of its power. Few men have had more impact on history than Mohammed. His religion split the old Mediterranean world and transformed the
5   civilization of the Middle East; his influence is felt today in a broad belt of territory stretching from West Africa to the East Indies. Islam was the last of the three great world religions to emerge, and for many centuries it was more vigorous than either of its rivals—Christianity in the West and Buddhism in the East.

The Early Arabs

Arabia had played no important role in history before the time of Mohammed. The huge
10   peninsula, about one-third the size of the United States, was like an arid wedge driven into the fertile lands of the Middle East. Most Arabs were nomads, driving their herds from one scanty patch of vegetation to another. A much smaller, but very influential, group was made up of traders who dealt in products from the southern part of the peninsula, notably frankincense, and in goods imported from India and the Far East.
15   Overland trade through Arabia was not extensive, but there was enough to support a few small towns along the southern and western sides of the peninsula.

    The early Arabs were thus in touch with all the civilizations of the East and had learned something from all of them. Since they themselves spoke a Semitic language, they had been most influenced by other peoples of this language group who lived in the Fertile
20   Crescent north of the peninsula. The Arabs developed a system of writing related, at least indirectly, to the Phoenician alphabet. They had the usual Semitic interest in religion, although it was expressed in almost indiscriminate polytheism. They had numerous tribal deities, and they had had contacts with the Christians and Jews who inhabited the northern part of the Arabian Peninsula. They honored poets, and the ideal Arab leader
25   was as ready to make verses as he was to make war. They knew a good deal about astronomy, for knowledge of the stars is as helpful in crossing the desert as it is in navigating the seas. At their best, the Arabs were imaginative and eager to absorb new

*LEARNING STRATEGY: Be able to describe Mohammed's struggle and his beliefs.

knowledge. They assimilated and profited from Greco-Roman civilization far more rapidly than did the Germans who took over the western part of the Roman Empire.

30 And yet there were grave defects in the social and political organization of the early Arabs. The nature of the country forced them to live in small, scattered tribes, and each tribe was almost constantly at war with its neighbors. The leading families within each tribe were often jealous of one another, so that blood-feuds were frequent and persistent. Weaker members of each tribe, and indeed of each family, were harshly treated by their

35 stronger relatives. Sickly children were often killed, and orphans had little hope of receiving their parents' property. Women had almost no rights; their fathers or their husbands controlled their lives and their property. Men who could afford it had many wives and could divorce any of them whenever they wished. The divorced woman was usually left without any property or regular income.

40 In spite of all this disunity, certain strong ties bound the Arabs together. They were great genealogists; the leaders of many tribes could trace their ancestry back to the same ancient families—families that were known and respected throughout Arabia. Most of the tribes accepted a few common religious observances. There was a sacred period in each year, for example, when fighting was suspended and when many Arabs made a pilgrimage

45 to the religious center of Mecca, a trading town near the west coast. In Mecca was the Kaaba, an ancient building full of images, including one of Christ. Here almost every god known to the Arabs could be worshiped. Here, too, was the most venerated object in the Arab world, the sacred Black Stone that had come from heaven. This habit of worshiping together at Mecca was the strongest unifying force in Arabia and one that was carefully

50 preserved by Mohammed.

Mohammed's Teaching

Mohammed was born about 570 in Mecca. We know little about his early years, except that he was a poor orphan (although his grandfather had been a successful merchant). When he reached adolescence he began to work for a woman named Khadija, the widow of a rich merchant. In her service he made many caravan trips, during which he may have

55 accumulated his information about the Jewish and Christian religions and his knowledge of the legends and traditions of other Arab tribes. He eventually married his employer, though she was considerably older than he, and the marriage gave him the wealth and leisure to meditate on religious problems.

Like many other Arabs, Mohammed had a sensitive mind, a deep appreciation of the

60 wonders of nature, and a strong interest in religion. These qualities were enhanced by mysterious seizures, to which he had been subject since childhood. During these attacks he seemed to be struggling to express ideas that were not yet fully formed in his own mind. He gradually came to believe that this was God's way of trying to communicate with him, but until he was about forty he had no clear idea of what he was meant to do.

65 Then he had his first revelation: a vision of the angel Gabriel, who commanded him to speak "in the name of the Lord, the Creator . . . the Lord who taught man what he did not know."

Mohammed was still doubtful about his mission, but as revelation succeeded revelation he became filled with the vision of the one, eternal God, the Lord of the world. He began

70 to appeal to his fellow citizens of Mecca to abandon their host of false deities and to worship the one, true God. These early revelations bear some resemblance to the Psalms, both in their poetic quality and in their appeal to the wonders of nature as proofs of God's greatness and mercy. The stars in the heavens, sunshine and rain, the fruits of the earth—"all are signs of God's power if you would only understand."

75　By now Mohammed was convinced that he was a prophet, the last and greatest in the succession of prophets whom God had sent to enlighten and save mankind. He never claimed to be more than a prophet and even denied that he could work miracles, although he admitted that some of his predecessors had had this gift. He also admitted the divine mission of the Jewish prophets and of Jesus, but he claimed that their

80　teachings had been distorted or misinterpreted. He was quite certain that the revelations he received superseded everything that had come before. The earlier prophets had had glimpses of the true religion, but he alone had received the full message. Their teachings were to be accepted only when they agreed with the final word of God, which had been revealed to him.

85　Mohammed at first made little progress in converting his countrymen. His wife, Khadija, believed in him and comforted him when he was despondent, and his cousin Ali was one of his first converts. But most Meccans of good family were hostile; most of his early followers were from poor and uninfluential families. Mohammed's attacks on idols angered those who believed that the prosperity of Mecca as a center of trade depended

90　also on its being the center of worship of all the known gods. Mohammed's followers were persecuted, and his own life was threatened. Finally he fled with his supporters to the city of Yathrib, some distance north of Mecca. The Mohammedan era begins with this flight, or Hegira, which took place in 622 A.D.*

Mohammed was welcomed as an arbitrator of local disputes in Yathrib. The town was

95　renamed Medinet-en-Nabi (Medina), the City of the Prophet. Jewish influence was strong there, and the Arabs of Medina found nothing strange in the doctrine of a single, all-powerful God. Mohammed soon gained many converts among the pagan and half-Jewish Arabs and became virtually the ruler of the community. He now became involved in political problems, and the revelations he received during this period dealt

100　largely with law and government. For example, it was at Medina that the rules about marriage, inheritance, and the punishment of criminals were laid down.

During the stay at Medina, Mohammed's reputation and power increased steadily. A desultory war between Medina and Mecca gradually became more serious, and by 630 Mohammed had gained so many supporters that he was able to capture Mecca with little

105　difficulty. He immediately destroyed the idols in the Kaaba, except for the Black Stone, and made the temple the center of his religion. He had long asserted that the Kaaba had been built by Abraham and that Abraham had placed the heavenly Stone there as a sign of God's power. Thus he was able to preserve Mecca as the religious center of Arabia.

The fall of Mecca convinced many Arabs that Mohammed really was a prophet or at

110　least that he was too strong to oppose. During his last years, most of the tribes of the peninsula acknowledged his spiritual and political leadership. Nevertheless, when Mohammed died in 632 Arabia was far from being a unified state, and many Arabs had only vague ideas about the religion they had accepted.

The Koran

Mohammed, however, had left a collection of his revelations, which became known as

115　the Koran. He had taught that the Koran was God's guide for the human race, that it had always existed in heaven, but that no one had been worthy of receiving it before his own appearance on earth.

*This does not mean that dates of the Moslem era can be converted to our reckoning simply by adding 622 years. The Moslem year is based on a lunar calendar, and so does not coincide with ours. Our year 1978 was 1398 A.H.

© Scott, Foresman and Company.

The religion taught in the Koran was easy to understand and easy to follow. The basic creed was simple: "There is no God but Allah and Mohammed is his prophet." The faithful must also believe in the resurrection and the day of judgment, when every man will be rewarded according to his merits. The Mohammedan hell is very like the Christian one, but the Mohammedan paradise is unmistakably Arabian—a green garden full of running water and fruit trees with beautiful damsels to wait on the souls in bliss. Finally, the Koran teaches predestination: "Every man's fate have We bound around his neck"—that is, all human events have been determined, once and for all, by the will of God. Mohammed's own name for his religion was Islam—"submission to the will of God"—and his followers were called Moslems—"those who submit."

The principal religious practices of Islam were as simple as its theology. Every Moslem was to pray five times a day and to fast during the daylight hours of the month of Ramadan. Alms giving was a religious duty. Finally, every believer was to make a pilgrimage, if possible, to Mecca. But "only he shall visit the Mosque of God who believes in God and the Last Day, and is constant in prayer, and gives alms and fears God alone."

The Koran forbade wine drinking, usury, and gambling, and a dietary law, somewhat like that of the Jews, banned certain foods, especially pork. There was also a rudimentary code of law designed to check the selfishness and violence that had prevailed among the Arabs. Arbitration was to take the place of the blood-feud, infanticide was condemned, and elaborate rules of inheritance safeguarded the rights of orphans and widows. Mohammed also made an effort to limit polygamy by ruling that no man might have more than four wives simultaneously. Divorce was still easy, but the divorced wife could no longer be sent away penniless. These and other provisions were enough to furnish a framework for a judicial system.   /2070

Stage 3: Recall

Stop and recall what you have read. Review your use of the thinking strategies. Did you use all five?

▥▨▥ Skill Development: Sentence Meaning

Answer the questions about the relationships of the following sentence parts.

1. A few years after the death of Justinian in 565, a child was born in Arabia who was to found a religion that spread more rapidly than Christianity and an empire that was larger than that of Rome at the height of its power.

   1. When was the child born? _____

   2. What did the child found? _____

   3. What "was larger than that of Rome"? _____

   4. "At the height of its power" modifies _____

2. He had taught that the Koran was God's guide for the human race, that it had always existed in heaven, but that no one had been worthy of receiving it before his own appearance on earth.

1. What was "God's guide for the human race"? _____

2. What "had always existed in heaven"? _____

3. Why had no one received the Koran before? _____

4. In "his own appearance on earth," *his* refers to _____

Using your own words, as well as those of the author, restate the main idea of the sentence in a manner that maintains the author's original focus.

3. Finally, the Koran emphasizes predestination: "Every man's fate have We bound around his neck"—that is, all human events have been determined, once and for all, by the will of God.

_____

_____

_____

4. But "only he shall visit the Mosque of God who believes in God and the Last Day, and is constant in prayer, and gives alms and fears God alone."

_____

_____

_____

5. These early revelations bear some resemblance to the Psalms, both in their poetic quality and in their appeal to the wonders of nature as proofs of God's greatness and mercy.

_____

_____

▌▌▌ Comprehension Questions

1. The main point that the author is trying to get across in this selection is _____

_____

_____

After reading the selection, answer the following questions with *a, b, c,* or *d.*

2. Prior to Mohammed, the Arabs predominantly believed in
   a. Islam
   b. Christianity
   c. Judaism
   d. many gods

3. According to the author, a primary factor in the political and social instability of the early Arab world before Mohammed was
   a. the emergence of small trading towns
   b. the tribal and nomadic way of life
   c. the Semitic interest in religion
   d. the custom of men having many wives

4. The author believes that prior to Mohammed, the pilgrimage of the Arabs to Mecca was
   a. a result of a desire to trace their ancestry
   b. the strongest unifying force in the Arab world
   c. an indication of their desire to worship one god
   d. a burden for tribal people in an arid land

5. In 622 A.D. the wealthy citizens of Mecca felt threatened by Mohammed because
   a. they were mostly Christians
   b. they were afraid he would conquer the city with military forces
   c. they felt that the present polytheism brought prosperity to the city
   d. they felt his teaching pitted the rich against the poor

6. After his revelations, Mohammed claimed that
   a. he was the last and greatest prophet of God
   b. he was the only prophet of God
   c. he could perform miracles
   d. he was sent by Jesus to save the Arab world

7. The author implies that Medina was a particularly receptive place for Mohammed teachings because
   a. the citizens were accustomed to the idea of worshipping a single god
   b. the Arabs were ill-treated by the Jewish community
   c. Mecca was at war with Medina
   d. the city was populated largely by the poor

8. The author believes that the capture of Mecca
   a. established Mohammed as an Arab military leader
   b. designated Medina as a religious capital
   c. gave Mohammed an opportunity to destroy the Black Stone
   d. influenced more Arabs to follow Mohammed

9. The Koran teaches that
   a. Mohammed is God
   b. Allah is the only God
   c. there is no hell
   d. divorce is against the law of God

10. The author portrays Mohammed as
    a. a selfish and insensitive leader
    b. a greedy and powerful prophet
    c. an inconsistent religious fanatic who insisted on constant prayer
    d. a concerned prophet who desired humane laws

Answer the following questions with *T* (true), *F* (false), or *CT* (can't tell).

_____ 11. The author suggests that Mohammed's marriage gave him the financial security needed to meditate.

_____ 12. Wine drinking is forbidden in the Koran.

_____ 13. The author feels that Mohammed's laws improve the plight of widows and orphans.

_____ 14. The author feels that Mohammed made a mistake in maintaining Mecca as a holy city.

_____ 15. Mohammed was the only child of a wealthy merchant.

▦ ▦ ▦ Vocabulary

According to the way the boldface word was used in the selection, indicate *a, b, c,* or *d* for the word or phrase that gives the best definition.

____ 1. "like an **arid** wedge (09)"
  a. thin
  b. dry
  c. friendly
  d. large

____ 2. "made a **pilgrimage** to (44)"
  a. commitment
  b. holiday
  c. prayer
  d. journey

____ 3. "the most **venerated** object (47)"
  a. revered
  b. popular
  c. talked about
  d. frequented

____ 4. "**superseded** everything that had come before (81)"
  a. fulfilled
  b. replaced
  c. converted
  d. verified

____ 5. "he was **despondent** (86)"
  a. unpopular
  b. disheartened
  c. afraid
  d. persecuted

____ 6. "A **desultory** war between (103)"
  a. bitter
  b. dragged out
  c. lacking organization
  d. bloody

____ 7. "The basic **creed** (119)"
  a. doctrine
  b. hypothesis
  c. notion
  d. purpose

____ 8. "**rudimentary** code of law (134)"
  a. complicated
  b. high
  c. beginning
  d. humane

___ 9. "violence that had **prevailed** (135)"
   a. predominated
   b. focused
   c. started
   d. infiltrated

___ 10. "**Arbitration** was to take the place of (136)"
   a. debating
   b. prayer
   c. autonomy
   d. judgment by impartial group

▐▌▐ Essay Question

Explain the religious beliefs held by Moslems by discussing the teachings of Islam. Use a sheet of notebook paper to record your answer.

ORGANIZING TEXTBOOK INFORMATION

ORGANIZING NOTES

Your first assignment in most college courses will be to read Chapter 1 of the appointed textbook, at which time you will immediately discover that a textbook chapter contains an amazing amount of information. Your instructor will continue to make similar assignments designating the remaining chapters in rapid succession. Your problem is to select the information that needs to be remembered and organize it to facilitate future study. In many cases, future study could be a midterm or a final exam which might be several weeks or months away. What are some of your options for efficiently and effectively organizing the material? This chapter will discuss five methods of organizing textbook information for future study: underscoring, summarizing, notetaking, outlining, and mapping.

UNDERSCORING

Which of the following would seem to indicate the most effective use of the textbook as a learning tool?

1. A text without a single mark—not even the owner's name has spoiled the sacred pages
2. A text ablaze with color—almost every line is adorned with a red, blue, yellow, and/or green magic marker
3. A text with a scattered variety of markings—underlines, numbers, and stars are interspersed with circles, arrows, and short, written notes

Naturally number three is the best, but unfortunately the first two are not just silly examples; they are commonplace in every classroom. The student's rationale for the first is probably for resale of the book at the end of the course. The reason for the second is procrastination in decision making which is a result of reading without thinking. In other words, the student underlines everything and relies on coming back later to figure out what is *really* important and worth remembering. Both of these extremes are inefficient and ineffective methods of using a college textbook.

Why Underscore?

The textbook is a learning tool and should be used as such; it should not be preserved as a treasure. A college professor requires a particular text because it contains information vital to your understanding of the course. The text places a vast body of knowledge in your hands, much more material than the professor

Dieter Hacker. *Cubes* (1963)

© Scott, Foresman and Company.

could possibly give in class. It is your job to wade through this information, to make some sense out of it, and to select the important points that need to be remembered.

Underscoring is a method of highlighting main ideas, significant supporting details, and key terms. By using a system of symbols and notations, you mark the text after the first reading so that a complete rereading will not be necessary. The markings indicate pertinent points to review for an exam.

Marking in the textbook itself is frequently faster than summarizing, outlining, or notetaking. In addition, rather than referring to separate notebooks, your material and personal reaction are all in one place and can be viewed at a glance for later study. Your textbook has become a workbook.

When to Underscore

Underscoring the words as they are first read is a mistake. The underscoring should be done after a unit of thought has been presented and the information can be viewed as a whole. This may mean marking after only one paragraph or after three pages; marking varies with the material. When you are first reading every sentence seems of major importance as each new idea unfolds, and the tendency is to underline too much. Overmarking serves no useful purpose and is a waste of both reading and review time. However, if you wait until a complete thought has been developed, the significant points will emerge from a background of lesser details. You will then have all the facts and can make decisions about what you want to remember later. At the end of the course your textbook should have that worn, but well-organized look.

How to Underscore

Develop a System of Notations. Highlighting material is not just underlining; it is circling and starring and numbering and generally making an effort to visually put the material into perspective. Notations vary with the individual, and each student develops a number of original creations. Anything that makes sense to you is a correct notation. The following are examples of a marking system:

—————————— Main idea
——————————

—————————— Supporting material

★ Major trend or possible essay exam question

✓ Important smaller point to know for multiple-choice item

$\bigcirc$ Word that you must be able to define

$\boxed{}$ Label of a key issue to remember

{ }   Section of material to reread for review

(1), (2), (3)   Numbering of important details under a major issue

?   Didn't understand and must seek advice

Topic, Def. or Ex.   Notes in the margin

How does it operate?   Questions in the margin

$\curvearrowright$ Indicating relationships

Examples of Underscoring   The following passage is taken from a biology textbook. Notice how the notations have been used to highlight main ideas and significant supporting details. This same passage on the circulatory systems will be used throughout this chapter to demonstrate each of the five methods of organizing textbook material.

What are characteristics of each?

CIRCULATORY SYSTEMS

When we examine the systems by which blood reaches all the cells of an animal, we find two general types, known as open and closed circulatory systems.

Def. I.

Open circulatory systems

The essential feature of the **open circulatory system** is that the blood moves through a body cavity—such as the abdominal cavity—and bathes the cells directly. The open circulatory system is particularly characteristic of insects and other arthropods, although it is also found in some other organisms.

In most insects the blood does not take a major part in oxygen transport. Oxygen enters the animal's body through a separate network of branching tubes that open to the atmosphere on the outside of the animal. (This type of respiratory system will be discussed in more detail in the next chapter.) Blood in an open circulatory system moves somewhat more slowly than in the average closed system. The slower system is adequate for insects because it does not have to supply the cells with oxygen.

Def. II. (Closed circulatory systems)

In a **closed circulatory system,** the blood flows through a well-defined system of vessels with many branches. In the majority of closed systems the blood is responsible for oxygen transport. To supply all the body cells with sufficient oxygen, the blood must move quickly through the blood vessels. A closed circulatory system must therefore have an efficient pumping mechanism, or heart, to set the blood in motion and keep it moving briskly through the body.

All vertebrates possess closed circulatory systems. Simple closed systems are also found in some invertebrates, including the annelid worms. A good example of such a simple closed circulatory system can be seen in the earthworm.

Victor A. Greulach and Vincent J. Chiapetta, eds., *Biology*

▥▤▥ Exercise 1: Underscoring

Using a variety of notations, underscore the following passages as if you were preparing for a quiz on the material. Remember, do not underscore as you read, but wait until you finish a paragraph or a section and then mark the important points.

A. Monopoly

Remember that one of the characteristics of competition is many small sellers producing identical products. In the real world, some markets are characterized by a *few large* sellers producing *differentiated* products. In such markets, the conclusions of Adam Smith's theoretical model may not be valid.

If there is only one large seller in a market, the firm is said to be a **monopoly.** There are few examples of *pure* monopoly, but many where a few large firms *behave* like a monopoly and achieve results similar to monopoly. When we speak of monopoly in this text, we will be referring to groups of noncompeting firms with power to affect price.

Monopoly can be achieved in several ways. The monopoly may be the first firm (or firms) in the industry, it may buy out all rival firms, or it may drive its competitors out of business. The monopoly firm must keep out price-cutting competitors in order to maintain control over supply. And it will try to increase demand so that there will be buyers at profitable prices.

A country fellow in the rural South had learned this lesson quite well—without ever attending business school! Some tourists were driving along a detour off the main road when they became hopelessly mired in the mud. A humble shack was the only sign of civilization, and the farmer's tractor was available (at a price) to pull their car from the ditch. As he handed the fellow a twenty, the tourist observed, "I'll bet you're busy night and day pulling cars from this mud, aren't you?"

"Nope," replied the farmer. "Night's when we haul the water."

(Single supplier—control of demand? It would be hard to beat that!)

Marilu Hurt McCarty, *Dollars and Sense*

From *Dollars and Sense,* Third Edition, by Marilu Hurt McCarty, pp. 67–68. Copyright © 1982 by Scott, Foresman and Company.

Review your underscoring. Have you sufficiently highlighted the main idea and the significant supporting details?

B. Purposes of the Peer Group

If you were to ask most teenagers why they have joined a particular clique, club, or gang, they would probably tell you it is because they like the people in the group, or they like the kind of things the group is doing. Actually, there are many other purposes fulfilled by membership in a peer group. Rogers (1977) has summarized a number of these:

The "radar" function. One peer group function is to help the members find out how well they are doing in life. Adolescents can try out some behaviors by "bouncing" them off their peers who act as a radar screen. They then receive a message back as to how well others feel they are performing, and can alter their behavior accordingly.

Replacement for father. Although many, perhaps most, teenagers try to repudiate their father's authority during adolescence, the need for a father figure remains. The group leader often replaces one's father during the transition toward independence.

Support for independence. Closely related is the need for support from others while struggling against parental authority. Most adolescents need to learn to assert themselves, which often gives them strong guilt feelings and fear that their parents will reject them. Mutual support can be relied on among those who have similar concerns.

Ego building. Adolescence is a time of confusion as to who one is. At this low ebb of self-confidence, the peer group often serves the purpose of making one feel at least minimally good about oneself.

Psychic attachment. All human beings experience a deep need for psychological closeness and intimacy with others. In the past, this need was met largely by one's family. Today one's peers, especially in adolescence, have largely taken over this role.

Values orientation. We like to think we select our values by carefully considering how we feel about things and coming to our own conclusions as to what we shall believe (see Chapter 13). In fact, if we were forced to make up our minds about most things without any outside information, we would find it very difficult indeed. The peer group serves as a setting for the discussion of values, so that one has a better chance of seeing a wide range of options and making better choices.

Status setting. All societies have their hierarchy of status, in fact, several of them. Each of us needs to know something about how others regard us in the hierarchy of life. The peer group allows adolescents to learn more about how dominant and subordinate they are, thus giving them a better image of how they appear to others.

Negative identity. Often, youth join groups not so much because they believe in the goals of the group, but because they want to demonstrate their antagonism toward someone else. For example, a person whose parents overcontrol him may join an unruly gang even though he dislikes the occasional violence the group engages in. Nevertheless, he may view membership in the group as proof that he is more independent than his parents believe he is.

The avoidance of adult requirements. When the requirements of the peer group conflict with the requirements of adult society, the latter may be shunted aside. For example, teachers may insist that their students spend a considerable amount of time on homework; being a member of the basketball team may make it difficult to schedule both

From *Adolescents Today,* Second Edition, by John S. Dacey, pp. 218–219. Copyright © 1982 by Scott, Foresman and Company.

homework and practice sessions. Therefore, belonging to the basketball team may serve the purpose of excusing the teenager, at least to himself, from doing the homework that he didn't want to do anyway.

John Dacey, *Adolescents Today*

Review your underscoring. Have you sufficiently highlighted the main idea and the significant supporting details?

SUMMARIZING

What Is a Summary?

A summary is a brief, concise statement in your own words of the main point and the significant supporting details. The first sentence should state the main point or thesis and subsequent sentences should incorporate the significant details. Minor details and material irrelevant to the learner's purpose should be deleted. The summary should be in paragraph form and should always be shorter than the material being summarized.

Why Summarize?

Summaries can be used for textbook study and are particularly useful in anticipating the organization of answers for essay exam questions. For writing research papers, summarizing is an essential skill. Using your own words and putting the essence of an article into concise sentences requires a thorough understanding of the material. As one researcher noted, "Since so much summarizing is necessary for writing papers, students should have the skill before starting work on research papers. How much plagiarism is the result of inadequate summarizing skills?"[1]

Writing a research paper may mean that you will have to read thirty articles and four books over a period of one or two months. After each reading you want to take enough notes so you can write your paper without returning to the library for another look at the original reference. Since you will be using so many different references, the notetaking should be carefully done. The complete sentences of a summary are more explicit than underscored text or the highlighted topic-phrase format of an outline. Your summary should demonstrate a synthesis of the information.

How to Summarize

1. Keep in mind the purpose of your summary. Your projected needs will determine which details are important and how many should be included.

[1]Taylor, Karl. Can College Students Summarize? *Journal of Reading,* vol. 26 (March 1983), pp. 540–544.

2. Decide on the main point the author is trying to convey. Make this main point the first sentence in your summary.
3. Decide on the major ideas and details that support the author's point. Include the major ideas in your summary and as many of the significant supporting details as your purpose demands.
4. Do not include irrelevant or repeated information in your summary.

Example of Summarizing

Read the following summary of the previous biology excerpt on the circulatory system. This summary is based on the same passage that was used to illustrate underscoring. Notice that the same material is highlighted and that studying the underscored passage would have made writing a summary an easier task.

There are two types of circulatory systems, the open and closed, by which blood reaches all the cells of an animal. In the open system, found mostly in insects and other anthropods, blood moves through the body and bathes the cells directly. The blood moves slower than in the closed system, and oxygen is supplied from outside air through tubes. In the closed system, blood flows through a system of vessels, oxygen is carried by the blood so it must move quickly, and the heart serves as a pumping mechanism. All vertebrates, as well as earthworms, have closed systems.

▦▣▥ Exercise 2: Summerizing

Write a summary on a sheet of notebook paper for each of the following passages. Your purpose in writing the summary is to note the main points for later reference. Be brief, but include the essential elements.

A. The Problem of Alienation

There was a parlor game making the rounds several years ago in which the players were asked to answer the question, "Who are you?" with three responses. Supposedly, deep psychological insights could be derived from the answers and their sequence. For example, a man who answers "I am an engineer, I am a Republican, I am a golfer" reveals much of his personal conception of self.

How frightening it would be to have no answers to the question! Without identity, one almost ceases to exist. And most of us in Western culture achieve our identities from our work. We *do,* therefore we *are!*

When modern manufacturing jobs became simplified, workers began to lose some of the self-identity associated with particular skills. Repeating one simple operation over and over reduces a worker's sense of pride of creativity and involvement in a finished product. At one time it may have been possible to reply in answer to the parlor question, "I am an automaker." But it is hardly uplifting to admit "I am a lever operator," or a "wrench twister," or a "windshield lifter."

From *Dollars and Sense,* Third Edition, by Marilu Hurt McCarty, p. 86. Copyright © 1982 by Scott, Foresman and Company.

Karl Marx called this problem *alienation*. Alienation is the separation of a worker from the product of his or her work. It diminishes a worker's sense of self-worth and the capacity for creative expression and personal growth. Also, alienation often leads to boredom, poor quality production, and reduced worker productivity.

These ill effects have produced a deliberate turnabout in some manufacturing firms, from the increasing simplification of jobs back to complexity. (Some might say it is contrived complexity.) In some plants, teams of workers are allowed to organize total production of a product as in the "old days" before the assembly line. The team is rewarded according to the quantity and quality of production. Total output may be less than under the assembly-line method, but there are compensating psychological benefits in improved employee morale and, frequently, better quality products as well.

Marilu Hurt McCarty, Dollars and Sense

Does your summary include the important points?

B. Adolescents' Attitudes Toward Their Bodies

Curiously, there is little recent research on the topic of adolescents' feelings about their own bodies (Clifford, 1971; Faust, 1960). The results of these studies are somewhat conflicting and now rather out of date. Therefore, with the help of some colleagues, the following questionnaire was developed and administered to 135 college freshmen who came from fifteen different states. The results of this survey follow, but first perhaps you might like to respond to it yourself.

In looking at the results of the freshman body-image study, we see that the majority of both men and women believe their bodies to be average. This is not surprising, because most people are average, by definition. Somewhat more men than women were willing to admit that they were smaller in overall size, but almost half the women in the study thought they were smaller than average in their bust size. It is unlikely that this is true, so this finding is probably more indicative of the sensitivity about possessing small breasts that has been created by our culture. There is reason to believe these attitudes are changing.

With the tremendous emphasis on slimness (especially female) in the media today, we could expect even those with average bodies to be dissatisfied, and they are. A considerably larger number of women were dissatisfied with their bodies than were men. Whether this is because women are more willing to admit they feel unhappy about their bodies or because they really do is impossible to say. Women were most concerned about their weight and legs. Yet, although 55 percent of the women felt bad about their weight, 70 percent of them thought their weight was average; 55 percent were dissatisfied with their legs, but 80 percent thought that their legs were average. Women were also bothered about the quality of their skin and about their figures in general. Perhaps not so surprising was the finding for female sports ability. Whereas 85 percent of the women thought that their ability was average, over a third of them felt bad about their ability. This is no doubt a reflection of the increased interest and support for sports activities among women. One further finding among the women that should be noted is the very high percentage who felt good about their eyes and faces. Perhaps self-acceptance is more crucial here.

From *Adolescents Today,* Second Edition, by John S. Dacey, pp. 102–103. Copyright © 1982 by Scott, Foresman and Company.

Men expressed more satisfaction with their body features. Surprisingly, what bothered men most was the quality of their hair; almost one-third said that they felt bad about their hair. Four other characteristics disturbed one-fourth of the freshmen men: their physiques, the amount of hair on their faces, the quality of their voices, and their overall looks. A high percentage of this sample felt they were bigger, larger, or better than average compared to others. The majority of women and the high majority of men said that they felt good about most aspects of their bodies. It is possible that these freshmen were not expressing their true feelings. It is also possible that college students actually are superior to others in their physical attributes. Terman found that those who were superior intellectually also tended to be superior in other aspects of their development. If this is true, then it is not surprising to find that college students feel relatively good about their bodies.

John Dacey, *Adolescents Today*

Does your summary include the important points?

NOTETAKING

What Is Notetaking?

Many students prefer to jot down brief sentence summaries to highlight important textbook information. These summaries can be further highlighted with marginal notes to indicate topics and key words. The students who prefer this method say that working with a pencil and paper while reading keeps them involved with the material and thus improves concentration.

How to Take Notes

One of the most popular systems of notetaking is called the Cornell Method and the steps are as follows:

1. Draw a line down your paper two and one-half inches from the left side to create a two and one-half inch margin for noting key words and a six inch area on the right for sentence summaries.
2. After you have finished reading a section, tell yourself what you have read and jot down sentence summaries in the six-inch area on the right side of your paper. Use your own words and make sure you have included the main ideas and significant supporting details. Be brief, but use complete sentences.
3. Review your summary sentences and underline key words. Write these key words in the column on the left side of your paper. These words can be used to stimulate your memory of the material for later study.

   The Cornell Method can be used for taking notes on classroom lectures. The following explanation, developed by Norman Stahl and James King, both explains the procedure and gives a visual display of the results.

Taking Class Notes: The Cornell Method[2]

← 2½ inches →	← 6 inches →
Reduce ideas to concise jottings and summaries as cues for reciting.	Record the lecture as fully and as meaningfully as possible.
Cornell Method	This sheet demonstrates the Cornell Method of taking classroom notes. It is recommended by experts from the Learning Center at Cornell University.
Line drawn down paper	You should draw a line down your notepage about 2½ inches from the left side. On the right side of the line simply record your classroom notes as you usually do. Be sure that you write legibly.
After the lecture	After the lecture you should read the notes, fill-in materials that you missed, make your writing legible and underline any important materials. Ask another classmate for help if you missed something during lecture.
Use the Recall Column Key Phrases	The recall column on the left will help you when you study for your tests. Jot down any important words or key phrases in the recall column. This activity forces you to rethink and summarize your notes. The key words should stick in your mind.
Five R's	The Five R's will help you take better notes based on the Cornell Method.
Record	1. Record any information given during the lecture which you believe will be important.
Reduce	2. When you reduce your information you are summarizing and listing key words/phrases in the recall column.
Recite	3. Cover the notes you took for your class. Test yourself on the words in the recall section. This is what we mean by recite.
Reflect	4. You should reflect on the information you received during the lecture. Determine how your ideas fit in with the information.
Review	If you review your notes you will remember a great deal more when you take your midterm.
Binder & Paper	Remember it is a good idea to keep your notes in a standard-sized binder. Also you should use only full-sized binder paper. You will be able to add mimeographed materials easily to your binder.
Hints	Abbreviations and symbols should be used when possible. Abbrev. & sym. give you time when used auto.

[2]Stahl, Norman A. and James King. "A Language Experience Model for Teaching College Reading, Study and Survival," 25th College Reading Association Annual Conference, Louisville, KY, 30 October 1981.

Example of Notetaking

The following example applies the Cornell Method of notetaking to the biology passage on the circulatory system. Notice the use of the previous sentence summaries and the addition of highlighted key words.

Circulatory System

Two types Open and Closed	There are two types, the open and the closed, by which blood reaches all the cells of an animal
Open	In the open system, found mostly in insects and other arthropods, blood moves through the body and
Bathes Cells	bathes the cells directly. The blood moves slower than in the closed
Oxygen from outside	system, and oxygen is supplied from outside air through tubes.
Blood vessels Blood carries oxygen	In the closed system, blood flows through a system of vessels, oxygen is carried by the blood so it must move quickly, and the heart
Heart pumps	serves as a pumping mechanism. All vertebrates, as well as earthworms, have closed systems

▥▥▥ Exercise 3: Notetaking

The textbook organization methods in this chapter are all more appropriately applied to longer reading selections such as a chapter or an article, rather than to one or two paragraphs. Space, however, is a consideration and thus many of the practice exercises in this book must be applied to less lengthy material than would be the case in a college course. For practice with somewhat longer selections, use the long readings at the end of the chapters or sections from your texts for other courses. Make sure to prepare some two-columned notetaking sheets. Read the material and then take notes using the Cornell Method.

OUTLINING

What Is an Outline?

The outline organizes and highlights major points and subordinates items of lesser importance. In a glance the indentations, the numbers, and the letters quickly show how one idea relates to another and how all aspects relate to the whole. The layout of the outline is simply a graphic presentation of main ideas and significant supporting details. To outline correctly you must have a thorough understanding of the underlying structure of the material. The outline forms the skeleton of ideas from which the writer or speaker originally planned and worked.

The following example is the picture-perfect version of the basic outline form. In practice your "working outline" would probably not be as detailed or as regular as this.

Title

I. First main idea
  A. Supporting idea
    1. Detail
    2. Detail
    3. Detail
      a. Minor detail
      b. Minor detail
  B. Supporting idea
    1. Detail
    2. Detail
  C. Supporting idea

II. Second main idea
  A. Supporting idea
  B. Supporting idea

Why Outline?

Some students find that outlining textbook material helps them study, while others prefer underscoring or notetaking and feel that textbook outlining is too time consuming. In actual practice, underscoring is probably the least active study preparation method, but all the methods require the same priority-setting skills. When the book does not belong to you, however, underscoring is not possible, and outlining offers an efficient method of recording material for later study.

Another use of the outline is to take notes from class lectures. During class most professors try to add to the material in the textbook and put it into perspective for students. Since the notes taken in class represent a large percentage of the material you need to know in order to pass the course, they are extremely important. While listening to a class lecture, you must almost instantly receive, synthesize, and select material and, at the same time, record something on paper for future reference. The difficulty of the task demands order and decision making. One of the most efficient methods of taking lecture notes is to use a modified outline form, a version with the addition of stars, circles, and underlines to further emphasize the levels of importance.

How to Outline

Professors say that they can walk around the classroom and look at the notes students have taken from the text or from a lecture and tell how well each has understood the lesson. The errors most frequently observed fall into the following categories:

1. Poor organization
2. Failure to show importance
3. Writing too much
4. Writing too little

To avoid these pitfalls the most important thing to remember in outlining is *"What is my purpose?"* You don't need to include everything and you don't need a picture-perfect version for study notes. Include only what you feel you will need to remember later and use the numbering system and the indentations to show how one thing relates to another. Several other important guidelines to remember are as follows:

1. Get a general overview before you start.
   (How many main topics do there seem to be?)
2. Use phrases rather than sentences.
   (Can you state it in a few short words?)
3. Put it in your own words.
   (If you cannot paraphrase it, do you really understand it?)
4. Be selective
   (Are you highlighting or completely rewriting?)

Example of Outlining

The following is an outline of the biology passage on the circulatory system. Notice how the numbers and letters, as well as the distance from the left side of the paper, show levels of importance.

I. Open circulatory system
   A. Blood moves through body and bathes cells directly

B. Found mostly in insects and other arthropods
C. Oxygen supplied from outside air through tubes
D. Slower blood movement since not supplying cells with oxygen
II. Closed circulatory system
   A. Blood flows through system of vessels
   B. Oxygen carried by blood so it must move quickly
   C. Heart serves as pumping mechanism
   D. Found in all vertebrates
   E. Found also in annelid worms (earthworms)

▮▮▮ Exercise 4: Outlining

Outline the key ideas in the selection as if you were planning to use your notes to study for a quiz.

A. Psychologists separate the memory system into three parts: *sensory, short-term,* and *long-term.* Sensory memory performs a screening function. Incoming information reaches it first and is preserved just long enough to be used in perceiving, comparing, judging, and so on. It lasts for only a very brief time while the brain decides whether or not it needs this information for present or future use. If it seems useful, it is passed on to the short-term memory. If not, it is discarded. Sensory memory employs a "file or forget" approach to its job.

Short-term memory performs a second screening operation on the retained information. You can think of it as a sort of desk-top memory. Data arriving in the "in" box is looked over, sorted out, and acted on. Everything is there in front of you. Like most desk tops, however, short-term memory often gets cluttered up with many different items, some of which are more important than others. Often, too, a new item in the "in" box interferes with something you are working on. You put the old item aside and can't find it later. Generally speaking, you can deal with no more than seven or eight items at any one time. (There are strategies, however, for expanding the capacity of short-term memory and prolonging its duration.) To make room for more information, you clean off your "desk" every few minutes, throwing the "junk" mail into the wastebasket and sorting your ideas into meaningful groups. What remains will be filed in the "out" box for transmission to long-term memory.

Long-term memory is more permanent, and has a theoretically unlimited capacity. It used to be thought of as a kind of "dead storage," made up of information to be retrieved at some future time. Psychologists now think that long-term memory is a dynamic process, continually interacting with short-term memory to provide *operational,* or working, memory. To make decisions, for example, you constantly refer to material that has been filed away. Long-term memories are reactivated, combined with short-term memories, and then filed away again, along with any new material that seems worth saving.

David Dempsey and Philip G. Zimbardo, *Psychology and You*

Title: _____

I. _____

   A. _____

   B. _____

   C. _____

II. _____

   A. _____

   B. _____

   C. _____

   D. _____

III. _____

   A. _____

   B. _____

   C. _____

Does your outline include all of the significant points that you will need for later study?

B. A fad is a product/service which is quickly accepted and then just as quickly rejected by a large number of consumers. The product life-cycle for a fad item is a highly compressed version of the typical product life-cycle. If the fad catches on, sales soar quickly in the introductory and growth phases. As the fad loses its novelty appeal, sales curves that went up quickly reverse their direction and decline with equal speed. Experienced marketers of novelty fad items understand the compressed product life-cycle and are ready to supply a high volume of units to the market place quickly. They know that product acceptability will be short-lived. Some companies introduce a large number of such products to the market, knowing that many of the products will fail or have only limited or temporary success. (Most such products are inexpensive to produce.) On occasion, however, a product catches on, becomes a fad, and reaps high sales and profits for a short period of time. Hula-hoops, message-bearing T-shirts, and frisbees are examples of successful fads.

The fashion product life-cycle is less compressed than the fad cycle. But, like fads, fashion items are subject to quick and sometimes unpredictable swings in popularity and profitability. Innovation and emulation play important roles in the fashion life-cycle. Innovative individuals or firms develop a fashion product in the hope and expectation that it will be taken up by opinion leaders and trend setters who are highly visible in the fashion and general news media. If it is accepted and touted by such persons, the general

From *Modern Marketing* by Edward J. Fox and Edward W. Wheatley, pp. 128, 184, 216–220. Copyright © 1978 by Scott, Foresman and Company.

public will likely emulate the fashion leaders and also demand the product. Mass production and marketing of the fashion will then ensue. (Recall the "diffusion of innovation" process discussed in Chapter 4: Understanding Consumer Behavior.) The process, however, is by no means automatic. Despite a good deal of media hoopla for midi-and maxi-length dresses in the 1970s, American women flatly rejected the innovative fashion.

Edward J. Fox and Edward W. Wheatley, Modern Marketing

Use a sheet of notebook paper to outline Selection B. Does your outline include all of the significant points that you will need for later study?

MAPPING

What Is Mapping?

Mapping is a visual system of condensing material to show relationships and importance. A map is a diagram of the major points, with their significant subpoints, that support a topic. The purpose of mapping as an organizing strategy is to improve memory by grouping material in a highly visual way. The map provides a quick reference for overviewing an article or a chapter.

How to Map

The following describe the steps to use in mapping.

1. Draw a circle or a box in the middle of a page and in it write the subject or topic of the material.
2. Determine the main ideas that support the subject and write them on lines radiating from the central circle or box.
3. Determine the significant details and write them on lines attached to each main idea. The number of details you include will depend on the material and your purpose.

Maps are not restricted to any one pattern, but can be formed in a variety of creative shapes as the following diagrams illustrate:

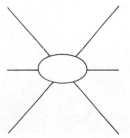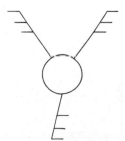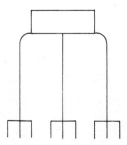

Example of Mapping

The following map highlights the biology passage on the circulatory system. Notice how the visual display emphasizes the groups of ideas supporting the topic.

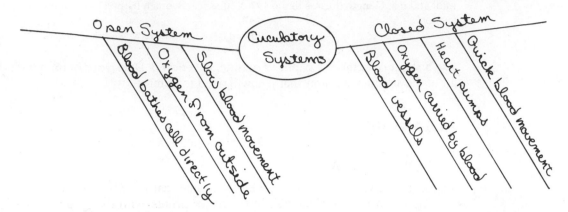

▌▐ ▐ ## Exercise 5: Mapping

Refer to Exercise 4 and design a map for each of the passages that you previously outlined. Use your outlines to help you in making the maps. Experiment with several different shapes for your map patterns on notebook or unlined paper.

Selection **1**

MARKETING

Ron Watts/First Light, Toronto

Stage 1: Preview

Preview the selection and complete the following sentence:

After reading this selection, I would like to know _____

_____

_____

Stage 2: Integrate Knowledge While Reading

Use the thinking strategies as you read:

1. Predict
2. Picture
3. Form analogies
4. Verbalize points
5. Fix up strategies

Skill Development: Underscoring, Outlining, and Mapping

Using a variety of notations, underscore the following selection as if you were organizing the material to study for a quiz. Remember, do not underscore as you read, but wait until you finish a section and then mark the important points. (After reading and underscoring, you will also be asked to outline the material and design a map.)

NEW PRODUCT PRICING*

Louis E. Boone and David L. Kurtz, from *Contemporary Business*

Pampers, the paper baby diaper, failed in its original market test because of pricing. Later, it became Procter & Gamble's second best-selling brand (the detergent Tide is first). When it was first introduced, Pampers sold for about ten cents each. This was more than the per use cost of buying a cloth diaper and washing it. When Pampers bombed in the
5 marketplace, Procter & Gamble reduced production costs to the point where Pampers could be priced at six cents each, and the product became a household word in families with infants.

    Procter & Gamble's experience with Pampers shows how difficult it is to select a price for a new product line. All such pricing decisions are risky; it is usually best to field test

*LEARNING STRATEGY: During the previewing step, you are formulating your learning strategy. Be able to explain the different factors to be considered in the pricing of products.

From *Contemporary Business* by Louis E. Boone and David L. Kurtz. Copyright © 1976 by the Dryden Press, a Division of Holt, Rinehart and Winston, CBS College Publishing. Reprinted by permission of Holt, Rinehart and Winston.

10   possible alternative prices with a sample group of consumers. Once the product is
      actually launched, it is difficult to modify its price during the introductory period.

          New product pricing can take one of two alternative strategies. One is to *price the new
      product relatively high compared to substitute goods, and then gradually lower it.* Du Pont,
      which offers many specialty items, has traditionally followed such a pattern. Du Pont's
15   polyester fiber, Dacron, was sold at $2.25 a pound in 1953. It now goes for about 40¢.
      Similarly, the price of Quiana, a synthetic silklike fiber, has fallen 35 percent in 5 years.
      This alternative is known as a **skimming price policy,** and is used where the market is
      segmented on a price basis. In other words, some may buy an item at $10; another, larger
      group will buy if it is priced at $7.50; and a still larger group will buy if the item sells for
20    $6.00. Color television and electronic calculators are examples of where this policy has
      been used effectively. Today's best-selling ballpoint pen sells for 25¢, but when this
      product was first introduced after World War II it sold for about $20. A skimming price
      policy allows the firm to recover its costs rapidly by maximizing the revenue it receives.
      But the policy has a disadvantage in that early profits tend to attract competition, and this
25   puts eventual pressure on prices.

          Soaps and toothpastes are often introduced using a **penetration price policy.** This
      means *the new product is priced low relative to substitute items in order to secure wide
      market acceptance.* Later it is hoped that brand acceptance will allow the firm to raise
      prices. Dow Chemical, which sells many commodity products, tends to be a penetration
30   pricer. Dow attempts to build its market share with lower prices, and then stay in a certain
      market for a long time.

          Penetration pricing discourages competition because of its low profits. It can also
      provide competitive opportunities against users of a skimming price policy. Wella-Balsam
      hair conditioner was introduced at $1.98 (compared to $1.19 for regular cream rinses).
35   Alberto-Culver Company countered with Alberto-Balsam at $1.49 and an advertising
      budget ten times the size of the one supporting Wella-Balsam. The Alberto-Culver
      product overtook Wella-Balsam in ten months, and now accounts for about 55–60 percent
      of hair conditioner sales.

Price Lining

      Price lining occurs when *a seller decides to offer merchandise at a limited number of
40   prices, rather than pricing each item individually.* For instance, a boutique might offer
      lines of women's sportswear priced at $60, $90, and $110. Price lining is a common
      marketing practice among retailers. The original five-and-ten-cent stores were an example
      of its early use.

          As a pricing strategy the concept of price lining prevents the confusion common to
45   situations where all items are priced individually. The pricing function is more easily
      managed. But marketers must clearly identify the market segments to which they are
      appealing. Three "high price" lines might not be appropriate to a store located in an area
      of young married couples.

          A disadvantage of price lining is that it is sometimes difficult to alter the price ranges
50   once they are set. This may be a crucial factor during a period of inflation when the firm
      must either raise the price of the line or reduce its quality. Consumers may resist either of
      these decisions. Price lining can be useful, but its implementation must be considered
      carefully.

Price-Quality Relationships

Numerous research studies have shown that the consumers' perception of product quality
55   is related closely to the item's price. The higher the price of the product, the better the
consumer perceives its quality. One study asked four hundred respondents what terms
they associated with the word *expensive*. Two-thirds of the replies referred to high
quality—such as *best* or *superior*.

Most marketers believe that the price-quality relationship exists over a relatively wide
60   range of prices. It also appears that there are extreme prices that can be viewed as either
too expensive or *too cheap*. Marketing managers need to study and experiment with prices
for their own particular products. The price-quality relationship can be of key importance
to a firm's pricing strategy.

Psychological Pricing

Many marketers feel that certain prices are more appealing to buyers than others.
65   Psychological pricing is widely used by industry throughout the world. The image pricing
goals mentioned earlier are an example of psychological pricing.

Have you ever wondered why retailers use prices like $39.95, $18.98, or $9.99? Why
don't the stores use $40, $19, or $10 instead? Years ago **odd pricing** (as this practice is
called) was employed to force clerks to make change. This was before the age of cash
70   registers, so odd pricing served as a cash control technique for retailers. It is now a
common technique in retail pricing. Many retailers believe that odd prices are more
attractive to consumers than even ones. In fact, some stores have now begun to use prices
ending in 2, 3, 4, or 7 to avoid the look of ordinary prices like $5.95, $10.98, and $19.99.
The "new" prices are more likely to be $2.22, $6.53, or $10.94.   /959

Stage 3: Recall

*Stop and recall what you have read. Review your use of the thinking strategies.
Did you use all five?*

▥▤▥ Skill Development: Outlining and Mapping

Outline the key ideas in the selection as if you were planning to use your notes
to study for a quiz. Use a sheet of notebook paper.

Design a map that groups the key ideas that you would need to study from
this selection. Draw it on a sheet of notebook paper or unlined paper.

Comparing these three methods of organizing textbook material (underscoring, outlining, and mapping), which do you think would work the best for you
in studying this selection? Why? Write your answer on a sheet of notebook paper.

1. The main point the author is trying to get across in this selection is _____

_____

_____

After reading the selection, answer the following questions with *a, b, c,* or *d.*

_____ 2. The final success of Pampers depended on all of the following except
    a. changing the price
    b. reducing production cost
    c. a skimming price policy
    d. a penetration price policy

_____ 3. In selecting the price for a new product, the authors recommend
    a. initial high pricing to gain early profits
    b. lower prices to develop a market
    c. expensive prices to imply quality
    d. testing several prices on selected consumers

_____ 4. The skimming price policy includes all of the following except
    a. unique product for which the consumer will pay a high price
    b. early profits to recover research costs
    c. a market that is segmented on a price basis
    d. no tendency toward attracting competition

_____ 5. The major reason for a penetration pricing policy is
    a. initial market acceptance
    b. raising prices later
    c. initial advertising costs
    d. the value of the product

_____ 6. The authors consider an advantage of price lining to be
    a. lower costs to the consumer
    b. easy management
    c. a tendency to guard against inflation
    d. the ease of entering higher price markets

_____ 7. The idea of price-quality relationships is based on
    a. consumer perception
    b. production cost
    c. only expensive items
    d. early development cost recovery

_____ 8. Odd pricing was first used as a cash control technique to
    a. increase the product price
    b. force the sale to be registered
    c. create a psychologically attractive price
    d. lower the product price

9. When introducing a new product, the best pricing technique to discourage competition is
   a. a skimming price policy
   b. a penetration price policy
   c. price lining
   d. odd pricing

10. It would seem that the greatest initial benefit to the consumer would come from
    a. skimming price policy
    b. a penetration price policy
    c. price lining
    d. odd pricing

Answer the following with *T* (true), *F* (false), or *CT* (can't tell).

11. The author implies that an item can be too cheap for a consumer to buy.
12. Many lower-priced substitutes for Quiana have now been marketed.
13. The author implies that odd pricing was initiated to keep clerks honest.
14. Even without the advertising, Alberto-Balsam still would have overtaken Wella-Balsam in market sales.
15. The author implies that the gradual demise of the five-and-ten-cent store is an example of the impact of inflation on price lining.

Vocabulary

According to the way the boldface word was used in the selection, indicate *a, b, c,* or *d* for the word or phrase that gives the best definition.

1. "When Pampers **bombed** (04)"
   a. destroyed
   b. exploded
   c. entered
   d. failed

2. "is actually **launched** (11)"
   a. started off
   b. withdrawn
   c. submerged
   d. designated

3. "is difficult to **modify** (11)"
   a. solidify
   b. change
   c. argue
   d. overlook

4. "**relatively** high (13)"
   a. comparatively
   b. favorably
   c. slowly
   d. outrageously

5. "many **commodity** products (29)"
   a. unnecessary
   b. luxury
   c. convenience
   d. expensive

6. "a **penetration** pricer (29)"
   a. retraction
   b. act of cutting through
   c. approximation
   d. agreeable

_____ 7. "a **crucial** factor (50)"
   a. informative
   b. enjoyable
   c. logical
   d. decisive

_____ 8. "its **implementation** must (52)"
   a. act of carrying out
   b. renewal
   c. motivation
   d. release

_____ 9. "the consumer **perceives** (56)"
   a. buys
   b. becomes aware
   c. directs
   d. acquires

_____ 10. "four hundred **respondents** (56)"
   a. customers
   b. workers
   c. persons who answer
   d. managers

▮▮▮▮ Essay Question

If you had just manufactured a new tennis racket, what factors would you consider in pricing it for sale in your store? Explain and relate each pricing factor to your situation. Use a sheet of notebook paper to record your answer.

Selection **2**

MARKETING

Copyright Sidney Harris

"It's delicious—just the thing for our nationwide franchise operation."

Stage 1: Preview

Preview the selection and complete the following sentence: After reading this

selection, I would like to know _____

_____

Stage 2: Integrate Knowledge While Reading

Use thinking strategies as you read:

1. *Predict*
2. *Picture*
3. *Form analogies*
4. *Verbalize points*
5. *Fix up strategies*

Skill Development: Notetaking

After reading the selection, use the Cornell Method of notetaking *to organize*
material for future study. Use a sheet of notebook paper on which you have
drawn a recall column.

FRANCHISES—A SPECIAL CASE*

Edward J. Fox and Edward W. Wheatley, from *Modern Marketing*

Holiday Inns, International House of Pancakes, Dairy Queen, McDonald's, U-Totem
Stores, the Aapco (car painting) Systems—all saw unmatched growth in the 1960s. For
marketers, that growth signified the opening of a new direct channel—franchising.

5   These operations and many more, some regional, some national, have the same general
pattern. The parent company first establishes a successful retail business. As it expands, it
sees a profit potential in offering others the right to open similar businesses under its
name. The parent company's methods and means of identification with consumers (color
schemes, layouts, point-of-purchase displays) are included in this right. The franchising
company supplies know-how, and may build and lease stores to franchisees. For these

10   advantages the franchisee pays the franchisor a substantial fee. Day-to-day operations are,
for the franchisor, similar to those of the manufacturer selling direct to independent
retailers. However, some of the advantages and disadvantages are different.

    By extending a "proven" marketing method, a parent can profit in several ways. First,
the franchisee's purchase price gives the parent an immediate return on the plan. Then,

---

*LEARNING STRATEGY: From a marketing point of view, how does franchising work? What are
the benefits to the franchisor and to the franchisee?

From *Modern Marketing* by Edward J. Fox and Edward W. Wheatley, pp. 128, 184, 216–220.
Copyright © 1978 by Scott, Foresman and Company.

15   the sale of supplies to the franchisee provides a continuing source of profits. As new
business are added and the company's reputation spreads, the value of the franchise
increases and sales of franchises become easier. The snowballing effect can be dramatic.
McDonald's, for example, once announced that commitments for new franchises were so
heavy it would not undertake more accounts for about 18 months. Such growth, too,
20   brings into play the economies of scale. Regional or national advertising that might
be financially impossible for a franchisor with 20 franchises could be profitable for one
with 40.

    The parent, then, finds immediate gains from the opportunity to expand markets on the
basis of reputation alone, without having to put up capital or take the risk of owning retail
25   outlets. Added to this advantage is a less obvious but material one. Skilled, conscientious
retail managers are rare. People who invest their capital in franchises, though, probably
come closer to the ideal than do paid managers. In effect, the franchisee is an
independent store operator working for the franchisor, but without an independent's
freedom to drop suppliers at will. Of course the factory's costs of selling supplies are less.
30   But also certainly the franchisee buying goods that have had broad consumer acceptance
will not casually change suppliers, even when the contract permits. If the hamburger or
french fries are not what customers expected, they may not return. Having paid for the
goodwill, the franchisee won't thoughtlessly jeopardize it.

    Our description of franchising may give you the idea that as a franchisor you need only
35   relax in your rocking chair. Few marketers can do that. Franchising, like any other
channel, has problems to be solved.

    Selling franchises is not simple. Buyers need not only capital to invest but also a
willingness to invest in and supervise what is in many ways a new outlet. Few franchisors
can easily round up such people. Franchisees who do not follow the format are threats to
40   both franchisors and themselves. Badly managed operations with poor service hurt the
image that is a major part of what a company is selling. Even when an agreement
specifically states the franchisee's obligations, enforcement can be impracticable. In fact,
the conformity problem could become so difficult that the firm might be forced to revert
to a company-owned operation. Reportedly, Howard Johnson stopped franchising its
45   restaurants primarily for this reason.

    Franchisors (who are, after all, manufacturers) often have little experience in some
aspects of the business. Suitable sites for outlets must be found and buildings
constructed. Vastly different types of franchisees in various areas must be counseled and
controlled. These and many other jobs all compete for management time and capital.
50   The immediate consumer for the franchisor's goods is, of course, the franchisee. Many of
these people could start a business of their own. Why, then, would someone who wanted,
say, a restaurant, choose to pay for the use of someone else's name and agree to all the
operating restrictions? The answer is probably an expectation of greater profits.
Franchisees' dollars buy, first, established names that are promoted continually at less
55   cost to them than the amount needed to promote an independent business. Second, they
buy an established line of products and procedures that have a proven track record. In
effect, they buy consumer acceptance that would have taken years to establish alone (or
perhaps never could have been established).

    Franchisees do take risks. New and untried franchises may well fail. Minnie Pearl's and
60   Broadway Joe's franchisees have not done well. Franchisees who invest in established
names—and pay the higher asking price—could fail, although the risks are lessened. No

one can predict with certainty if or how consumer tastes might change or sites deteriorate to the point of unprofitableness. "Investigate before you invest" is old, wise advice.

65 Although franchising grew up in the 1960s, relatively few companies (concentrated in a few products and services) have taken the franchise route to consumers. Most of these companies apparently started from a strong nucleus of company-owned operations. They have been well financed and have vigorously promoted the franchises. And because of their continual heavy advertising, franchisees have been able to attract consumers.

70 The range of products and services a franchise offers is limited. Although these products and services vary among franchises from 15¢ hamburgers to over $100 transmission services, the companies do have some things in common. Since operations can be standardized, people need few skills to manage and service them. Franchisees need no great buying or supervising skills (workers at hamburger or pizza counters need be neither high-powered salespeople nor master chefs).

75 The offerings are of a kind to which consumers can be attracted by advertising. Few car owners, for example, can judge in advance whether a paint job will be worth the price. Advertising for an established name, though, lends confidence to a choice. Too, a large market exists for most franchise offerings. Marketers of highly specialized or expensive products would have little use for this channel (diamond producers don't sell franchises).

80 Prompt volume sales must be expected.

How much of the growth in franchising is a basic trend, how much is fad, only time will show. As better locations become scarce and competition among franchised operations sharpens, the method will be tested. Evidence already shows much disillusionment. Clearly, however, the new franchising is firmly established. Almost gone

85 are the old "franchised dealers" who pay nothing for the privilege. They operate under their own names, may or may not have exclusive areas, and may sell both competing and noncompeting products.

The new franchising, though, has a lot going for it. Population and incomes are expanding. Retailing is becoming more and more automated. Longevity is increasing and

90 retirees and others are seeking new channels for both energy and capital. The new franchising, then, could be for more marketers the answer to "which channel shall I choose?"   /1169

Stage 3: Recall

Stop and recall what you have read. Review your use of the thinking strategies. Did you use all five?

▦ ▦ ▦ Skill Development: Summarizing

Write a summary on a sheet of notebook paper noting the main points of this selection for later reference. Be brief, but include the essential elements.

Comparing the two methods of organizing textbook material (notetaking and summarizing), which do you think would work better for you for this selection? Why?

▌▌▌▌ Comprehension Questions

1. The main point the author is trying to get across in this selection is _____

_____

_____

After reading the selection, answer the following questions with *a, b, c,* or *d.*

_____ 2. The author's main purpose in this selection is
   a. to favorably influence the reader toward franchise investing
   b. to warn the public of the dangers of franchise investing
   c. to give an example of a decrease in marketing competition in the 60s
   d. to explain the advantages and disadvantages of franchising

_____ 3. The franchising operation might best be defined as a successful parent company
   a. selling name-brand goods to a private investor
   b. renting proven ideas and techniques for investment capital
   c. selling an independent investor the right, as well as the guidance, to open a business under its name
   d. assuming management and advertising responsibility for individual investors

_____ 4. The advantages of franchising to the parent company are all the following except
   a. the ownership of additional retail outlets
   b. an immediate investment return
   c. the development of a future market for sale of supplies
   d. the opportunity for more extensive advertising

_____ 5. The advantages of franchising to the franchisee are all of the following except
   a. use of proven procedures
   b. insurance of greater profits
   c. greater advertising than an independent could afford
   d. starting out with customer acceptance of the product

_____ 6. According to the author, a significant danger of franchising to the franchisor is
   a. overspending advertising dollars on regional markets
   b. establishing a line of products that the franchisee does not want to sell
   c. the bad image a franchisee can give to the total business
   d. the franchisee deciding to open an independent business operation without the parent company

_____ 7. According to the author a business that would lend itself well to franchising usually has all of the following characteristics except
   a. limited products and services
   b. standardized operations

c. cheap locations

d. no need for highly skilled employees

8. According to the author, the trend of franchising may continue to grow because

a. fads continue for many years

b. good locations are becoming scarce

c. competition is keen

d. retailing is becoming more automated

9. The snowballing effect in franchising referred to by the author is best stated as

a. success breeds success

b. the first is the easiest

c. overextending causes failure

d. greater quality increases volume

10. An important motivating and management key on which franchising capitalizes is

a. cheap labor

b. parent company leasing

c. individual ownership

d. local marketing controls

Answer the following with *T* (true), *F* (false), or *CT* (can't tell).

11. In the author's opinion, a franchisor should sell to anyone who has the capital to invest.

12. The author implies that franchisees of the Howard Johnson restaurants did not always meet the standards of the parent company.

13. According to the author, as the franchisor becomes more established, the price of a franchise usually becomes higher.

14. McDonald's is the number one franchising business in the world.

15. Minnie Pearl's and Broadway Joe's franchisees failed because of inferior products.

▌▐▐ Vocabulary

According to the way the boldface word was used in the selection, indicate *a, b, c,* or *d* for the word or phrase that gives the best definition.

1. "sees a profit **potential** (06)"

a. area

b. undeveloped power

c. reality

d. notion

2. "The **parent** company's methods (07)"

a. original

b. responsible

c. independent

d. family

_____ 3. "The **snowballing** effect (11)"
    a. chilling
    b. accumulating
    c. circling
    c. playful

_____ 4. "**conscientious** retail managers (25)"
    a. willing to learn
    b. specifically trained
    c. intelligent
    d. honest and hardworking

_____ 5. "won't thoughtlessly **jeopardize** it (33)"
    a. endanger
    b. forget
    c. fail
    d. slander

_____ 6. "follow the **format** (39)"
    a. manner
    b. plan
    c. legality
    d. leadership

_____ 7. "the franchisee's **obligations** (42)"
    a. payments
    b. practices
    c. commitments
    d. privileges

_____ 8. "from a strong **nucleus** (66)"
    a. energy area
    b. center of growth
    c. research base
    d. module

_____ 9. "shows much **disillusionment** (84)"
    a. animosity
    b. fantasy
    c. disenchantment
    d. bitterness

_____ 10. "**Longevity** is increasing (89)"
    a. available money
    b. length of loans
    c. interest rate
    d. long life

Essay Question

Describe how franchising helped McDonald's grow into a bigger and better company than might otherwise have been possible. In answering the question, relate the strengths and weaknesses of franchising to McDonald's Corporation. Use a sheet of notebook paper to record your answer.

Selection **3**

PSYCHOLOGY

Stage 1: Preview

Preview _the selection and complete the following sentence: After reading this selection, I would like to know_ _____

_____

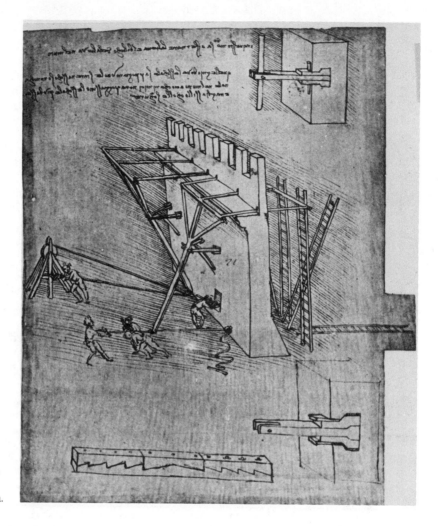

Architectural sketches
by Leonardo da Vinci.
Biblioteca Ambrosiana.

Stage 2: Integrate Knowledge While Reading

1. *Predict*
2. *Picture*
3. *Form analogies*
4. *Verbalize points*
5. *Fix up strategies*

Skill Development: Underscoring

Using a variety of notations, underscore *the following selection as if you were organizing the material to study for a quiz. Remember, do not underscore as you read, but wait until you finish a section and then mark the important points.*

CREATIVE THINKING AND CRITICAL THINKING*

Gardner Lindzey, Calvin Hall, and Richard F. Thompson, from *Psychology*

Creative thinking is thinking that results in the discovery of a new or improved solution to a problem. *Critical thinking* is the examination and testing of suggested solutions to see whether they will work. Creative thinking leads to the birth of new ideas, while critical thinking tests ideas for flaws and defects. Both are necessary for effective problem-
5 solving, yet they are incompatible—creative thinking interferes with critical thinking, and vice versa. To think creatively we must let our thoughts run free. The more spontaneous the process, the more ideas will be born and the greater the probability that an effective solution will be found. A steady stream of ideas furnishes the raw material. Then critical judgment selects and refines the best ideas, picking the most effective solution out of the
10 available possibilities. Though we must engage in the two types of thinking separately, we need both for efficient problem-solving.

Inhibitions of Creative Thinking

Conformity—the desire to be like everyone else—is the foremost barrier to creative thinking. A person is afraid to express new ideas because he thinks he will make a fool of himself and be ridiculed. This feeling may date back to his childhood, when his
15 spontaneous and imaginative ideas may have been laughted at by parents or older people. During adolescence, conformity is reinforced because young people are afraid to be different from their peers. Then, too, history teaches us that innovators often are laughed at and even persecuted.

Censorship—especially self-imposed censorship—is a second significant barrier to
20 creativity. External censorship of ideas, the thought-control of modern dictatorships, is dramatic and newsworthy; but internal censorship is more effective and dependable. External censorship merely prevents public distribution of proscribed thoughts; the thoughts may still be expressed privately. But people who are frightened by their thoughts tend to react passively, rather than think of creative solutions to their problems.
25 Sometimes they even repress those thoughts, so that they are not aware they exist. Freud called this internalized censor the *superego*.

A third barrier to creative thinking is the rigid *education* still commonly imposed upon children. Regimentation, memorization, and drill may help instill the accepted knowledge of the day, but these classroom methods cannot teach students how to solve
30 new problems or how to improve upon conventional solutions. On the other hand, the progressive movement in education often has been criticized on the ground that its emphasis on creative thinking also encourages intellectual nonconformity and radicalism. Such critics fear that new ideas may threaten the established order. Others simply believe that creative thinking must be balanced by critical thinking if it is to be useful.
35 A fourth barrier to creative thinking is the great *desire to find an answer quickly*. Such a strong motivation often narrows one's consciousness and encourages the acceptance of early, inadequate solutions. People tend to do their best creative thinking when they are

*LEARNING STRATEGY: Be able to describe the factors involved in both creative and critical thinking and explain how the two interact.

From *Psychology* by Gardner Lindzey, Calvin Hall and Richard F. Thompson, pp. 291–295. Copyright © 1975 by Worth Publishers, Inc. Reprinted by permission.

released from the demands and responsibilities of everyday living. Inventors, scientists, artists, writers, and executives often do their most creative thinking when they are not
40   distracted by routine work. The value of a vacation is not that it enables a person to work better on his return but rather that it permits new ideas to be born during the vacation.

The daydreamer often is criticized for wasting his time. Yet without daydreams, society's progress would be considerably slower, since daydreaming often leads to the discovery of original ideas. This is not to suggest that all daydreaming or leisurely
45   contemplation results in valid and workable ideas—far from it. But somewhere, among the thousands of ideas conceived, one useful idea will appear. Finding this one idea without having to produce a thousand poor ones would achieve a vast saving in creative thinking. But such a saving seems unlikely, especially since creative thinking is generally enjoyable whether its results are useful or not.

Critical Thinking

50   Creative thinking must be followed by critical thinking if we want to sort out and refine those ideas that are potentially useful. Critical thinking is essentially an idea-testing operation. Will it work? What is wrong with it? How can it be improved? These are questions to be answered by a critical examination of newly hatched ideas. You may be highly creative, but if you cannot determine which ideas are practical and reasonable,
55   your creativity will not lead to many fruitful consequences. In order to make such distinctions, you must maintain some distance and detachment, so that you can appraise your own ideas objectively.

Critical thinking requires some criteria by which to judge the practicality of the ideas. For example, if a community wants to do something about crime, it must decide what
60   limitations are to be imposed upon the measures that are suggested. One limitation is the amount of money available; many proposals for curbing crime cost more than the community is willing or able to pay. Critical thinking must always take such realities into account.

What barriers stand in the path of critical thinking? One is the *fear of being aggressive*
65   *and destructive*. We learn as children not to be critical, not to differ with what someone says, especially an older person. To criticize is to be discourteous.

A closely related barrier is the *fear of retaliation*. If I criticize your ideas, you may turn about and criticize mine. This often involves yet another barrier, the *overevaluation* of one's own ideas. We like what we have created, and often we are reluctant to let others
70   take apart our creation. By and large, those who are least secure hang on most tenaciously to their original ideas.

Finally, we should note again that if too much emphasis is placed upon being creative, the critical faculty may remain underdeveloped. In their zeal to stimulate creativity in their pupils, teachers often are reluctant to think critically. This is unfortunate, since for
75   most people life requires a balance between creative and critical thinking.

Critical Attitudes.   There is an important distinction between critical thinking and a *critical attitude*. Critical thinking tries to arrive at a valid and practical solution to a problem. However much it may reject and discard, its final goal is constructive. A critical attitude, on the other hand, is destructive in intent. A person with a critical attitude tends
80   to criticize solely for the sake of criticizing. Such an attitude is emotional rather than cognitive.

The Creative Person

In recent years, psychologists have studied creativity intensively. The first challenge they faced was how to define and recognize creativity. One common solution to this problem is to ask knowledgeable people to name the most creative individuals in their own field.
85   Architects are asked to identify the most creative members of their profession or authors are asked to name the most creative writers. These highly creative people then are studied by means of interviews, questionnaires, tests, and other devices to see how they differ from less creative members of the same profession. These studies show that exceptionally creative people are characteristically:

1. flexible

2. intuitive

3. perceptive

4. original

5. ingenious

6. dedicated

7. hardworking

8. persistent

9. independent

10. unconventional

11. courageous

12. uninhibited

13. moody

14. self-centered

15. self-assertive

16. dominant

17. eccentric

90   Creative people often have vivid and sometimes even flamboyant personalities. They prefer complexity to simplicity. And those who are males accept the feminine side of their nature without being effeminate (Barron, 1959).

Isolating such characteristics of highly creative people may be useful. If these traits are related to creativity, child training and educational procedures may be tailored to produce more creative people. Still, we are only assuming that these traits have anything to do with being creative. They may merely be associated with creativity, rather than being determinants of it. Or, they may be necessary but not sufficient conditions for being creative. Flexibility, originality, and hard work, for example, may be requirements for creativity but they certainly are not sufficient to insure it. The creative genius displayed by Shakespeare, Leonardo da Vinci, Einstein, and Beethoven remains a mystery that has so far eluded scientific analysis.   /1340

Stage 3: Recall

Stop and recall what you have read. Review your use of the thinking strategies. Did you use all five?

▦▦ Skill Development: Outlining and Summarizing

Outline the key ideas in the selection as if you were planning to use your notes to study for a quiz. Use a piece of notebook paper to record your outline.

Write a summary of the selection noting the main points for later reference. Be brief, but include the essential elements. Use a sheet of notebook paper to record your answer.

Compare the three methods of organizing textbook material (underscoring, outlining, and summarizing). Which do you think would work better for you for this selection? Why? Use a sheet of notebook paper to record your answer.

▦▦ Comprehension Questions

1. The main point the author is trying to get across in this selection is _____

_____

_____

After reading the selection, answer the following questions with *a, b, c,* or *d.*

_____ 2. According to the author, creative thinking includes all of the following except
  a. improved solutions to old problems
  b. the birth of new ideas
  c. a spontaneous flow of free thoughts
  d. an evaluation of effective alternatives

_____ 3. The author implies that critical thinking could be characterized as all of the following except
  a. selective   c. spontaneous
  b. judgmental   d. organized

_____ 4. Of the following barriers to creative thinking, the single individual would probably have the most control over
  a. conformity   c. education
  b. external censorship   d. the desire for a quick answer

_____ 5. Of the following statements, the author would agree that
  a. in general, today's educational system encourages creativity
  b. creative people must dare to be different
  c. dictatorships cannot stop creative ideas
  d. daily duties do not interfere with creativity

_____ 6. The author believes that daydreaming
  a. is a waste of time
  b. slows society's progress

c. fosters creative thinking

d. saves time in problem solving

_____ 7. The author would agree with all of the following statements except

a. creative thinking comes before critical thinking

b. critical thinking requires guidelines for evaluating ideas

c. critical thinking must be realistic

d. creative thinking should be done by one person and critical thinking by another

_____ 8. All of the following are barriers to critical thinking except

a. the threat of returned criticism

b. the chance of offending someone

c. an aggressive desire for improvement

d. the possible destruction of cherished ideas

_____ 9. The author feels that a critical attitude is

a. desirable   c. unintentional

b. cognitive   d. destructive

_____ 10. The author believes that highly creative people

a. cannot isolate the determinants of creativity

b. tend to be effeminate

c. make simple solutions complicated

d. do not need to work hard

Answer the following with *T* (true), *F* (false), or *CT* (can't tell).

_____ 11. The author believes that rest is the most important result of a vacation.

_____ 12. The author suggests that the progressive movement in education should be followed.

_____ 13. The author implies that a teacher's constructive criticism helps students develop critical thinking.

_____ 14. The author feels that conformity is at its worst during adolescence.

_____ 15. The author feels that creative thinking is fun.

▌▌▌ **Vocabulary**

According to the way the boldface word was used in the selection, indicate *a, b, c,* or *d* for the word or phrase that gives the best definition.

____ 1. "yet they are **incompatible** (05)"

a. untouched

b. not understood

c. similar in nature

d. unsuitable together

____ 2. "The more **spontaneous** the process (06)"

a. demanding

b. momentarily impulsive

c. reliable

d. advantageous

_____ 3. "**Inhibitions** of Creative
Thinking (12)"
   a. variations
   b. objections
   c. motivators
   d. restraints

_____ 4. "**Innovators** often are laughed
at (17)"
   a. clowns
   b. introducers of the new
   c. people who fail
   d. adventurers

_____ 5. "nonconformity and
radicalism (32)"
   a. conservatism
   b. extremism
   c. isolationism
   d. romanticism

_____ 6. "leisurely **contemplation**
(45)"
   a. relaxation
   b. conversation
   c. meditation
   d. manipulation

_____ 7. "maintain some distance and
detachment (56)"
   a. outside advice
   b. separation
   c. sophistication
   d. emotional involvement

_____ 8. "hang on most **tenaciously**
(70)"
   a. strongly
   b. loosely
   c. quickly
   d. quietly

_____ 9. "in their **zeal** to stimulate
(73)"
   a. attempt
   b. goal
   c. rush
   d. eagerness

_____ 10. "**flamboyant** personalities
(90)"
   a. annoying
   b. likeable
   c. showy
   d. intelligent

▦ ▦ ▦ Essay Question

Define creative and critical thinking and discuss activities in which you feel a
teacher can create a desirable balance between the two in the classroom. Use a
sheet of notebook paper to record your answer.

INFERENCE

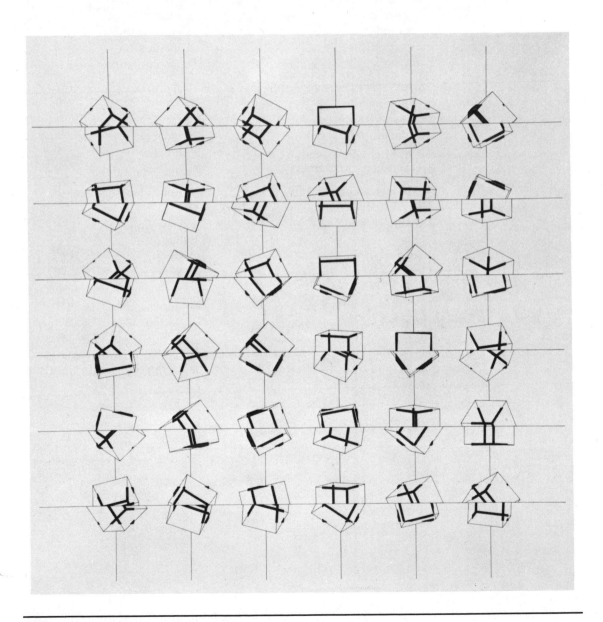

WHAT IS AN INFERENCE?

In categorizing reading skills, the first and most basic level of reading is the literal level, that is, what are the facts? In reacting to a literal question, you can actually point to the words on the page that answer the question. Reading, however, progresses beyond this initial stage. A second and more sophisticated level of reading deals with motives, feelings, and judgments; this is the inferential level. At this level you no longer can point to the answer, but instead must form opinions from suggestions within the selection. In a manner of speaking, the reader must "read between the lines" for the implied meaning.

Rather than directly stating, authors often subtly suggest and thus manipulate the reader. Suggestion can be a more effective method of getting the message across than a direct statement. Suggestion requires greater writing skill, and it is also usually more artistic, creative, and entertaining. The responsible reader searches beyond the printed word for insights into what was left unsaid.

For example, in cigarette advertisements the public is enticed through suggestion, not facts, into spending millions of dollars on a product that is presumably unhealthful. According to the choice of a particular brand, smoking offers the refreshment of a mountain stream or the sophisticated elegance of the rich and famous. Never in the ads is smoking directly praised or pleasure promised; the positive aspects are implied. A lawsuit for false advertising is out of the question because nothing tangible has been put into print. The emotionalism of the full-page advertisement is so overwhelming that the consumer hardly notices the warning peeking from the hillside at the bottom of the page— "Warning: The Surgeon General Has Determined That Cigarette Smoking is Dangerous to Your Health."

▚▙▜ Exercise 1: Implied Meaning in Advertisements

A. Look at the following cigarette advertisements and answer these questions:

1. What is directly stated about each?

   a. Marlboro _____

   b. Newport _____

   c. Virginia Slims _____

2. What is suggested by the name of each cigarette?

   a. Marlboro _____

   b. Newport _____

   c. Virginia Slims _____

Manfred Mohr. *P-197H.* (1979) Courtesy of The McCrory Collection.

3. What does the advertisement imply about each cigarette?

   a. Marlboro _____

   b. Newport _____

   c. Virginia Slims _____

4. Describe the potential consumer for each cigarette.

   a. Marlboro _____

   b. Newport _____

   c. Virginia Slims _____

5. What characteristics do all three advertisements have in common?

   _____

6. Why do you think a Marlboro smoker would or would not switch to Newport or Virginia Slims?

   _____

   _____

B. For a different approach, look at the following ad and answer the same kind of questions.

   1. What makes this ad particularly eye-catching?

   _____

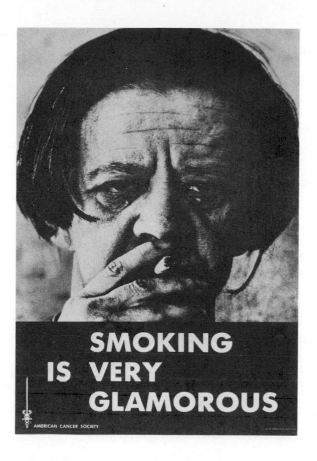

SMOKING
IS VERY
GLAMOROUS

AMERICAN CANCER SOCIETY

2. To whom is this ad appealing?

_____

_____

3. What is directly stated about smoking?

_____

_____

4. What is implied about smoking?

_____

_____

   In this ad, the message is exactly the opposite of the direct statement. Although you can point to the words, the ad is certainly not saying that smoking is glamorous.

Authors and advertisers have not invented a new comprehension skill; they are merely capitalizing on an already highly developed skill of daily life. When asked by a co-worker, "How do you like your boss?", the employee might answer, "I think she wears nice suits," rather than "I don't like my boss." A lack of approval has been suggested, while the employee has avoided a direct negative statement. In everyday life, we make inferences about people by examining what people say, what they do, and what others say about them. The intuition of everyday life applied to the printed word is the inferential level of reading.

CONNOTATION OF WORDS

Notice the power of suggested meaning in responding to the following questions:

1. Which is the sexiest?
   a. lingerie
   b. underwear
   c. undergarments
2. Which would you find in a small town?
   a. movies
   b. flickers
   c. picture shows
3. Who probably earns the most money?
   a. a businessperson in a dark suit, white shirt, and tie
   b. a businessperson in slacks and a sport shirt
   c. a businessperson in a pale blue uniform

Can you prove your answers? It's not the same as proving when the Declaration of Independence was signed, yet you still have a feeling for how each question should be answered. Even though a right or wrong answer is more difficult to explain in this type of question, certain answers can still be supported as correct—they are *a, c,* and *a.* The answers are based on feelings, attitudes, and knowledge commonly shared by society. Perhaps you can't prove lingerie is sexier than underwear, but everyone has a feeling that it must be.

Seemingly an innocent tool, the writer's choice of words is the first indication of implied meaning. For example, if a person is skinny, he is unattractive, but if he is slender or slim he must be attractive. All three words might refer to the same underweight person, but *skinny* communicates a negative feeling while *slender* or *slim* communicates a positive one. This feeling or emotionalism surrounding a word is called *connotation. Denotation* is the specific meaning of a word, but the connotative meaning goes beyond this to reflect certain attitudes and prejudices of society. Even though it may not seem premeditated, writers select words, just as advertisers select symbols and models, to manipulate the reader's opinions.

▧▨▥ Exercise 2: Connotation of Words

In each of the following word pairs, write the letter of the word that connotes a more positive emotional feeling:

_____	1. (a) guest	(b) boarder
_____	2. (a) surplus	(b) waste
_____	3. (a) conceited	(b) proud
_____	4. (a) buzzard	(b) robin
_____	5. (a) heavyset	(b) obese
_____	6. (a) Richard	(b) Elmer
_____	7. (a) house	(b) mansion
_____	8. (a) song	(b) serenade
_____	9. (a) calculating	(b) clever
_____	10. (a) neglected	(b) deteriorated
_____	11. (a) colleague	(b) accomplice
_____	12. (a) ambition	(b) greed
_____	13. (a) kitten	(b) cat
_____	14. (a) courageous	(b) audacious
_____	15. (a) contrived	(b) designed
_____	16. (a) flower	(b) orchid
_____	17. (a) distinctive	(b) peculiar
_____	18. (a) baby	(b) kid
_____	19. (a) persuasion	(b) propaganda
_____	20. (a) gold	(b) tin
_____	21. (a) slump	(b) decline
_____	22. (a) lie	(b) misrepresentation
_____	23. (a) janitor	(b) custodian
_____	24. (a) offering	(b) collection
_____	25. (a) soldiers	(b) mercenaries

▧▨▥ Exercise 3: Connotation in Textbooks

For each of the underlined words in the following sentences, indicate whether the connotation is positive or negative and explain why.

1. While the unions fought mainly for better wages and hours, they also championed various social reforms.

Leonard Pitt, *We Americans*

_____

2. The ad was part of the oil companies' program to sell their image rather than their

product to the public. In the ad they <u>boasted</u> that they were reseeding all the disrupted areas with a newly developed grass that grows five times faster than the grass that normally occurs there.

Robert Wallace, Biology: The World of Life

---

3. Old Henry Reifsneider and his wife Phoebe were a loving couple. You perhaps know how it is with simple natures that fasten themselves like <u>lichens</u> on the stones of circumstance and weather their days to a <u>crumbling</u> conclusion.

Theodore Dreiser, The Lost Phoebe

---

4. America's youthful <u>exuberance</u> and its <u>greed</u> for land were embedded in Manifest Destiny.

Leonard Pitt, We Americans

---

5. Where do all the locust that suddenly appear to <u>ravage</u> African crops come from? Certain populations seem to <u>blossom</u> for some mysterious reason, and we hear of "invasions" or "plagues."

Robert Wallace, Biology: The World of Life

---

6. She was bare-headed; but she balanced in her hand a large parasol, with a deep border of embroidery; and she was <u>strikingly</u>, <u>admirably</u> pretty.

Henry James, Daisy Miller

---

7. Lots that sold for $75 in 1833 brought a <u>whopping</u> $7,500 in 1837.

Leonard Pitt, We Americans

---

8. The cities were <u>garbage-filled</u> and <u>overrun</u> with rats. The <u>stench</u> was devastating. Life in the country was not much better, with the scattered hamlets being little more than isolated slums inhabited by people of <u>numbing</u> ignorance.

Robert Wallace, Biology: The World of Life

9. Mr. Emerson was a <u>seedy</u> little bit of a chap—red headed. Mr. Holmes was as fat as a <u>balloon</u>—he weighed as much as three hundred, and had double chins all the way down to his stomach.

Mark Twain, Whittier Birthday Dinner Speech

---

10. Not since Wilson had tried to <u>ram</u> the League of Nations through the Senate had any president put more on the line.

Leonard Pitt, We Americans

FIGURATIVE LANGUAGE

Figurative language, in a sense, is another language because it is a different way of using "regular language" words so that they take on new meaning. For example, "It was raining buckets" or "raining cats and dogs" is a lively, figurative way of describing a heavy rain. A young child, however, who comprehends only on a literal level, might look up in the sky for the descending pails or animals. The two expressions give an exaggerated, humorous effect, but, on the literal level, they do not make any sense. Figurative expressions add zest, surprise, and beauty to our language.

Although the types of figurative expressions overlap, some of the variations are:

1. **Idiom:** an expression that does not make sense grammatically, but has taken on a new generally accepted meaning over many years of use.

She tried to *keep a stiff upper lip* during the ordeal.
His eyes were *bigger than his stomach.*

2. **Simile:** a comparison of two unlike things using the words *like* or *as.*

He appeared at the meeting *like a wolf in sheep's clothing.*
She fought *like a tiger* for her rights.

3. **Metaphor:** a direct comparison of two unlike things (without using like or as).

He was a *wet blanket.*
She *was a tiger* in the court room.

4. **Personification:** attributing human characteristics to nonhuman things.

The *birds speak* from the forest.
Time marches on.

▪▪▪ Exercise 4: Figurative Language

Find the definition of each of the following figurative expressions and indicate the letter of the definition in the blank.

_____	1. eat humble pie	a. small problem that spoils fun
_____	2. leave no stone unturned	b. overcome stiffness between strangers
_____	3. a sacred cow	c. person who cannot be criticized
_____	4. lock, stock, and barrel	d. to be well prepared
_____	5. a feather in one's cap	e. make every effort
_____	6. a fly in the ointment	f. something of which to be proud
_____	7. to hit the nail on the head	g. admit your error
_____	8. get down to brass tacks	h. entirely, completely
_____	9. break the ice	i. guess something correctly
_____	10. loaded for bear	j. get to the real problem

▪▪▪ Exercise 5: Figurative Language in Textbooks

The figurative expressions in the following sentences are underlined. Define each expression so that it makes sense in the sentence.

1. He cast his lot with the British, who at one point gave him command over a redcoat army.

Leonard Pitt, *We Americans*

_____

_____

2. Obviously, a bird must be able to manage it pretty well on the first attempt, or the bird will crash to the ground as surely as would a launched mouse.

Robert Wallace, *Biology: The World of Life*

_____

_____

3. Often they were the jacks-of-all trades who worked with simple tools and equipment and displayed a knack for solving practical problems.

Leonard Pitt, *We Americans*

_____

4. A familiar example is the two hands of a clock that move at different rates within the same twenty-four-hour period, but are driven by the same mechanism.

Robert Wallace, *Biology: The World of Life*

_____

© Scott, Foresman and Company.

5. Contrary to myth, it was the towns rather than the farms that <u>spearheaded</u> the westward movement.

Leonard Pitt, We Americans

_____

6. This Dreaming, this <u>Somnambulism</u> is what we on Earth call Life; wherein the most indeed undoubtingly wander, as if they <u>knew right hand from left</u>; yet they only are wise who know that they know nothing.

Thomas Carlyle, Sartor Resartus

_____

_____

7. The government urged women to fill the gaps in the assembly line as well as the empty desk chairs in the offices. Millions responded. <u>Rosie-the-Riveter</u> was welcomed into every plant.

Leonard Pitt, We Americans

_____

_____

8. As a trained nurse working in the immigrant slums of New York, she knew that <u>table-top</u> abortions were common among poor women, and she had seen some of the tragic results.

Leonard Pitt, We Americans

_____

_____

9. The oppression of the thought that all <u>feeling was dead</u> within me, was gone. I was no longer hopeless—I was not a stock or a <u>stone</u>.

John Stuart Mill, Autobiography

_____

_____

_____

10. The <u>Moving Finger</u> writes; and, having writ,
    Moves on; nor all your <u>Piety nor Wit</u>
    Shall lure it back <u>to cancel half a Line,</u>
    Nor all your <u>Tears wash out a Word of it.</u>

The Rubaiyat of Omar Khayyam

_____

_____

_____

IMPLIED MEANING

Reading would be rather dull if the author stated every idea, never giving you a chance to figure things out for yourself. For example, in a mystery novel you carefully weigh each word, each action, each conversation, each description, and each fact in an effort to identify the villain and solve the crime before it is revealed at the end. Although textbook material may not have the Sherlock Holmes' spirit of high adventure, authors use the same techniques to imply meaning. The following examples, factual and fictitious, show how authors use suggestion, and from the clues given, you can deduce the facts.

Exercise 6: Inference from Description

Looking back on the Revolutionary War, one cannot say enough about Washington's leadership. While his military skills proved less than brilliant and he and his generals lost many battles, George Washington was the single most important figure of the colonial war effort. His original appointment was partly political, for the rebellion that had started in Massachusetts needed a commander from the South to give geographic balance to the cause. The choice fell to Washington, a wealthy and respectable Virginia planter with military experience dating back to the French and Indian War. He had been denied a commission in the English army and had never forgiven the English for the insult. During the war he shared the physical suffering of his men, rarely wavered on important questions, and always used his officers to good advantage. His correspondence with Congress to ask for sorely needed supplies was tireless and forceful. He recruited several new armies in a row, as short-term enlistments gave out.

Leonard Pitt, *We Americans*

Answer the following with *T* (true), *F* (false), or *CT* (can't tell).

_____ 1. The author regards George Washington as the most brilliant military genius in American history.
_____ 2. A prime factor in Washington's becoming President was a need for geographic balance.
_____ 3. Washington resented the British for a past injustice.
_____ 4. The Revolutionary War started as a rebellion in the northeast.
_____ 5. The author feels that Washington's leadership was courageous and persistent even though not infallible.

Exercise 7: Inference from Action

When he came to the surface he was conscious of little but the noisy water. Afterward he saw his companions in the sea. The oiler was ahead in the race. He was swimming strongly and rapidly. Off to the correspondent's left, the cook's great white and corked

Pitt: *We Americans,* Second Edition. Copyright © 1984 Kendall/Hunt Publishing Company. Reprinted with permission.

back bulged out of the water, and in the rear the captain was hanging with his one good hand to the keel of the overturned dinghy.

There is a certain immovable quality to a shore, and the correspondent wondered at it amid the confusion of the sea.

Stephen Crane, The Open Boat

Answer the following with *a, b, c,* or *d.*

_____ 1. The reason that the people are in the water is because of
   a. a swimming race
   b. an airplane crash
   c. a capsized boat
   d. a group decision

_____ 2. In relation to his companions, the correspondent is
   a. closest to the shore
   b. the second or third closest to the shore
   c. farthest from the shore
   d. in a position that is impossible to determine

_____ 3. The member of the group that had probably suffered a previous injury is the
   a. oiler
   b. correspondent
   c. cook
   d. captain

_____ 4. The uninjured member of the group that the author seems to regard as the least physically fit is the
   a. oiler
   b. correspondent
   c. cook
   d. captain

_____ 5. The story is being told through the eyes of the
   a. oiler
   b. correspondent
   c. cook
   d. captain

■■■ Exercise 8: Inference from Figurative Language

<blockquote>
He clasps the crag with crooked hands;
Close to the sun in lonely lands,
Ringed with the azure world, he stands.

The wrinkled sea beneath him crawls;
He watches from his mountain walls
And like a thunderbolt he falls.
</blockquote>

Alfred Lord Tennyson, "The Eagle"

© Scott, Foresman and Company.

Answer the following with *a, b, c,* or *d.*

_____ 1. For an overall effect in this poem the author wants the reader to see the eagle as
   a. majestic
   b. violent
   c. lonely
   d. frightened

_____ 2. Using *wrinkled* and *crawls* to describe the sea suggests
   a. the harsh force of the ocean waves
   b. the eagle's dominance over the sea
   c. the eternal age of the sea
   d. the changing ocean tides

_____ 3. The "crooked hands" suggest a relationship between the eagle and
   a. a deformed person
   b. a dishonest villain
   c. an aging monarch
   d. other birds of prey

_____ 4. "Close to the sun" is suggestive primarily of the eagle's
   a. superb flying ability
   b. superiority over earthly things
   c. warm-hearted manner
   d. bald head

_____ 5. *Thunderbolt* suggests all of the following except
   a. speed
   b. destruction
   c. power
   d. failure

■ ■ ■ Exercise 9: Inference from Factual Material

Except for some minor internal disturbances in the nineteenth century, Switzerland has been at peace inside stable boundaries since 1815. The basic factors underlying this long period of peace seem to have been (1) Switzerland's position as a buffer between larger powers, (2) the comparative defensibility of much of the country's terrain, (3) the relatively small value of Swiss economic production to an aggressive state, (4) the country's value as an intermediary between belligerents in wartime, and (5) Switzerland's own policy of strict and heavily armed neutrality. The difficulties which a great power might encounter in attempting to conquer Switzerland have often been popularly exaggerated since the Swiss Plateau, the heart of the country, lies open to Germany and France, and even the Alps have frequently been traversed by strong military forces in past times. On the other hand, resistance in the mountains might well be hard to thoroughly extinguish. In World War II Switzerland was able to hold a club over the head of Germany by mining the tunnels through which Swiss rail lines avoid the crests of the Alpine passes. Destruction of these tunnels would have been very costly to Germany, as well as to its military partner, Italy, since the Swiss railways were depended on to carry much traffic between them.

Wheeler, Kostbade and Thoman, *Regional Geography of the World*

Answer the following with *T* (true), *F* (false), or *CT* (can't tell).

_____ 1. In 1814 Switzerland was fighting a war with its neighbors.

_____ 2. The most important economic area of Switzerland is protected from its neighbors by the Alps.

_____ 3. In World War II Germany did not invade Switzerland primarily because of the five basic factors listed by the author.

_____ 4. The maintenance of a neutral Swiss position in World War II was due in part to a kind of international blackmail.

_____ 5. If it had not been for the railroad access to Italy through Switzerland, Germany would have been defeated sooner.

Selection **1**

POETRY

Wayne Bladholm

Stage 1: Preview

Preview *the selection and complete the following sentence: After reading this selection, I would like to know* _____

_____

_____

Since the selection is a poem, read it twice: once for meaning and once for feeling.

Stage 2: Integrate Knowledge While Reading

Use thinking strategies as you read:

1. *Predict*
2. *Picture*
3. *Form analogies*

4. *Verbalize points*
5. *Fix up strategies*

THE DEATH OF THE HIRED MAN*

Robert Frost

    Mary sat musing on the lamp-flame at the table
    Waiting for Warren. When she heard his step,
    She ran on tip-toe down the darkened passage
    To meet him in the doorway with the news
5   And put him on his guard. "Silas is back."
    She pushed him outward with her through the door
    And shut it after her. "Be kind," she said.
    She took the market things from Warren's arms
    And set them on the porch, then drew him down
10 To sit beside her on the wooden steps.

    "When was I ever anything but kind to him?
    But I'll not have the fellow back," he said.
    "I told him so last haying, didn't I?
    'If he left then,' I said, 'that ended it.'
15 What good is he? Who else will harbour him
    At his age for the little he can do?
    What help he is there's no depending on.
    Off he goes always when I need him most.
    'He thinks he ought to earn a little pay,
20 Enough at least to buy tobacco with,
    So he won't have to beg and be beholden.'
    'All right,' I say, 'I can't afford to pay
    Any fixed wages, though I wish I could.'
    'Someone else can.' 'Then someone else will have to.'
25 I shouldn't mind his bettering himself
    If that was what it was. You can be certain,

*LEARNING STRATEGY: Visualize the scene and try to piece together the character of the hired man as the parts unfold one by one.

When he begins like that, there's someone at him
Trying to coax him off with pocket-money,—
In haying time, when any help is scarce.
30   In winter he comes back to us. I'm done."

"Sh! not so loud: he'll hear you," Mary said.

"I want him to: he'll have to soon or late."

"He's worn out. He's asleep beside the stove.
When I came up from Rowe's I found him here,
35   Huddled against the barn-door fast asleep,
A miserable sight, and frightening, too—
You needn't smile—I didn't recognize him—
I wasn't looking for him—and he's changed.
Wait till you see."

40   "Where did you say he'd been?"

"He didn't say. I dragged him to the house,
And gave him tea and tried to make him smoke.
I tried to make him talk about his travels
Nothing would do: he just kept nodding off."

45   "What did he say? Did he say anything?"

"But little."

                   "Anything? Mary, confess
He said he'd come to ditch the meadow for me."

"Warren!"

50   "But did he? I just want to know."
"Of course he did. What would you have him say?
Surely you wouldn't grudge the poor old man
Some humble way to save his self-respect.
He added, if you really care to know,
55   He meant to clear the upper pasture, too.
That sounds like something you have heard before?
Warren, I wish you could have heard the way
He jumbled everything. I stopped to look
Two or three times—he made me feel so queer—
60   To see if he was talking in his sleep.
He ran on Harold Wilson—you remember—
The boy you had in haying four years since.
He's finished school, and teaching in his college.
Silas declares you'll have to get him back.
65   He says they two will make a team for work:

© Scott, Foresman and Company.

Between them they will lay this farm as smooth!
The way he mixed that in with other things.
He thinks young Wilson a likely lad, though daft
On education—you know how they fought
70   All through July under the blazing sun,
Silas up on the cart to build the load,
Harold along beside to pitch it on."

"Yes, I took care to keep well out of earshot."

"Well, those days trouble Silas like a dream.
75   You wouldn't think they would. How some things linger!
Harold's young college boy's assurance piqued him.
After so many years he still keeps finding
Good arguments he sees he might have used.
I sympathise. I know just how it feels
80   To think of the right thing to say too late.
Harold's associated in his mind with Latin.
He asked me what I thought of Harold's saying
He studied Latin like the violin
Because he liked it—that an argument!
85   He said he couldn't make the boy believe
He could find water with a hazel prong—
Which showed how much good school had ever done him.
He wanted to go over that. But most of all
He thinks if he could have another chance
90   To teach him how to build a load of hay—"

"I know, that's Silas' one accomplishment.
He bundles every forkful in its place,
And tags and numbers it for future reference,
So he can find and easily dislodge it
95   In the unloading. Silas does that well.
He takes it out in bunches like big birds' nests.
You never see him standing on the hay
He's trying to lift, straining to lift himself."

"He thinks if he could teach him that, he'd be
100   Some good perhaps to someone in the world.
He hates to see a boy the fool of books.
Poor Silas, so concerned for other folk,
And nothing to look backward to with pride,
And nothing to look forward to with hope,
105   So now and never any different."

Part of a moon was falling down the west,
Dragging the whole sky with it to the hills.
Its light poured softly in her lap. She saw it
And spread her apron to it. She put out her hand

110 Among the harp-like morning-glory strings,
   Taut with the dew from garden bed to eaves,
   As if she played unheard some tenderness
   That wrought on him beside her in the night.
   "Warren," she said, "he has come home to die:
115 You needn't be afraid he'll leave you this time."

   "Home," he mocked gently.
         "Yes, what else but home?
   It all depends on what you mean by home.
   Of course he's nothing to us, any more
120 Than was the hound that came a stranger to us
   Out of the woods, worn out upon the trail."

   "Home is the place where, when you have to go there,
   They have to take you in."
         "I should have called it
125 Something you somehow haven't to deserve."

   Warren leaned out and took a step or two,
   Picked up a little stick, and brought it back
   And broke it in his hand and tossed it by.
   "Silas has better claim on us you think
130 Than on his brother? Thirteen little miles
   As the road winds would bring him to his door.
   Silas has walked that far no doubt to-day.
   Why didn't he go there? His brother's rich.
   A somebody—director in the bank."

135 "He never told us that."

         "We know it though."
   "I think his brother ought to help, of course.
   I'll see to that if there is need. He ought of right
   To take him in, and might be willing to—
140 He may be better than appearances.
   But have some pity on Silas. Do you think
   If he had any pride in claiming kin
   Or anything he looked for from his brother,
   He'd keep so still about him all this time?"

145 "I wonder what's between them."
         "I can tell you.
   Silas is what he is—we wouldn't mind him—
   But just the kind that kinsfolk can't abide.
   He never did a thing so very bad.
150 He don't know why he isn't quite as good
   As anybody. Worthless though he is,
   He won't be made ashamed to please his brother."

"I can't think Si ever hurt anyone."

"No, but he hurt my heart the way he lay.
155   And rolled his old head on that sharp-edged chair-back.
He wouldn't let me put him on the lounge.
You must go in and see what you can do.
I made the bed up for him there to-night.
You'll be surprised at him—how much he's broken.
160   His working days are done; I'm sure of it."

"I'd not be in a hurry to say that."

"I haven't been. Go, look, see for yourself.
But, Warren, please remember how it is:
He's come to help you ditch the meadow.
165   He has a plan. You mustn't laugh at him.
He may not speak of it, and then he may.
I'll sit and see if that small sailing cloud
Will hit or miss the moon."

It hit the moon.
170   Then there were three there, making a dim row,
The moon, the little silver cloud, and she.

Warren returned—too soon, it seemed to her,
Slipped to her side, caught up her hand and waited.

"Warren?" she questioned.

"Dead," was all he answered.   /1402

Stage 3: Recall

Stop and recall what you have read.
Review your use of the thinking strategies. Did you use all five?

▰▰▰ Skill Development: Implied Meaning

According to the implied meaning in the selection, answer the following with
T (true), *F* (false), or *CT* (can't tell).

_____ 1. Warren had just come back from the grocery store.
_____ 2. Silas always asked Warren for higher wages than the other workers.
_____ 3. Silas had gone to see his brother before coming to Mary and Warren's farm.
_____ 4. Each year when Silas returned he always said the same thing to Warren about
          why he had come back.

_____ 5. Silas wanted to teach Harold to load hay only to enhance his own ego, and not at all for Harold's benefit.

_____ 6. This time Warren probably would have absolutely made Silas leave if he had not been dead.

_____ 7. Silas' brother probably has more money than Mary and Warren.

_____ 8. Mary seems to understand Silas better than Warren.

_____ 9. Warren had been told, not by Silas but by his brother, that the two were kin.

_____ 10. Mary was particularly fond of Silas because she did not have any children.

▥ ▩ ▥ Summarizing

Write a summary of the poem on a sheet of notebook paper noting the main points for later reference. Be brief, but include the essential elements.

▥ ▩ ▥ Comprehension Questions

1. The main point the author is trying to get across in this selection is _____

_____

_____

After reading the selection, answer the following questions with *a, b, c,* or *d.*

_____ 2. If this selection were presented in exactly the same format as a stage play, the number of characters seen on stage would be
   a. two
   b. three
   c. four
   d. five

_____ 3. Warren does not want to hire Silas again because of Silas' past history of
   a. arguing with Warren
   b. deserting Warren at harvest time
   c. causing unpleasant friction with Harold
   d. doing careless and unsatisfactory work

_____ 4. Silas said he had come back "to ditch the meadow" and "clear the upper pasture" because
   a. he knew it needed to be done
   b. he had always done it in the past
   c. he knew they expected him to say it
   d. he wanted to feel as if he had an important reason for being there

_____ 5. The author suggests that Harold probably thought of Silas as all of the following except
   a. an uneducated man

b. a failure

c. an expert teacher of haying technique

d. an argumentative know-it-all

_____ 6. The author's major purpose in contrasting Harold Wilson and Silas is to show that

a. Silas was not respected for his one accomplishment and had little hope for the future

b. Harold was too well educated to be working in haying for the rest of his life

c. a young person needs more than book learning to become educated

d. Silas was not able to teach his expertise to anyone

_____ 7. In his life, as well as in his resting position by the stove, Silas is compared to

a. a gypsy

b. a family member

c. a hound dog

d. a lonely child

_____ 8. Mary and Warren define home as a place that must be

a. accepting

b. approving

c. deserved

d. welcoming

_____ 9. Silas did not go to his brother's house because

a. his brother would make him feel shame at his failure

b. he and his brother had an argument over money

c. his brother threw him out of the house

d. his brother is a banker and does not want Silas around

_____ 10. The feeling that Mary and Warren had for Silas was

a. respect for his ability to work

b. dislike for his worthlessness

c. pretended belief that he was better than he was

d. understanding and acceptance of what he was

Answer the following with *T* (true), *F* (false), or *CT* (can't tell).

_____ 11. Mary had been at home all day.

_____ 12. The setting for the story is the porch steps of a farmhouse.

_____ 13. The time-setting of the poem is sunset.

_____ 14. The author implies that Silas probably knew he was going to die.

_____ 15. Mary and Warren did not care that Silas had died.

▥ ▧ ▨ **Vocabulary**

According to the way the boldface word was used in the selection, indicate *a, b, c,* or *d* for the word or phrase that gives the best definition.

_____ 1. "Mary sat **musing** (01)"
a. dozing
b. pondering
c. weaving
d. warming

_____ 2. "Trying to **coax** him off (28)"
a. persuade
b. force
c. steal
d. rush

_____ 3. "Some **humble** way (53)"
a. sly
b. secret
c. desperate
d. lowly

_____ 4. "**daft** on education (68)"
a. foolish
b. capable
c. intelligent
d. spoiled

_____ 5. "young college boy's **assurance** (76)"
a. agility
b. knowledge
c. confidence
d. mannerism

_____ 6. "**piqued** him (76)"
a. interested
b. endangered
c. flattered
d. provoked

_____ 7. "**taut** with the dew (111)"
a. shining
b. covered
c. tightly stretched
d. wet

_____ 8. "from garden bed to **eaves** (111)"
a. barns
b. edges of the roof
c. windows
d. trees

_____ 9. "he **mocked** gently (116)"
a. attacked
b. realized
c. ridiculed
d. questioned

_____ 10. "kinsfolk can't **abide** (148)"
a. put up with
b. respect
c. forget
d. invite

▮▮▮ Essay Question

Discuss the character traits of the hired man and explain why he felt that Mary and Warren's place was his home.

LITERATURE

Wisconsin Center for Film and Theater Research

Stage 1: Preview

Preview the selection and complete the following sentence: After reading this selection, I would like to know _____

_____

Stage 2: Integrate Knowledge While Reading

Use thinking strategies as you read:

1. *Predict*
2. *Picture*
3. *Form analogies*

4. *Verbalize points*
5. *Fix up strategies*

COL. GRANGERFORD*

Mark Twain, from *Huckleberry Finn*

There was another caln of aristocracy around there—five or six families—mostly of the name of Shepherdson. They was as high-toned and well born and rich and grand as the tribe of Grangerfords. The Shepherdsons and Grangerfords used the same steamboat landing, which was about two mile above our house; so sometimes when I went up there
5 with a lot of our folks I used to see a lot of the Shepherdsons there on their fine horses.
   One day Buck and me was away out in the woods hunting, and heard a horse coming. We was crossing the road. Buck says:
   "Quick! Jump for the woods!"
   We done it, and then peeped down the woods through the leaves. Pretty soon a
10 splendid young man came galloping down the road, setting his horse easy and looking like a soldier. He had his gun across his pommel. I had seen him before. It was young Harney Shepherdson. I heard Buck's gun go off at my ear, and Harney's hat tumbled off from his head. He grabbed his gun and rode straight to the place where we was hid. But we didn't wait. We started through the woods on a run. The woods warn't thick, so I
15 looked over my shoulder to dodge the bullet, and twice I seen Harney cover Buck with his gun; and then he rode away the way he come—to get his hat, I reckon, but I couldn't see. We never stopped running till we got home. The old gentleman's eyes blazed a minute—'twas pleasure, mainly, I judged—then his face sort of smoothed down, and he says, kind of gentle:
20 "I don't like that shooting from behind a bush. Why didn't you step into the road, my boy?"
   "The Shepherdsons don't, father. They always take advantage."
   Miss Charlotte she held her head up like a queen while Buck was telling his tale, and her nostrils spread and her eyes snapped. The two young men looked dark, but never
25 said nothing. Miss Sophia she turned pale, but the color come back when she found the man warn't hurt.
   Soon as I could get Buck down by the corncribs under the trees by ourselves, I says:
   "Did you want to kill him, Buck?"
   "Well, I bet I did."
30 "What did he do to you?"
   "Him? He never done nothing to me."
   "Well, then, what did you want to kill him for?"
   "Why, nothing—only it's on account of the feud."
   "What's a feud?"
35 "Why, where was you raised? Don't you know what a feud is?"
   "Never heard of it before—tell me about it."
   "Well," says Buck, "a feud is this way: A man has a quarrel with another man, and kills *him*; then that other man's brother kills *him;* then the other brothers, on both sides, goes for one another; then the *cousins* chip in—and by and by everybody's killed off, and
40 there ain't no more feud. But it's kind of slow, and takes a long time."
   "Has this one been going on long, Buck?"
   "Well, I should *reckon!* It started thirty years ago, or som'ers along there. There was

*LEARNING STRATEGY: Imagine the scenes in your mind and try to understand Huck's difficulty in accepting Buck's philosophy and way of life. Look for the irony in each situation.

Samuel Clemens, *The Adventures of Huckleberry Finn*, 1844.

trouble 'bout something, and then a lawsuit to settle it; and the suit went agin one of the men, and so he up and shot the man that won the suit—which he would naturally do, of

45   course. Anybody would."

    "What was the trouble about, Buck?—land?"

    "I reckon maybe—I don't know."

    "Well, who done the shooting? Was it a Grangerford or a Shepherdson?"

    "Laws, how do *I* know? It was so long ago."

50   "Don't anybody know?"

    "Oh, yes, pa knows, I reckon, and some of the other old people; but they don't know now what the row was about in the first place."

    "Has there been many killed, Buck?"

    "Yes; right smart chance of funerals. But they don't always kill. Pa's got a few buckshot

55   in him; but he don't mind it 'cuz he don't weigh much anyway. Bob's been carved up some with a bowie, and Tom's been hurt once or twice."

    "Has anybody been killed this year, Buck?"

    "Yes; we got one and they got one. 'Bout three months ago my cousin Bud, fourteen year old, was riding through the woods on t'other side of the river, and didn't have no

60   weapon with him, which was blame' foolishness, and in a lonesome place he hears a horse a-coming behind him, and sees old Baldy Shepherdson a-linkin' after him with his gun in his hand and his white hair a-flying in the wind; and 'stead of jumping off and taking to the brush, Bud 'lowed he could outrun him; so they had it, nip and tuck, for five mile or more, the old man a-gaining all the time; so at last Bud seen it warn't any use,

65   so he stopped and faced around so as to have the bullet holes in front, you know, and the old man he rode up and shot him down. But he didn't git much chance to enjoy his luck, for inside of a week our folks laid *him* out."

    "I reckon that old man was a coward, Buck."

    "I reckon he *warn't* a coward. Not by a blame' sight. There ain't a coward amongst

70   them Shephersons—not a one. And there ain't no cowards amongst the Grangerfords either. Why, that old man kep' up his end in a fight one day for half an hour against three Grangerfords, and come out winner. They was all a-horseback; he lit off of his horse and got behind a little woodpile, and kep' his horse before him to stop the bullets; but the Grangerfords stayed on their horses and capered around the old man, and peppered away

75   at him, and he peppered away at them. Him and his horse both went home pretty leaky and crippled, but the Grangerfords had to be *fetched* home and one of 'em was dead, and another died the next day. No, sir; if a body's out hunting for cowards he don't want to fool away any time amongst them Shepherdsons, becuz they don't breed any of that *kind.*"

    Next Sunday we all went to church, about three mile, everybody a-horseback. The men

80   took their guns along, so did Buck, and kept them between their knees or stood them handy against the wall. The Shepherdsons done the same. It was pretty ornery preaching—all about brotherly love, and such-like tiresomeness; but everybody said it was a good sermon, and they all talked it over going home, and had such a powerful lot to say about faith and good works and free grace and preforeordestination, and I don't

85   know what all, that it did seem to me to be one of the roughest Sundays I had run across yet.

                                                /1134

Text to the right, rotated: © Scott, Foresman and Company.

Stage 3: Recall

Stop and recall what you have read. Review your use of the thinking strategies. Did you use all five?

▣▣▣ Skill Development: Implied Meaning

According to the implied meaning in the selection, answer the following with
T (true), *F* (false), or *CT* (can't tell).

_____ 1. Huck is probably not a member of the Grangerford family.
_____ 2. The Shepherdsons owned more land than the Grangerfords.
_____ 3. Miss Sophia's reaction indicates that she might had had a feeling of affection for Harney Shepherdson.
_____ 4. Miss Charlotte probably would have been pleased if Harney Shepherdson had been killed.
_____ 5. When he first heard that Buck had shot at Harney, Buck's father seemed rather happy.
_____ 6. The author feels that Harney probably does not know exactly what caused the feud.
_____ 7. The author probably feels that both the Shepherdsons and Grangerfords are cowards.
_____ 8. The author feels that the church service softened the hearts of the feuding families and gave them a hope of peace.
_____ 9. Buck seems to admire the courage of Baldy Shepherdson even though he killed an unarmed boy.
_____ 10. In a previous encounter Buck had killed a Grangerford.

▣▣▣ Summarizing

Write a summary of the selection on a sheet of notebook paper noting the main points for later reference. Be brief, but include the essential elements.

▣▣▣ Comprehension Questions

1. The main point the author is trying to get across in this selection is _____
_____
_____

After reading the selection, answer the following questions with *a, b, c,* or *d.*

_____ 2. All of the following are untrue about the shooting incident between Buck and Harney Shepherdson except
   a. to Huck's surprise Buck stepped into the road and shot at Harney
   b. Buck shot from behind a bush and then ran away
   c. Harney provoked Buck into an attack
   d. Huck took pleasure in the excitement of the surprise attack

3. Harney's reaction to the surprise attack was to
   a. shoot at Buck and Huck
   b. shoot only at Huck
   c. pick up his hat and run away
   d. chase the boys all the way home

4. The author implies that Pa Grangerford is primarily concerned with
   a. the well-being of his sons
   b. the honor of the family name
   c. teaching his family the Christian way of life
   d. finding a solution to the feud

5. In Buck's explanation of the feud, all of the following are true except
   a. it started before he was born
   b. the original conflict between the families was heard in a court of law
   c. no one now living remembers the exact reason for the lawsuit
   d. the disagreement was definitely over land claims

6. Bud was killed by Baldy Shepherdson because
   a. Bud had killed his cousin
   b. Bud jumped off his horse and ran into the brush
   c. Bud was not able to outrun the pursuing Baldy
   d. Baldy was intimidated by Bud's face-to-face confrontation

7. The author suggests that Huck interpreted the killing of Bud as
   a. a lucky break for Baldy Shepherdson
   b. a cowardly old man killing an unarmed boy
   c. a foolish mistake on the part of Bud
   d. his friend Buck interpreted it

8. The incident in which the three Grangerfords were chasing after Baldy resulted in
   a. Baldy's being killed
   b. the death of Baldy's horse
   c. the death of two Grangerfords
   d. the death of all three Grangerfords

9. The author's purpose in including a description of the Sunday church service is to show
   a. the hypocrisy of the situation
   b. that Huck didn't like to go to church
   c. that a good sermon can change a person's life
   d. that the feuding families were religious at heart

10. In the author's characterizaton of the two boys, Huck is portrayed as
    a. less mature in moral concerns than Buck
    b. innocent while Buck is portrayed as evil
    c. a person with little understanding of life who now has Buck as a teacher
    d. more understanding of human values than Buck

Answer the following with *T* (true), *F* (false), or *CT* (can't tell).

_____ 11. The steamboat landing was neutral territory in which no killing was allowed.

_____ 12. No guns were allowed inside the church.

_____ 13. When the shooting incident with Harney Shepherdson occurred, Buck and Huck had been hunting in the woods for rabbits.

_____ 14. The women in the feuding families were never killed.

_____ 15. Buck's mother was dead and Miss Charlotte was the female head of the family.

▦ ▰ ▥ Vocabulary

According to the way the boldface word or phrase was used in the selection, indicate _a, b, c,_ or _d_ for the word or phrase that gives the best definition.

_____ 1. "clan of **aristocracy** (01)"
   a. believers
   b. warriors
   c. country people
   d. privileged upper class

_____ 2. "his gun across his **pommel** (11)"
   a. stomach
   b. lap
   c. saddle front
   d. shoulder pads

_____ 3. "on account of the **feud** (33)"
   a. lawsuit
   b. quarrel for revenge
   c. secret mission
   d. compromise

_____ 4. "what the **row** was (52)"
   a. dispute
   b. line
   c. oar
   d. race

_____ 5. "carved up some with a **bowie** (56)"
   a. sword
   b. hunting knife
   c. kitchen carver
   d. hatchet

_____ 6. "**nip and tuck** for five mile (63)"
   a. uneven
   b. familiar territory
   c. exhausting
   d. closely contested

_____ 7. "**capered** around the old man (73)"
   a. combined
   b. spread out
   c. frisked
   d. organized

_____ 8. "pretty **ornery** preaching (81)"
   a. inspiring
   b. low-down
   c. high-minded
   d. relevant

_____ 9. "and such-like **tiresomeness** (82)"
   a. boredom
   b. cleverness
   c. dishonesty
   d. commonness

_____ 10. "free grace and **preforeordestination** (84)"
   a. spiritual leadership
   b. the holy spirit
   c. forgiveness
   d. mispronunciation of _predestination_

Selection **3**

POLITICAL SCIENCE

Jean Claude Lejeune

Stage 1: Preview

Preview the selection and complete the following sentence: After reading this

selection, I would like to know _____

_____

© Scott, Foresman and Company.

Stage 2: Integrate Knowledge While Reading

Use thinking strategies as you read:

1. *Predict*
2. *Picture*
3. *Form analogies*

4. *Verbalize points*
5. *Fix up strategies*

Underscoring

Using a variety of notations, underscore *the following selection as if you were preparing for a quiz on the material. Remember, do not underscore as you read, but wait until you finish a section and then mark the important points.*

THE NATURE OF POLITICS: *

Charles P. Sohner, from *American Government and Politics Today*

What's It All About?

Aristotle, often called the father of political science, wrote that man is a political animal. One can argue about whether this was a compliment or an insult. As the United States (a political creation) approaches its two-hundredth birthday, most Americans seem to believe that politicians are a pretty bad lot. According to a 1973 Harris survey, 60 percent
5 feel that "most elective officials are in politics for all they personally can get out of it for themselves." Fifty-five percent believe that our leaders really don't care what happens to the average person. In addition, 74 percent think that "special interests get more from the government than the people do."[1] Given these attitudes, it is not surprising that nearly two-thirds of the people, the highest percentage in 20 years, would not like to see their
10 children go into politics.[2] If the survival of a free nation depends on faith and confidence, as Walter Lippmann said in the quotation on page 1, then America is in trouble. Only about a third of the people put much faith in those running the national government or sitting on the Supreme Court.[3]

Yet Americans have contradictory feelings about their political leaders. They reserve
15 their greatest respect for Washington, Lincoln, and other famous presidents. Even among the living, a 1974 Gallup poll showed that eight out of the ten most admired men were politicians. A ninth, Secretary of State Henry Kissinger, was appointed by a politician.[4]

*LEARNING STRATEGY: Be able to explain why people feel a sense of alienation toward government and how this affects our social system.

From *American Government and Politics Today,* 2nd Edition, by Charles P. Sohner, pp. 2–6. Copyright © 1976 by Scott, Foresman and Company.

[1] *Confidence and Concern: Citizens View American Government* (Cleveland: Regal Books/King's Court Communications, 1974), pp. 6–7. This pamphlet is a summary of a poll by Lou Harris and Associates.

[2] Gallup Poll, *Los Angeles Times,* Oct. 14, 1973, Part IX, p. 4, and Feb. 3, 1974, p. 3.

[3] *Confidence and Concern,* p. 8.

[4] *Los Angeles Times,* Dec. 29, 1974, p. 4. The only one not connected with the government was the Reverend Billy Graham, a friend of both President Johnson and President Nixon.

What is the truth of the matter? Is politics a "dirty game" or a "noble calling"? Probably the best answer is that it is neither. Like a stick of dynamite, politics can be used for good
20   purposes or bad ones, to build tunnels or to kill people. Such an answer is not a cop-out. It recognizes that an accurate picture of politics is painted with few blacks and whites but with many shades of gray. It is a portrait full of shadows. To understand it one must develop what social scientists call a "tolerance of ambiguity," in other words, a willingness to live with complexity and contradictions. To accept these may be the mark
25   of an educated human being.

With such acceptance, one can ask an even more important question: Can politics be made better? Can it be used more frequently for noble purposes? This book is written with the conviction that it can. Whether it will depends on all of us.

Corruption and Alienation

The death of democracy is not likely to be an assassination from ambush. It will be a slow
30   extinction from apathy, indifference, and undernourishment.

Robert M. Hutchins

The sentiments expressed in the polls cited on page 2 indicate that while most people may still have a strong loyalty to the nation and its form of government, they distrust its political leaders. They feel cut off from the process of government, sensing that their faith in the system has somehow been betrayed. They believe they are powerless to control the
35   institutions that affect their lives. This is the essence of what is often called *alienation*.

The Politician as Crook

Corruption is one of the major causes of alienation, recently dramatized by a single word: Watergate. Scarcely a week went by in 1973 and 1974 when television channels and newspapers did not sicken the American public with reports of new scandals, accusations of official misconduct, and charges of criminal deceit. The president to whom we gave
40   more votes than anyone else in the nation's history resigned in disgrace. It was disclosed that two of the government's most secret bodies, the Federal Bureau of Investigation (F.B.I.) and the Central Intelligence Agency (C.I.A.), used their vast powers not only to fight domestic crime and foreign threats, but also to harass and discredit the political opponents of those in office.
45   Corruption in government is not limited to Watergate crimes. It seems like a spreading cancer, creeping into every branch and level of the political system. In 1974, two New York congressmen were found guilty of accepting money in return for political influence.[5] The same year, ten former or current state legislators in Illinois were indicted for similar offenses.[6] Other instances of misconduct are discussed in the following chapter and
50   elsewhere in this book.

The Roots of Alienation

Corruption, of course, is not the only cause of alienation. Another contributing factor has been the "credibility gap" of the late 1960s—a belief that officials were not telling the

[5] *Los Angeles Times,* Jan. 2, 1974, p. 9 and July 20, 1974, p. 2. They were Representatives Bertram L. Podell and Frank J. Brasco, both Democrats.
[6] Ibid., Dec. 5, 1974, p. 18. They included six Republicans and four Democrats.

truth, especially about the Vietnam war. In the mid 1970s, the situation has been
worsened by the apparent inability of the government to cope with such basic problems
55 as unemployment, prices, and crime rates which were too high and energy supplies
which were too low.

Also contributing to the growing alienation of people is the "future shock" or change,
the dizzying speed with which old and familiar attitudes have had to be readjusted or
replaced. In little more than a generation, abortion was legalized, pot became popular,
60 and Germany and Japan rose from destitute and defeated enemies to prosperous and
peaceful allies. Television entered the living room, computers entered the office, blacks
entered all-white schools, topless dancers entered bars, men entered outer space, and
Richard Nixon, staunch foe of communists in America, entered Peking as a guest of the
Communists in China. Within just four months, President Ford recommended a tax
65 increase to fight inflation and then a tax cut to fight recession. Worst of all, perhaps, an
economy of abundance suddenly became one of scarcity, and a politics of speech-making
and baby-kissing became one of spying and burglary. Many people looked to their leaders
to provide at least some cushion against these startling changes. But they often looked in
vain, while the trauma of change joined with corruption, loss of credibility, and unsolved
70 economic problems in further alienating people from their government. A big segment of
the population had the feeling that somehow public officials were too powerful to
control yet too weak or indifferent to solve the country's problems.

The Effects of Alienation

We have just attempted to explain some of the causes of alienation. Equally important are
its effects. What happens when people lose faith in their government? Three things, all of
75 them bad. First, this reduces participation in politics. Voter turnout at the 1972 and 1974
elections, which will be discussed further in Chapter 9, dropped to its lowest levels since
the 1940s. A 1974 poll of college freshmen disclosed that only 36.6 percent, the lowest in
9 years, think it important to keep informed about political events. Only 12.5 percent
want to try to influence political affairs themselves.[7] Since 61 percent of the total
80 population seem to believe that what they think doesn't count much any more,[8] it is not
surprising that many college students also "don't want to get involved." Many, no doubt,
would follow the recommendation of Gordon Strachan, a former aide in the Nixon White
House. He advised young people to "stay away" from government service. They don't
have the necessary experience, he later explained, "to deal with such a crummy
85 business." If this advice is heeded, however, the nation will surely lose the services of
some of its most able and honorable citizens.[9]

Such a loss would lead to worse government, a second result of alienation. If good
people are not involved in politics, corruption is likely to increase,[10] and even more
problems are likely to go unsolved. It was the involvement of Rachel Carson, Ralph
90 Nader, and Martin Luther King, Jr., along with thousands of others, that led to regulations
on dangerous pesticides,[11] bans on automobile safety hazards, and new civil rights
legislation. T. V. Smith, a philosopher and congressman, said it well: "Democracy is
government by politicians for citizens who too often reward them with disdain. This

[7]Ibid., Jan. 12, 1975, p. 12. The poll was conducted by the American Council on Education.
[8]*Confidence and Concern*, p. 6.
[9]*Los Angeles Times*, March 11, 1975, p. 7.
[10]See Chapter 2, pp. 43–44 of this book.
[11]Rachel Carson, *Silent Spring* (Greenwich Conn.: Fawcett Publications, 1962).

disdain of politicians is a dangerous disease. . . . Politicians, of course, are not perfect—
95   not yet. They may be improved and should be improved. . . . Disdain, however, is a poor
improver. Understanding is much better. . . . From it will flow replacement of the weak
and corrupt. From it will flow larger participation in politics by the strong and the
good."[12]

The third effect of alienation is a decrease in the authority of government. If people
100   disdain their political system, they will be less likely to obey even ordinary laws
regulating things like fire hazards and traffic safety. This weakens the whole principle of
rule of law which is so important in limiting excessive use of power in a democracy. It
could also undermine government efforts in an emergency such as a flood or enemy
attack, when respect for government authority might be the key to survival itself.   /1419

Stage 3: Recall

Stop and recall what you have read. Review your use of the thinking strategies.
Did you use all five?
Review your underscoring. Have you sufficiently highlighted the main idea
and the significant supporting details?

▥▦▨ Skill Development: Implied Meaning

According to the implied meaning in the selection, answer the following with
T (true), *F* (false), or *CT* (can't tell).

_____   1. The author believes that politics can be used more frequently for noble
purposes.
_____   2. The author implies that government officials did not tell the truth about the
Vietnam War.
_____   3. The author implies that the FBI and the CIA should be abolished.
_____   4. The author is probably an American citizen.
_____   5. The quote by Robert Hutchins implies that lack of involvement threatens
democracy.
_____   6. The author does not respect Nixon's presidency.
_____   7. The author feels that more corruption exists at the state level of government
than at the federal level.
_____   8. The author would like for more people to become interested in politics as a
career.
_____   9. The author feels that there is more corruption in the government of the
United States than exists in other democracies.
_____   10. The author believes that some political crooks are needed to make the
system work.

[12]T. V. Smith, *The Legislative Way of Life* (Chicago: The University of Chicago Press, 1940), pp. ix-x.

▨▬▬ Comprehension Questions

1. The main point the author is trying to get across in this selection is ＿＿＿＿＿

_____

_____

After reading the selection, answer the following questions with *a, b, c,* or *d.*

＿＿＿＿＿＿ 2. The author's opinion about the future of politics in America might best be
described as
   a. optimistic
   b. pessimistic
   c. fatalistic
   d. antagonistic

＿＿＿＿＿＿ 3. According to the author, America is in the biggest trouble politically if
   a. corruption in the government continues
   b. citizens cannot tolerate ambiguity
   c. politics does not become a more noble calling
   d. the American people lack confidence in the government

＿＿＿＿＿＿ 4. The author points out that the 1973 Harris survey and the 1974 Gallup polls
are contradictory because
   a. the data were collected in two different years
   b. one professes disdain and the other admiration for the same group of
people
   c. different questions were asked in the two different studies
   d. the Presidents who were most admired are now dead

＿＿＿＿＿＿ 5. The candidate who received the highest number of votes in a presidential
election in American history is
   a. Washington
   b. Lincoln
   c. Nixon
   d. Ford

＿＿＿＿＿＿ 6. According to the author, the "credibility gap" causes alienation because
   a. people do not want to fight an unpopular war
   b. citizens no longer believe what the government says
   c. unemployment exists on a national level
   d. the cities suffer from crime

＿＿＿＿＿＿ 7. According to the author "future shock" breeds political alienation because
people feel
   a. topless dancers should not enter bars
   b. past enemies cannot become political friends
   c. our country is a land of abundance
   d. politicians do not provide adequate leadership in the face of change

8. The author feels that the reason fewer college students expressed an active interest in politics in the 1974 polls is because
   a. they comprise a small percent of the total population
   b. they had lost faith in their ability to influence government
   c. Gordon Strachan advised against involvement
   d. politics in general is a "crummy business"

9. The author uses Rachel Carson as an example of
   a. involvement that decreases corruption
   b. political disdain
   c. supporters of civil rights litigation
   d. alienation of philosophers

10. The author sees running a red light as a possible chain reaction effect of
    a. alienation
    b. power
    c. democracy
    d. rule by law

Answer the following with *T* (true), *F* (false), or *CT* (can't tell).

11. The author believes that corruption in the country began with Watergate.
12. The author implies that the FBI and CIA were used as political pawns.
13. Two New York congressmen were indicted in 1974 for accepting bribes from a major oil company.
14. The author feels that Nixon should not have gone to China.
15. T. V. Smith believes politicians need more understanding from the public.

▌▌▌ Vocabulary

According to the way the boldface word was used in the selection, indicate *a, b, c,* or *d* for the word or phrase that gives the best definition.

1. "tolerance of **ambiguity** (23)"
   a. confidence
   b. more than one meaning
   c. mismanagement
   d. the unexpected

2. "This is the **essence** (35)"
   a. name
   b. formula
   c. choice
   d. fundamental nature

3. "charges of criminal **deceit** (39)"
   a. lying
   b. suicide
   c. negligence
   d. murder

4. "**credibility** gap (52)"
   a. responsibility
   b. believability
   c. reliability
   d. indoctrination

    5. "to **cope** with (54)"
        a. agree
        b. solve
        c. argue
        d. contend

    6. "growing **alienation** of people (57)"
        a. anger
        b. involvement
        c. selfishness
        d. estrangement

    7. "**prosperous** and peaceful allies (60)"
        a. thriving
        b. helpful
        c. ambitious
        d. likeable

    8. "the **trauma** of change (69)"
        a. moment
        b. noise
        c. shock
        d. assault

    9. "dangerous **pesticides** (91)"
        a. bug killers
        b. politicians
        c. animals
        d. infections

    10. "automobile safety **hazards** (91)"
        a. risks
        b. headaches
        c. controls
        d. requirements

▐▌▪▐▌ Essay Question

Discuss the specific causes and effects of alienation and explain why the author feels that America is in trouble if people lose faith in the government. Use a sheet of notebook paper to record your answer.

BIAS

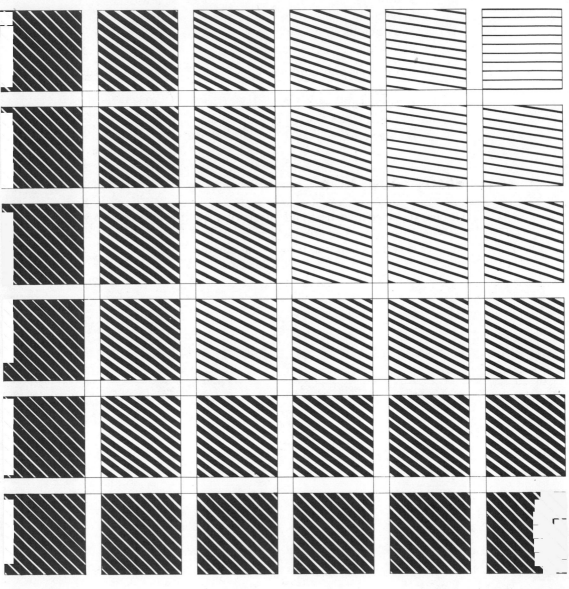

ARE TEXTBOOKS BIASED?

How many of the following statements are true?
1. Textbooks contain facts and not opinions.
2. The historical account of an incident is based on fact and thus does not vary from one author to another.
3. Except for the style of the author, freshman biology textbooks do not vary in their informational content.
4. Textbooks are supposed to be free from author's interpretation.

Unfortunately, too many students tend to answer *"true"* to *all of the above.* Paying big money for a thick history book with lots of facts and an authoritative title does not mean, contrary to student belief, that the text is an unbiased chronicle of the nation's past. No purity rule applies to textbook writing. In the case of history, the author portrays the past from a personal and unique perspective. The name of the first President of the United States does not vary from one text to another, but the emphasis on the importance of Washington's administration might.

WHAT IS BIAS?

Authors of factual material, like authors of fiction, have opinions, theories, and prejudices that influence their presentation of the subject matter. When facts are slanted, though not necessarily distorted, toward the author's personal beliefs, the written material reflects the *biases* of that author. A bias is a prejudice, a mental leaning, or an inclination. Authors show their biases through their treatment of the material. Bias is not an indication of evil intent; it is merely a signpost to the aware and responsible reader.

Exercise 1: Bias

Read the following two descriptions of Mary of Scotland from two different history books. While both include positive and negative comments, the second author obviously finds the subject more engaging and has chosen to include more positive details.

Passage A

Mary Stuart returned to Scotland in 1561 after her husband's death. She was a far more charming and romantic figure than her cousin Elizabeth, but she was no stateswoman. A convinced Catholic, she soon ran head-on into the granitelike opposition of Knox and the Kirk. In 1567 she was forced to abdicate, and in the following year she fled from Scotland and sought protection in England from Elizabeth. No visitor could have been more unwelcome.

Joseph R. Strayer et al., The Mainstream of Civilization

Passage B

Mary Stuart was an altogether remarkable young woman, about whom it is almost impossible to remain objectively impartial. Even when one discounts the flattery that crept into descriptions of her, one is inclined to accept the contemporary evidence that Mary was extraordinarily beautiful, though tall for a girl—perhaps over six feet. In addition to beauty, she had almost every other attractive attribute in high degree: courage, wit, resourcefulness, loyalty, and responsiveness, in short everything needful for worldly greatness save discretion in her relations with men and a willingness to compromise, if need be, on matters of religion. She was a thoroughgoing Roman Catholic, a good lover, and a magnificent hater.

Shepard B. Clough et al., from A History of the Western World

1. How are the two descriptions alike? _____

_____

_____

2. How do the two descriptions differ? _____

_____

_____

3. Which do you like better and why? _____

_____

_____

4. What clues signal that the author of the second description is more biased than the first? _____

_____

_____

WHAT IS THE AUTHOR'S POINT OF VIEW?

Bias and point of view are very similar and are sometimes used interchangeably. A bias, in a sense, creates a particular point of view. For example, would a London professor write the same account of American history during the revolutionary period as a native Philadelphia scholar? Probably not, because they look at the problem from different angles—one as a colonial uprising on a distant continent and the other as a struggle for personal freedom and survival. The two authors are writing from different points of view and expressing particular biases because they have different ways of looking at the subject.

Identifying each particular viewpoint helps you evaluate material. How would you evaluate the validity of the descriptions of your blind date for Friday night by the following three persons: (1) the date's mother, (2) the person setting up the date, (3) someone who dated the person last weekend?

To objectively evaluate, you need to ask, "What are the biases and beliefs of the author or speaker and how do they affect the presentation of the information?" In addition, question the author's background and ask yourself if there is another side to the issue that is not presented.

▉▉▉ Exercise 2: The Author's Point of View

Read the following passage from a history text and notice how the author tries to appear unbiased by presenting two different points of view.

Queen Elizabeth 1 (1558–1603) is generally accounted the greatest of the Tudors and one of England's ablest rulers, though to some critics she was simply a stingy and narrow-minded woman. Whatever the judgment, England was immeasurably stronger at her death than at her accession, and she died beloved by the great majority of her people. At twenty-five, when she came to the throne, she had already lived through disgrace, humiliation, and even danger of execution during her sister Mary's reign. She had seen how Mary had lost the love of her people by marrying a foreigner and by burning heretics. These early experiences left her a strong-willed and shrewd young woman, aware of how precarious both her own situation and that of her nation were, determined to put politics before religion and to follow a purely national policy.

Joseph R. Strayer et al., *The Mainstream of Civilization*

1. The author presents three different points of view. What are they?

   _____

   _____

   _____

2. Is the author biased? Give reasons for your answer.

   _____

   _____

   _____

Excerpt from *The Mainstream of Civilization*, Fourth Edition, by Joseph R. Strayer and Hans W. Gatzke, copyright © 1984 by Harcourt Brace Jovanovich, Inc. Reprinted by permission of the publisher.

WHAT ARE THE TECHNIQUES OF PROPAGANDA?

Propaganda is a systematic and deliberate attempt to persuade others to a particular doctrine or point of view. The word propaganda has taken on a negative connotation and conjures up visions of communists or religious fanatics trying to infiltrate through deception. In reality, propaganda can be both positive and negative. On the college campus, cheerleaders, the football team, and the fight song are all a part of a propaganda campaign to make you think, "My college is the best."

Television commercials propagandize us with cleanliness, and nations manipulate using the same techniques, with our acceptance depending on our own particular point of view. Americans revel in patriotic propaganda on the Fourth of July, whereas, Russia's May Day celebration is viewed with skepticism by Americans.

The following are propaganda techniques used to manipulate opinions and persuade readers. Recognizing these techniques allows the reader to logically decide an issue rather than emotionally react.

Choice of Words

In shaping opinion, certain words trigger emotional, rather than logical, reactions, and authors deliberately choose such words to elicit positive or negative responses. The positive words are called "glittering generalities" and the negative are called "name calling." Notice the emotionalism surrounding the following words:

Positive—the free world, efficient, patriotic, the American people, freedom loving

Negative—industrialist, opportunism, punk rocker, capitalism, socialistic tendencies

Testimonials

If a celebrity says an idea is correct, does that make you more likely to believe it? Testimonials are endorsements, which are actually no more than opinions, from well-known and respected people. Acceptance of these opinions depends on your respect for the one giving the testimonial, but you should remember that often the endorser is paid. You as a reader must evaluate the person's credentials for making the statement.

Example: If movie star X always drinks brand Z coffee; should that make you more likely to drink it?

Transfer

Transfer is a deliberate association with someone or something that is positive to lend an aura of good feeling.

Example: Including a quote from Abraham Lincoln in a political article does not mean that Lincoln agrees with the author. Lincoln's name, however, associates respect and authority with the writing.

Card Stacking

If you want to persuade someone, should you present all sides of the issue? Card stacking refers to "stacking the cards" in your favor and only presenting the facts and figures that are favorable to your particular side of the issue.

Example: Tobacco companies do not volunteer unfavorable cancer research in advertisements for smoking.

The Bandwagon

The bandwagon approach is to give the impression that everybody is doing it and you will be left out if you do not quickly "jump on the bandwagon" and join the crowd.

Example: Cola commercials usually show large crowds of happy people enjoying soft drinks together as if "everybody were doing it."

Plain Folks

Politicians use this technique to associate their names with average, plain people.

Example: A politician appearing in a field with farmers in casual clothes recounting anecdotes of earlier days of poverty gives the impression that "I'm just one of you."

WHAT IS A FACT AND WHAT IS AN OPINION?

Both fact and opinion are used persuasively to support positions. It is up to you to determine which is which and then to judge the issue accordingly. Adding the quoted opinion of a well-known authority to a few bits of evidence does not improve the data, yet this is an effective persuasive technique. Even though the opinion may be valid, it should not be viewed as fact.

A fact is a statement based on actual evidence or personal observation. It can be checked objectively with empirical data and proved to be either true or false. On the other hand, an opinion is a statement of personal feeling or a judgment. It reflects a belief or an interpretation rather than an accumulation of evidence, and it cannot be proved true or false. Both fact and opinion play a role in evaluation and in decision making, but you need to tell the difference between the two.

Examples:

Fact: Freud developed a theory of personality.
Fact: Freud believed that the personality is divided into three parts.
Opinion: Freud constructed the most complete theory of personality
   development.
Opinion: The personality is divided into three parts: the id, the ego, and the
   superego.

▥▤▥ Exercise 3: Fact of Opinion

Read each of the following and indicate *F* for fact and *O* for opinion.

_____ 1. For women locked into socioeconomic situations that cannot promise
   financial independence, liberation is relatively meaningless and sometimes
   suggests the denial of femininity as a goal.
   Reece McGee et al., *Sociology: An Introduction*

_____ 2. The territorial base from which Soviet ambitions proceed is the largest
   country in area on the globe.
   Wheeler, Kostbade and Thoman, *Regional Geography of the World*

_____ 3. Company sources attribute Coors' success to product quality, boasting that it
   "is the most expensively brewed beer in the world."
   Louis Boone and David L. Kurtz, *Contemporary Business*

_____ 4. If you wish to "break the hunger habit" in order to gain better control over
   your own food intake, you might be wise to do so slowly—by putting
   yourself on a very irregular eating schedule.
   James V. McConnell, *Understanding Human Behavior*

_____ 5. The first step in running for the nomination is to build a personal
   organization, because the party organization is supposed to stay neutral until
   the nomination is decided.
   James M. Burns, J. W. Peltason and Thomas E. Cronin, *Government by the People*

_____ 6. It is true that American politics often rewards with power those who have
   proved that they can direct the large institutions of commerce and business,
   of banking, and of law, education, and philanthropy.
   Kenneth Prewitt and Sidney Verba, *An Introduction to American Government*

_____ 7. Precipitation is not uniform, and neither is the distribution of population.
   Robert J. Foster, *Physical Geology*

_____ 8. What Caesar wanted most of all was a military command that would give him
   a reputation equal to that of Pompey.
   Joseph R. Strayer et al, *The Mainstream of Civilization*

_____ 9. At least 10 percent of the world's available food is destroyed by pests, waste,
   and spoilage somewhere between the marketplace and the stomach of the
   consumer.
   Robert Wallace, *Biology: The World of Life*

10. Women, young girls, and even mere children were tortured by driving needles under their nails, roasting their feet in the fire, or crushing their legs under heavy weights until the marrow spurted from their bones, in order to force them to confess to filthy orgies with demons.

Edward M. Burns, Western Civilizations

WHAT IS THE AUTHOR'S PURPOSE?

An author always has a purpose in mind when putting words on paper. In textbook writing, the reader expects that the author's purpose will be to inform or explain and, in general, this is true. At times, however, texts can slip from factual explanation to persuasion. The sophisticated reader recognizes this shift in purpose and thus is more critical in evaluating the content. A persuasive paragraph for or against birth control alerts the reader to be more skeptical and less accepting than a paragraph explaining how birth control methods work. Be aware that a textbook author can shift from an objective and factual explanation of a topic to a subjective and opinionated treatment of the facts. Recognizing the author's purpose does not mean that you won't buy the product; it just means that you are a more cautious, well-informed consumer.

Exercise 4: Author's Purpose

Read the following passage from a biology textbook and notice how the explanation is mixed with persuasion.

Minamata is a small fishing village on the southern Japanese island of Kyushu. It is also the home of the Chisso chemical company whose founder is credited with saying, "Treat the workers like cows and horses." But they did worse. They polluted Minamata Bay so drastically that the beautiful sea was turned into a veritable sludge dump of industrial poisons. Years ago the people found that their fish catches were falling off and blamed the company, which eventually paid each fisherman a token amount and continued to pollute. Finally, in the early 1950s a mysterious disease began to take the citizens of the town. It was called the "strange disease" because no one knew what caused it. When anyone accused the company, Chisso would produce a gallery of "expert witnesses" who would faithfully exonerate it. It blocked every effort to stop its dumping. Once, when it began to dump in a new place, people there began to fall ill. Finally, one of its researchers could keep quiet no longer. The agent was mercury from the company's drains.

"Minamata Disease" begins with a tingling around the lips. Then numbness sets in and speech blurs. Finally blindness engulfs the victims even as their movements become jerky and uncoordinated and they shout uncontrollably. Many die. The famous essay photographer, W. Eugene Smith, went to Minamata to shoot pictures of the victims' plight and at a demonstration received a broken back by the hands of thugs for his trouble. What he found were helpless people, cared for by their families, people who would never recover because they had eaten fish from Minamata Bay. Autopsies showed the brains of the victims were soft and spongy because the cells had deteriorated, the result of methyl-poisoning. The culprit was unveiled when a company researcher fed effluent to the now-famous "cat number 400" and it developed the disease. The company immediately censured the researcher and hid his findings. Chisso continued to pollute the water until 1968 when the mercury method of production became outmoded. But people continued to fall ill. Kumamoto University doctors have suggested that the number may reach 10,000.

Robert Wallace, Biology: The World of Life

1. What is the author's purpose in this passage?

   _____

2. Does the author use facts or opinions to persuade the reader? Explain your answer and mark the sentences in the passage that are statements of opinion.

   _____

   _____

   _____

   _____

   _____

WHAT IS THE AUTHOR'S TONE?

The tone of an author's writing is similar to the tone of a speaker's voice. For listeners, it is fairly easy to tell the difference between an angry tone and a romantic tone by noticing the speaker's voice. Distinguishing between humor, sarcasm, and irony, however, may be more difficult. Humorous remarks are designed to be comical and amusing while sarcastic remarks are designed to cut or give pain. Ironic remarks, on the other hand, express something other than the literal meaning and are designed to show the incongruity between the actual and the expected. Making such precise distinctions requires more than just listening to sounds; it requires a careful evaluation of what is said. Since the sound of the voice is not heard in reading, clues to the tone must come from the writer's presentation of the message. The reader's job is to look for clues to answer the question, "What is the author's attitude toward the topic?"

The following is a list of some of the words that can be used to describe the author's tone. Can you imagine an example for each?

angry	depressing	happy	hostile
bitter	enthusiastic	hateful	humorous
cynical	fearful	hopeful	hypocritical
defensive	gloomy	horrifying	hysterical

insulting	loving	pessimistic	scornful
intellectual	miserable	professional	serious
ironic	nostalgic	respectful	sincere
jovial	objective	sarcastic	sympathetic
lonely	optimistic	satirical	threatening

▮▤▮ Exercise 5: Author's Tone

Read the following passage to determine the author's attitude toward the topic.

Columbus

The human mind is affected with a singular disability to get a sense of an historical event without a gigantic figure in the foreground overtopping all his fellows. As surely as God liveth, if one hundred congenital idiots were set adrift in a scow to get rid of them, and, borne by favoring currents into eyeshot of an unknown continent, should simultaneously shout, "Land ho!", we should have one of them figuring in history ever thereafter with a growing glory as an illustrious discoverer of his time. I do not say that Columbus was a navigator and discoverer of that kind, nor that he did anything of that kind in that way; the parallel is perfect only in what history has done to Columbus; and some seventy millions of Americans are authenticating the imposture all they know how. In this whole black business hardly one element of falsehood is lacking.

The Sardonic Humor of Ambrose Bierce

1. What is the author's attitude toward the topic?

_____

2. What is the tone? _____

3. How do the choice of words and the choice of details establish the tone? Give examples.

_____

_____

_____

_____

POLITICAL CARTOONS

Political cartoons vividly illustrate how an author or an artist can effectively communicate bias without making a direct verbal statement. Through their drawings, cartoonists have great freedom to be extremely harsh and judgmental. For example, cartoonists take position on local and national news events and frequently depict politicians as crooks, thieves, or even murderers. Since the accusations are implied rather than directly stated, the cartoonist communicates a bias but is still safe from libel charges.

To illustrate, study the cartoon on the Internal Revenue Service to determine what the cartoonist feels and is saying about the agency. Use the following steps to help you analyze the implied meaning and the bias.

1. Glance at the cartoon for an overview and then read the caption.
2. Answer the question, "What is this about?" to determine the general topic.

_____

3. Return to the drawing to study the symbolism. Look at the dress and facial expressions of the characters. Answer the question, "Who or what does each person represent?"

   Family: _____

   _____

   Pirates: _____

   _____

4. Move to the objects, signs, and other supporting details and answer the question, "How do these things contribute to the general topic?"

   1. _____

   2. _____

   3. _____

   4. _____

   5. _____

5. With all the information in mind, answer the question, "What is the main point the cartoonist is trying to get across?"

   _____

   _____

6. Taking the message into consideration, answer "What is the cartoonist's purpose?"

   _____

   _____

7. What is the tone of the cartoon?

   _____

Reprinted by permission of United Features Syndicate.

8. What is the cartoonist's point of view?

_____

_____

To summarize, the cartoonist feels that the Internal Revenue Service has no mercy, and is even masochistic, in torturing and stripping the taxpayer. The tone is sarcastic and bitter, the purpose is to ridicule, and the point of view is strongly anti-IRS.

▞▞▞ Exercise 6: Political Cartoons

Use the same steps to analyze the message and answer the questions on the next cartoon. Be sensitive that only one side of the issue is being presented.

1. What is the general topic of this cartoon?

_____

Reprinted by permission of United Features Syndicate.

2. Who or what does each person represent?

   Side 1: _____

   _____

   Side 2: _____

   _____

3. How do the objects, signs, and details contribute to the general topic?

   Side 1: _____

   _____

   Side 2: _____

   _____

4. What is the main point the cartoonist is trying to convey?

   _____

   _____

5. What is the cartoonist's purpose?

_____

6. What is the tone of the cartoon?

_____

7. What is the cartoonist's point of view?

_____

As stated in the beginning of the chapter, even in college textbooks, the authors' attitudes and biases slip through. It is the reader's responsibility to be alert for signs of manipulation and to be ready to question interpretations and conclusions. Sophisticated readers are aware and draw their own conclusions based on their own interpretation of the facts. The following exercises use examples from different subject-matter areas. Notice how the authors' biases creep into the seemingly factual presentations.

▦▤▥ Exercise 7: Government

Propaganda has been treated as an unmitigated evil, but that is a simplistic approach. Indeed, it is hard to say just where propaganda ends and education starts. Effective education may include some propaganda (in favor, say, of democratic values, the virtues of which must be taken in part on faith). And if propaganda is defined as a "method used for influencing the conduct of others on behalf of predetermined ends," then almost every person who writes or talks with a purpose becomes a propagandist. Lasswell has described propaganda as a technique for social control—"the manipulation of collective attitudes by the use of significant symbols (words, pictures, and tunes) rather than violence, bribery, or boycott." Obviously propaganda in these terms may be used for good causes as well as bad.*

Burns, Peltason and Cronin, *Government by the People*

_____ 1. The author's major objective in this paragraph is to point out
  a. the good side of propaganda
  b. the bad side of propaganda
  c. both the good and bad sides of propaganda
  d. how education can combat propaganda

_____ 2. The author is assuming that the reader is already greatly aware of all of the following except
  a. the benefits of propaganda
  b. the dangers of propaganda
  c. the traditional definition of propaganda
  d. the techniques of propaganda

*Burns/Peltason/Cronin, *Government by the People*, National, State and Local Edition, 9th Edition, © 1975, pp. 267. Reprinted by permission of Prentice-Hall, Inc., Englewood Cliffs, NJ.

3. Which of the following sentences, except for a few emotive words, is a statement of fact?
   a. "Propaganda has been . . . ."
   b. Effective education may . . . ."
   c. "And if propaganda . . . ."
   d. none of the above
4. The author's primary reason for using the quotation by Lasswell is to
   a. give an unbiased, authoritative definition of propaganda
   b. show the good and bad in propaganda
   c. add credibility to his own argument by quoting an authority
   d. give a modern definition to an overused word
5. Which of the following words, as used in this paragraph, is the least emotional?
   a. *evil*
   b. *democratic*
   c. *virtues*
   d. *education*

▥▤▥ Exercise 8: Science

The seas contain very few animals outwardly as unattractive as the oyster. Misshapen, drab, practically motionless, and devoid of expression, the oyster presents little to stir in the imagination or aesthetic sensibilities. Nevertheless, in its prosaic way, the oyster contributes more to the welfare of man than any other invertebrate of the sea, and its geologic history is long and informative. Kilometer after kilometer of oyster banks and reefs fringe the warmer borders of the continents, furnishing food and raw materials for man. The approximate annual world production of oyster meat approaches 54 million kilograms, and in several countries, especially the United States, France, the Netherlands, Japan, and Australia, oyster fishing is an important industry. Oyster shells are dredged by the thousands of tons from shallow banks and used for construction material and other purposes. A number of mollusks popularly called oysters are not really members of the genus Ostrea; among these are "pearl oysters," genus Melagrina. More than 1,000 species of oysters, including fossil and living species are known.

William Lee Stokes, *Essentials of Earth History*

1. The author's major objective in this paragraph is to emphasize the
   a. unattractive appearance of the oyster
   b. importance of the oyster to man
   c. many different species of oysters
   d. many ways in which oyster shells are used
2. Which of the following sentences is a statement of fact?
   a. "The seas contain . . . ."
   b. "Nevertheless, in its . . . ."
   c. The approximate annual . . . ."
   d. none of the above

3. Which of the following words, as used in this paragraph, is the least emotional?
   a. *unattractive*   c. *invertebrate*
   b. *drab*   d. *welfare*
4. By stating that the "pearl oyster" is not really a member of the genus *Ostrea,* the author is trying to do all of the following except
   a. relate to what the reader already knows
   b. dispel a myth
   c. show that everything that looks like an oyster isn't one
   d. explain the process of pearl formation
5. The author seems to be most intrigued with the oyster's
   a. geologic history
   b. practically motionless position in the sea
   c. annual production of food for the world
   d. contrasting bad looks and extreme importance

▥ ▤ ▥ Exercise 9: Literature

love, *n.* A temporary insanity curable by marriage or by removal of the patient from the influences under which he incurred the disorder. This disease, like caries and many other ailments, is prevalent only among civilized races living under artificial conditions; barbarous nations breathing pure air and eating simple food enjoy immunity from its ravages. It is sometimes fatal, but more frequently to the physician than to the patient.

Ambrose Bierce, *The Devil's Dictionary*

1. The author's major objective in this selection is to
   a. praise love
   b. ridicule love
   c. condemn love
   d. promote love
2. The author feels that marriage is
   a. the beginning of love
   b. the end of love
   c. the continuation of love
   d. the vehicle of a greater growth of love
3. The author believes that love is
   a. a social necessity
   b. a part of the natural order
   c. a disease like tooth decay
   d. a lasting bond of affection
4. The author believes that the most dangerous position is
   a. to be in love
   b. to be loved by someone
   c. not to be loved
   d. to try to cure love

5. Which of the following words, as used in the paragraph, is the least emotional?
   a. *insanity*
   b. *barbarous*
   c. *races*
   d. *ravages*

Exercise 10: History

The surprising thing about the War of Independence when you compare it with other wars of liberation is not that the Americans won, but that they did not win more easily. All they had to do to gain independence was to hold what they had. The British, on the contrary, had to reconquer a vast territory in order to win. To get troops in action against the 'rebels' of 1775–83, the British government had to send them by bulky, slow-moving sailing vessels which never took less than four weeks (and often ten) to cross the Atlantic. Moreover, those who 'came three thousand miles and died, to keep the Past upon its throne,' had to be armed, clothed, and even partly fed from England, which meant more shipping, more delays, more losses at sea, and such expense as had never been known in English history.

Morison, Commager and Leuchtenburg, *A Concise History of the American Republic*

_____ 1. By using the terms, "War of Independence" and "other wars of liberation," the author indicates that he
   a. wishes that the British had won
   b. understands the American point of view
   c. is an impartial observer
   d. is careful to use the correct terminology

_____ 2. The author's major objective in this paragraph is to
   a. show the dedication of the British to the war
   b. emphasize the difficulties confronting the British in the war
   c. minimize the American accomplishments in the war
   d. chastise the Americans for their inefficiency

_____ 3. The author is assuming that the reader
   a. has a preconceived bias in favor of the American war effort
   b. has a preconceived bias in favor of the British
   c. is unbiased in viewing the war
   d. is trying to decide which side deserved to win

_____ 4. Which of the following sentences, except for a few emotive words, is a statement of fact?
   a. "The surprising thing . . . ."
   b. "All they had . . . ."
   c. "To get troops . . . ."
   d. none of the above

5. Which of the following words, as used in this paragraph, is the least emotional?
   a. *surprising*   c. *vessels*
   b. *'rebels'*   d. *liberation*

LITERATURE

William Hogarth. *Gin Lane.*
The Metropolitan Museum of Art,
Harris Brisbane Dick Fund.

Stage 1: Preview

Preview the selection and complete the following sentence: After reading this

selection, I would like to know _____

_____

Stage 2: Integrate Knowledge While Reading

Use thinking strategies as you read:

1. *Predict*
2. *Picture*
3. *Form analogies*

4. *Verbalize points*
5. *Fix up strategies*

A MODEST PROPOSAL*
for Preventing the Children of Poor People in Ireland From Being a Burden to Their Parents or Country, and for Making Them Beneficial to the Public.

Jonathan Swift

It is a melancholy object to those who walk through this great town or travel in the country, when they see the street, the roads, and cabin doors, crowded with beggars of the female sex, followed by three, four, or six children, all in rags, an importuning every passenger for an alms. These mothers, instead of being able to work for their honest
5 livelihood, are forced to employ all their time in strolling to beg sustenance for their helpless infants, who, as they grow up, either turn thieves for want of work, or leave their dear native country, to fight for the Pretender in Spain, or sell themselves to the Barbadoes.

    I think it is agreed by all parties that this prodigious number of children in the arms, or
10 on the backs, or at the heels of their mothers, and frequently of their fathers, is in the present deplorable state of the kingdom a very great additional grievance; and therefore whoever could find out a fair, cheap, and easy method of making these children sound and useful members of the common-wealth, would deserve so well of the public as to have its statue up for a preserver of the nation.
15   But my intention is very far from being confined to provide only for the children of professed beggars; it is of much greater extent, and shall take in the whole number of infants at a certain age, who are born of parents in effect as little able to support them, as those who demand our charity in the streets.

    As to my own part, having turned my thoughts, for many years, upon this important
20 subject, and maturely weighed the several schemes of other projectors, I have always found them grossly mistaken in their computation. It is true, a child just dropt from its dam, may be supported by her milk for a solar year with little other nourishment, at most not above the value of two shillings, which the mother may certainly get, or the value in scraps, by her lawful occupation of begging; and it is exactly at one year old that I
25 propose to provide for them in such a manner, as, instead of being a charge upon their parents, or the parish, or wanting food and raiment for the rest of their lives, they shall, on the contrary, contribute to the feeding and partly to the clothing of many thousands.

*LEARNING STRATEGY: Look for the irony in this selection. What is the difference between what Swift is saying and what he really means?

There is likewise another great advantage in my scheme, that it will prevent those voluntary abortions, and that horrid practice of women murdering their bastard children, alas! too frequent among us—sacrificing the poor innocent babes, I doubt, more to avoid the expense than the shame—which would move tears and pity in the most savage and inhuman breast.

The number of souls in this kingdom being usually reckoned one million and a half, of these I calculate there may be about two hundred thousand couples whose wives are breeders; from which number I subtract thirty thousand couples, who are able to maintain their own children, although I apprehend there cannot be so many, under the present distresses of the kingdom; but this being granted, there will remain an hundred and seventy thousand breeders. I again subtract fifty thousand, for those women who miscarry, or whose children die by accident or disease within the year. There only remain an hundred and twenty thousand children of poor parents annually born: The question therefore is, How this number shall be reared, and provided for: which, as I have already said, under the present situation of affairs, is utterly impossible by all the methods hitherto proposed; for we can neither employ them in handicraft or agriculture; we neither build houses (I mean in the country) nor cultivate land: They can very seldom pick up a livelihood by stealing till they arrive at six years old, except where they are of towardly parts, although, I confess, they learn the rudiments much earlier; during which time they can however be properly looked upon only as probationers; as I have been informed by a principal gentleman in the county of Cavan, who protested to me, that he never knew above one or two instances under the age of six, even in a part of the kingdom so renowned for the quickest proficiency in that art.

I am assured by our merchants, that a boy or a girl before twelve years old, is no saleable commodity, and even when they come to this age, they will not yield above three pounds, or three pounds and a half a crown at most, on the exchange; which cannot turn to account either to the parents or kingdom, the charge of nutriment and rags having been at least four times that value.

I shall now therefore humbly propose my own thoughts, which I hope will not be liable to the least objection.

I have been assured by a very knowing American of my acquaintance in London, that a young healthy child well nursed is at a year old a most delicious nourishing and wholesome food, whether stewed, roasted, baked, or boiled; and I make no doubt that it will equally serve in a fricasee, or a ragout.

I do therefore humbly offer it to public consideration, that of the hundred and twenty thousand children, already computed, twenty thousand may be reserved for breed, whereof only one-fourth part to be males; which is more than we allow to sheep, black cattle, or swine; and my reason is that these children are seldom the fruits of marriage, a circumstance not much regarded by our savages; therefore one male will be sufficient to serve four females. That the remaining hundred thousand may, at a year old, be offered in the sale to the persons of quality and fortune through the kingdom; always advising the mother to let them suck plentifully in the last month, so as to render them plump and fat for a good table. A child will make two dishes at an entertainment for friends; and when the family dines alone, the fore or hind quarter will make a reasonable dish, and seasoned with a little pepper or salt will be very good boiled on the fourth day, especially in winter.

I have reckoned upon a medium that a child just born will weight 12 pounds, and in a solar year, if tolerably nursed, increaseth to 28 pounds. I grant this food will be somewhat dear, and therefore very proper for landlords, who, as they have already devoured most of the parents, seem to have the best title to the children.

Infants' flesh will be in season throughout the year, but more plentiful in March, and a little before and after; for we are told by a grave author, and eminent French physician, that fish being a prolific diet, there are more children born in Roman Catholic countries about nine months after Lent than at any other season; therefore, reckoning a year after Lent, the markets will be more glutted than usual, because the number of popish infants is at least three to one in this kingdom; and therefore it will have one other collateral advantage, by lessening the number of papists among us.

I have already computed the charge of nursing a beggar's child (in which list I reckon all cottagers, laborers, and four-fifths of the farmers) to be about two shillings per annum, rags included; and I believe no gentleman would repine to give ten shillings for the carcass of a good fat child, which, as I have said, will make four dishes of excellent nutritive meat, when he hath only some particular friend or his own family to dine with him. Thus the squire will learn to be a good landlord, and grow popular among his tenants; the mother will have eight shillings net profit, and be fit for work till she produces another child.

Those who are more thrifty (as I must confess the times require) may flay the carcass, the skin of which artificially dressed will make admirable gloves for ladies, and summer boots for fine gentlemen.

As to our city of Dublin, shambles may be appointed for this purpose in the most convenient parts of it, and butchers we may be assured will not be wanting; although I rather recommend buying the children alive and dressing them hot from the knife, as we do roasting pigs.

I can think of no one objection that will possibly be raised against this proposal, unless it should be urged that the number of people will be thereby much lessened in the kingdom. This I freely own, and 'twas indeed one principal design in offering it to the world. I desire the reader will observe that I calculate my remedy for this one individual kingdom of Ireland, and for no other that ever was, is, or, I think, ever can be upon earth. Therefore let no man talk to me of expedients: of taxing our absentees at five shillings a pound: of using neither clothes, nor household furniture, except what is of our own growth and manufacture: of utterly rejecting the materials and instruments that promote foreign luxury: of curing the expensiveness of pride, vanity, idleness, and gaming in our women: of introducing a vein of parsimony, prudence and temperance: of learning to love our country, where in we differ even from Laplanders, and the inhabitants of Topinamboo: of quitting our animosities, and factions, not act any longer like the Jews, who were murdering one another at the very moment their city was taken: of being a little cautious not to sell our country and consciences for nothing: of teaching landlords to have at least one degree of mercy towards their tenants. Lastly, of putting a spirit of honesty, industry, and skill into our shop-keepers, who, if a resolution could now be taken to buy only our native goods, would immediately unite to cheat and exact upon us in the price, the measure, and the goodness, nor could ever yet be brought to make one fair proposal of just dealing, though often and earnestly invited to it.

I profess, in the sincerity of my heart, that I have not the least personal interest in endeavoring to promote this necessary work, having no other motive than the public good of my country, by advancing our trade, providing for infants, relieving the poor, and giving some pleasure to the rich. I have no children by which I can propose to get a single penny; the youngest being nine years old, and my wife past child-bearing.   /1869

Stage 3: Recall

Stop and recall what you have read. Review your use of the thinking strategies. Did you use all five?

▥▤▥ Skill Development: Detecting Bias

Answer the following with *T* (true), *F* (false), or *CT* (can't tell).

_____ 1. The author's major purpose in this selection is to make the reader laugh.
_____ 2. The author uses statistics to add credibility to his proposal.
_____ 3. The author's organizational strategy is to sell the reader on the need and advantages of his plan before explaining it.
_____ 4. The author feels that poor families take advantage of landlords.

Which of the following word(s), as used in this selection, is the least emotional?

_____ 5. a. *cabin doors*
              b. *honest livelihood*
              c. *helpless infants*
              d. *a beggar's child*
_____ 6. a. *parties*
              b. *prodigious*
              c. *great*
              d. *deplorable*
_____ 7. a. *breeders*
              b. *miscarry*
              c. *stealing*
              d. *agriculture*

For each of the following excerpts, indicate *F* for fact and *O* for opinion.

_____ 8. "It is true, a child just dropt from its dam, may be supported by her milk for a solar year with little other nourishment . . . ."
_____ 9. "The number of souls in this kingdom being usually reckoned one million and a half . . . ."
_____ 10. "I have no children by which I can propose to get a single penny . . . ."

▥▤▥ Comprehension Questions

1. The main point the author is trying to get across in this selection is _____
_____
_____

© Scott, Foresman and Company.

After reading the selection, answer the following questions with *a, b, c,* or *d.*

2. The author states that he intends his proposal to apply to the children of
   a. professional beggars only
   b. the rich and poor alike
   c. parents who cannot afford them
   d. beggars and politicians

3. The major reason the author proposes the age of one year for the sale of a child is because the child would then
   a. be most plump and tender
   b. not yet be educated in the ways of thievery
   c. be taken away before parental attachment develops
   d. bring the greatest profit for the least expense

4. The author feels that abortion is mainly due to
   a. unfeeling mothers
   b. financial necessity
   c. shame
   d. the country's laws regarding unwed mothers

5. The author proposes, through careful calculation, that the number of children to be sold for food each year should be
   a. two hundred thousand
   b. one hundred and seventy thousand
   c. one hundred and twenty thousand
   d. one hundred thousand

6. In the author's proposal the sex ratio of the children who are to be sold for food at the age of one year
   a. should be half male and half female
   b. should be one fourth male and three fourths female
   c. should be largely female
   d. is not determined

7. The author implies that landlords
   a. have good taste and deserve the best
   b. take unfair advantage of the poor
   c. are popular among their tenants
   d. teach mercy to their tenants

8. Underlying the satire of this selection, the author seriously proposes all of the following solutions to the poverty problems of Ireland except
   a. a form of absentee taxation
   b. the purchase of native goods before foreign imports
   c. a national concern for thrift and a love of country
   d. an extermination of the poor similar to the murdering of Jews

9. The irony of the author's final statements is that
   a. his concern is purely for the good of the country

b. he will not be affected by the cruelty of his proposal

c. he cannot realize any profits from his own proposal

d. he does not care about the poor or the country

_____ 10. The author uses satire in this selection for all of the following reasons except

a. to dramatize the horror and desperation of the problem

b. to entertain

c. to lessen the impact of the problem

d. to shock

Answer the following with *T* (true), *F* (false), or *CT* (can't tell).

_____ 11. The author feels that the Irish should leave their country and fight for the Pretender of Spain

_____ 12. The author implies that Americans are somewhat savage.

_____ 13. The author implies that there is an unemployment problem in Ireland.

_____ 14. The Roman Catholics composed a minority of the Irish population.

_____ 15. The author has lived in Ireland all of his life.

▥▤▥ Vocabulary

According to the way the boldface word was used in the selection, indicate *a, b, c,* or *d* for the word that gives the best definition.

___ 1. "**importuning** every passenger (03)"

a. begging

b. welcoming

c. introducing

d. attacking

___ 2. "for an **alms** (04)"

a. sympathy

b. job

c. money

d. flower

___ 3. "to beg **sustenance** (05)"

a. shelter

b. food

c. forgiveness

d. mercy

___ 4. "**prodigious** number of children (09)"

a. increasing

b. unmanageable

c. enormous

d. solitary

___ 5. "the present **deplorable** state (11)"

a. unfortunate

b. convincing

c. remorseful

d. unstable

___ 6. "wanting food and **raiment** (26)"

a. money

b. lodging

c. pension

d. clothing

7. "more **glutted** than usual (82)"
   a. depleted
   b. expensive
   c. flooded
   d. popular

8. "one other **collateral** advantage (85)"
   a. opposite
   b. accompanying
   c. antagonistic
   d. redeeming

9. "would **repine** to give (89)"
   a. fail
   b. request
   c. neglect
   d. complain

10. "introducing a vein of **parsimony** (111)"
   a. stinginess
   b. trust
   c. loyalty
   d. pride

▪▪▪ Essay Question: Interpreting Illustrations

Although the illustration that accompanies "A Modest Proposal" describes an English street scene, how does it compare in purpose to Swift's essay? Use a sheet of notebook paper to record your answer.

Selection **2**

HISTORY

PUCK.

LET THEM HAVE IT ALL, AND BE DONE WITH IT!

© Scott, Foresman and Company.

Culver Pictures

Stage 1: Preview

Preview the selection and complete the following sentence: After reading this

selection, I would like to know _____

_____

Stage 2: Integrate Knowledge While Reading

Use thinking strategies as you read:

1. *Predict*   4. *Verbalize points*
2. *Picture*   5. *Fix up strategies*
3. *Form analogies*

THE RUTHLESS POWER OF BIG BUSINESS*

Leonard Pitt, from *We Americans*

Natural resources and technological ability alone would probably not have made America
the leading industrial nation. Big business was a vital link. America's new wealth came
primarily from manufacturing. Most impressive were the advances in railroads,
steamships, farm tools, and the steel and chemical industries.

5   The railroad was the first to leap ahead. In the spring of 1869 at Promontory Point,
Utah, a golden spike was driven into the rail that completed the first transcontinental line.
Chugging across flat plains and through high mountain passes, scattering the buffalo in
their paths, railroads could now carry goods and passengers from coast to coast.
      The new east-west rail line did more than mark the finish of the first railroad to cross

10 the continent. It also opened the Age of Big Business. The railroads were the first of the
giant corporations that were to assume such a commanding place in American life. Their
owners—the empire builders whose vision spanned the continent—needed more capital
and labor than ever before. Banks and financial syndicates sprang up to lend them
money. Construction companies were organized to carry out their plans. New and bigger

15 unions were formed to organize railroad workers. The government set up the first
regulatory agencies to control the lines. As their finances increased, the railroads
organized their own subsidiaries to store grain, drill oil, cut timber, or mine coal and ore
on their own land. They spent millions in lobbying—and graft—to get grants of money
and land from federal and state governments. And they also sold and leased the land on a

20 huge scale.
      The era gave rise to a new type of business leader. Called "robber barons" or
"tycoons," they were known for their ruthless competition and their indifference to the
needs of either their workers or the public. "The public be damned!" Cornelius

*LEARNING STRATEGY: Look critically at how the ruthless power of big business was both an
advantage and a disadvantage to the nation and its creation of wealth.

Pitt: *We Americans,* Second Edition. Copyright © 1984 Kendall/Hunt Publishing Company. Reprinted
with permission.

Vanderbilt once exclaimed. Vanderbilt and Collis P. Huntington in railroads, Andrew
25 Carnegie in steel, John D. Rockefeller in oil, Phillip D. Armour in meat packing, Cyrus
McCormick in farm machinery, and Jay Cooke and J. P. Morgan in finance controlled
enormous chunks of money and power. They considered themselves rugged
individualists. A few rose from rags to riches, but most worked their way up from
moderately comfortable surroundings.
30   While the new tycoons were thought of as self-made men, it is misleading to ignore the
help they got from Uncle Sam and from state governments. Some of the largest fortunes
in railroads, oil, timber, water power, coal, cattle, and land were made from the public
domain. The federal government granted 131 million acres of public land to the railroads,
and the states added another 40 million acres.
35   Andrew Carnegie, who emigrated from Scotland with his poor parents in 1848, amassed
a fortune in iron and steel. In 1872 he began using the new Bessemer process to make
steel for railroad tracks. Seven years later he had virtually cornered the market on steel
production. His own barges and railroad cars carried mountains of iron ore and coal to
his giant mills in Pennsylvania. The secret to his success, Carnegie said, was to control the
40 resources:

> Two pounds of ironstone mined upon Lake Superior and transported nine hundred miles to
> Pittsburgh; one pound and one-half of lime, mined and transported to Pittsburgh; a small amount
> of manganese ore mined in Virginia and brought to Pittsburgh—and these four pounds of
> materials manufactured into one pound of steel, for which the consumer pays one cent.

45   Some tycoons built their fortunes by ruthlessly destroying the competition. A classic
example was John D. Rockefeller. He organized Standard Oil in 1870 and in 1882 formed
the Standard Oil Trust—the first trust ever organized—which represented a combination
of 77 different oil companies. A master of cutthroat competition, Rockefeller also
organized the South Improvement Company, a transportation business that has been
50 called by Stewart Holbrook "the boldest, most naked attempt at dry-land piracy" in all of
history. It contracted for special rebates with leading eastern railroads that shipped its oil.
From them it got in exchange secret information about competitors, as well as secret
rebate payments for shipping the oil of competitors. In effect it was getting some of the
profit of competing firms. When necessary, the early Rockefeller companies used hired
55 goons to dynamite the refineries of competitors and bribed various elected officials in
New Jersey and Pennsylvania. Six U.S. senators were on the company payroll (one
received a salary of $100,000) and were expected to favor Standard Oil with special laws.
The company contracted with more than a hundred Ohio newspapers to print only stories
that put Standard Oil in a favorable light. By these methods—and through new
60 technology and efficient management—Rockefeller amassed a personal fortune of $800
million and created a billion-dollar industrial corporation. A devout Baptist, Rockefeller
felt convinced that "God gave me my money" and that the South Improvement Company
was "right between me and my God."
    When the captains of industry retired or died off, many of the major corporations they
65 had formed remained in existence. These large corporate organizations were not
dependent on a single leader nor limited to the time span of one life. They took
advantage of a simple fact: the bigger the output, the cheaper the unit cost. By gaining
nationwide and, when possible, worldwide markets, they magnified profits. Even greater
profits could be earned if competition could be cut out. Sometimes competing
70 companies agreed to limit production or to charge the same prices. These agreements

© Scott, Foresman and Company.

were not legally binding, and the "pools," as they were called, broke down when one member pulled out.

A lawyer for Standard Oil invented a stronger device—the trust. Competing companies were "invited" to have their securities administered by a common board of trustees while
75 keeping the profits for themselves. In this way they coordinated their operations instead of competing with one another. Soon there were trusts controlling petroleum, cottonseed oil, whiskey, sugar, lead, and other products. When the trusts were attacked by state and federal governments, they reorganized into holding companies. A corporation was formed to hold a controlling interest in a group of related companies. These arrangements were
80 legal. The simple merger, where one company bought out another, was yet another route. In the late 1890s a wave of mergers hit the manufacturing and mining industries.

So strong was the trend toward concentration that in a number of industries it looked as if one company would completely dominate the field by the end of the century. In 1870 there were nineteen locomotive makers; thirty years later there were only two.
85 Standard Oil of Ohio refined 80 to 90 percent of the oil in 1879. At first bigness resulted in lower prices for the consumer. But when a producer established a monopoly, consumers had to pay any price the company set.

Say what one will of the "robber barons"—that they were crude and ruthless and exploited their workers mercilessly—it is also true that they contributed in a
90 revolutionary way to the creation of new material wealth. They did so by bringing together labor power, resouces, and intelligence at a particular moment in time when they could make a lasting mark on American history. /1308

Stage 3: Recall

Stop and recall what you have read. Review your use of the thinking strategies. Did you use all five?

Skill Development: Detecting Bias in the Cartoon

Return to the political cartoon and answer the following questions:

1. What is the general topic of this cartoon?

   _____

2. Who or what does each person represent?

   _____

   _____

3. How do the objects, signs, and details contribute to the general topic?

   _____

   _____

4. What is the main point the cartoonist is trying to get across?

_____

_____

5. What is the cartoonist's purpose?

_____

6. What is the tone of the cartoon?

_____

7. What is the cartoonist's point of view?

_____

▥▤▥ Skill Development: Detecting Bias in the Text

Answer the following with *T* (true), *F* (false), or *CT* (can't tell).

_____   1. The author's intent in this selection is to show the positive force of big business on America's industrial development.

_____   2. The author includes Vanderbilt's quotation, "The public be damned!" to illustrate the public's indifference to big business.

_____   3. The author mentions that Rockefeller was a devout Baptist and quotes him in order to dramatize the irony between his philosophy and his practices.

_____   4. The author implies that the railroads engaged in corruption to obtain land from the government.

Which of the following word(s), as used in this selection, is the least emotional?

_____   5. a. *ruthless power*
     b. *empire builders*
     c. *different oil companies*
     d. *robber barons*

_____   6. a. *graft*
     b. *management*
     c. *rebates*
     d. *cutthroat competition*

_____   7. a. *worldwide market*
     b. *goons*
     c. *lobbying*
     d. *exploited their workers*

For each of the following sentences, indicate *F* for fact and *O* for opinion.

8. "The railroads were the first of the giant corporations that were to assume such a commanding place in American life."

9. "While the new tycoons were thought of as self-made men, it is misleading to ignore the help they got from Uncle Sam and from state governments."

10. "Standard Oil of Ohio refined 80 to 90 percent of the oil in 1879."

Comprehension Questions

1. The main point the author is trying to get across in this selection is _____

_____

_____

After reading the selection, answer the following questions with *a, b, c,* or *d.*

2. According to the author the railroad spurred a cause-and-effect relationship with all of the following except
   a. lending institutions
   b. labor unions
   c. government regulatory agencies
   d. natural resources

3. By organizing subsidiaries to store grain, drill oil, etc., the railroad's main purpose was to
   a. contribute to America's growth
   b. get the maximum profit from its land holdings
   c. create additional jobs for its labor force
   d. force the government to give it more land

4. According to the author the railroads acquired government land by
   a. trading oil, timber, and iron ore
   b. paying the market price
   c. organizing subsidiaries
   d. illegally influencing political figures

5. The author primarily includes the quoted paragraph beginning with "Two pounds of . . . ." to illustrate
   a. Pittsburgh's function as an industrial center
   b. Carnegie's control of the resources
   c. the cheap price paid by the consumer for steel
   d. the diversity of ingredients used in steel manufacturing

6. The author implies that Rockefeller made his fortune through all of the following except
   a. bribery   c. espionage
   b. coercion   d. religion

7. The major purpose of establishing a trust is to
   a. eliminate competition, control price, and increase profits
   b. shift to central management for policy decisions
   c. stimulate competition among businesses of common interest
   d. secure control in order to lower consumer prices

8. Trusts were primarily attacked by the federal government because they
   a. bribed politicians   c. offered rebates
   b. established monopolies   d. earned profits

9. The primary rationale for trusts and holding companies was the desire of a large company to
   a. control the marketplace   c. avoid government regulations
   b. open worldwide markets   d. shelter tax benefits

10. The reduction in the number of locomotive makers from nineteen to two in a thirty-year period is an example of
    a. the inefficiency of small companies
    b. the need for industrial centralization
    c. the control of big business
    d. the restrictions of regulatory agencies

Answer the following with *T* (true), *F* (false), or *CT* (can't tell).

11. The east and west railroad lines were joined together at Promontory Point, Utah.

12. The author implies that most of the leading business tycoons rose to success from very meager beginnings.

13. Without the need for railroad tracks, Andrew Carnegie would not have become a tycoon.

14. The general public was not aware that Standard Oil illegally paid salaries to six U.S. Senators.

15. Major corporations formed by the robber barons today continue the same ruthless practices of their predecessors.

▌▌▌ ▌ ▌ **Vocabulary**

According to the way the boldface word was used in the selection, indicate *a, b, c,* or *d* for the word or phrase that gives the best definition.

_____ 1. "the first **transcontinental** line (06)"
   a. oceanic
   b. international
   c. worldwide
   d. across the continent

_____ 2. "**vision** spanned the continent (12)"
   a. eyeballs
   b. influence
   c. foresight
   d. commands

3. "their own **subsidiaries** (17)"
   a. warehouses
   b. labor leaders
   c. freight cars
   d. auxiliary companies

4. "The **era** gave rise to (21)"
   a. period of time
   b. year
   c. timetable
   d. trend

5. "their **ruthless** competition (22)"
   a. keen
   b. efficient
   c. pitiless
   d. magnanimous

6. "rugged **individualists** (28)"
   a. Westerners
   b. believers in self-expression
   c. slaves to industry
   d. freedom fighters

7. "the new **tycoons** (30)"
   a. wealthy financiers
   b. pioneers
   c. sophisticates
   d. workers

8. "secret **rebate** payments (53)"
   a. sale-priced
   b. retroactive
   c. kickback
   d. reusable

9. "a wave of **mergers** (76)"
   a. antitrusts
   b. bankruptcies
   c. syndications
   d. combination of companies

10. "**exploited** their workers (84)"
    a. took unethical advantage
    b. mistrusted
    c. physically abused
    d. criminally attacked

Essay Question

Explain how the ruthless power of big business could be considered a vital factor in increasing America's wealth. Use a sheet of notebook paper to record your answer.

Summarizing

Write a summary of the selection noting the main points for later reference on a sheet of notebook paper. Be brief, but include the essential elements.

POLITICAL SCIENCE

"*A Senator Fulbright to see you, sire. Seems he can't reconcile himself to your infallibility.*"

Copyright Paul Szep

Stage 1: Preview

Preview the selection and complete the following sentence: After reading this

selection, I would like to know _____

_____

Stage 2: Integrate Knowledge While Reading

Use thinking strategies as you read:

1. *Predict*
2. *Picture*
3. *Form analogies*

4. *Verbalize points*
5. *Fix up strategies*

Outlining

Outline the key ideas in the selection as if you were planning to use your notes to study for a quiz. Use a sheet of notebook paper to record your outline.

THE EFFECTS OF THE PRESIDENCY ON THE PRESIDENT*

Richard Saeger, from *American Government and Politics*

One of the principal criticisms that students of the presidency have leveled at the executive office is that its recent occupants have become isolated, insulated, arrogant, and out of touch with the public and with reality. How valid is this criticism? It can reasonably be argued, I think, that one person's isolation or insulation is another's protection.

5 Presidents have to be insulated to some extent from all those disgruntled taxpayers and courtiers and favor-seekers who would monopolize a President's time if they could. Presidents must also be insulated, and indeed isolated, from all the petty day-to-day details and minor decisions that are best delegated to others. Presidents who insist on attending to such minutiae oftentimes get bogged down in them.

Delegation or Insulation?

10 One mark of an effective President is that he can delegate responsibility to others, thus conserving his time and energy for the most important decisions. FDR, for example, was a master of this art. Nixon, who insisted on planning menus for state dinners and selecting uniforms for the White House guards, was not. Neither was Carter, who prided himself on knowing all the details of his Administration's operations.

15 One responsibility, however, that all recent Presidents have delegated to their aides is the one of limiting access to the Oval Office. Nixon set up a "palace guard," to screen all requests for audiences with the President and all memoranda to the President. Only those persons and communications that his staff felt the President should see got through, and often that did not include members of the President's own cabinet, or influential

20 members of Congress, or their communications.**

The Arrogance of the Office

Is it in the very nature of the presidential office that its occupants appear to be so arrogant? There is a story told about Lyndon Johnson that once, while he was walking

*LEARNING STRATEGY: Look for how the author feels the power of the presidency affects the person who is president. What personality types make good presidents?

**Of course, by delegating so much "gatekeeping" authority to his staff, Nixon could later claim to have had no direct knowledge of the Watergate affair and to buck the blame for that fiasco back to them. If it is true that Nixon knew nothing about Watergate, although his own tapes make his ignorance appear to be feigned, it does illustrate a very useful aspect of a President's choosing to be isolated: "What a President doesn't know, can't hurt him." It is much easier for him to deny wrongdoing or miscalculation if someone else is delegated the task of doing the "dirty work." Presidents then can stand above the fray and remain unsullied by what their subordinates do.

From *American Government and Politics* by Richard T. Saeger, pp. 304–308. Copyright © 1978 by Scott, Foresman and Company.

across an airfield toward what he thought was his helicopter, a young airman came running over to the President to inform him that he was heading toward the wrong
25   helicopter—that *his* helicopter was "over there." Johnson replied, not unkindly, "Son, they're *all my* helicopters."

Surrounded by the trappings of power—helicopters, Air Force One, Camp David, limousines, the Marine Band playing "Hail to the Chief"—is it surprising that Presidents become arrogant? Should it come as a surprise to hear Richard Nixon reply to a question
30   posed by his interviewer, David Frost, as to why he had authorized "illegal" wiretapping and burglaries: "Well, when a President does it, that means that it is not illegal"?

The personal power of the presidency is so awesome that most mere mortals are reduced to quivering, quaking, flattering toadies in the presence of the "Great One." Normally fearless reporters shake when they ask the President questions at press
35   conferences, and seem to be grateful even for evasive answers. Antiwar students who hated Nixon with a passion and who wished for a confrontation with him were content to listen to him ramble on at the Lincoln Memorial about Coach Woody Hayes and Ohio State football. Even the President's closest aides will tell the President what they think he wants to hear, and bring him only good news to ingratiate themselves with him,
40   seemingly for fear that bringing him bad news would cause him, as the kings of old, to lop off their heads.

Former press secretary to Lyndon Johnson, George Reedy, described this phenomenon well.[1] Regardless of how open a President intends to be at the outset of his Administration, the trappings of office, the bowing, scraping, and sycophancy of his aides,
45   and the isolation and insulation of the job will ultimately affect him. Richard Nixon promised an open Administration, but ended up with one of the most closed ones in history. Gerald Ford, at first, made his own English muffins for breakfast and disclaimed any interest in seeking a second term, arguing that he really didn't care to shoulder the burdens of the presidency for another four years. But later he allowed that he was
50   beginning to enjoy the power, perquisites, and adulation that come with being President. And even humble, self-effacing, "aw shucks" Jimmy Carter, who carried his own suit bag during the campaign and early on in his Administration, who refused to allow "Hail to the Chief" to be played in his presence, who sold off the presidential yacht, *Sequoia,* and who appeared on television in jeans and a cardigan sweater—even this President began to
55   change. By 1980, the jeans, cardigan sweater, and suit bag were done, and "Hail to the Chief" was back. In 1980 also, the President's trips into the nation's hinterland to solicit the wise counsel of "just folks" had become part of the history of the Carter Administration. Arguing that the international crises in Iran and Afghanistan were forcing him to remain close to the Oval Office, Carter even refused to campaign for reelection,
60   employing the same strategy that his 1976 opponent, Gerald Ford, had used and which Carter, *qua* 1976 candidate, had criticized as a campaigning "from the Rose Garden."

The Presidential Personality

It seems that in recent history only Harry Truman remained virtually unaffected by the trappings of presidential power. Why that "plain speaking" gentleman from Missouri was so different from all of his successors in the White House has much to do with his
65   personality. James David Barber and other political scientists, political psychologists, and amateur psychoanalysts have suggested that an examination of psychological traits of

[1] George E. Reedy, *The Twilight of the Presidency* (New York: New American Library, 1970).

would-be presidential contenders would tell us much about the people who might someday be President.[2] Perhaps, if we were to scrutinize more closely the characters of these persons, the potentially isolated, insulated, arrogant, and out-of-touch types could be weeded out.

But we had twenty years to observe Richard Nixon, and we still elected him. Most of us had never heard of Jimmy Carter prior to the 1976 campaign, and thus had no chance to observe him at all. Besides, if we looked into the backgrounds of would-be presidential contenders, what would we find? That they had unhappy childhoods? That they grew up poor? That they were ambitious? Some of our best and some of our worst Presidents came from relatively unhappy childhoods, grew up poor, and were ambitious. Moreover, if we had psychological tests that every person who aspired to the presidency had to pass, it is quite possible that either no one would pass or that those who did couldn't be elected.

Years ago, political scientist Harold Lasswell described the kinds of persons who go into politics.[3] By the standards of what we consider normal, political types are frequently abnormal, and it is their abnormality that "drives" them into politics in the first place. They "need" attention, they "need" to achieve, they "need" to be fulfilled; they may even have delusions of grandeur. Thus, those from whom we select our Presidents may not be the most "normal" people in our society. And those who are "normal" are often not very colorful; those who lack color seldom get elected.

One other problem with such examinations as Barber's of presidential personality types is that they contain thinly veiled assumptions about what makes a good President and what makes a bad one. The best Presidents are assumed to be the *active-positive* types who want to accomplish great deeds and who enjoy the office. Less desirable personality types are *active-negative* Presidents who are preoccupied with acquiring and maintaining power for the sake of power, but who don't really enjoy exercising it. *Passive-positive* Presidents are those who want most to be loved and admired, but who choose to do little as President. *Passive-negative* Presidents have a profound sense of civic virtue and moral rectitude (i.e., they are suckers for duty), and neither do much as Presidents nor enjoy doing it.

Presidential Types Along Ideological Lines.　Since social scientists who write about the presidency are disproportionately liberals who support a strong presidency, conventional wisdom among them has long favored the active-positive types. In their judgment, then, the great or near great Presidents have been active-positives: Theodore and Franklin Roosevelt, Truman, and Kennedy (all liberals). The worst Presidents have been passive-negatives, Coolidge and Eisenhower (both conservatives). The active-negatives, Wilson, Hoover, Johnson, and Nixon, are the most tragic in that they usually get the nation and themselves into trouble (two are liberal, two conservative). And the passive-positives, Taft and Harding, are the least noteworthy. Although Ford had active-negative and active-positive traits, Barber decided that overall he was an active-positive. Carter appears clearly to have been an active-negative in the style of Wilson (Although Barber predicted he would be an active-positive).

So Ford, a conservative, joins the liberals in the active-positive ranks, but Ford did little or nothing to reverse the liberal agenda. He was a caretaker President who pretty much

[2]James David Barber, *The Presidential Character: Predicting Performance in the White House.* 2nd ed. (Englewood Cliffs, N.J.: Prentice-Hall, 1977).

[3]*See* Harold D. Lasswell, *Psychopathology and Politics* (New York: The Viking Press, 1960) and *Power and Personality* (New York: The Viking Press, 1962).

protected and preserved the status quo. But what about Reagan? Although it may be
110   premature, it appears that Reagan is not only committed to having his Administration
accomplish prodigious feats, but that he is also enjoying the job immensely. Thus, he
shows great promise of becoming an active-positive President.
      But a genuinely conservative active-positive? That seems almost a contradiction in
terms. Active-positives use the power of the presidency to expand the role of the federal
115   government, not contract it. The Barber typology seems somehow ill-suited to an
active-positive conservative President. One wonders what the liberal social scientists who
have become enamored of this kind of psychohistory will do. Will they decide that
perhaps the best Presidents are really passive-positives, who will leave well enough
alone? Will they fashion a new typology? Or will they merely consider Reagan an aberrant
120   example of an active-positive? We'll just have to wait and see.

Presidential Types Not Seen.   We might consider ourselves fortunate that the history
of the presidency yields no examples of Hitlers, Stalins, Napoleons, or other
megalomaniacs. But "fortunate" may not be the proper word. Such people are seldom
elected anywhere, and certainly not in political systems where the lengthy process of
125   campaigning exposes candidates to as much scrutiny as ours does. Moreover, as awesome
as our President's power is, it is nevertheless checked. Even relatively minor abuses of
power can result in a President's ouster, as the example of Nixon clearly shows. Hence, it
is not from *fortune* but from *design* that our Presidents, regardless of their backgrounds
and characters, have been better-than-average leaders. Few truly great men have occupied
130   the White House, but that may be a blessing, for "greatness" may be considered both a
positive and a negative quality; Winston Churchill was a great leader, but so was Adolf
Hitler. Both were isolated, insulated, arrogant, and out of touch with the public and, in
greater or lesser degrees, with political reality. One, however, was regarded as the savior
of his country and the free world; the other, his country's and the free world's destroyer.
135   Our system does not produce leaders with the greatness of Churchill; but neither does it
produce those with the greatness of Hitler.   1838

Stage 3: Recall

Stop and recall what you have read. Review your use of the thinking strategies.
Did you use all five?

▰▰▰ **Skill Development:
Detecting Bias in the Cartoon**

Return to the political cartoon and answer the following questions:

1. What is the general topic of this cartoon?

   _____

2. Who or what does each person represent?

   _____

3. How do the objects, signs, and details contribute to the general topic?

_____

_____

4. What is the main point the cartoonist is trying to get across?

_____

_____

5. What is the cartoonist's purpose?

_____

6. What is the tone of the cartoon?

_____

7. What is the cartoonist's point of view?

_____

▥▤▥ Skill Development: Detecting Bias in the Text

Answer the following with T (true), F (false), or CT (can't tell).

_____ 1. The author's intent in this selection is to point out the psychological effects that come from being President.

_____ 2. The author's tone is bitter and resentful.

_____ 3. The author feels that "Hail to the Chief" should not be played.

4. In referring to Jimmy Carter as "aw shucks," the author is implying that Carter employed the "plain folks" propaganda technique.

Which of the following phrases, as used in this selection, is the least emotional?

_____ 5. a. courtiers and favor-seekers
    b. those who lack color
    c. "palace guard"
    d. members of the President's own cabinet

_____ 6. a. ingratiate themselves
    b. evasive answer
    c. presidential personality types
    d. a caretaker President

_____ 7. a. thinly-veiled assumptions
    b. preserved the status quo
    c. savior of the world
    d. history of the presidency

For each of the following sentences, indicate *F* for fact and *O* for opinion.

_____ 8. "Presidents must also be insulated, and indeed isolated, from all the petty day-to-day details and minor decisions that are best delegated to others."

_____ 9. "Normally fearless reporters shake when they ask the President questions at press conferences, and seem to be grateful even for evasive answers."

_____ 10. The worst Presidents have been passive-negatives Coolidge and Eisenhower (both conservatives).

▦▦▦ Comprehension Questions

1. The main point the author is trying to get across in this selection is _____

_____

_____

After reading the selection, answer the following questions with *a, b, c,* or *d.*

_____ 2. The author feels that isolation can be dangerous to a President because
  a. he can spend more time on big issues
  b. his time will then be wasted on petty details
  c. he can lose touch with reality
  d. his time will be monopolized with favor-seekers

_____ 3. The author believes that Presidential arrogance
  a. gradually evolves if not already there
  b. is a striking part of each President when he first comes to office
  c. is symbolized by jeans and a cardigan sweater
  d. can be avoided by those who enjoy power

_____ 4. The author believes that in recent history the President least affected by the trappings of power was
  a. Nixon
  b. Carter
  c. Ford
  d. Truman

_____ 5. The author states that most social scientists who analyze and write about the presidency are
  a. biased liberals
  b. biased conservatives
  c. unbiased patriots
  d. unbiased liberals

_____ 6. In Barber's examination of presidential personality types, the best Presidents are assumed to be
  a. active-positive

      b. active-negative

      c. passive-positive

      d. passive-negative

_____ 7. The author feels that the Presidents of the United States have been

      a. truly great men

      b. megalomaniacs

      c. better-than-average leaders

      d. the most qualified people in the country

_____ 8. The author's view of Nixon is

      a. objective

      b. subjective

      c. positive

      d. sympathic

_____ 9. The author's main purpose in relating the anecdote about Lyndon Johnson and the helicopters is to show

      a. the sense of humor of the President

      b. the extent of the Presidential power

      c. the extent of the arrogance that comes with power

      d. that the President is Commander-in-Chief

_____ 10. The author's main purpose in mentioning Carter's pride in knowing all the details is to illustrate

      a. Carter's arrogance

      b. Carter's inability to delegate

      c. Carter's excellence as an administrator

      d. Carter's attempt to remain "just folks"

Answer the following questions with *T* (true), *F* (false), *CT* (can't tell).

_____ 11. The author implies that planning the menus for state dinners is too trivial a matter to occupy a President's time.

_____ 12. The author implies that Carter used the same "Rose Garden" campaign tactic which he had criticized when it was used earlier against him.

_____ 13. The author feels that on psychological tests Presidents would most likely be classified as "normal."

_____ 14. The author believes that observing the character of a potential President would "weed out" the bad ones.

_____ 15. The author respects George Washington more than Abraham Lincoln.

▌≡▐ **Vocabulary**

According to the way the boldface word was used in the selection, indicate *a, b, c,* or *d* for the word or phrase that gives the best definition.

_____ 1. "those **disgruntled** taxpayers (05)"
   a. poor
   b. cheated
   c. discontent
   d. malicious

_____ 2. "**courtiers** and favor-seekers (06)"
   a. lawyers
   b. flatterers
   c. voters
   d. jurors

_____ 3. "insist on attending to such **minutiae** (09)"
   a. policy
   b. decision making
   c. concepts
   d. minor details

_____ 4. "**sycophancy** of his aides (44)"
   a. sincere attention
   b. charm
   c. fawning flattery
   d. honesty

_____ 5. "enjoy the power, **perquisites**, and adulation (50)"
   a. conveniences
   b. privileges
   c. fame
   d. requirements

_____ 6. "**scrutinize** more closely the characters (68)"
   a. isolate
   b. criticize
   c. examine
   d. overemphasize

_____ 7. "may even have delusions of **grandeur** (83)"
   a. religions power
   b. greatness
   c. wealth
   d. grace

_____ 8. "accomplish **prodigious** feats (111)"
   a. necessary
   b. complicated
   c. needy
   d. amazing

_____ 9. "an **aberrant** example of (119)"
   a. atypical
   b. interesting
   c. active
   d. well qualified

_____ 10. "can result in a President's **ouster** (127)"
   a. embarrassment
   b. disgrace
   c. confession
   d. expulsion

GRAPHIC ILLUSTRATION

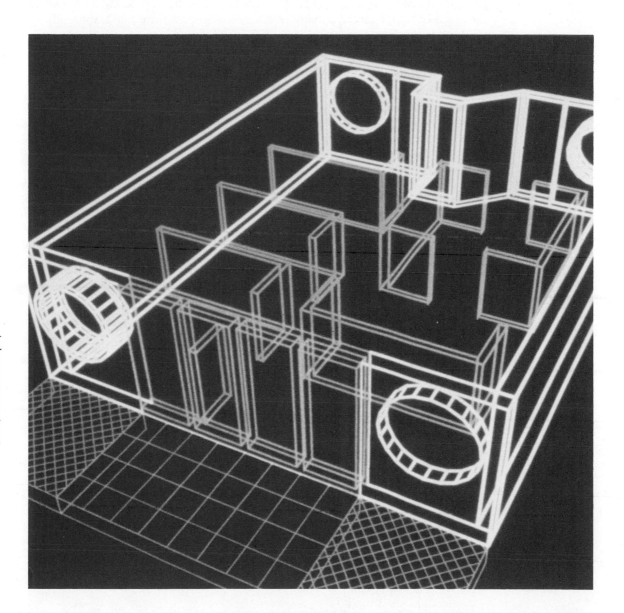

WHAT GRAPHICS DO

If a picture is worth a thousand words, a graphic illustration is worth at least several pages of facts and figures. Graphics express complex interrelationships in simplified form. Instead of plodding through repetitious data, you can glance at a chart, a map, or a graph and immediately see how everything fits together as well as how one part compares with another. Instead of reading several lengthy paragraphs and trying to visualize comparisons, you can study an organized design. For understanding many small bits of information, the graphic illustration is a logically constructed aid.

Graphic illustrations are generally used for the following reasons.

1. **To condense**
   Pages of repetitious, detailed information can be organized into one explanatory design.
2. **To clarify**
   Processes and interrelationships can be more clearly defined through visual representations.
3. **To convince**
   Developing trends and gross inequities can be forcefully dramatized.

There are five kinds of graphic illustrations? (1) diagrams, (2) tables, (3) maps, (4) graphs, and (5) flowcharts. All are used in textbooks, and the choice of which is best to use depends on the type of material presented. Study the following explanations of the different graphic forms.

HOW TO READ GRAPHIC MATERIAL

1. Read the title and get an overview. What is it about?
2. Look for footnotes and read italicized introductory material.
   Identify the who, where, and how.
   How and when were the data collected?
   Who collected the data?
   How many persons were included on the survey?
   Do the researchers seem to have been objective or biased?
   Considering the above information, does the study seem valid?
3. Read the labels.
   What do the vertical columns and the horizontal rows represent?
   Are the numbers in thousands or millions?
   What does the legend represent?
4. Notice the trends and find the extremes.
   What are the highest and lowest rates?
   What is the average rate?

Courtesy Precision Visuals, Inc.

© Scott, Foresman and Company.

How do the extremes compare with the total?
What is the percentage of increase or decrease?
5. Draw conclusions and formulate future exam questions.
What does it mean?
What needs to be done with the information?
What wasn't included?
Where do we go from here?

This chapter contains explanations and exercises for five types of graphic illustration. Read the explanations, study the illustrations, and respond to the statements as instructed.

Exercise 1: Diagram

A diagram is an outlined drawing or picture of an object or a process. It shows the labeled parts of a complicated form such as the muscles of the human body, the organizational make-up of a company's management and production teams, or the directional flow of a natural ecological system. Notice in the following diagram that the lines indicate areas on a sphere rather than specific points on a flat surface.

Human eye

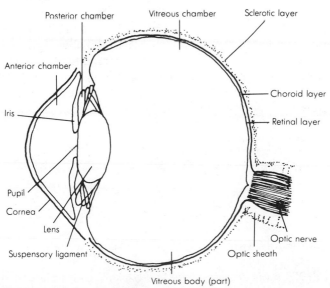

Willis H. Johnson et al., *Essentials of Biology*

From *Essentials of Biology*, 2nd Edition, by Willis H. Johnson, Louis E. Delany, Thomas A. Cole and Austin E. Brooks, pp. 194, 537. Copyright © 1969, 1974 by Holt, Rinehart and Winston, Inc. Reprinted by permission of Holt, Rinehart and Winston, CBS College Publishing.

Write a summary statement for this diagram.

_____

_____

_____

Answer the following with *T* (true), *F* (false), or *CT* (can't tell).

_____ 1. The cornea covers the front of the eye.
_____ 2. The retinal layer is directly touching the sclerotic layer.
_____ 3. The vitreous chamber or the vitreous body are one and the same as indicated by the diagram.
_____ 4. The iris of the eye regulates the size of the pupil.
_____ 5. The front of the lens is called the pupil.
_____ 6. The anterior chamber and the vitreous chamber are filled with the same type of jelly-like material.
_____ 7. An optic sheath surrounds the optic nerve.
_____ 8. The lens is supported by suspensory ligaments.
_____ 9. The cornea encircles the vitreous chamber.
_____ 10. The image is reflected on the retina.

▌▋▐▐ Exercise 2: Table

A table is a listing of facts and figures in columns for quick and easy reference. The information in the columns are usually labeled in two different directions. First read the title for the topic and then read the footnotes to judge the source. Determine what each column represents and how they interact. In the following table the **D** stands for Democrats and the **R** stands for Republicans. Notice that congressmen and senators are listed for more than one occupation.

Write a summary statement for this table.

_____

_____

_____

Answer the following with *T* (true), *F* (false), or *CT* (can't tell).

_____ 1. In 1973 more congressmen had backgrounds in law than any other occupational area.
_____ 2. The majority of the members of the 1973 Senate at some time served in the U.S. military.

Occupational Backgrounds of the Members of the House and Senate, 1973

Occupation	House			Senate		
	D	R	Total	D	R	Total
Agriculture	14	24	38	4	7	11
Business or banking	72	83	155	12	10	22
Education	41	18	59	7	3	10
Engineering	1	1	2	2	0	2
Journalism	16	7	23	4	1	5
Labor leader	3	0	3	0	0	0
Law	137	84	221	42	26	68
Law enforcement	1	1	2	0	0	0
Medicine	3	2	5	1	0	1
Public service/politics	201	152	353	55	42	97
Minister	2	2	4	0	0	0
Scientist	2	0	2	0	0	0
Veteran	175	142	317	42	31	73

*Senate total = 100; House total = 435, Data from **Congressional Quarterly Weekly Report,** January 6, 1973, p. 3, Reprinted by permission.

3. Congressmen were allowed to list more than one occupational background for this study.

4. In 1973 only three Republican congressmen had occupational backgrounds as labor leaders.

5. Because of the occupational background of its members, the House has passed more bills than the Senate that are favorable to business and banking interests.

6. According to this data a minister would seem to be less likely than a journalist to be elected to the House.

7. In the 1973 Congress more Democrats than Republicans were employed in law firms.

8. Most of the senators who listed public "service/politics" as a previous occupation also listed at least two other occupational areas.

9. In 1973, two hundred eighty-nine of the Democratic congressmen had occupational backgrounds in law.

10. In this study about fifty percent of the House members listed occupational backgrounds in education.

▥▤▥ Exercise 3: Map

A map shows a geographic designation or distribution. It shows differences in physical terrain, direction, or variations over a specified area. The legend of a map, which usually appears in a corner box, explains the coding for symbols, distance, and shading. Use the legend on the following map to help you answer the questions.

Geographical Review

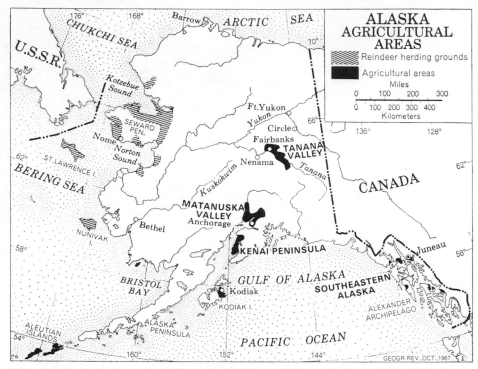

FIG. 1—Agricultural areas. *Sources:* Alaska Crop and Livestock Reporting Service and the Bureau of Indian Affairs, Juneau.

Write a summary statement for this map.

_____

Answer the following with *T* (true), *F* (false), or *CT* (can't tell).

_____ 1. The major concentration of reindeer-herding grounds in Alaska is on Seward Peninsula.

_____ 2. There are no major highways in Alaska north of Anchorage.

_____ 3. Bethel is the largest city in Alaska.

_____ 4. Anchorage is less than 300 miles from Juneau.

_____ 5. The Matanuska Valley and the Tanana Valley are two of the major agricultural areas in Alaska.

_____ 6. The Yukon River extends into Canada.

_____ 7. Eskimos live in the areas around Nome and Barrow.

8. Reindeer herding is more prevalent than agriculture on the islands in the Bering Sea.

9. No farming exists in Southeastern Alaska.

10. The northernmost city in the United States is Fort Yukon.

▰▰▰ ## Exercise 4: Pie Graph

A **pie graph** is a circle that is divided into wedge-shaped slices. The complete pie or circle represents a total of 100 percent. Each slice is a percent or fraction of that whole. Budgets, such as the annual expenditure of the federal or state governments, are frequently illustrated by pie graphs.

In the following graphs, notice that the figures are percents and not numbers of people. We cannot assume that the male and female population is equal. We only know percents, not numbers.

Virginia in 1625: an age profile

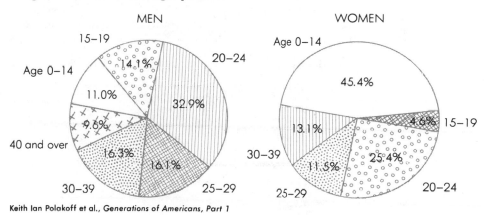

Keith Ian Polakoff et al., *Generations of Americans, Part 1*

Write a summary statement for these graphs.

_____

Answer the following with *T* (true), *F* (false), or *CT* (can't tell).

1. The majority of the children arriving in Virginia from England were females.

2. There were more men than women in Virginia in 1625.

3. Only approximately one quarter of the men in Virginia in 1625 were thirty years or more of age.

Reprinted from *Generations of Americans: A History of the United States* by Keith Ian Polakoff, et. al. Copyright © 1976 by St. Martin's Press, Inc. Reprinted with permission of the publisher.

© Scott, Foresman and Company.

_____ 4. The population of Virginia in 1625 was thirty percent younger than Virginia's population today.

_____ 5. Almost half the women in Virginia in 1625 were under eighteen years of age.

_____ 6. A greater number of women than men in Virginia in 1625 were 20–24 years of age.

_____ 7. According to the graph there were no women in Virginia in 1625 over 40 years of age.

_____ 8. More women than men left the Virginia colony.

_____ 9. There was a greater number of men than women between the ages of 30–39 in Virginia in 1625.

_____ 10. Because of the availability of females, men married women much younger than themselves in the Virginia colony.

▮▬▮▮ Exercise 5: Bar Graph

A **bar graph** is a series of horizontal bars in which the length of each bar represents a particular amount of what is being discussed. A series of different items can be quickly compared by noting the different bar lengths. In the following graph notice that the bars represent increases and decreases, not total numbers.

Projected Percentage Increase in Occupations: 1970–1980

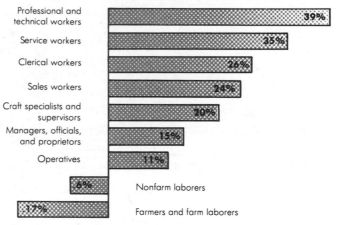

Louis E. Boone and David L. Kurtz, *Contemporary Business*

Write a summary statement for this graph.

_____

_____

From *Contemporary Business* by Louis E. Boone and David L. Kurtz, pp. 259, 306–309. Copyright © 1976 by The Dryden Press. Reprinted by permission of Holt, Rinehart and Winston, CBS College Publishing.

Answer the following with T (true), F (false), or CT (can't tell).

_____ 1. The decrease in farmers and farm laborers will be greater than the increase in managers, officials, and proprietors.

_____ 2. The greatest projected increase will be in professional and technical workers.

_____ 3. The greatest projected increase will be in nonfarm laborers.

_____ 4. A greater number of people will be working in the towns and cities than on the farms.

_____ 5. Farmers will be moving to the cities and becoming managers.

_____ 6. The projected increase in operative positions is approximately one third the increase in service worker positions.

_____ 7. In 1980, twenty-six percent of all workers will be clerical workers.

_____ 8. This graph was published to help people find jobs.

_____ 9. There will be a greater demand for service workers than for sales workers in 1980 because more things will need to be fixed.

_____ 10. The combined projected increase in sales and clerical workers will be greater than the projected increase in professional and technical workers.

▮▮▮ Exercise 6: Column Graph

A **column graph** is like a bar graph that is standing upright and measures not only horizontally, but vertically. Thus, the column graph gives two kinds of information. It can compare an item at different time intervals or at different stages of development.

In the graph on page 302 notice how much different information is presented for a quick comparison. Also note that each column represents the mean or average income for a group; each person in the group did not necessarily make the average income.

Write a summary statement for this graph.

_____

_____

Answer the following with T (true), F (false), or CT (can't tell).

_____ 1. Only a person between 45 and 54 years of age with a college education made over $20,000 in 1972.

_____ 2. For all ages over twenty-five in 1972, the average income of college graduates was higher than the average income of noncollege graduates.

_____ 3. The greatest difference in the average income of college graduates and noncollege graduates is in the 35 to 44 age group.

_____ 4. In 1972 the average 25-to-34-year-old college graduate made approximately $2500 more than the average high-school graduate of the same age.

Mean income of men by level of education and age, 1972

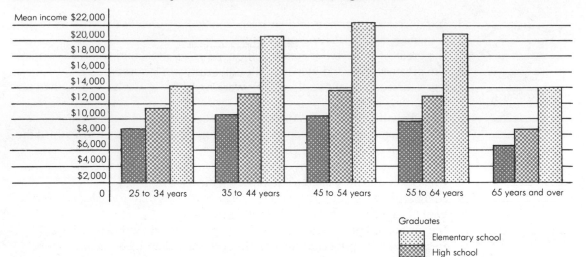

Mean income

| | $22,000 |
| $20,000 |
| $18,000 |
| $16,000 |
| $14,000 |
| $12,000 |
| $10,000 |
| $8,000 |
| $6,000 |
| $4,000 |
| $2,000 |

0   25 to 34 years   35 to 44 years   45 to 54 years   55 to 64 years   65 years and over

Graduates
Elementary school
High school
College

Reece McGee et al., *Sociology: An Introduction*

_____ 5. According to this information a college education on the average means more financially at 50 than it does at 30.

_____ 6. In 1972 the average high-school graduate reached his peak earning potential at 54 years.

_____ 7. The 1972 figures show that, on the average, more education means more money.

_____ 8. In 1972 the average college graduate made about the same at age 65 as a college graduate would make at age 30.

_____ 9. In the 1972 figures an average elementary-school graduate never made as much as an average college graduate.

_____ 10. College graduates work harder than noncollege graduates and thus have higher incomes.

▓▓▓ Exercise 7: Line Graph

A **line graph** is a continuous curve or frequency distribution. The horizontal scale measures time and the vertical scale measures amount. As the data fluctuate, the line will change direction and with extreme differences become very jagged.

In the following graph note the variations in the population movement.

From *Sociology: An Introduction* by Reece McGee and Others, pp. 222, 314. Copyright © 1977 by The Dryden Press. Reprinted by permission of Holt, Rinehart and Winston, CBS College Publishing.

U.S. population by place of residence, 1910–1970

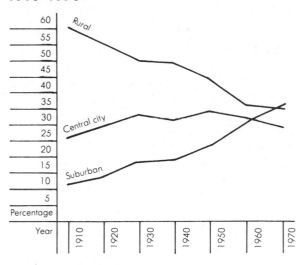

The percentage of the population living in rural areas declined drastically during the period shown. The percentage in central cities rose steadily until 1950, except for a slight decline during the Depression of the 1930s. The percentage in suburban areas grew throughout this period, and particularly so after 1940. Since 1940, suburban living has gained so steadily at the expense of both central city and rural living that by 1970 there were more suburbanites than either of the other two groups.

Reece McGee et al., *Sociology: An Introduction*

Write a summary statement for this graph.

_____

_____

Answer the following with *T* (true), *F* (false), or *CT* (can't tell).

_____ 1. In 1910 about six times more people lived in rural areas than lived in suburban areas.

_____ 2. The greatest growth in population since 1918 has been in suburban areas.

_____ 3. The percentage of the population living in the central city in 1910 and in 1970 is exactly the same.

_____ 4. Since 1910, the periods of the least decline in rural population were in the 1930s and 1960s.

_____ 5. The graph shows the number of people leaving the farms to become factory workers.

_____ 6. In 1920 about half of the U.S. population lived in rural areas.

_____ 7. In 1970 more people work in suburban areas than in the central city.

_____ 8. The increase in suburban population was greater in the 1930s than in the 1950s.

From *Sociology: An Introduction* by Reece McGee and Others, pp. 222, 314. Copyright © 1977 by The Dryden Press. Reprinted by permission of Holt, Rinehart and Winston, CBS College Publishing.

_____ 9. The suburban population approximately tripled between 1910 and 1960.

_____ 10. More of the people who left the rural areas between 1910 and 1970 went to suburban areas than central city areas.

■▦▥ Exercise 8: Flow Chart

Flow charts provide a diagram of a writer's ideas. Elements can be seen as parts of a whole, rather than as isolated points. Their original use was in computer programming. Key ideas are stated in boxes, along with supporting ideas which are linked by arrows. Arrows pointing downward or to the right indicate sequence or mean "leads to" while arrows pointing upward or to the left mean "supports" or "relates to." For the following flow chart, read the passage that discusses the charted information since the diagram is an elaboration of the ideas in the text.

The Many Faces of QWL

QWL [Quality of Work Life] is not an exact science or approach. While all its programs are aimed at reducing absenteeism and improving productivity and morale through the development of a better work climate, in practice QWL can have many faces.

Quality of Work Life Elements

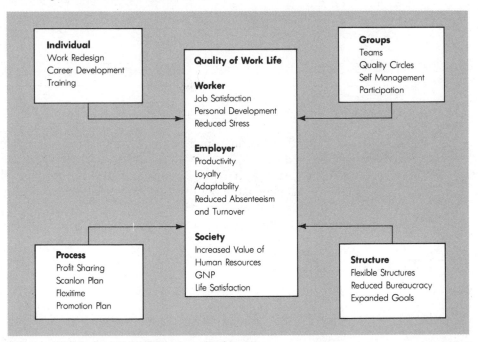

Szilagyi and Wallace, **Organizational Behavior and Performance**

From _Organizational Behavior and Performance,_ 3rd Edition, by Andrew D. Szilagyi, Jr., and Marc J. Wallace, Jr., p. 589. Copyright © 1983 by Scott, Foresman and Company.

It can involve work teams like those at General Foods, where the isolated worker who did one task repeatedly is now doing group projects in which responsibility for a variety of tasks is shared.

It can be quality circles, where workers at Westinghouse and other companies help to solve work-related problems through group interaction.

It can mean a company gives its workers as much information as it gives stockholders.

It can take the form of more flexible working schedules, so workers have time to go to the dentist or see their children's teacher—the sort of errand time usually available only to management.

It can mean less supervision, as at G.M.'s Buick plants, in which production teams, operating without direct supervision, help select and train new team members, forecast material and manpower requirements, and evaluate their own performance.

It can be in-house training courses, free tuition for higher education, or a firm policy of promoting from within.

Answer the following *T* (true), *F* (false), or *CT* (can't tell).

_____ 1. QWL is designed to benefit both the workers and the employer.
_____ 2. Employees can work individually or as a team in the QWL plan.
_____ 3. Increased loyalty is a desired element of QWL.
_____ 4. Wages are higher under the QWL plan.
_____ 5. A major emphasis of QWL is job satisfaction.
_____ 6. Group needs command more emphasis than individual needs in the QWL plan.
_____ 7. The goals of QWL attempt to meet individuals' needs on three different levels.
_____ 8. The chart implies that self management benefits workers but not the employer or society.
_____ 9. Profit sharing is designed to benefit the worker, the employer, and society.
_____ 10. In QWL both the group and the individual are involved in goal setting.

ECONOMICS

Stage 1: Preview

Preview *the selection and complete the following sentence: After reading this*

*selection, I would like to know*_____

_____

_____

Stage 2: Integrate Knowledge While Reading

Use thinking strategies as you read:

1. Predict   *4. Verbalize points*

2. Picture   *5. Fix up strategies*

3. Form analogies

Underscoring

Using a variety of notations, underscore *the following selection as if you were preparing for a quiz on the material. Remember, do not underscore as you read, but wait until you finish a section and then mark the important points.*

INFLATION*

Marilu Hurt McCarty, from *Dollars and Sense*

It has been said that if you ask five economists for their opinion on a subject, you will get six opinions—one can't make up his (or her) mind.

Inflation Since 1860

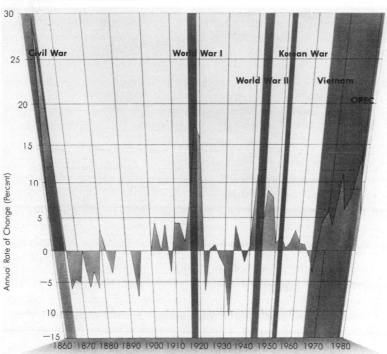

Source: **U.S. Department of Labor, Bureau of Labor Statistics.**

This figure highlights the various inflationary periods experienced by the United States since 1860. The majority of these periods have occurred during extended military hostilities; however, although the 1970s and early 1980s were relatively peaceful, the price level crept up briskly.

From *Macroeconomics,* Second Edition, by Ralph T. Byrns and Gerald W. Stone, p. 147. Copyright © 1984 by Scott, Foresman and Company.

*LEARNING STRATEGY: Be able to define inflation, identify the possible causes, and explain the effects of inflation on different groups.

From *Dollars and Sense,* Second Edition, by Marilu Hurt McCarty, pp. 155–157. Copyright © 1979 by Scott, Foresman and Company.

This is particularly true of the subject of inflation. Because the sources of inflation are difficult to pinpoint, it is often hard to choose the proper policy for correcting the problem. Before policy alternatives can be evaluated, the problem must be carefully analyzed and the process by which it travels through the system understood. If the problem is approached haphazardly, any action may bring about results opposite from those intended.

Inflation can be defined as a general rise in the price level of goods and services. Prices are rising and falling all the time. As long as the *average* price level remains the same, inflation is not a problem. When the average price level for all goods and services increases, we have inflation.

Primitive Production

Early humans had to struggle just to stay alive. Because groups were isolated, they had to be self-sufficient. A group produced its entire reserve of game, grain, shelter, and cloth or skins. Later, some groups began to specialize and trade with neighboring tribes. Specialization made possible greater production so that the entire community could enjoy rising standards of living. Material gains were accomplished at the expense of self-sufficiency, but that was a small price to pay.

Specialization and trade required the use of money to overcome the difficulties of barter. Primitive tribes used as money whatever tokens they found at hand—special beads and stones and rare shells. As long as the supply of money remained in balance with the supply of goods, there was no problem of rising prices. There was just enough money to exchange for goods at their customary prices.

Economic Development

As knowledge expanded, however, output grew. More money was needed to symbolize the greater values. A paradox arose: Money had to be of a scarce material to prevent misuse, but it also had to be expansible if it was to be exchanged for a growing supply of goods. Gold fulfilled both requirements for many centuries. But eventually, fewer new sources of gold (as well as the difficulty of hauling it around in one's pockets) made it necessary to find a substitute. Paper money "tied" to gold was the result.*

Balancing the supply of money and goods grew more difficult as economic life became more complex. This might be seen as a problem of *form* versus *substance*. On the one hand, the supply of goods (substance) might grow faster than the supply of money (form). Or, what is more common, the supply of money might grow faster than the real substance of goods.

When the supply of money increases faster than the supply of goods, holders of money will bid for the smaller quantity of goods. Prices will tend to rise; the economy will experience *inflation*. When the supply of money increases more slowly than the supply of goods, sellers will compete for the smaller quantity of money. Prices will tend to fall; the economy will experience *deflation*.

*Our money is no longer tied to gold except in a very limited sense. When the U.S. Treasury buys newly mined gold, it may issue currency in payment. However, most of our currency is issued by the Federal Reserve banks which are not limited by the supply of gold.

Why All the Fuss About Inflation?

40 Why should inflation concern us? A one-dollar bill and a ten look pretty much the same. Why should it matter whether a day's welding, a truckload of soybeans, a college course, or a suit of clothes is counted as ten or one?

It matters if a day's welding *today* at forty dollars is to be exchanged in ten years for a suit of clothes. By that time the value of forty dollars may have evaporated and a suit
45 might cost as much as *five* days' welding. Inflation is especially hard on those people who depend on *stored* money value: savers, the elderly, pensioners. (We'll all be there one day!)

It matters, too, if the price of a college course, for example, rises more slowly than the price of a truckload of soybeans. Those groups who depend on income from the sale of
50 college courses may be unfairly penalized by uneven price changes. Inflation means a lower standard of living for people whose occupations or incomes are relatively *fixed:* teachers, civil servants, low-skilled or technically obsolete workers, and those who depend on government transfer payments.

Inflation interferes with our ability to plan for the future. We have been taught to save
55 part of our income to provide security for out retirement years. Our savings may earn interest of up to, say, 7 percent a year. But suppose the value of our money is declining at the rate of 10 percent a year because of inflation. The thrifty saver will actually *lose* 3 percent in purchasing power. The saver will be worse off than the scoundrel who squanders money on frivolous living!
60 What may be even more disturbing is the fact that the saver's interest earnings of 7 percent are taxed as part of personal income. In effect, he or she is being taxed twice for being virtuous—once through inflation and once by the Internal Revenue Service!

Those who make loans and borrow money (creditors and debtors) are also affected by inflation. In fact, inflation may benefit the debtor, who pays back less in actual purchasing
65 power than originally borrowed. Lenders are understandably reluctant to lock themselves into long-term loans when interest rates may not compensate for inflation.

Rampant inflation is often followed by recession or depression. During expansion, there is feverish spending for capital investment and production of goods and services. The result may be overproduction and stockpiling inventories. Investment and
70 production will eventually fall off, and unemployment and economic distress follow.

Stage 3: Recall

Stop and recall what you have read.
Review your use of the thinking strategies. Did you use all five?
Review your underscoring. Have you sufficiently highlighted the main idea and the significant supporting details?

▥▤▥ Skill Development: Reading Graphs

Refer to the inflation graph and answer the following items with *T* (true), *F* (false), or *CT* (can't tell).

_____ 1. Inflation has been on a steady rise since 1860.
_____ 2. Inflation in the United States reached its highest peak during World War II.
_____ 3. In the 1930s the inflation rate reached 10 percent.
_____ 4. Inflation tends to increase during extended periods of war.
_____ 5. During the Civil War the inflation rate was above ten percent.
_____ 6. The inflation rate in 1980 was more than twice the annual rate of 1960.
_____ 7. The rate of inflation was higher during World War I than during World War II.
_____ 8. War causes an uncertain world economy which creates inflation.
_____ 9. Since the 1860s, the highest inflation rate was during the Civil War.
_____ 10. The annual inflation rate has never been less than one percent.

Interpreting Cartoons

After reading the selection for background knowledge, return to the cartoon and answer the following questions.

1. What is the main idea implied in this cartoon? _____

_____

_____

2. How do the details contribute to the main idea? _____

_____

Comprehension Questions

1. The main point the author is trying to get across in this selection is _____

_____

_____

After reading the selection, answer the following questions with *a, b, c,* or *d.*

_____ 2. The author's main purpose in this selection is to
   a. explain the causes and effects of inflation
   b. argue for policies to stop inflation
   c. discuss how to control inflation
   d. offer alternatives to the inflationary cycle

_____ 3. In early human history the need for money was created by
   a. self-sufficiency
   b. isolation
   c. agricultural production
   d. specialization

_____ 4. All of the following are desirable characteristics of material used for money except
   a. exhaustibility
   b. handiness
   c. scarcity
   d. expansibility

_____ 5. Applying the concept of _form_ versus _substance_, inflation occurs when there are
   a. more mink coats and more money
   b. fewer mink coats and more money
   c. more mink coats and less money
   d. fewer mink coats and less money

_____ 6. Inflation definitely penalizes all of the following except
   a. savers
   b. social security recipients
   c. post-office workers
   d. debtors

_____ 7. According to the author putting $1,000 in the bank at 7 percent a year, with an inflation rate of 10 percent a year, will result in a loss (because of inflation) for that year of
   a. less than $30
   b. $30
   c. $300 plus tax
   d. $3.00

_____ 8. The author implies that during an inflationary period she would
   a. lend money
   b. produce fewer goods
   c. save money
   d. not want to tax interest earnings

_____ 9. The reader can conclude that all of the following represent an oversupply of goods except
   a. inflation
   b. deflation
   c. recession
   d. depression

_____ 10. The author points out that the irony of inflation is that it
   a. penalizes overindulgence
   b. raises the standard of living for everyone
   c. decreases product production
   d. hurts those who have conserved money prudently

Answer the following with _T_ (true), _F_ (false), or _CT_ (can't tell).

_____ 11. Inflation is defined by the average price level rather than by an immediate price increase.

_____ 12. Specialization raised the standard of living in early times because more products were available.

_____ 13. More people rather than more products means that more money must be put into circulation.

_____ 14. In the United States the paper currency issued by Federal Reserve banks is directly tied to the supply of gold.

_____ 15. Economists predict a continued rise in the rate of inflation.

■■■ ## Vocabulary

According to the way the boldface word was used in the selection, indicate _a, b, c,_ or _d_ for the word or phrase that gives the best definition.

_____ 1. "is approached **haphazardly** (07)"
a. logically
b. maliciously
c. harshly
d. randomly

_____ 2. "had to be **self-sufficient** (14)"
a. selfish
b. productive
c. independently maintained
d. self-disciplined

_____ 3. "**Specialization** made possible (16)"
a. concentration of endeavor
b. generalization of needs
c. mechanization
d. technology

_____ 4. "difficulties of **barter** (20)"
a. primitive deflation
b. taxation
c. trading by exchange of goods
d. growing interest rates

_____ 5. "technically **obsolete** workers (52)"
a. out-of-date
b. impoverished
c. sick
d. aimless

_____ 6. "taxed twice for being **virtuous** (62)"
a. dishonest
b. unskillful
c. morally responsible
d. evasive

_____ 7. "(**creditors** and debtors) (63)"
a. money lenders
b. authorities
c. originators
d. stockbrokers

_____ 8. "may benefit the **debtor** (64)"
a. money manager
b. one who owes money
c. one who lends money
d. inflation controller

_____ 9. "**Rampant** inflation (67)"
a. local
b. exaggerated
c. modified
d. widespread

_____ 10. "stockpiling of **inventories** (69)"
a. paper money
b. supply of goods
c. investment capital
d. services

■ ■ ■ **Essay Question**

Explain how inflation affects buying power and wages and discuss the financial difficulties that workers on fixed incomes experience during times of inflation. Use a sheet of notebook paper to record your answer.

Selection **2**

POLITICAL SCIENCE

Jeannie Taylot/Michael Sullivan & Associates

Stage 1: Preview

Preview *the selection and complete the following sentence: After reading this selection, I would like to know* _____

_____

_____

Stage 2: Integrate Knowledge While Reading

Use thinking strategies as you read:

1. *Predict*   4. *Verbalize points*
2. *Picture*   5. *Fix up strategies*
3. *Form analogies*

MILLIONS OF NONVOTERS*

James H. Burns, J. W. Peltason, and Thomas E. Cronin, from *Government by the People*

On the average, the proportion of Americans who vote is smaller than that of the British, French, Italians, West Germans, Scandinavians, or Canadians. Talk as we will about democratic suffrage, the fact remains that millions of Americans do not choose to vote or somehow fail to get to the polls on election day. Our record has not always been so poor.

5   Voting was generally high (among those legally *able* to vote) during the latter nineteenth century; in 1876, 86 percent of the adult enfranchised males voted. In this century our voting ratio has been erratic. Turnout dropped between the early 1900s and the mid-twenties, rose in the late 1920s and 1930s, declined in the mid- and late 1940s, climbed in 1952 and 1956, and has decreased in the last three presidential elections—three

10   elections, incidentally, that were thought to be unusually significant and compelling.

Americans have an absolute right *not* to vote. But in a democracy where voting is considered a civic virtue and a prudent means of self-defense, the extent of nonvoting is startling. In the last two presidential elections about 40 percent of the eligible voters did not go to the polls. *Over 60 percent* of them stayed home in the congressional elections

15   of 1974. Participation in state and local elections is usually even *lower.*

Why do people fail to vote? Aside from outright denials of the right to vote—happily no longer a significant factor—important reasons are registration requirements and being absent from the voting district on election day. As we noted in Part Three, registering to vote (not required in many other democracies) is bothersome and time-consuming and

20   often compels a potential voter to initiate action long before he or she faces election issues.[1] Although the Supreme Court has ruled that states may not impose residency requirements of longer than fifty days, almost a third of the potential voters are not even registered to vote. Disturbed by the low turn-out, Congress in 1970 established for *presidential elections* a uniform thirty-day residency requirement and set simpler

25   procedures for absentee voting.

The *prime* reasons for not voting, however, are not institutional. They are *personal.* Millions of Americans are just not interested enough to go to the polls to vote for president, and even fewer vote for state and local candidates. They feel—if they think about the matter at all—that politics is not important, or that there is no real choice

30   between candidates, or that they do not know enough to vote, or that they are "disgusted with politics." Some fear losing business or wages if they go to the polls. Much nonvoting

*LEARNING STRATEGY: Be able to describe who the nonvoters are and why they are not going to the polls.

[1]See Stanley Kelley, Jr., Richard E. Ayres, and William G. Bowen, "Registration and Voting: Putting First Things First," *American Political Science Review* (June 1967), pp. 359-77.

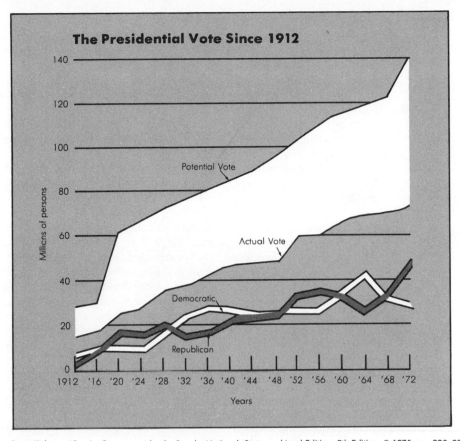

The Presidential Vote Since 1912

Millions of persons

Potential Vote

Actual Vote

Democratic

Republican

1912 '16 '20 '24 '28 '32 '36 '40 '44 '48 '52 '56 '60 '64 '68 '72

Years

Burns/Peltason/Cronin, *Government by the People*, National, State and Local Edition, 9th Edition, © 1975, pp. 280–284. Reprinted by permission of Prentice-Hall, Inc., Englewood Cliffs, NJ.

probably results from a combination of low interest and inconvenience: An elderly person might vote if the polls were around the corner—but actually they are two miles away and he or she lacks transportation. Of course, sometimes the inconvenience is
35   simply a rationalization for basic lack of interest.

Should such apathy surprise us? When students mobilized for action after President Nixon's Cambodia "incursion" of 1970, it was estimated that half a million of them would take part in the ensuing national elections. In fact only a tiny minority was active. That minority was effective in a number of congressional elections, but the vast majority of
40   interested students did more talking than electioneering. Some were alienated from the whole election process; most were simply not interested in the issues of the day.[2] Indeed, of all major categories of voters, the lowest percentage of voter turnout in the 1964 and 1968 presidential elections was among the eighteen to twenty-year-olds in the states that permitted them to vote.

[2]Walter T. Murphy, Jr., "Student Power in the 1970 Elections: A Preliminary Assessment," *Political Science* (Winter 1971), pp. 27–32. See also Sidney Hyman, *Youth in Politics* (Basic Books, 1972).

Who Fails to Vote?

45 The extent of voting varies among different types of persons, areas, and elections. Voting studies generally agree on the following patterns, which are listed here roughly in order of declining importance:

1. People with high incomes are more likely to vote than people with low ones. Why do low-income people vote in fewer numbers than the wealthy? They have less economic
50 security; they feel less of a sense of control over their political environment; they feel at a disadvantage in social contacts; and their social norms tend to deemphasize politics. Their nonvoting thus is part of a larger political and psychological environment that discourages political activity, including voting.[3]

2. The college-educated are more likely to vote than the noncollege-educated. High
55 school alumni are more likely to vote than those with only a grade school education. "Practically speaking," writes Warren Miller, "almost everybody who has been to college votes."[4] Even college-educated persons who profess little interest in or knowledge about political issues turn out to vote. People with college backgrounds exist in a climate of opinion in which voting is considered a civic duty; they tend to be more exposed to
60 ideas, active people, newspapers, political leaders. The college education itself may have an independent effect in exposing the graduates to political ideas and personalities.

3. Middle-aged people are more likely to vote than the younger and older. Many young people are busy getting established, moving about, having babies, raising young children. The new husband is occupied with getting ahead; the young wife is immersed in home
65 affairs, or has a job of her own. They find little time for politics. The more established, between thirty-five and fifty-five, are more active; then voting falls off sharply in the sixties and seventies, owing partly to the infirmities of old age.

4. Men are more likley to vote than women. This variation—not very great in most elections—exists in many foreign countries as well. In recent presidential elections about
70 61 in every 100 women have voted, about 75 in every 100 men. Women feel less social pressure to vote than men. Morality issues such as birth control, however, generally bring out a high women's vote, and college-educated women tend to be more active in political party work than college-educated men. There are indications that the traditional difference in the rate of voting between men and women is decreasing.

75 5. Partisans are more likely to vote than independents. "By far the most important psychological factor affecting an individual's decision to vote is his identification with a political party."[5] When the election outcome is doubtful, strong partisanship is even more likely to induce a person to vote. A partisan is likely to have a personal interest and to be concerned about the outcome. If partisanship has this influence, however, the recent
80 decline in party feeling and loyalty could bring a decline in voting turnout.

6. Persons who are active in organized groups are more likely to vote. This is especially true when the organized groups are themselves involved in community activity.[6] People in groups are more likely to be exposed to stimuli that engage them with civic and political problems.

[3]See Angus Campbell, Philip E. Converse, Warren E. Miller, and Donald E. Stokes, *The American Voter* (John Wiley, 1960).

[4]Warren Miller, "Political Behavior of the Electorate," *American Government Annual, 1960–1961* (Holt, Rinehart & Winston, 1960), p. 50.

[5]*Report of the President's Commission on Registration and Voting Participation* (U.S. Government Printing Office, 1963), pp. 9–10.

[6]Sidney Verba and Norman H. Nie, *Participation in America* (Harper & Row, 1972), pp. 197–200.

85   Summing up, if you are a young woman with a low income and little sense of partisanship, the chances that you will turn out even for an exciting presidential election are far less than if you are a wealthy man in your fifties, a strong partisan, and a member of a civic group. Thus nonvoting influences are cumulative. But there also appear to be psychological or attitudinal differences between nonvoters and voters. Even when sex,
90 age, education, and income are controlled, the chronic nonvoter, more characteristically than the voter, is a person with a sense of inadequacy, more inclined to accept authority, more concerned with personal and short-range issues, less sympathetic toward democratic norms, and less tolerant of those who differ from himself.   /1164

Stage 3: Recall

Stop and recall what you have read.
Review your use of the thinking strategies. Did you use all five?

▌▌▤▌▌ Skill Development: Reading Graphs

Study the graph and then respond to the following statements with *T* (true), *F* (false), or *CT* (can't tell).

_____   1. In 1956 almost half of the potential voters actually voted in the presidential election.
_____   2. In 1920 a greater percentage of the nonvoters were registered Republicans than registered Democrats.
_____   3. The approximately equal turnout of Republican and Democratic voters for the 1948 presidential election accounts for a leveling off in the total vote from the previous election year.
_____   4. More votes were cast for the Republican candidate in 1936 than for the Democratic one.
_____   5. Approximately 60 million people voted in the presidential election of 1952.
_____   6. In the presidential election of 1972 there were more total voters as well as more total nonvoters than in any other presidential election since 1912.
_____   7. Between 1916 and 1920 the number of potential American voters doubled.
_____   8. In the 1924 presidential election more of the nonvoters were registered Democrats than registered Republicans.
_____   9. In the presidential election of 1940 there were approximately 80 million nonvoters.
_____   10. Republicans have enjoyed a steady, uninterrupted increase in presidential votes since 1912.

▌▌▤▌▌ Outlining

Outline the key ideas in the selection on a sheet of notebook paper as if you were planning to use your notes to study for a quiz. After studying your outline, answer the comprehension questions.

▌▐▌ Comprehension Questions

1. The main point the author is trying to get across in this selection is _____

_____

_____

After reading the selection, answer the following questions with *a, b, c,* or *d.*

_____ 2. In the following, the only definitely true statement about the American voter is
    a. more people voted in 1876 than in any of the last three presidential elections
    b. voter turnout has been on a continual decline since the early 1900's
    c. In 1974 voter turnout was lower for state and local elections than for congressional elections
    d. about the same number of people voted in the late 1920s as voted in 1952.

_____ 3. The author feels that the major cause for the high number of nonvoting Americans is
    a. registration requirements
    b. absenteeism
    c. failure to register
    d. apathy

_____ 4. The effect at the polls of President Nixon's Cambodia "incursion" of 1970 was
    a. equal to the amount of student protest
    b. less than anticipated
    c. an example of the powerful influence of a discontented voter group in a presidential election
    d. a strong danger to Nixon when he ran for reelection

5. According to the author, wealthy people are more likely to vote than people with low incomes because of all of the following except
    a. a greater feeling of control over their political environment
    b. less trouble in getting time off from work
    c. a stronger emphasis on voting in their social group
    d. greater financial security

_____ 6. Voting studies show that generally the most important of the following comparative factors in describing voters and nonvoters is
    a. education
    b. income
    c. political party affiliation
    d. sex

7. According to the selection, all of the following are true of the college educated except
   a. they are more likely to vote than those who have not been to college
   b. the men are less likely to be involved in political party work than the non-college-educated men
   c. they seem to vote even if they are not interested in the political issues
   d. they are more likely to have high incomes

8. The author feels that women are less likely to vote than men because of
   a. education
   b. less social pressure
   c. raising young children
   d. morality issues

9. The author believes that the most important characteristic distinguishing the voter from the nonvoter is
   a. education
   b. sex
   c. attitude
   d. income

10. Of the following, the author would probably feel that Americans
   a. should all fulfill a civic duty and go to the polls and vote
   b. should vote only if they feel that their actual vote can make a difference
   c. should penalize the citizens who fail to vote
   d. should launch a massive campaign in the six listed areas to insure greater voter turnout

Answer the following with *T* (true), *F* (false), or *CT* (can't tell).

11. All democracies require voters to be registered before the actual day of voting in the election.
12. Fewer eighteen- to twenty-year-olds voted in the 1972 presidential election than in the presidential election of 1968.
13. Members of civic organizations are more likely to vote than sixty- or seventy-year-olds.
14. The author implies that there has been a recent feeling toward voter independence as opposed to political-party membership.
15. The author believes that most nonvoters use inconveniences as an excuse.

▌▌▤▐ **Vocabulary**

According to the way the boldface word was used in the selection, indicate *a, b, c,* or *d* for the word or phrase that gives the best definition.

_____ 1. "adult **enfranchised** males
(06)"
a. educated
b. enlisted in the military
c. endowed with a vote
d. certified

_____ 2. "has been **erratic**
(07)"
a. enormous
b. unsteady
c. regular
d. erroneous

_____ 3. "a **prudent** means of self-
defense (12)"
a. wise
b. satisfactory
c. encouraged
d. continuing

_____ 4. "to **initiate** action
(20)"
a. complete
b. begin
c. regulate
d. terminate

_____ 5. "students **mobilized** for action
(36)"
a. assembled
b. got into automobiles
c. rioted
d. shouted

_____ 6. "Cambodia **incursion**
(37)"
a. mistake
b. concession
c. invasion
d. adventure

_____ 7. "**ensuing** national elections
(38)"
a. previous
b. illegal
c. contested
d. following

_____ 8. "High school **alumni**
(55)"
a. graduates
b. seniors
c. teachers
d. students

_____ 9. "stong **partisanship** (77)"
a. friendship
b. adherence to a political
party
c. civic involvement
d. business affiliations

_____ 10. "influences are **cumulative**
(88)"
a. important
b. added one to another
c. predictable
d. relevant

■ ■ ■ **Essay Question**

Explain why millions of Americans fail to vote by discussing general reasons and specific examples of types of persons, areas, and elections. Use a sheet of notebook paper to record your answer.

BIOLOGY

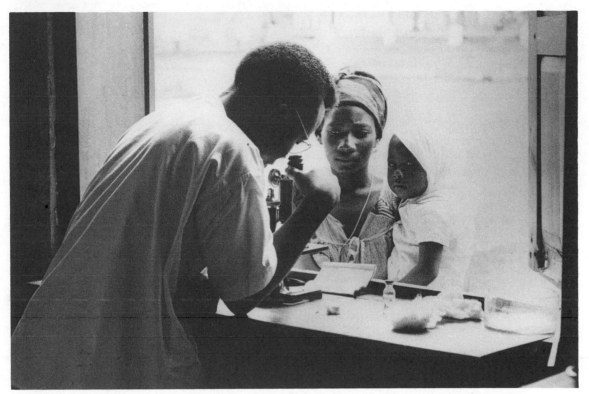

World Health Organization

Stage 1: Preview

Preview *the selection and complete the following sentence: After reading this selection, I would like to know* _____

_____

_____

Stage 2: Integrate Knowledge While Reading

Use thinking strategies as you read:

1. Predict
2. Picture
3. Form analogies

4. Verbalize points
5. Fix up strategies

Underscoring

Using a variety of notations, underscore *the following selection as if you were preparing for a quiz on the material. Remember, do not underscore as you read, but wait until you finish a section and then mark the important points.*

REPRODUCTION RATE*

Robert Wallace, from *Biology: The World of Life*

There is an argument among biologists regarding whether mechanisms are operating that maintain population numbers within certain limits—mechanisms that only occasionally break down. It seems, however, that the relative stability of so many species would indicate that some sort of stabilizing influence is operating. This influence, if it exists,
5 could theoretically operate at two levels by affecting: (1) how many offspring are produced, and (2) the longevity or mortality of organisms in the population.

How Many Offspring Are Produced?

The reproductive potential of most species, even the slowest breeding ones, is incredibly high. Charles Darwin estimated that a single pair of elephants could leave over 19,000,000 descendents in only 750 years. The fact that the entire world was not teeming with
10 elephants indicated to him that some elephants were not reproducing, and that the reproducers were somehow "selected" by the environment.

Whereas elephants are very slow breeders, other species are more prolific. For example, the reproductive potential, for a *single year,* of the housefly is shown in Table 1.

Table 1   Projected populations of the housefly *Musca domestica* for one year, a period that encompasses about seven generations. Do all these offspring survive? The numbers are based on each female laying 120 eggs per generation, each fly surviving just one generation, and half of these being females.

Generation	Numbers If All Survive
1	120
2	7,200
3	432,000
4	25,920,000
5	1,555,200,000
6	93,312,000,000
7	5,598,720,000,000

Edward Kormondy, **Concepts of Ecology,** © 1969, page 63. Reprinted by permission of Prentice-Hall, Inc., Englewood Cliffs, NJ.

*LEARNING STRATEGY: Look for factors that influence the reproductive rate in humans.

From *Biology: The World of Life,* 3rd Edition, by Robert A. Wallace. Copyright © 1981 by Scott, Foresman and Company.

But what determines the rate at which an organism reproduces? It should be apparent
15 that simple laws of energy would not allow an elephant to become pregnant several times
a year. There is just no way that a female could find enough food to produce that many
offspring. And what would happen to the helpless baby elephants already born as new
brothers and sisters appeared on the scene?

It may seem puzzling, then, to learn that each animal theoretically reproduces to its
20 biological limit. Can it be true that animals leave as many offspring as possible? You
might intuitively agree when you recall that any generation is primarily made up of the
offspring of the most successful reproducers. The next question we might ask regards
method. How does an organism maximize its reproductive success?

Humans

The reproductive strategies of any species evolve on the basis of its own particular
25 environmental circumstances, so let's consider the factors that might have determined our
own reproductive capacity. The human female has the ability to produce one child each
year for over thirty years. However, does this mean that humans are physiologically and
psychologically prepared to rear thirty children? Or is our reproductive ability an
evolutionary adjustment to a historically rigorous life in which most, or even all, of the
30 offspring were not likely to survive? In other words, the ability of the human female to
reproduce prolifically may have evolved in response to a traditionally high death rate for
children.

All this is highly hypothetical but the system might work like this. During its early years,
the human is unequipped physically or mentally to deal effectively with the problems of
35 the world. It is among the most helpless of mammalian offspring and one of the slowest
to reach self-sufficiency. During this time it must be cared for by adults who strive to
provide it with food, keep it warm, protect it from predators, and see to it that it doesn't
harm itself. But such care can only have miminal effects on reducing the incidence of
disease and parasitism in these vulnerable years. The precariousness of its first years
40 might be reflected in a high mortality rate. Even today, in highly stressful situations, the
first to die are the very young, the very old, and the sick.

Should an infant die during its first year, the mother could be expected to replace the
child rather quickly by becoming pregnant again. If the child continues to survive,
however, she might not reproduce again quite so soon. One reason is that in many
45 women, suckling somehow inhibits the secretion of FSH and LH from the pituitary,
especially if the diet is minimal, so pregnancy cannot occur as long as they are nursing. In
some cultures the period of nursing is extended for as long as three years, since milk
production will continue that long if the child continues to suckle.

The high reproductive capability of humans might also be a response to bleak
50 prospects of an adult surviving through the entire reproductive period, a span of
approximately 30 years (from 15 to 45). There is evidence that in some earlier
civilizations, the life expectancy was only about 30 years (Table 2). In risky
environmental situations in which there is a good possibility of an individual meeting
death at any age, natural selection might place a higher premium on reproductive output
55 even at the expense of the overall well-being of the individual.

I should add here that this business of calculating age expectancies is deceptive. For
example, when the U.S. Constitution was written, the average life expectancy was 40, but
the requirements for the presidency included not only great virtue but the attainment of
the age of 35 as well. Did this mean that the president was expected to die in the first

Table 2 Estimated Average Life Span in Human Populations

Population	Years
Neanderthal	29.4
Upper Paleolithic	32.4
Mesolithic	31.5
Neolithic Anatolia	38.2
Austrian Bronze Age	38
Classic Greece	35
Classic Rome	32
United States, 1900–1902	48
United States, 1950	70
United States, 1975	72

After E. S. Deevey, "The Probability of Death." Copyright © 1950 by **Scientific American**, Inc. All rights reserved.

60   year of his second term? Our founding fathers may, in their wisdom, have had just such
an event in mind, but it wasn't likely. They were old men themselves. The nation was full
of old people. It turns out that the 40-year expectancy was due to a great number of
people dying very young. *However*, if a person could make it to age 20, his or her chances
of growing old were very good (Table 3). In fact, even in 1850, if you could make it to 20,
you could probably make it to 60. And if you could make it to 60, you were likely to make
it to 76. And at present *your chances are no better*. Our progress has all been at the young
end. We have apparently not learned much about keeping old people alive.

Earlier we found that cells age and self-destruct. But it has also been suggested that old
people do not live longer because they have been subjected to long-term, low doses of
70   numerous substances that the human body simply cannot tolerate for extended periods.
We can kill bacteria, but we can't kill lead in the air. In 1900, most adults died from
disease (particularly pneumonia, flu, TB, and intestinal inflammation) and their life
expectancy was 49 years. In 1950, the leading causes of death for adults were chronic and
degenerative conditions such as heart disease, cancer, and brain hemorrhage, and the life
75   expectancy was 68 years. Do you think this shift can be correlated with differences in the
kind of world in which the people lived?

But what about now? As Table 4 shows, a child born in developed countries these days

Table 3 Life Expectancy. U.S. White Male's Probability of Achieving a Specified Age in Any Given Year of His Life

In the year:	0 years	20 years	40 years	60 years
		Your life expectancy would be:		
1850	38	60	68	76
1890	42	61	67	75
1930	59	66	69	75
1950	66	69	71	76
1980	68	70	72	76

Source: Statistical Bureau of the Metropolitan Life Insurance Co. compiled from various publications of the **Division of Vital Statistics, National Center for Health Statistics,** and **Bureau of the Census.**

Table 4 Population Under Age 15, Growth Rate, Infant Mortality Rates, and Life Expectancy, for Selected Populous Countries[a]

Country	Population Under 15 Years Old		Growth Rate of Population, 1976 (percent)	Infant Mortality Rate	Expectation of Life at Birth (both sexes)
	Year or Period	Percent of total population			
Afghanistan	1972–73	45	1.8–2.5	217–235	35–39
Algeria	1966	47	3.3–3.5	142	53
Argentina	1970	29	1.3	59	66
Australia	1971	29	1.0	14	71
Austria	1975	23	–	18	76
Bangladesh	1974	46	2.6–3.0	153	42
Brazil	1970	44	2.5–2.9	102	54
Canada	1975	26	1.3	15	73
Colombia	1973	45	2.1–2.3	98	59
Cuba	1975	37	1.4	23	70
Egypt	(X)	(NA)	2.6	108	53
Ethiopia	1971	45	2.2–2.6	155–200	36–44
France	1977	23	.3	13	73
German Dem. Rep.	1976	19	–.2	14	71
Germany, Fed. Rep. of	1976	21	–.3	17	71
Greece	1975	24	1.3	22	72
Guatemala	1973	44	2.5–2.6	75	53
India	1971	41	2.1	134	47
Indonesia	1971	43	1.8–2.3	126	42
Iran	1973–76	46	3.0	104	57
Italy	1976	24	.5	19	72
Japan	1976	24	1.0	10	74
Kenya	1969	48	3.4–3.7	119	49
Korea, Republic of	1975	39	1.8–1.9	47	64
Malaysia	1970	45	2.4–2.5	32	68
Mexico	1970	48	2.9–3.5	71	61
Netherlands	1976	25	.6	11	75
Nigeria	1953	44	2.4–3.0	178	37
Pakistan	1972	44	3.0–3.1	139	46
Phillippines	1970	46	2.2–2.6	80	58
Poland	1977	24	1.0	24	71
South Africa	1970	42	2.3–2.5	88–95	57
Spain	1970	28	1.1	16	72
Sweden	1977	21	.3	8	75
Switzerland	1977	22	–.6	11	73
Taiwan	1975	36	2.1	25	70
United States	1970	28	.7	15	72

[a]**Growth rate:** Annual increase (or decrease) to the population resulting from a surplus or deficit of births over deaths and a surplus or deficit of migrants into or out of the country, expressed as a percentage of the base population. **Infant mortality rate:** Number of deaths of children under 1 year of age per 1,000 live births in a calendar year for latest available year. **Life expectancy at birth:** Number of years to be lived by persons born in a certain year if mortality rates for each age group remain constant in the future. Minus sign (–) denotes decrease.

is very likely to live through its first critical years. In humans today, mortality rate decreases after the first year and is very low through the teens, then it increases gradually
80   until about age 60, when it rises rather rapidly. This is especially true in developed countries, such as the United States, but less true in certain poorer countries. Those with the highest infant mortality rate are Guatemala, Pakistan, Turkey, Colombia, Ecuador, Peru, Egypt, and the Sahel countries of West Africa.

    The means by which the human species has increased the likelihood of survival are
85   almost universally viewed as good and desirable. For example, we have specific medicines to combat various maladies that, in earlier days, would have proven fatal. We also have therapeutic and corrective devices to aid the sick. If someone in our midst is unable to provide for himself, that person will usually be cared for, however minimally. We have laws that state that not only must the mentally deficient be allowed to remain in
90   the population, but that their reproductive abilities must not be tampered with. Also, our society often provides for those who, in harsher days, would have been selected against. A person doesn't have to be keen of wit and physically agile in order to cross a busy street. He simply waits for a light—a light that means it's safe to cross leisurely. The result of our social care has been a negation of many of the influences of natural selection. However,
95   at the same time that we have ceased selection for swiftness, strength, and intelligence, we have increased the variation in our species. Thus we find among us myriad interests, talents, tendencies, and appearances. The point is that our society attempts to ensure every individual that he will live and reproduce. With our reproductive potential so high, we may be placing our species in an untenable position by our uncontrolled breeding.

100   To sum up then, reproductive rates are subject to natural selection, and the reproductive potential of humans has been established through the eons of our development. We have recently altered our environment so that the direction and strength of natural selection has been changed, but we are left with a reproductive capacity that better fits our earlier situation.

105   If this is true, or even if it isn't, we might be led to ask ourselves a number of questions. Are large families with many children "natural"? Has the relaxation of natural selection resulted in our species increasing to the extent that we are physically or psychologically unable to deal effectively with the resulting swell of our own numbers? Do crowds make you uneasy? What might be the pressures on a social system in which
110   parents are unable to carefully rear each of their children as individuals? Perhaps the most important questions involve the future. Where do we go from here? What can we expect? How much social change will be necessary to solve the problems resulting from an overbreeding population? How much social change can we tolerate?   /1592

© Scott, Foresman and Company.

Stage 3: Recall

Stop and recall what you have read.
Review your use of the thinking strategies. Did you use all five?
Review your underscoring. Have you sufficiently highlighted the main idea and the significant details?

▥▤▥ Skill Development: Reading Tables

1. Summarize the information in Table 1.

_____

_____

_____

2. Summarize the information in Table 2.

_____

_____

_____

Refer to Table 3 and answer the following items with T (true), F (false), or CT (can't tell).

_____ 3. The life expectancy of a person who is 60 years old is the same today as it was in 1850.

_____ 4. Today your life expectancy at 40 years of age is two years longer than that of a 20 year old.

_____ 5. A baby's life expectancy is higher than that of a 60 year old man.

Refer to Table 4 and answer the following items with T (true), F (false), or CT (can't tell).

_____ 6. The countries listing a life expectancy of over 70 years also have an infant mortality rate of less than 20.

_____ 7. The infant mortality rate is highest in Afghanistan and lowest in the United States.

_____ 8. Of the countries listed, Mexico and Kenya have the highest percent of the total population under 15 years of age.

_____ 9. Of the countries listed, Algeria experienced the highest rate of population growth.

_____ 10. Famine in Ethiopia caused the infant mortality rate to be high.

▥▤▥ Comprehension Questions

_____ 1. The main point that the author is trying to convey in this selection is _____

_____

_____

After reading the selection, answer the following questions with a, b, c, or d.

_____ 2. Regarding population, the author seems to feel that
    a. stabilizing mechanisms exist within our environment to influence reproduction and longevity
    b. reproduction is not influenced by longevity
    c. high reproduction should be coupled with high longevity
    d. the environment does not influence reproduction and longevity

_____ 3. Charles Darwin used the example of the elephant's high reproductive capability to prove that
    a. slow breeders reproduce higher numbers
    b. the environment selects and rejects reproducers
    c. elephants tend to achieve their calculated maximum reproduction level
    d. elephant reproduction is inefficient

_____ 4. In humans nursing a child tends to do all of the following except
    a. inhibit pregnancy
    b. change the mother's hormone secretions
    c. enhance the child's chance of survival in primitive cultures
    d. provide a natural selection factor that works against the child

_____ 5. The author implies that the high human reproductive capacity is probably a natural response to
    a. improved medical treatment
    b. risky environmental situations in earlier civilizations
    c. the rise in life expectancy
    d. the need to limit population expansion

_____ 6. As you become older, your life expectancy
    a. increases
    b. decreases
    c. remains the same as it was at birth
    d. cannot be calculated beyond age 60

_____ 7. At the time the U.S. Constitution was written the author implies that
    a. most people died at 40
    b. a high infant mortality rate reduced the life expectancy
    c. the life expectancy of a 20 year old was only 40 years
    d. life expectancy from 60 is lower than it is today

_____ 8. In the early 1900s most adults died from
    a. air pollution
    b. degenerative conditions
    c. disease
    d. cancer

_____ 9. The author feels that society's efforts to ensure life and reproduction are resulting in
    a. overbreeding
    b. underbreeding

c. more risks to human survival

d. less opportunity for divergent development of individual interests

_____ 10. The author seems to feel that

    a. people today should have more children

    b. people today should have fewer children

    c. infant mortality rates in undeveloped countries should not be reduced

    d. we should have fewer therapeutic and corrective devices to aid the sick

Answer the following questions with *T* (true), *F* (false), or *CT* (can't tell).

_____ 11. The author suggests that if the human death rate were higher, a human female would be able to produce more than one child every year for thirty years.

_____ 12. The human child is among the most helpless of mammalian offspring.

_____ 13. The U.S. Constitution requires that a president be at least 35 years of age.

_____ 14. Pneumonia is a greater cause of death than cancer in today's poorer countries.

_____ 15. The author suggests that the age requirements for modern presidents should be changed.

▌▐▐ ▌ **Vocabulary**

According to the way the boldface word was used in the selection, indicate *a*, *b*, *c*, or *d* for the word or phrase that gives the best definition.

____ 1. "**stabilizing** influence is operating (04)"

    a. reversing

    b. calming

    c. fascinating

    d. questioning

____ 2. "was not **teeming** with elephants (09)"

    a. frightened

    b. raining

    c. irritated

    d. overflowing

____ 3. "to reproduce **prolifically** (31)"

    a. abundantly

    b. briefly

    c. innately

    d. completely

____ 4. "in these **vulnerable** years (39)"

    a. early

    b. susceptible to injury

    c. unsuitable

    d. harmful

____ 5. "**precariousness** of its first year (39)"

    a. loneliness

    b. seclusion

    c. unhappiness

    d. dangerousness

____ 6. "diet is **minimal** (46)"

    a. meager

    b. repetitious

    c. safe

    d. caloric

_____ 7. "**degenerative** conditions (74)"
  a. curable
  b. induced by accidents
  c. organ deterioration
  d. long lasting

_____ 8. "find among us **myriad** interests (96)"
  a. few
  b. innumerable
  c. innovative
  d. different

_____ 9. "in an **untenable** position (99)"
  a. unpopular
  b. awkward
  c. unteachable
  d. indefensible

_____ 10. "**eons** of our development (101)"
  a. several eras
  b. channels
  c. stages
  d. phases

▥▤▥ Essay Question

Discuss any stabilizing influences that you see operating in the human population. Use a sheet of notebook paper to record your answer.

READING FLEXIBILITY

ASSESSING READING RATE

Reading specialists say that the average adult reading speed on relatively easy material is approximately 250 words per minute at 70 percent comprehension. The rate for college students tends to be a little higher, averaging about 300 words per minute on the same type of material with 70 percent comprehension. These figures, however, are misleading for a number of reasons.

Anyone who says to you, "My reading rate is 500 words per minute," is not telling the whole story. The questions that immediately come to mind are, "Is that the rate for reading the newspaper or for the world history textbook?" In addition, you wonder, "Is that the rate when studying for an exam or reading a mystery novel for pleasure?" For an efficient reader, no one reading rate serves for all purposes for all materials. Efficient readers demonstrate their flexibility by varying rate according to their own purpose for reading or according to the difficulty of the material being read.

VARY RATE ACCORDING TO PURPOSE

Before starting on the first word and moving automatically on to the second, third, and fourth at the same pace, take a minute to ask yourself, "Why am I reading this material?" and, based on your answer vary your speed according to your purpose. Do you want 100 percent, 70 percent, or 50 percent comprehension? In other words, figure out what you want to know when you finish and read accordingly. If you are studying for an examination, you probably need to read slowly and carefully, taking time to monitor your comprehension as you progress. Since 100 percent comprehension is not always your goal, be willing to switch gears and move faster over low priority material even though you may sacrifice a few details. If you are reading only to get an overview or to verify a particular detail, read as rapidly as possible to achieve your specific purpose.

For the next two passages, vary your speed according to the designated purpose for reading. Read the first passage to locate a detail and the second to explain the main idea. Time your reading for each, and then calculate and compare your rates.

▥▤▥ Exercise 1: Matching Rate and Purpose

Rapidly read the following passage to determine the two types of industries in which the two monopolies existed. Time your reading.

Starting time = _____

From *Design and Planning 2* edited by Martin Krampen and Peter Seitz. © 1967 Doon School of Fine Arts.

© Scott, Foresman and Company.

Two Monopolies in American History

During the earliest stages of industrialization following the Civil War, there was cutthroat competition among American business firms. (The donkeys were still struggling to get at the hay.)

In the building of the railroads, early industrialists like Cornelius Vanderbilt fought ruthlessly to drive their competitors out of business. Where a competing parallel line served the same two cities, Vanderbilt would lower his rates below costs. He would make up the loss on other routes where he faced no competition. When the competing line was forced into bankruptcy, Vanderbilt would buy it cheaply. Eventually the Vanderbilt network took control of freight service over most of the industrialized Northeast.

In the petroleum industry, John D. Rockefeller began with several small oil refineries. However, he realized he could make more profit if he controlled the oil from well to final distributor. Rockefeller's Standard Oil was able to buy the major pipelines and establish a monopoly in the transport of crude oil. As the only buyer of crude oil from well owners, he would pay a low price. Then the oil would be transported over Rockefeller pipelines. Finally, as the only seller of oil to refiners, he could demand a high price. Economic profits were substantial.

As well owners were forced out of business on the one hand and refiners and distributors on the other, Rockefeller's Standard Oil could buy them up. In this way a major part of the petroleum industry was brought within one enterprise. Whenever rivals could not be forced out of business or could not be merged with the dominant company, cooperative agreements were often made. (The donkeys agreed to share the hay!)

These two cases illustrate *vertical* and *horizontal* combinations to achieve monopoly. Can you identify each?

Marilu McCarty, *Dollars and Sense*

Time*	Rate**	Time*	Rate**
0:10	1,788	0:40	447
0:20	894	0:50	358
0:30	596	1:00	298

*Time is measured in minutes and seconds.
**Rate is in words per minute.

Finishing time = _____

Total reading time = _____

Rate = _____ words per minute

In which two types of industries did the two monopolies exist? _____

_____

From *Dollars and Sense,* Third Edition, by Marilu Hurt McCarty. Copyright © 1979 by Scott, Foresman and Company.

Describe your strategy for reading this passage. _____

_____

▥▤▦ Exercise 2: Matching Rate and Purpose

Rapidly read the following passage to explain what is meant by "monopoly in monopoly" and what companies and products are involved. Time your reading.

Starting time = _____

Monopoly in Monopoly

It's not whether you win or lose; it's how you name the game!

That's the problem in the antitrust dispute over Monopoly.

You won't meet many Americans who aren't familiar with the game of Monopoly. Legend has it that the game was devised around the turn of the century by a Virginia Quaker, Elizabeth Magee. It was known as "The Landlord's Game." For years, several versions were played on painted oilcloth.

In 1933 a retired hotel manager from Georgia became interested in the game and bought rights to the idea. After some updating and standardizing, the patent and trademark were eventually sold to Parker Brothers. Today Parker Brothers is the world's largest producer of games and Monopoly is its star. More than 80 million games have been sold worldwide.

Such success could not forever go unchallenged. Many other manufacturers have come up with similar ideas hoping to grab a share of the market, but Parker Brothers has fought them all. Generally the company has been successful in preventing other firms from using any ideas similar to the original, one-and-only Monopoly. It was successful, that is, until 1973 when an economics professor from California came out with a new game he called Anti-Monopoly.

Professor Ralph Anspach is a specialist in antitrust law. His game is similar to the original, but instead of **building** monopoly its objective is to break it up. His idea caught on, and in the first two years he sold 280,000 games for revenues of about a million dollars. This was after investing only $5000 to set up his own company!

By law the Monopoly trademark belongs exclusively to Parker Brothers. Theirs is a **legal** monopoly. Therefore Parker Brothers is suing Professor Anspach for illegal use of their property. In turn, the professor is suing Parker Brothers over the validity of the trademark itself. He points out that some trademarks eventually become a part of the language itself and are free to be used by any firm. Kleenex, Kodak, aspirin, and even checkers are examples of brand names which now have meanings far broader than a single firm's product. And besides, he says, Anti-Monopoly does not involve competition with Monopoly at all.

Once the trademark case is settled, the right to a monopoly on Monopoly will probably be contested under the Sherman Act. The outcome cannot be considered of tremendous

From *Dollars and Sense,* Third Edition, by Marilu Hurt McCarty. Copyright © 1979 by Scott, Foresman and Company.

importance in the development of antitrust policy. But it's bound to be of interest to Monopoly lovers everywhere!

Marilu McCarty, *Dollars and Sense*

Time	Rate	Time	Rate
:30	820	1:20	307
:40	615	1:30	273
:50	492	1:40	246
1:00	410	1:50	223
1:10	350	2:00	205

Finishing time = _____

Total reading time = _____

Rate = _____ words per minute

Explain what the title means and discuss the companies and products involved.

_____

_____

Describe your strategy for reading this passage. _____

_____

VARY RATE ACCORDING TO DIFFICULTY OF THE MATERIAL

One reason textbooks usually require slower reading than newspapers is that textbooks are more difficult; the vocabulary, the sentences, and usually the information is new, and prior knowledge is limited. Given the same purpose for reading, your speed should vary according to the level of difficulty of the material. For easy material, speed up your reading and for the more challenging, complex selections, slow your pace.

One method of determining the difficulty level of the material is to use a formula that combines the length of the sentences and the number of syllables in the words. The longer sentences and words indicate a more difficult level of reading. Freshman textbooks vary greatly in difficulty from field to field and from book to book. Some freshman texts are written at levels as high as 16th grade level (senior in college), whereas others may be on the 11th or 12th grade level. Even within a single textbook the levels vary; some sections and paragraphs are at a more difficult level and require a slower rate than others. Unfamiliar technical vocabulary can bring a reader to a complete stop. Complex sentences are more difficult to read than simple, concise statements. Sometimes the difficulty is caused by the complexity of the ideas expressed and sometimes it is created by, perhaps unnecessarily, the complexity of the author's style of writing.

An additional factor contributing to difficulty is the reader's level of familiarity with the subject. If you already have a lot of knowledge on a topic, you can usually read about it at a faster rate than if you are exploring a totally new subject. For example, a student who is already involved in advertising will probably be able to work through the advertising chapter in the business textbook at a faster rate than the chapter on a less familiar topic, like supply-side economics. For the economics chapter, the same student may need to slow to a crawl at the beginning of the chapter in order to understand the new concepts, but, as the economics ideas become more familiar, the student can perhaps read at a faster rate toward the end of the chapter.

For the next two passages, vary your speed according to the difficulty of the material. The purpose for reading both will be to write a summary stating the main idea and including the significant supporting details. Time your reading for each, and then calculate and compare your rates.

▮▤▦▮ Exercise 3: Vary Rate According to Difficulty

Read the following passage and write a summary stating the main idea and the significant supporting details. Time your reading.

Starting time = _____

Language Affects Your Perceptions

If we label something "attractive" or "pleasant," we are already predisposed to perceive it in a certain way, probably with interest and enjoyment. If we think of people in terms of how much we like them rather than how little we hate them, we will probably respond more favorably to those individuals. Language shapes our ideas—the labels we attach to things are likely to affect the attitudes we hold. Doesn't a weather forecast of "partly sunny" make you feel better than "partly cloudy"?

To show how labels affect our responses, think of the possible confusion that might result if the person we label "professor" was also the person we label "best friend." If we are not accustomed to responding to "professors" in the same way as "best friends," conflicts occur and perceptual adjustments must be made.

Think about a person who seems to have a negative attitude toward life. Can you recall any conversations you've had with this person? What kinds of words did he or she use? Bob, a person with a pessimistic attitude if ever there was one, tends to label things as being different degrees of "awful." His perceptions cannot help but be reinforced by this

From *Understanding Interpersonal Communication*, Third Edition, by Richard L. Weaver, II, pp. 112–117, 142–144. Copyright © 1984 by Scott, Foresman and Company.

© Scott, Foresman and Company.

labeling. Bob cannot approach a person he has labeled "abusive" without fearing emotional or physical injury. Think how often we describe things as "not bad" when what we really mean is "great." Changing the labels we use to describe things is sometimes the first step toward changing our attitudes.

Examples abound of how language shapes the way we perceive things. In a grocery store, labeling techniques can trick us into thinking an item is "first" or "A-number-one" when it is really a third- or fourth-quality item. How, for example, is a shopper supposed to identify different grades of beef? Jennifer Cross, in *The Supermarket Trap,* explains the dilemma:

> The fact is that "Blogg's Blue Ribbon-Gold Ribbon-Gourmet-Good-Better-Best" has no objective meaning at all. It bears no relation to any U.S. Department of Agriculture meat grade, though in high quality stores "Blogg's Finest" is mostly choice, and occasionally prime. Elsewhere it could be choice, or even a lower grade like good or standard.

The problem is in identifying different levels of quality without making one level appear to be inferior. When we buy "U.S. No. 1" fresh fruits and vegetables or "U.S. Grade A" butter, we are getting second grade, because "U.S. Fancy" is first grade for most fruits and vegetables and "U.S. Grade AA" is first for butter. When we buy "U.S. Extra" nonfat dry milk we get first grade but "U.S. Extra" dry whole milk is second grade, and "U.S. Extra No. 1" in cucumbers or peaches is also second grade.

When we purchase clothes, we want labels that make us feel comfortable or good about our selves. We want a "Fine Linen Handkerchief," not a "Nose Rag." Schools that came under fire when they offered courses in "Sex Education" received fewer protests when the same material was taught as "Social Hygiene" or "Family Health." At work, most people will try much harder and be much happier if they have a title. Think how much more motivated you would be if you were called an "assistant manager" as opposed to a "sales clerk," or in a theater, a "ticket-taker." Ever wonder why large corporations have so many vice-presidents? The difference between "Vice-President in Charge of Widgets" and "Widget Director" may sound slight to an outsider, but it can make a great difference to those involved. The way things are labeled leads us to respond to them in a certain way.

Richard Weaver, *Understanding Interpersonal Communication*

Time	Rate	Time	Rate
:30	1,220	1:50	332
:40	915	2:00	305
:50	732	2:10	280
1:00	610	2:20	261
1:10	521	2:30	243
1:20	457	2:40	228
1:30	406	2:50	215
1:40	366	3:00	203

Finishing time = _____

Total reading time = _____

Rate = _____ words per minute

Write a summary of the passage on a sheet of notebook paper.

▮▤▥ Exercise 4: Vary Rate According to Difficulty

Read the following passage and write a summary stating the main idea and the significant supporting details. Time your reading.

Starting time = _____

Rhythms

Why does an apartment-dwelling cat become restless as evening draws on? How is it that some people are able to wake up at whatever time they want to, almost to the minute? Or better yet, how does a potato know what time it is? Questions about timing in living things have been asked for years, and in some cases for hundreds of years. Of course, scientists have come up with all sorts of data and theories, but the fundamental questions just haven't been answered yet.

The rhythmic nature of life should not be unexpected, in view of the cyclic nature of the world around us. The earth revolves around the sun with regularity, and it rotates at a constant rate on its tilted axis. And the moon has a predictable and recurring relationship with the earth. Our lives are segmented by daily periods of light and dark and seasonal periods of cold and warmth. Since the earth itself functions in rhythmic cycles, we should not be surprised that, through the eons of evolution, a certain rhythmicity or sensitivity to environmental rhythm has winnowed into the sensitive cytoplasm of living things.

About 300 years before Aristotle, men described plants that raise their leaves during the day and lower them at night. About 2,400 years passed, however, before anyone noticed that the leaves would continue their "sleep movements" even when the plant was placed inside and apparently deprived of its environmental information concerning the time of day. The basic question hinges here. Some organisms continue to show rhythmic behavior after they are placed under "constant" conditions. Is the rhythm a response to environmental clues of which we are not aware, or do the organisms have their own *internal* cycles? If an organism takes its timing cues from the environment, it is said to be under *exogenous* control. If it has its own innate internal cycle that operates independently of the environment, its control is *endogenous*.

Part of the difficulty in determining the mechanisms of biological rhythms is the fact that there is such a profusion of these cycles. There are rhythms in the staccato firing of neurons. Hibernating animals such as bears build up layers of fat every autumn. Human births are most likely to occur in the early morning hours than in the early evening. Cytoplasmic substrates and enzymes ebb and surge with a certain regularity.

Most of the rhythms that have been studied are those that occur in a daily cycle, or

From *Biology: The World of Life,* 3rd Edition, by Robert A. Wallace. Copyright © 1981 by Scott, Foresman and Company.

approximately every twenty-four hours. It is undoubtedly not coincidental that this is about the length of the solar day. Interestingly, when organisms with a twenty-four-hour cycle are placed under constant laboratory conditions, their rhythms may drift to a twenty-three- or a twenty-five-hour cycle. These periods of about a day are called *circadian rhythms* (from *circa,* meaning "about," and *diem,* meaning "day").

Circadian rhythms have led most researchers to agree that timing is internal. It is suggested that *approximate* twenty-four-hour clocks are built into circadian organisms, but that environmental cues, such as day length, are needed to keep the clock precisely set. In other words, the rhythm is innate, but the fine tuning is environmentally dependent. The fact that some rhythms go through several cycles every twenty-four hours while others are monthly or annual does not upset the theory at all. It is suggested that these rhythms either are governed by some other internal clocks or are based on a circadian clock but have some longer or shorter cycle. A familiar example is the two hands of a clock that move at different rates within the same twenty-four-hour period, but are driven by the same mechanism. If you were to stick you finger in you ear every three minutes, the cycle of this behavior would be three minutes, but the timing would still be done with a twelve-hour clock. Another example is people who keep different hours. Some people are "day people" and others seem to be "night people," but they both use the same twelve-hour clock—and they usually marry each other.

Robert Wallace, *Biology: The World of Life*

Time	Rate	Time	Rate
1:00	673	2:40	253
1:10	574	2:50	237
1:20	504	3:00	224
1:30	447	3:10	212
1:40	403	3:20	202
1:50	366	3:30	191
2:00	336	3:40	183
2:10	309	3:50	175
2:20	289	4:00	168
2:30	269		

Finishing time = _____

Total reading time = _____

Rate = _____ words per minute

Write a summary of the passage on a sheet of notebook paper.

SKIMMING

Skimming is a technique of selectively reading for the gist or the main idea. Since it involves processing material at rates around 900 words per minute, it is not defined by some experts as reading. Skimming involves skipping words, sentences, paragraphs, and even pages. It is a method of quickly overviewing material to answer the question, "What is this about?"

Skimming and previewing are very similar in that both involve getting an overview. Previewing sets the stage for later careful reading, whereas, skimming is a substitute for a complete reading. Skimming is useful for material that you want to know about but don't have the time to read. For example, you might want to skim some of the supplemental articles for a course that have been placed on reserve in the library because you know your professor is only interested in your understanding the main idea of each article and a complete reading would be unnecessary. Sometimes you may want to pick up a book and just "get the idea," but not make a complete reading. Skimming is a useful tool. The technique is as follows:

1. Read the title, subheadings, italics, and boldface print to get an idea of what the material is about.
2. Try to get an insight into the organization of the material to help you anticipate where the important points will be located. Some of the organizational patterns and their functions are:
   a. Listing: explains items of equal value
   b. Definition and Examples: defines a term and gives examples to help the reader understand the term
   c. Time Order or Sequence: presents items in chronological order
   d. Comparison-Contrast: items are compared for their similarities and differences
   e. Description: characteristics of an item are explained
   f. Cause and Effect: one item is shown to have produced another
   g. Problem-Solution: explains the problem, causes, and effects as well as suggests a solution
   h. Opinion-Proof: gives an opinion and then supports it with proof (See Appendix B for examples of organizational patterns.)
3. If the first paragraph is introductory, read it. If not, skip to a paragraph that seems to introduce the topic.
4. Moving rapidly, let your eyes float over the words trying to grasp main ideas and the significant supporting details.
5. Notice first sentences in paragraphs and read them if they seem to be summary statements.
6. Skip words that seem to have little meaning like *a, an,* and *the.*
7. Skip sentences or sections that seem to contain the following:
   a. Familiar ideas

b. Unnecessary details

c. Superfluous examples

d. Restatements or unneeded summaries

e. Material irrelevant to your purpose

8. If the last paragraph of a section is a summary, read it if you need to check your understanding.

▌▓▐ Exercise 5: Skimming

Skim the following passage to be able to state the point the author is making about conflict. Time your reading.

Starting time = _____

Conflict

Many therapists assume that anxiety is generally a sign of some underlying conflict. **Conflict** is described as opposing needs or goals that tend to pull an individual in two different directions. In order to relieve the anxiety, it is important for the individual to develop an understanding about the nature of the conflict. A child may want to be independent but also be protected by his or her parents. The opposing needs would pull the child in different directions and would probably result in anxiety.

As part of his theory of personality, psychologist Kurt Lewin described three types of conflict. These are **approach-approach, avoidance-avoidance,** and **approach-avoidance conflicts.**

Approach-Approach Conflict. This type of conflict involves the presence of two equally attractive alternatives. The person cannot have both. The fable of the donkey standing between two delicious bales of hay illustrates an approach-approach conflict. Supposedly, the donkey could not make up his mind which bale of hay he should choose, so he starved to death. Humans may have to choose between pie and cake for dessert, or whether to spend the afternoon at the beach or playing tennis. Unlike donkeys, humans generally resolve approach-approach conflicts rather quickly and with relatively little anxiety. Some individuals may become slightly flustered when they cannot decide between cake and pie, but most of us will pause only slightly before making a decision. This is probably the least serious form of conflict.

Avoidance-Avoidance Conflict. This type of conflict involves the presence of two or more equally unattractive choices. Again, the person is in a situation where a decision must be made. The person cannot avoid facing one of the unpleasant consequences. An example of this type of conflict might be a student who must choose between studying for a boring course or failing a final examination. Both alternatives are equally undesirable.

Avoidance-avoidance conflict can be quite serious. Consider children whose parents

From *Personal Adjustment,* Second Edition, by Valerian J. Derlega and Louis H. Janda, pp. 100–102. Copyright © 1981 by Scott, Foresman and Company.

constantly scold them, telling them to grow up and act their ages. Suppose that every time these children make an effort to be independent or to develop more mature interests, they are punished by their parents. Such children are in a "can't win" situation. Because they are so powerless in relation to their parents, these children experience intense anxiety, which in turn can lead to serious psychological problems.

Avoidance-avoidance conflicts are difficult to resolve because as individuals make a tentative decision, they move closer to one of the unattractive goals and so become more anxious. The student who decides to take a chance and not study for the final exam begins to worry about failing the course. The child who decides to be more independent worries about the parent's reactions. This action causes the individual to retreat and then approach the alternative, or second, goal, which is equally unpleasant.

One typical method of dealing with avoidance-avoidance conflicts is to remove oneself from the situation entirely. Students may try to find a way of dropping a boring course even though the deadline for doing so has passed. Children may run away from home. Humans will try to find a way to avoid having to make decisions between two unattractive alternatives. Often it is not possible to do so. Students must still face the exam, and children will usually be found and returned to their parents.

Approach-Avoidance Conflict.   The third type of conflict situation involves a single goal that has both desirable and undesirable characteristics. In such situations people are likely to describe themselves as having "mixed feelings." Consider the student who would like to become involved with student government because of the exciting opportunities this experience would provide. But the student is afraid to speak in front of large groups of people; therefore campaigning would be a difficult experience. This form of conflict can also result in anxiety.

Derlega and Janda, *Personal Adjustment*

Time	Rate	Time	Rate
:30	1,254	1:50	341
:40	940	2:00	313
:50	752	2:10	288
1:00	627	2:20	270
1:10	535	2:30	251
1:20	469	2:40	236
1:30	416	2:50	221
1:40	376	3:00	209

Finishing time =_____

Total reading time = _____

Rate = _____ words per minute

What is the author's point about conflict? _____

_____

SCANNING

Since scanning is a process of searching for a single bit of information, it is more of a locating skill than a reading skill. A common use of scanning is looking up a number in a telephone book. When scanning for information, you do not need to understand the meaning of the material, but instead you merely need to pinpoint a specific detail. For example, you might find that after reading a chapter on pricing in your marketing textbook that you cannot recall the definition of *price lining*. To locate the information, you would not reread, but scan the chapter to find the key phrase "price lining" and then review the definition.

A combination of skimming and scanning is used by researchers. If you are working on a research paper on paranoia, you might have a list of thirty books and articles to read. A complete reading of each reference, however, is probably unnecessary. Instead, you can scan to locate the information relevant to your topic and skim to get the main idea.

The techniques of scanning are:

1. Figure out the organization of the material.
   Get an overview of which section will probably contain the information you are looking for.
2. Know specifically what you are looking for.
   Decide on a key expression that will signal your information, but be ready to switch to a related idea if that doesn't work.
3. Repeat the phrase and hold the image in your mind.
   Concentrate on the image so that you will recognize it when it comes into view.
4. Move quickly and aggressively.
   Remember, you are scanning, not reading.
5. Verify through carefully reading. After locating your information, read carefully to make sure you have really found it.

▌▌▌▌ Exercise 6: Scanning

Scan the following passage only to find the organizational difference in the way chimps and baboons move around in groups. Time your reading. What term will

you scan for? _____

Starting time = _____

Variations in Social Organization Among the Primates

Interactions create, maintain, and change patterns of social organization. As we have noted, however, there are parameters to social organization, such as previous social patterns, personality characteristics, ecological/biological factors, and of course, existing values, beliefs, technology, and other cultural forces. Although chimpanzees are our closest primate relative, they did not have to live and evolve on the African savannah. They evolved in the lower parts of the trees next to the savannah. They could thus take refuge in the trees when danger presented itself. However, a very distant relative—the baboon—did evolve on the savannah under conditions similar to those facing our ancestors. The differences in chimp and baboon social organization reflect, to some degree, the different environments in which they evolved. But more than this is involved: baboons are monkeys with smaller brains and with less capacity to brachiate, or swing with their arms than chimps (who are apes). Baboons thus entered the savannah with a much different biological legacy, which certainly influenced the evolution of their social patterns. We can compare chimp and baboon "societies" to appreciate some of the differences that ecology, biology, and perhaps personality make in the evolution of social organization.

Chimps are highly vocal, baboons are much less vocal. Chimps reveal very loose, free-floating social relationships. Baboons show clear patterns of male dominance and authority. Chimps are much less sexually dimorphic—that is, they reveal fewer differences in size and strength between males and females—than baboons. Male baboons are much bigger and stronger than females. Chimps move about in a somewhat chaotic fashion; baboons move in "formation" with dominant males at the front, back, and sides of the troops, encircling females, children, and nondominant males. Chimps flee in an "each-chimp-for-itself" fashion when danger presents itself, whereas dominant male baboons are more likely to stand and collectively attack aggressively a dangerous predator. Chimps are sexually promiscuous, engaging in sex regularly and easily—for example, males have been seen to "line up" and "wait their turn" for access to a receptive female. Dominant male baboons aggressively protect "their females," although females often "sneak off" to mate with lower-ranking males.

Jonathan Turner, *Sociology*

Time	Rate	Time	Rate
:10	2,742	1:10	390
:20	1,371	1:20	342
:30	914	1:30	303
:40	685	1:40	274
:50	548	1:50	248
1:00	457	2:00	228

From *Sociology: Studying the Human System* by Jonathan Turner, pp. 117, 136, 213, 294. Copyright © 1981 by Random House, Inc. Reprinted by permission of Random House, Inc.

Finishing time = ⎯⎯⎯⎯⎯

Total reading time = ⎯⎯⎯⎯⎯

Rate = ⎯⎯⎯⎯⎯ words per minute

Describe the organizational difference in the formational movement of chimps and baboons.

⎯⎯⎯⎯⎯⎯⎯⎯⎯⎯⎯⎯⎯⎯⎯⎯⎯⎯⎯⎯⎯⎯⎯⎯⎯⎯

⎯⎯⎯⎯⎯⎯⎯⎯⎯⎯⎯⎯⎯⎯⎯⎯⎯⎯⎯⎯⎯⎯⎯⎯⎯⎯

⎯⎯⎯⎯⎯⎯⎯⎯⎯⎯⎯⎯⎯⎯⎯⎯⎯⎯⎯⎯⎯⎯⎯⎯⎯⎯

Selection **1**

SPEECH

Jean-Claude Lejeune

Skill Development: Skimming and Scanning

Skim *the selection as if you were planning to use a brief summary of it in a research paper. Use three or four sentences to write a summary that you could use in your paper. Record your summary on a sheet of notebook paper. Describe the organization of the selection and time your reading. Allow no more than five minutes for this exercise.*

Scan *the selection to answer the following questions and record your total time: Allow no more than two minutes for this exercise.*

1. *What are the usual effects of the withdrawing style?*

_____

2. *How many styles of feedback are listed?*

_____

3. *How does the reassuring style operate?*

_____

Stage 2: Integrate Knowledge While Reading

Now carefully read the selection to organize the material for future study and to answer some comprehension questions. Select the method of organizing textbook material that you feel is most helpful to you and most appropriate for remembering the information in this selection. Explain why you chose either underscoring, summarizing, the Cornell Method of notetaking, outlining, or mapping.

THE EFFECTS OF FEEDBACK*

Richard Weaver, from *Understanding Interpersonal Communication*

If you ever think that your feedback is insignificant and makes no difference, remember that in a two-person interpersonal situation, you are the *only* source of reactions for the other person. Without you, there is no one else. If you do not provide feedback, the other person can't know how well he or she is getting through. It's up to you to help the other
5 person make the message as accurate as possible: your influence is felt strongly. How much feedback you give is also important.

In a landmark study, researchers investigated how differing amounts of feedback affected how the message was conveyed. In all cases, students were to draw geometric patterns according to directions given to them by the instructors. In one situation the
10 researchers allowed no feedback between the instructor and the students. In a second situation, the students and teacher could see each other, but ask no questions. In a third environment, students could answer yes or no to the instructor's questions. In a fourth circumstance, students could ask any questions and get information—a free-feedback situation. The researchers discovered that as the amount of allowed feedback increased, it
15 took students longer to complete their tasks but they also drew their geometric figures more accurately. And they felt far more confident about their success in drawing the figures in this condition of free feedback. We can conclude from this that feedback in an interpersonal communication encounter takes extra time but results in more accurate message transmission and more confidence in the message-transmission process.

*LEARNING STRATEGY: Be able to discuss and evaluate each kind of feedback.

From *Understanding Interpersonal Communication,* Third Edition, by Richard L. Weaver, II. Copyright © 1984 by Scott, Foresman and Company.

Style of Feedback

20 Feedback begins within us. **Internal feedback** takes place all the time as we communicate with others. As we speak, we anticipate certain responses from the other person; our process of getting set depends on internal feedback. As we receive feedback from another person, we adapt and correct our own message; the process of adapting and correcting depends on internal feedback.

25 Giving feedback to another person begins with our own internal feedback. If we want to give someone feedback as he or she speaks, we must first be very attentive to that person's communications. We can't give helpful feedback if we aren't listening effectively to start with. To be ready to respond appropriately we must be alert to the other person's overall message—we should try hard to see where he or she is coming from so that our

30 feedback is not insensitive or confusing.

Thomas Gordon, in *Parent Effectiveness Training*, suggests twelve kinds of response styles for giving feedback. Other authors list only five. The following scheme provides for six ways. Even though all the styles are listed—to give us a way to classify typical ways of responding—the final method is strongly recommended. The six are called withdrawing,

35 judging, analyzing, questioning, reassuring, and paraphrasing.

Withdrawing. The **withdrawing response** simply tries to separate the other person from the problem. "Just forget about it" or "Let's not talk about it now" are common examples of this style. Withdrawing also could take the form of distracting. When a friend comes to you with a problem about one of her professors, you might ask her, "Say, how is

40 your boyfriend, I haven't heard much about him lately?" If that appears too blatant and obvious you could ease into the distraction with a related comment or question, "That's the professor you liked so much last week?"

Withdrawing responses are weak because they do not address the problem at hand. Although they may allow the other person time to think, in most cases, the reason the

45 other person is coming to you is for a response of some kind. Also, they may reveal lack of concern, poor listening, or callousness on the part of the responder. With so many other possible responses available, this is not considered a positive method for successful interaction.

Judging.   The **judging response** is one of the most common responses we make when

50 trying to help others. We give advice or make a judgment without realizing we are being evaluative, corrective, or suggestive. By telling people that their idea or behavior is good or bad, appropriate or inappropriate, effective or ineffective, or right or wrong, we imply what they might do to solve their problem, or how they ought to behave. Judging responses often begin with "If I were you, I would," "You know, you should . . . ," or

55 "The thing you might consider doing is . . . ."

One reason a judging response can hinder a relationship is that it can appear threatening. What is your immediate reaction when someone tells you that something you did, or an idea that you have, is wrong? You probably get defensive; defensiveness causes closed-mindedness, rejection, and resistance. You want to stop exploring, change subjects, retreat, or escape. When people judge, they imply that their evaluation is

60 superior to someone else's. Someone with a problem does not want to feel inferior.

Further, judging responses are quick ways to deal with others' problems. They do not necessarily reveal genuine concern—if that is your intent. If others perceive that you are trying to deal with them in a quick or easy way, rejection is likely to follow. Nobody wants to be brushed off.

65   Finally, when you give advice often you encourage others not to take responsibility for their own problems. You provide an escape route—an "easy out." If others can ask and get advice whenever they are face-to-face with problems, why should they bother to take responsibility for or solve their own problems? In addition, if you give advice they could blame you when your evaluation or suggestion does not work out. You set yourself up as a convenient scapegoat.

70

Analyzing.   If you rephrase your response above so that it explains the other's action or dissects it, you are **analyzing**—and the situation is not greatly improved. "You know, the reason you are disturbed is . . . " or "Your situation is simply . . . " are likely to be analyzing responses. In these cases you end up trying to instruct others or to tell them
75   what their problems mean. It is as if you have assumed the role of psychiatrist: "Your problem implies (or indicates) that . . . ." The difference between the judging and analyzing responses is small. When analyzing others' problems we imply what they ought to think. We are supplying the motives, justifications, or rationale for their behavior— once again, providing them a convenient "out."
80   The drawbacks, too, are similar to those for the judging response. Analyzing the behavior of others can make them defensive and less likely to reveal thoughts and feelings—thus preventing them from further interpretation or analysis. Although analyzing takes longer than judging, it still can seem to "brush others off" because with a single analysis, we may explain their behavior. It may encourage others *not* to take
85   responsibility for their own problems; analyzing supplies answers which keeps them from thinking through and trying to approach their own problems. Also, it can convey superiority: "I know more about what makes you tick than you do."

Questioning.   A questioning response may draw out the other person. The purpose of questioning feedback is to get him or her to discuss the problem. A questioning response
90   is a good beginning, too, because it gives us information about the nature of the problem. It provides a better base to act on and an emotional release for the other person at the same time. This response takes the form of a question: "What makes this situation so upsetting to you?" or "What do you suppose caused this to happen?" An implied question might be phrased, " . . . and you expect the situation to get worse, not better . . . ."
95   In questioning, we don't want to be threatening or accusatory. Phrasing our questions carelessly can cause more problems than we solve. For example, we would probably not ask, "How did you ever get into this mess?" because that puts a value judgment on the experience and changes the response to a judging one. Questions like, "Didn't you know that was wrong?" or "You really weren't thinking, were you?" are also judging. Again we
100   don't want to imply what that person should have done or ought to do.
In using the questioning response, communicators should avoid questions beginning with *why. Why* questions create defensiveness. When asked, "Why did you do that?" our immediate impulse is to defend ourselves. It automatically indicates disapproval: "You shouldn't have done that." Criticism and advice tend to be threatening. *What, where,*
105   *when, how,* and *who* questions are more helpful in opening others up. They encourage specificity, precision, and more self-disclosure.

Reassuring.   If a friend comes to us with an upsetting problem, we probably want to reassure him or her that all is not lost. Pointing out alternatives he or she may not have thought of would be **reassuring**. Our response should be calming, to reduce the intensity
110   of our friend's feeling. Initially, our reassurance may be no more specific than a look or a

touch that says, "I'm on your side." A reassuring response may reveal agreement. Once a friend knows that we are empathic, we can discuss actions to correct the problem.

To provide reassurance we should first reduce the intensity of the feeling. A comment like, "That is a serious problem, and I can see why you are upset . . . " is a good
115 beginning. Reassurance means acknowledging the seriousness of the other person's feelings. It does not need to reveal agreement, but we don't want to argue or suggest that these emotions are inappropriate.

Although reassuring responses may be stronger than many of the preceding styles, they can come across negatively, too. If by tone of voice or phrasing we imply that others
120 should not feel the way they do, once again, we have turned our response into a judging one, and the weaknesses of the judging response become operative.

Paraphrasing.   Our first comment to our friend could be, "I can see you're very upset about this problem. It must mean a great deal to you." In **paraphrasing** the other person's remarks we show that we understand. Thus, paraphrasing can show that we care about
125 correctly understanding our friend's situation. When we reinforce our remarks with nonverbal cues—eye contact, facial expressions of sincerity, touching, tone of voice—this response is very supportive.

You might ask, why paraphrase? Why restate in your own words what others have just
130 said? First, paraphrasing helps make certain that you have understood what others are saying. In a sense, it gives you a second chance to make sure you are understanding them. Second, it can begin a clarifying process—drawing others out, gaining more information, and talking things out more extensively. Both talk and time allow communicators opportunities to gain clearer understanding of themselves and the
140 implications of their feelings and thoughts. Third, paraphrasing can serve as a summarizing process—covering the main points of a situation more concisely, or trying to add things up—as others reflect and review. Fourth, it assures others that you did, indeed hear what they said. You are alert, responsive—involved. And finally it shows others that you are trying to understand their thoughts and feelings. It helps legitimize
145 your efforts as a concerned, caring person.

In positive response styles we avoid judging the other person and the situation. Our **intentional communication**, our choice of words, for example, is not as crucial as is our **unintentional communication**, our nonverbal cues that reveal our honest effort to understand the other person's problem and feelings. The idea is to indicate acceptance
150 and respect for the other person. As the feelings are reflected back to us, an atmosphere of mutual respect, support, and trust develops. And our interpersonal relationships are likely to become more satisfying.

Stage 3: Recall

Stop and recall what you have read.
Review your use of the thinking strategies. Did you use all five?

▪▪▪ Organizing Textbook Material

Write a summary, take notes, outline, or map this selection on a sheet of notebook paper. Explain your choice for organizing the information in "Feedback."

© Scott, Foresman and Company.

▐▌▐▌▐▌ Comprehension Questions

1. The main point that the author is trying to get across in this selection is _____

_____

After reading the selection, answer the following questions with a, b, c, or d.

_____ 2. In the study measuring the effects of differing amounts of feedback on student ability to draw geometric patterns, researchers found that
   a. increased feedback was faster and more accurate
   b. decreased feedback was fast but totally inaccurate
   c. increased feedback took more time but resulted in greater accuracy.
   d. the amount of feedback influenced attitude but did not determine accuracy

_____ 3. The style of feedback that says "If I were you, I would . . ." is called
   a. withdrawing
   b. judging
   c. analyzing
   d. reassuring

_____ 4. The questioning style of feedback primarily indicates a desire to
   a. draw the other person out
   b. raise distractions
   c. assess blame
   d. determine right or wrong

_____ 5. The type of feedback that says, "Let's forget about it" is
   a. withdrawing
   b. judging
   c. analyzing
   d. reassuring

_____ 6. The type of feedback most preferred by the author is
   a. analyzing
   b. questioning
   c. judging
   d. paraphrasing

_____ 7. The reassuring type of feedback focuses on
   a. agreeing with the other person's views
   b. changing the other person's opinion
   c. acknowledging the seriousness of the other person's feelings
   d. finding the reasons for the other person's attitude

_____ 8. In the questioning style of feedback, the question to be avoided is
   a. who
   b. what
   c. when
   d. why

9. The author feels that the paraphrasing style of feedback is particularly effective because of all the following except
   a. it serves as a summarizing process
   b. it can be a clarifying process
   c. it assures others that you understood the message
   d. it allows both sides to be heard so that an evaluation can be made

10. The author indicates that his choice in the six types of feedback styles
    a. was determined by Thomas Gordon
    b. varies from other authors
    c. is the number accepted by most researchers
    d. is based on a research study with college students

Answer the following questions with T (true), F (false), or CT (can't tell).

11. Internal feedback occurs constantly as we communicate with others.
12. The author considers the withdrawing style of feedback a weak, but positive, method for successful interaction.
13. The author feels that the analyzing style of feedback can supply too many answers and encourage others not to take responsibility for their own problems.
14. Paraphrasing is the style of feedback used by most communicators.
15. The author believes that we bear no responsibility for our unintentional communication.

▥▤▥ Vocabulary

According to the way the boldface word was used in the selection, indicate *a, b, c,* or *d* for the word or phrase that gives the best definition.

_____ 1. "In a **landmark** study (07)"
   a. modern
   b. turning point
   c. interesting
   d. thorough

_____ 2. "how the message was **conveyed** (08)"
   a. communicated
   b. written
   c. concluded
   d. solved

_____ 3. "appears too **blatant** and obvious (40)"
   a. loud
   b. offensively conspicuous
   c. pessimistic
   d. obviously embarrassed

_____ 4. "**callousness** on the part of the responder (46)"
   a. unfeeling toughness
   b. closed mindedness
   c. irrationality
   d. ignorance

—— 5. "as a convenient **scapegoat** (70)"
   a. consultant
   b. animal
   c. dishonest counselor
   d. person to blame

—— 6. "to be threatening or **accusatory** (95)"
   a. leveling charges
   b. legal
   c. frightening
   d. disagreeable

—— 7. "knows that we are **emphatic** (112)"
   a. definite
   b. sympathetic
   c. sincere
   d. open

—— 8. "the weakness of the judging response become **operative** (121)"
   a. obsolete
   b. in use
   c. forgiven
   d. tangible

—— 9. "helps **legitimize** your efforts (143)"
   a. pay for
   b. lengthen through litigation
   c. refine
   d. make legal

—— 10. "our **intentional** communication (146)"
   a. done by design
   b. intelligent
   c. healthy
   d. rehearsed

■ ■ ■ Essay Question

Describe each of the six types of feedback and discuss the effects of each. Use a sheet of notebook paper to record your answer.

Selection **2**

BIOLOGY

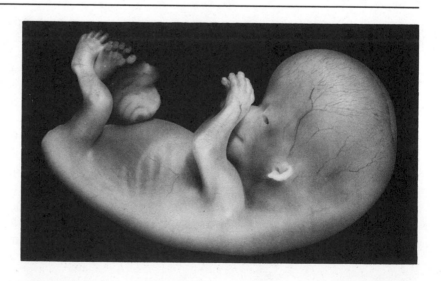

Skill Development: Skimming and Scanning

Skim *the selection as if you were planning to use a brief summary of the information in a research paper. Write a three or four sentence summary that you could use in your paper. Describe the organization of the selection and time your reading. Allow no more than five minutes for this exercise.*

Scan *the selection to answer the following questions and record your total time. Allow no more than two minutes for this exercise.*

1. What is the amniotic fluid? _____

_____

2. What is the approximate length of a normal pregnancy? _____

_____

3. What is "lightening"? _____

_____

Stage 2: Integrate Knowledge While Reading

Now carefully read the selection to organize the material for future study and to answer some comprehension questions. Select the method of organizing textbook material that you feel is most helpful to you and most appropriate for remembering the information in this selection. Explain why you chose either underscoring, summarizing, the Cornell Method of notetaking, outlining, or mapping.

PREGNANCY AND BIRTH

Robert Wallace, from *Biology: The World of Life**

Descriptions in bus-station novels notwithstanding, fertilization occurs with the mother-to-be totally unaware of the event. If there are sperm cells thrashing around in the genital tract at any time within forty-eight hours before ovulation to about twelve hours after, the odds are very good that pregnancy will occur. As soon as the egg is touched by the head
5 of a spern, it undergoes violent pulsating movements which unite the twenty-three chromosomes of the sperm with its own genetic complement. From this single cell, about 1/175 of an inch in diameter, a baby weighing several pounds and composed of trillions of cells will be delivered about 266 days later.

For convenience, we will divide the 266 days, or nine months, into three periods of

*LEARNING STRATEGY: Be able to describe the changes in both fetus and mother during each trimester.

From *Biology: The World of Life*, 3rd Edition, by Robert A. Wallace. Copyright © 1981 by Scott, Foresman and Company.

10　three months each. We can consider these *trimesters* separately, since each is characterized by different sorts of events.

The First Trimester

In the first trimester the embryo begins the delicate structural differentiations that will lead to its final form. It is therefore particularly susceptible during this period to any number of factors that might influence its development. In fact the embryo often fails to
15　survive this stage.

The first cell divisions result in cells that all look about alike and have roughly the same potentials. In other words, at this stage the cells are, theoretically anyway, interchangeable. Seventy-two hours after fertilization, the embryo will consist of sixteen such cells. (So, how many divisions will have taken place?) Each cell will divide before it
20　reaches the size of the cell that has produced it; hence the cells will become progressively smaller with each division. By the end of the first month the embryo will have reached a length of only ⅛ inch, but it will consist of millions of cells.

In the second month the features of the embryo become more recognizable. Bone begins to form throughout the body, primarily in the jaw and shoulder areas. The head
25　and brain are developing at a much faster rate than the rest of the body, so that at this point the ears appear and open, lidless eyes stare blankly into the amniotic fluid. The circulatory system is developing and blood is pumped through the umbilical cord out to the chorion, where it receives life-sustaining nutrients and deposits the poisons it has removed from the developing embryo. The nitrogenous wastes and carbon dioxide filter
30　into the mother's bloodstream, where they will be circulated to her own kidneys and lungs for removal. At about day 46 the primordial reproductive organs begin to form, either as testes or ovaries, and it is now, for the first time, that the sex of the embryo becomes apparent. Near the end of the second month fingers and toes begin to appear on the flattened paddles which have formed from the limb buds. By this time the embryo is
35　about two inches long and is more or less human in appearance; it is now called a *fetus*. Growth and differentiation continue during the third month, but now the fetus begins to move. It breathes the amniotic fluid in and out of bulblike lungs and swallowing motions become distinct. At this point individual differences can be distinguished in the behavior of fetuses. The clearest differences are in their facial expressions. Some frown a lot; others
40　smile or grimace. It would be interesting to correlate this early behavior with the personality traits that develop after birth.

The Second Trimester

In the second trimester the fetus grows rapidly, and by the end of the sixth month it may be about a foot long, although it will weigh only about a pound and a half. Whereas the predominant growth of the fetus during the first trimester was in the head and brain
45　areas, during the second trimester the body grows at a much faster relative rate than the brain and begins to catch up in size with the head.

The fetus is by this time behaving more vigorously. It is able to move freely within its sea of amniotic fluid and the delighted mother can feel it kicking and thrashing about. Interestingly, the fetus must sleep now, so there are periods when it is inactive. It is
50　capable of reacting to more types of stimuli as time passes. For example, by the fifth month the eyes are sensitive to light, although there is still no sensitivity to sound. Other organs seem to be complete, but remain nonfunctional. For example, the lungs are

developed, but they cannot exchange oxygen. The digestive organs are present, but they cannot digest food. Even the skin is not prepared to cope with the temperature
55 changes in the outside world. In fact, at the end of the fifth month the skin is covered by a protective cheesy paste consisting of wax and sweatlike secretions mixed with loosened skin cells (*vernix caseosa*). The fetus is still incapable in nearly all instances of surviving alone.

By the sixth month the fetus is kicking and turning so constantly that the mother often
60 must time her own sleep periods to coincide with her baby's. The distracting effect has been described as similar to being continually tapped on the shoulder, but not exactly. The fetus moves with such vigor that its movements are not only felt from the inside, but can be seen clearly from the outside. To add to the mother's distraction, the fetus may even have periods of hiccups. By this stage it is so large and demanding that it places a
65 tremendous drain on the mother's reserves.

At the end of the second trimester the fetus has the unmistakable appearance of a human baby (or a very old person, since its skin is loose and wrinkled at this stage). In the event of a premature birth around the end of this trimester, the fetus may be able to survive.

The Third Trimester

70 During the third trimester the fetus grows until it is no longer floating free in its amniotic pool. It now fills the abdominal area of the mother. The fetus is crowded so tightly into the greatly enlarged uterus that its movement is restricted. In these last three months the mother's abdomen becomes greatly distended and heavy, and her posture and gait may be noticeably altered in response to the shift in her center of gravity. The mass of tissue
75 and amniotic fluid that accompanies the fetus ordinarily weighs almost twice as much as the fetus itself. Toward the end of this period, milk begins to form in the mother's mammary glands, which in the previous trimester have undergone a sudden surge of growth.

At this time, the mother is at a great disadvantage in several ways in terms of her
80 physical well-being. About 85 percent of the calcium she eats goes to the fetal skeleton, and about the same percentage of her iron intake goes to the fetal blood cells. Of the protein she eats, much of the nitrogen goes to the brain and other nerve tissues of the fetus.

Some interesting questions arise here. If a woman is unable to afford expensive
85 protein-rich foods during the third trimester, what is the probability of a lowered I.Q. in her offspring? On the average the poorer people in this country show lower I.Q. scores. Are they poor because their I.Q.'s are low, or are I.Q.'s low because they are poor? Is there a self-perpetuating nature about either of these alternatives?

In the third trimester, the fetus is large. It requires increasingly greater amounts of
90 food, and each day it produces more poisonous wastes for the mother's body to carry away. Her heart must work harder to provide food and oxygen for two bodies. She must breathe, now, for two individuals. Her blood pressure and heart rate rise. The fetus and the tissues maintaining it form a large mass that crowds the internal organs of the mother. In fact, the crowding of the fetus against the mother's diaphragm may make breathing
95 difficult for her in these months. Several weeks before delivery, however, the fetus will change its position, dropping lower in the pelvis (called "*lightening*") and thus relieve the pressure against the mother's lungs.

There are important changes occuring in the fetus in these last three months, and

© Scott, Foresman and Company.

some of these are not very well understood. The effects of these changes, however, are reflected in the survival rate of babies delivered by Caesarian section (an incision through the mother's side). In the seventh month, only 10 percent survive; in the eighth month, 70 percent; and in the ninth, 95 percent survive.

Interestingly, there is another change in the relationship of the fetus and mother at this time. Whereas measles and certain other infectious diseases would have affected the embryo during the first trimester of pregnancy, at this stage the mother's antibodies confer an immunity to the fetus, a protection that may last through the first few weeks of infancy.

At some point about 255 to 265 days from the time of conception the life-sustaining placenta begins to break down. Certain parts shrink, the tissue structure begins changing, and the capillaries begin to disintegrate. The result is a less hospitable environment for the fetus, and premature births at this time are not unusual. At about this time the fetus slows its growth, and drops into position with its head toward the bottom of the uterus. Meanwhile, the internal organs undergo the final changes that will enable the newborn to survive in an entirely different kind of world. Its home has been warm, rather constant in its qualities, protected, and confining. It is not likely to encounter anything quite so secure again.

Birth

The signal that there will soon be a new member of the earth's most dominant species is the onset of *labor*, a series of uterine contractions that usually begin at about half-hour intervals and gradually increase in frequency. Meanwhile, the sphincter muscle around the cervix dilates, and as the periodic contractions become stronger, the baby's head pushes through the extended cervical canal to the opening of the vagina. The infant is finally about to emerge into its new environment, one that, in time, may give it the chance to propel its own genes into the gene pool of the species.

Once the baby's head emerges, the pattern of uterine contractions changes. The contractions become milder and more frequent. After the head gradually emerges through the vaginal opening, the smaller shoulders and the body appear. Then with a rush the baby slips into a new world. As soon as the baby has emerged, the umbilicus by which it is attached to the placenta is tied off and cut. The placenta is expelled by further contractions as the *afterbirth*. The mother recovers surprisingly rapidly. In other species, which deliver their young unaided, the mother immediately chews through the umbilicus and eats the afterbirth so that it will not advertise to predators the presence of a helpless newborn. Fortunately, the behavior never became popular in our own species.

The cutting of the umbilicus stops the only source of oxygen the infant has known. There is a resulting rapid buildup of carbon dioxide in the blood, which affects a breathing center in the brain. An impulse is fired to the diaphragm, and the baby gasps its first breath. Its exhaling cry signals that it is breathing on its own.

In American hospitals the newborn is then given the first series of the many tests it will encounter during its lifetime. This one is called the *Apgar test series,* in which muscle tone, breathing, reflexes, and heart rate are evaluated. The obstetrician then checks for skin lesions and evidence of hernias. If the infant is a boy, it is checked to see whether the testes have properly descended into the scrotum. A footprint is then recorded as a means of identification, since the new individual, despite the protestations of proud parents, does not yet have many other distinctive features that would be apparent to the casual observer. And there have been more than a few cases of accidental baby-switching.

/1981

Stage 3: Recall

Stop and recall what you have read.
Review your use of the thinking strategies. Did you use all five?

■▤▥ Organizing Textbook Material

Write a summary, take notes, outline, or map "Pregnancy and Birth" on a sheet of notebook paper. Explain your choice for organizing the information the way you did.

▥▤■ Comprehension Questions

_____ 1. The main point that the author is trying to get across in this selection is _____

_____

After reading the selection, answer the following questions with a, b, c, or d.

_____ 2. All of the following are true about fertilization except
     a. the twenty-three chromosomes of the sperm unite with the egg
     b. the egg and the sperm form a single cell
     c. the mother can feel the egg and sperm touch
     d. sperm can live for several hours in the genital tract

_____ 3. All of the following are true of the first trimester except
     a. the jaw bone begins to develop
     b. changes in facial expressions occur
     c. the eyes open and close
     d. fingers and toes begin to appear

_____ 4. All of the following are true of the second trimester except
     a. the mother can feel the fetus kicking
     b. oxygen is taken in through the lungs
     c. the fetus sleeps
     d. the fetus can have the hiccups

_____ 5. All the following are true of the third trimester except
     a. the fetus requires great amounts of calcium and protein
     b. the fetus floats freely with room to move in the uterus
     c. milk forms in the mother's mammary glands
     d. the mother's center of gravity may shift

6. During which of the trimesters does the author imply that the mother's body works the hardest?
   a. first
   b. second
   c. third
   d. equally in all
7. According to the author during which of the following periods would the fetus be able to survive in the event of a premature birth?
   a. the first trimester
   b. the beginning of the second trimester
   c. the fifth month
   d. the beginning of the third trimester
8. According to the author the embryo is considered a fetus at
   a. conception
   b. the end of the first month
   c. the end of the second month
   d. not until the third trimester
9. "Lightening" means that
   a. the baby has dropped lower in the pelvis
   b. delivery must be by Caesarian section
   c. the pressure is relieved on the baby's lungs
   d. the heart rate of the fetus begins to rise
10. The baby is forced to breathe when
   a. the head pushes through the canal
   b. the cervix dilates
   c. the unbilicus is cut
   d. labor begins

Answer the following questions with *T* (true), *F* (false), or *CT* (can't tell).

11. A normal pregnancy is approximately 266 days in length.
12. Babies are footprinted as a means of identification.
13. The fetus is most susceptible to measles during the last trimester.
14. Intelligence is determined when the egg and the sperm meet.
15. The author implies that hospitals have seldom, if ever, failed to identify babies properly.

▮▯▮ **Vocabulary**

According to the way the boldface word was used in the selection, indicate a, b, c, or d for the word or phrase that gives the best definition.

1. "**thrashing** around in the genital tract (02)"
   a. floating
   b. tossing about
   c. pushing
   d. resting

2. "**correlate** this early behavior (40)"
   a. compare
   b. contrast
   c. repeat
   d. consider

3. "becomes greatly **distended** and heavy (73)"
   a. crowded
   b. irritated
   c. expanded
   d. engorged

4. "**gait** may be noticeably altered (73)"
   a. breathing
   b. walk
   c. posture
   d. attitude

5. "sudden **surge** of growth (77)"
   a. feeling
   b. moment
   c. swell
   d. signal

6. "**confer** an immunity to the fetus (106)"
   a. seize
   b. replace
   c. represent
   d. bestow

7. "less **hospitable** environment (110)"
   a. varied
   b. normal
   c. comfortable
   d. complex

8. "the cervix **dilates** (120)"
   a. opens
   b. collapses
   c. becomes red
   d. deepens

9. "**propel** its own genes (124)"
   a. alter
   b. pushes
   c. remodel
   d. manage

10. "**apparent** to the casual observer (143)"
    a. intriguing
    b. unwelcomed
    c. visible
    d. humorous

▚▚▚ Essay Question

Discuss the major changes that occur in both the fetus and the mother during each of the trimesters of pregnancy.

HISTORY

U.P.I.

Skill Development: Skimming and Scanning

Skim *the selection as if you were planning to use a brief summary of the information in a research paper. Write a three or four sentence summary that you could use in your paper. Describe the organization of the selection and time your reading. Allow no more than five minutes for this exercise.*

Scan *the selection to answer the following questions and record your total time. Allow no more than two minutes for this exercise.*

1. *When was Tuskegee Institute founded?*

_____

2. *Where did DuBois go to college?*

_____

3. *Was Washington a leader in the NAACP?*

_____

© Scott, Foresman and Company.

Stage 2: Integrate Knowledge While Reading

Now carefully read the selection to organize the material for future study and to answer some comprehension questions. Select the method of organizing textbook material that you feel is most helpful to you and most appropriate for remembering the information in this selection. Explain why you chose either underscoring, summarizing, the Cornell Method of notetaking, outlining, or mapping.

WASHINGTON AND DUBOIS*

Leonard Pitt, *We Americans*

During Reconstruction, blacks joined the American body politic for the first time. Reconstruction failed because it tried to impose a solution from the top down, from the outside in. While giving blacks the vote, it disfranchised many whites, thus alienating those whose compliance was essential for success. The Radicals pushed for *legal* equality
5   but never came to grips with the underlying poverty and social inequality of blacks. From Reconstruction until the 1950s blacks—and other racial minorities—made little progress in acquiring civil rights. Lincoln's "new birth of freedom" had yet to materialize.

Booker T. Washington and Accommodation

Reacting to violence and to Jim Crow restrictions, abandoned by liberal white friends, and ignored by Congress, the White House, and the courts, the black community turned in
10   upon itself, looking for solutions through self-help. Now that their civil rights were dead, blacks hoped that accommodating the whites would save them.

    Booker T. Washington (1856–1915), an educated ex-slave, became the oracle of moderate black America. Washington believed in full equality, but for the time being, Jim Crow was a reality that had to be lived with. As long as Negroes remained poor, ignorant,
15   and unskilled, they would be despised by whites. They must turn to vocational education, hard work, and thrift in order to improve themselves. Washington warned that it was unwise for blacks to leave the rural South for the cities or for the North. "Cast down your bucket where you are," he urged in a famous address at Atlanta in 1895. On the other side of the coin, he held that whites should give blacks a hand by hiring them rather than
20   European immigrants whenever possible. Washington also worked actively with southern Negro merchants who were attempting to gain the good will of southern whites. Privately he fought segregation and took a vital interest in politics and patronage, although in public he urged Negroes not to use these tactics.

    Washington had graduated from Hampton Institute, Virginia, a Negro vocational school
25   founded in 1865, and was convinced that Negroes trained in farming, handicrafts, home economics, carpentry, and other manual careers would advance farther in the world than those who might try to elbow their way into white-dominated professions. In 1881 he founded Tuskegee Normal and Industrial Institute in Alabama to train Negroes as

*LEARNING STRATEGY: Look for similarities and differences between Washington and DuBois.

Pitt: *We Americans,* Second Edition. Copyright © 1984 Kendall/Hunt Publishing Company. Reprinted with permission.

teachers, farmers, and skilled workers. The school's success was due in part to the work of
George W. Carver, an agricultural chemist who joined its faculty in 1896. He developed
numerous by-products from the peanut, sweet potato, and soybean. Carver's work with
the peanut had particular impact in diversifying southern agriculture, which had become
too dependent on a single crop, cotton.

A man of great charm and eloquence, Washington had the ear of prominent whites.
Philanthropists Andrew Carnegie and George F. Peabody generously endowed Tuskegee.
President Theodore Roosevelt invited him to lunch at the White House. His
autobiography *Up From Slavery* (1901) became a classic of Negro American writing. Many
whites considered him the "chief spokesman for his race."

Yet Washington led his people down a fruitless path. Few trained Negro craftsmen
could find decent jobs. Even the best trained black farmers could seldom escape debt or
sharecropping. Often they drifted away to the cities, even northern cities, against
Washington's advice. Northern white employers preferred white European laborers to
blacks. Meanwhile, accommodation by blacks seemed to inflame rather than calm
southern whites. Racist mobs continued to lynch blacks—nine hundred were lynched
between 1900 and 1910.

Stereotyping of blacks reached its most vicious extreme during the era of
accommodation. Nonwhites had always been portrayed as children or savages (or both),
who required the civilizing example of whites. Minstrel shows carried on the image of
happy-go-lucky, banjo-playing Black Sambo (impersonated by whites in "blackface"). But
this picture of blacks was only one side of the coin: whites were increasingly obsessed by
the "black brute." He was dangerous precisely because he was not under white control.
He "did not know his place," stole jobs from white men, and raped white women.
Running for governor in Mississippi, James K. Vardaman in 1903 assured his audience that
the black was a "lazy, lying, lustful animal which no conceivable amount of training can
transform into a tolerable citizen. We would be justified," he claimed, "in slaughtering
every Ethiop on earth to preserve unsullied the honor of one Caucasian home." *The
Klansman* (1905) by Thomas Dixon Ryan, Jr., became the basis for D. W. Griffith's classic
movie *Birth of a Nation,* which included several scenes of the "black brute" during
Reconstruction.

The Beginnings of Militancy

The realities of lynching and discrimination mocked Booker T. Washington's blueprint for
improving the status of blacks. Whites seemed to take advantage of accommodation. This
made Washington suspect to young blacks. His most articulate black critic was William E.
B. Du Bois (1868–1963), a northern-born, Harvard-trained scholar. Du Bois insisted that
blacks must stop waiting for white charity and seek full equality. A professor of sociology
at black Atlanta University, Du Bois had little regard for Washington's philosophy of
vocational training. He wanted the "talented tenth" of blacks to assert racial pride and
independence and seek the best education available.

Du Bois and other militants founded the Niagara Movement in 1905. In a flaming
manifesto they protested the denial of the vote, civil rights, economic opportunities, and
higher education to blacks. Booker T. Washington sensed a threat to his leadership.
Fearing that white philanthropists would stop supporting black schools, he pulled strings
to deny the upstarts access to the press. Soon the Niagara Movement ceased to function.

Yet time was on the militants' side. They helped form the National Association for the

Advancement of Colored People (NAACP) in 1909, which became the first line of legal
75 defense for victims of race riots, lynchings, and Jim Crow policies. By now most black
leaders rejected Washington's leadership. The NAACP lobbied for antilynching laws and
sued in the courts to eliminate grandfather clauses, white primaries, segregated schools,
discrimination in housing, and other infringements on the Fourteenth Amendment. It
won its first major court victory in 1915, when the U.S. Supreme Court agreed to nullify
80 Oklahoma's grandfather clause.

The Progressive era as a whole produced no great benefits for blacks. Few white
Progressives believed in racial equality. Even those who did usually found it expedient to
compromise with white supremacist politicians. Woodrow Wilson refused to end black
segregation in the Post Office and other federal agencies.

85 During the First World War the emerging northern ghettos began to attract attention.
Wartime jobs opened up for blacks in northern factories. By the war's end 500,000
southern black men and women had moved north of Dixie. A great migration of blacks
from southern plantations to northern cities was under way. In the cities poverty and
housing discrimination were creating large black ghettos. On the fringes of these ghettos
90 racial violence flared. A serious clash occurred in East St. Louis, Illinois, in 1917. This
prompted a silent march of blacks along New York's Fifth Avenue, the first such protest.

Meantime 200,000 blacks entered the armed services. Two Negro divisions served
overseas. While most were placed in noncombat positions and labor battalions, many
others fought. Some blacks were decorated by the French government. But almost none
95 rose above the rank of captain. Discrimination against black troops was common. In
Houston in August 1917 black infantrymen rioted against repressive action by police.
Seventeen whites were killed and thirteen blacks executed. Nevertheless, the war created
new black voters, industrial workers, and community leaders. World War I also gave
nationwide scope to racial issues formerly identified as strictly southern.   /1269

Stage 3: Recall

Stop and recall what you have read.
Review your use of the thinking strategies. Did you use all five?

▌▌▌ **Organizing Textbook Material**

Write a summary, take notes, outline, or map "Washington and DuBois." Explain
your choice for organizing the information the way you did.

▌▌▌ **Comprehension Questions**

_____   1. The main point the author is trying to get across in this selection is _____

_____

_____

After reading the selection, answer the following questions with *a, b, c,* or *d.*

© Scott, Foresman and Company.

_____ 2. The philosophy of accommodation was said to include all of the following except:
   a. self-help for blacks
   b. white charity
   c. jobs in professions
   d. gaining respect for blacks

_____ 3. In the author's opinion, World War I produced all of the following results except
   a. more job discrimination than during the accommodation era
   b. national publicity for what was previously a local concern
   c. black ghettos
   d. more concrete change than Booker T. Washington's philosophy had effected

_____ 4. It can be inferred from this selection that the author feels that Booker T. Washington
   a. was the greatest black leader since the Civil War
   b. provided leadership but did not dramatically improve opportunities for black people
   c. deserves more credit as a black leader than he usually gets.
   d. should not be thought of as a great leader

_____ 5. Job opportunities for a large number of blacks emerged primarily because of
   a. the Progressive era
   b. wartime needs
   c. the accommodation philosophy
   d. racial riots

_____ 6. The reader can infer that Jim Crow laws were
   a. permissive
   b. incriminating
   c. justifiable
   d. discriminatory

_____ 7. The organization of militants lead by DuBois was
   a. sabotaged by Washington
   b. successfully organized in the first attempt
   c. stereotyped and ridiculed
   d. supported by white philanthropists

_____ 8. Black Americans were portrayed as happy and friendly but nonproductive in
   a. minstrel shows
   b. _Birth of a Nation_
   c. _The Klansman_
   d. _Up from Slavery_

_____ 9. The work of George Washington Carver led directly to
   a. agricultural diversification
   b. the decline of cotton
   c. less discrimination
   d. jobs for blacks

_____ 10. All of the following contributed to the success of Booker T. Washington
except
a. DuBois
b. George Washington Carver
c. Andrew Carnegie
d. Theodore Roosevelt

Answer the following with _T_ (true), _F_ (false), or _CT_ (can't tell).

_____ 11. World War I was indirectly responsible for the two racial riots of 1917.
_____ 12. Booker T. Washington encouraged blacks to seek job opportunities in the
North.
_____ 13. Both DuBois and Washington were products of the kind of educational
background that they each advocated.
_____ 14. Blacks were decorated by the French government in World War I.
_____ 15. Washington was a strong supporter of the NAACP.

▬▬▬ **Vocabulary**

According to the way the underlined word was used in the selection, indicate _a,
b, c,_ or _d_ for the word or phrase that gives the best definition.

____ 1. "the **oracle** of moderate black
America (12)"
a. source of wise counsel
b. harbinger of evil
c. vehicle for travel
d. optimist

____ 2. "turn to **vocational** education
(15)"
a. professional
b. compensatory
c. teacher training
d. relating to a skill or trade

____ 3. "interest in **politics and
patronage** (22)"
a. agriculture
b. support of wealthy persons
c. force
d. national organizations

____ 4. "**Philanthropists** Andrew
Carnegie (35)"
a. humanitarians
b. novelists
c. politicians
d. philosophers

____ 5. "generously **endowed**
Tuskegee (35)"
a. granted permission
b. given income
c. summoned to appear
d. denied entrance

____ 6. "most **articulate** black critic
(62)"
a. distasteful
b. renown
c. well-spoken
d. argumentative

_____ 7. "in a flaming **manifesto** (69)"
   a. public declaration of principles
   b. proclamation of war
   c. doctrine of rebellion
   d. declaration of discrimination

_____ 8. "**infringements** on the Fourteenth Amendment (78)"
   a. additions
   b. variations
   c. modifications
   d. violations

_____ 9. "found it **expedient** to compromise (82)"
   a. disgraceful
   b. politic
   c. meaningless
   d. unnecessary

_____ 10. "the **fringes** of these ghettos (89)"
   a. opposite areas
   b. central gathering points
   c. streets
   d. borders

▎▇▎ ## Essay Question

Explain how the philosophies of Washington and DuBois differed. Use a sheet of notebook paper to record your answer.

TEST TAKING STRATEGIES

Receiving a passing grade on a test should not be the result of a trick; your grade should be a genuine assessment of the mastery of a skill or the understanding of a body of information. High scores, therefore, should depend on preparation, both mental and physical, and not on schemes involving length of responses or the likelihood of b or c being the right answer. Research has proven many such gimmicks don't work.[1] Tricks will not get you through college. For a well-constructed examination, the only magic formula is mastery of the skill and an understanding of the material being tested.

The purpose of this material is to help you become more aware of how *not* to lose points on a test and thereby gain an edge. The following suggestions cover both mental and physical preparation as well as discussing certain technical aspects of test construction.

BEFORE TAKING A TEST

1. Get Plenty of Sleep the Night Before

How alert can you be with inadequate sleep? Would you want a physician operating on you who only had a few hours sleep the night before? The mental alertness that comes from a good night's sleep could add two, four, or even six points to your score and mean the difference between passing or failing the course. Why take a chance by staying up late and gambling at such high stakes?

2. Arrive Five or Ten Minutes Early and Get Settled

If you run in flustered at the last second, you will spend the first five minutes of the test calming yourself rather than getting immediately to work. Do your nerves a favor and arrive early. Find a seat, get settled with a pen or pencil and paper, and relax with some small talk about the weather to a neighbor.

[1]Brozo, W. G., Schmelzer, R. V., ahd Hiller A. Spires. "A Study of Test-Wiseness Clues in College and University Teacher-Made Tests with Implications for Academic Assistance Centers. College Reading and Learning Assistance (Technical Report 84–01).

3. Know What to Expect on the Test

Check beforehand to see if the test will be essay or multiple-choice so that you can anticipate the format. Research studies have shown that studying for both types should stress main ideas, and that it is as difficult to get a good grade on one as it is on another.[2]

4. Have Confidence in Your Abilities

The best way to achieve self-confidence is to be well prepared. Be optimistic and approach the test with a positive mental attitude. Lack of preparation breeds anxiety, but positive testing experiences tend to breed confidence. Research shows that students who have frequent quizzes during a course tend to do better on the final exam.[3]

5. Know How the Test Will Be Scored

Find out if there is a penalty for guessing and, if so, what it is. Since most test scores are based on answering all of the questions, you are usually better off to guess than to leave items unanswered. Research shows that guessing can add points to your score.[4] Know the answers to the following questions and act accordingly:

Will the items omitted count against you?
Is there a penalty for guessing?
Are some items worth more points than others?

DURING THE TEST

1. Concentrate

Tune out both internal and external distractions and focus your attention on the material on the test. Visualize and integrate old and new knowledge as you work. Read with curiosity and an eagerness to learn something new. If you become anxious or distracted, close your eyes and take a few deep breaths to relax and get yourself back on track.

[2]Clark, P. M., "Examination Performance and Examination Set," in D. M. Wark, ed., *Fifth Yearbook of the North Central Reading Association.* Minneapolis: North Central Reading Association, 1968, 114–122.
[3]Fitch, M. L., Drucker, A. J., and Norton, J. A. Frequent Testing as a Motivating Factor in Large Lecture Classes. *Journal of Educational Psychology,* 1951, *42,* 1–20.
[4]Preston, R. C., Ability of Students to Identify Correct Responses Before Reading. *Journal of Educational Research,* 1964, *58,* 181–83.

2. Schedule Your Time

Wear a watch and plan to use it. When you receive your copy of the test, look it over, size up the task, and allocate your time. Determine the number of sections to be covered and organize your time accordingly. As you work through the test, periodically check to see if you are meeting your time goals.

3. Work Rapidly

On a test every minute counts. Do not waste the time that you may need later by pondering at length over an especially difficult item. Mark the item with a check or a dot and move on to the rest of the test. If you have a few minutes at the end of the test, return to the marked items for further study.

4. Think

Use knowledge, logic, and common sense in responding to the items. Be aggressive and alert in moving through the test.

5. Don't Be Intimidated by Students Who Finish Early

Research shows that there is no correlation between high scores and the time students finish a test.[5] Even though some students work more rapidly than others, it does not mean that they work more accurately. If you have time, review areas of the test where you felt a weakness. If your careful rethinking indicates another response, change your answer to agree with your new thoughts. Research shows that scores can be improved by making such changes.[6]

MULTIPLE-CHOICE TESTS

1. Consider All Alternatives

Do not rush to record an answer without considering all the alternatives. Be careful, not careless, in considering all options.

2. Anticipate Answers

As you read the beginning of a multiple-choice item, anticipate what you would write for a correct response. Develop an answer in your mind before you read the options, and then look for a response that corroborates your thinking.

[5]Barch, Abram M., The Relation of Departure Time and Retention to Academic Achievement. *Journal of Educational Psychology,* 1957, *48,* 352–358.
[6]Berrien, F. K., Are Scores Increased on Objective Tests by Changing the Initial Decision? *Journal of Educational Psychology,* 1940, *31,* 64–67.

3. Be Alert to Key Words

A response that contains always or never is seldom correct; rarely can a statement be so definitely inclusive or exclusive. These key words are qualifiers and require special attention.

all	except	rarely	sometimes
no	always	never	every
only	none	often	necessary
must	generally	few	may
little	seldom	much	perhaps

4. Be Alert to Grammatical Clues

In reviewing options, you can eliminate responses that do not have subject-verb agreement; a singular subject requires a singular verb and vice versa. Verb tense and modifiers such as *a* or *an* can also give clues to the correct response.

5. Use Information from Other Parts of the Test

Sometimes you will find clues from other items on a test that will help you answer a particular question. Use the clues to your advantage.

6. Eliminate Absurd Options

Eliminating one option will allow you to spend more of your energy deciding among the remaining choices. If an option is unreasonable or unsound, eliminate it and consider the rest.

7. Eliminate Two Similar Options

If *both* is not a possible answer and two items say basically the same thing, then neither can be correct. Eliminate the two and spend you time on the others.

8. All of the Following Except . . .

In this type of question, you must recognize several responses as correct and find the one that is incorrect. Corroborate each response and by process of elimination fid the one that does not fit.

9. True Without Exception

A statement is true only if it is completely true. If a statement is half true and half false, mark it false.

© Scott, Foresman and Company.

10. Can't Tell from Clues

Mark an item can't tell only if there are not clues on which to base an assumption. In other words, there is no evidence to indicate either true or false for the statement.

READING TESTS

1. Main Idea Items

For the "best title" or the "best statement of the main idea" questions, the incorrect responses will fall into two categories. Some responses will be too broad, covering much more than is included in the passage. Others will be details within the passage that support the main idea. To get some perspective on the main idea, try rereading the first and last sentences in hopes that one or the other will be a topic sentence and thus give you an overview of the main idea.

2. Corroborate Details

Detail questions are the only kind that can be answered without a clear understanding of the passage. Ideally, you will understand the material, but if you are unsure of a detail, glance back over the passage to quickly corroborate an answer. Beware of a response that uses a catchy phrase from the passage. Often such distractors are tempting because the reader says, "Oh yes, I saw those words in the passage."

3. Implied Meaning Questions

Do not expect to answer questions on implied meaning if you have not understood the passage. Rarely can you go back and point to such an answer. A correct response on inference items depends on an ability to pick up hints from the material and then make assumptions and draw conclusions.

4. Words in Context

To correctly identify the definition of a vocabulary word, reread the sentence in which the word appears. Although a word may have multiple meanings, only one meaning would be correct in the sentence in which it is used.

5. Anticipate the Types of Questions

The content of a passage influences the kind of questions that can be asked. Science passages tend to be rather detailed, and thus you can expect a number of detail questions to follow. On the other hand, a passage from literature would be more likely to deal with emotions and motives, so you would anticipate more inference questions. Almost all passages are followed by a main idea question.

ESSAY EXAMINATIONS

1. Write with Purpose

Your answer should be in response to the question that is asked and not a summary of everything you know about a particular subject. Write with purpose so that the reader can understand your views and relate your points to the subject. "Padding" your answer by repeating the same idea or including irrelevant information is recognized by graders and seldom appreciated.

2. Use an Appropriate Style

Use simple, straightforward vocabulary and express your ideas in a clear, concise, and logical style.

3. Organize Your Response

Do not write the first thing to pop into your head. Take a few minutes to brainstorm and jot down ideas. Number the ideas in the order that you wish to present them and use this plan as your outline for writing.

In your first sentence, establish the purpose and direction of your response. Then list specific details that support, explain, prove, and develop your point. Reemphasize the points in a concluding sentence and restate your purpose. Whenever possible, use numbers or subheadings to simplify your message for the reader. If time runs short, use an outline or a diagram to express your remaining ideas.

4. Be Aware of Appearance

Research has shown that on the average, essays written in a clear, legible hand receive a grade level higher score than essays written somewhat illegibly.[7] Be particular about appearance and considerate of the reader. Proofread for correct grammar, punctuation, and spelling.

5. Practice

Predict possible essay items by using the table of contents and subheadings of your text to form questions. Practice brainstorming to answer these questions.

[7]James, H. W., The Effect of Handwriting upon Grading. *English Journal*, 1927, *16*, 180–185.

Review old exams for an insight both into the questions and the kinds of answers that received good marks. Do as much thinking as possible to prepare yourself to take the test before you sit down to begin writing.

6. Notice Key Words in Essay Questions

This is a list of key words of instruction that appear in essay questions with hints for responding to each word:

Compare: note the similarities between things
Contrast: note the differences between things
Criticize: state your opinion and stress the weaknesses
Define: state the meaning so that the term is understood
Describe: state the characteristics so that the image is vivid
Diagram: make a drawing that demonstrates relationships
Discuss: define the issue and elaborate on the advantages and disadvantages
Evaluate: state positive and negative views and make a judgment
Explain: show cause and effect and give reasons
Illustrate: provide examples
Interpret: explain your own understanding of a topic which includes your opinions.
Justify: give proof or reasons to support an opinion
List: record a series of numbered items
Outline: sketch out the main points with their significant supporting details
Prove: use facts as evidence in support of an opinion
Relate: connect items and show how one influences another
Review: overview with a summary
Summarize: retell the main points
Trace: move sequentially from one event to another

ORGANIZATIONAL PATTERNS OF PARAGRAPHS

Anticipating the order in which the material will be presented helps you put the facts into perspective and see how the parts fit into the whole. For example, if the selection begins by indicating that there are four important components of management, you are alert to look for four key phrases to mark and remember. Likewise, if a comparison is suggested, you want to note the points that are similar in nature. For material that shows cause and effect, you need to anticipate the linkage and note the relationship.

The importance of these patterns is that they signal how the facts will be presented. They are blueprints for you to use.

In textbook reading the number of details can be overwhelming. The mind responds to a logical pattern; relating the small parts to the whole simplifies complexities of the material and makes remembering easier.

Although key signal words help in identifying the particular type of pattern, a single paragraph can be a mixture of different patterns. Your aim is to anticipate the overall pattern and thus place the facts into a broad perspective.

The following examples are the patterns of organization that are most frequently found in textbooks.

SIMPLE LISTING

Items are randomly listed in a series of supporting facts or details. These supporting elements are of equal value, and the order in which they are presented is of no importance. Changing the order of the items does not change the meaning of the paragraph.

Signal words often used for simple listing: *in addition, also, another, several, for example, a number of.*

The year 1879 isn't as famous as many other dates in history, but a number of notable things did occur during that year. Thomas A. Edison invented the incandescent lamp; F. W. Woolworth opened the first five- and ten-cent store, the state of California prohibited employers from hiring Chinese people, W. C. Fields first saw the light of day; and the science of psychology was born. For it was in the year 1879 that a scientist named Wilhelm Wundt set up the world's first psychology laboratory in Leipzig, Germany.

Douglas Matheson, Introductory Psychology

DEFINITION

Frequently in textbook reading an entire paragraph is devoted to defining a complex term or idea. The concept is initially defined and then further expanded with examples and restatements.

The preoperational phase is often referred to as the symbolic period, for this is the time of appearance for communicative language, which uses a shared set of symbols. It is at this age also that children most enjoy symbolic play, or make-believe. You can probably think of many preschoolers who spend hours playing house, pretending they are mommy or daddy, or talking on a nonexistent telephone. This is also the time in which deferred imitation first appears. By this Piaget means the child's mimicking of a series of actions he has observed earlier, such as another child's temper tantrum or a song from a TV show. In order to mimic, the child must be able to remember and then recreate what he has previously experienced.

Douglas Matheson, Introductory Psychology

DESCRIPTION

Description is like listing; the characteristics that make up a description are no more than a simple listing of details.

Watch a baby explore the world from his crib. When a moving object is dangled above him, he will follow it with his eyes. If he can reach, he will touch it with his hands. If the object makes a noise when he shakes it, he will shake it again. Finally, he will try to put it in his mouth, which he uses to explore everything in his world. The baby is actively seeking information about his environment; he is getting to know the things around him. Seeing, hearing, tasting, smelling, body position, and touching are basic to all behavior.

Douglas Matheson, Introductory Psychology

TIME ORDER OR SEQUENCE

Items are listed in the order in which they occurred or in a specifically planned order in which they must develop. In this case, the order is important and changing it would change the meaning.

Signal words often used for time order or sequence: *first, second, third, after, before, when, until, at last, next later*

From *Introductory Psychology: The Modern View* by Douglas Matheson, pp. 3, 103, 135. Copyright © 1975 by The Dryden Press, a division of Holt, Rinehart and Winston. Reprinted by permission of the author.

On June 1, 1812, President Madison asked Congress to declare war on Great Britain, listing the catalog of British offenses over the past years, none of major importance but adding up to an intolerable total. on June 18 Congress responded with a declaration of war. The vote was close in the Senate—19 to 13—and not overwhelming in the House, 79 to 49, with New England and the Middle Atlantic states against, the South and West for. Ironically, unknown to Madison, Parliament had already on June 16 revoked the orders restricting neutral trade with France—orders which had so stirred American resentment— and there were signs that the British might be willing to negotiate differences further.

Carl N. Degler et al., *The Democratic Experience*

COMPARISON-CONTRAST

Items are presented according to similarities and differences. They are related according to the comparisons and the contrasts that exist.

Signal words often used for comparison-contrast: *different, similar, on the other hand, but, however, bigger than, in the same way, parallels.*

It does not take much thinking to come up with real life parallels to the Milgram experiment. Images of Nazi Germany and My Lai massacre in Vietnam immediately come to mind. Indeed Milgram showed in another experiment (5) that normal, healthy American men will give severe shocks to a kindly old man at the command of the experimenter. Even though subjects complained vigorously to the experimenter, sweated, trembled, and bit their lips, most continued to shock the learner. Evidently the pressures of either the group or an authority figure (the experimenter) can overcome the subjects' sense of morality. In fact, many of the subjects felt no guilt or responsibility for their actions. In their minds, it was not they themselves who were delivering the shocks, even though they actually pushed the button. They viewed themselves as the tools of others and explained their actions in words highly reminiscent of the Nuremberg war trials: "I was only following orders."

Carl Degler et al., *The Democratic Experience*

CAUSE AND EFFECT

In this pattern, one item is showed as having produced another element. One is the *cause* or the "happening" that stimulated the particular result or *effect.*

Signal words often used for cause and effect: *for this reason, consequently, on that account, hence, because, made.*

Groups demand conformity because deviance threatens their social consensus about beliefs and opinions and their ability to obtain desired goals. As we pointed out earlier, people validate their opinions through social consensus. However, deviants threaten this consensus by holding conflicting views; this destroys the other group members' sense of confidence in the group's "official ideology." Since people find it uncomfortable to be unsure of what is right and wrong, they tend to react with hostility toward anyone who threatens the consensus. Also, particular norms are needed to ensure that the group can obtain its goals. Obviously, if each person on a basketball team came and left practice whenever he felt like it, the team would not be very effective.

Carl Degler et al., *The Democratic Experience*